HEBREW GRAMMAR.

A

GRAMMAR

OF

THE HEBREW LANGUAGE.

BY

MOSES STUART

Associate Professor of Sacred Literature in the Theological Institution at Andover.

FOURTH EDITION CORRECTED AND ENLARGED.

Wipf & Stock
PUBLISHERS
Eugene, Oregon

Wipf and Stock Publishers
199 W 8th Ave, Suite 3
Eugene, OR 97401

A Grammar of the Hebrew Language
By Stuart, Moses
ISBN: 1-59752-191-4
Publication date 5/16/2005
Previously published by Flagg & Gould, 1831

PREFACE.

The present edition of my Hebrew Grammar retains all the essential features of the third edition, and in nearly every case the same notation of sections with their respective subdivisions. In some respects I wished for a change here; but I did not hold myself at liberty to make any important one, on account of the references every where made to the third edition, in my *Course of Hebrew Study*. In the very few cases where some change in the notation was a matter of expediency or of necessity, in the present edition, no serious embarrassment will be experienced by the student, in finding what is referred to in the Course of Hebrew Study.

I have revised the present edition throughout, and have made a multitude of additions and corrections of a subordinate kind. No page of the third edition has escaped some change; although, for the most part, the alterations are of such a nature as will not attract the notice of readers in general. The encouragement which has been given to the work, is such as lays upon me an imperious obligation to do all in my power to render it as complete as possible. I have availed myself, in order to accomplish this purpose, of the latest editions of the grammars of Gesenius and Ewald.

The reader who takes the pains to compare the present edition with the preceding one, will see that a change has been made in the theory of classifying the vowels, the *medial* ones being now omitted. My convictions in regard to this subject remain as before; but the inconvenience of the division in question to the learner, and its disagreement with the division of vowels in other languages, united with a conviction that 'the trouble is more than a balance for the advantage,' have occasioned my return *practically* to the old theory of long and short vowels only.

As a specimen of the additions and changes made in the present edition, §§ 421. 424. 432. 453*a*. 514, may be consulted and compared.

Throughout the whole work, more than the former facility of being consulted has been aimed at, and I trust secured, by the mode of printing. The titles and catch-words have every where been rendered more conspicuous. Owing to this principally, the size of the work has been somewhat increased.

In regard to the copiousness of the present grammar, it does not exceed the number of pages in the *abridged* edition of Gesenius' Hebrew Grammar, which has now gone through nine editions. I do not aim at making a *skeleton* grammar, but a somewhat complete, although compressed one. Experienced teachers, who have a thorough knowledge of the Hebrew, and who wish to communicate a radical knowledge of it to their pupils, will never employ a skeleton grammar. The testimony of such scholars as J. D. Michaelis, Vater, Gesenius, Hoffmann, and many others, against this practice, is sufficient to render it very doubtful; and the nature of the case decides altogether against it. Whoever uses a synoptical grammar merely, must either remain ignorant of more than one half of the grammatical phenomena of a language, or he must consume his time in filling up, by means of his teacher or of other grammars, the skeleton which he uses. How much loss of time and how much perplexity and discouragement, this would occasion, it is not difficult to foresee.

To avoid the evil, however, of obliging the learner to occupy himself too much, and for too long a time, with the dry details of grammar, before he comes to know any thing particular of the use of them, I have marked a great part of the passages in the present grammar with *brackets*, which may be *omitted* the *first* time that the contents are passed over. These brackets are put at the beginning and end only of sections or such parts of them as may be omitted. They are continued only so far as the Syntax. On the *first* going over, the student need not commit any thing more of the paradigms, than the first one of the regular verb. Let all the rest be learned in the way of *practice*, gradually, and not by burdening the mind at once with all the minutiae of the language. I would refer teacher and learner to my Hebrew Chrestomathy, where in the introductory remarks to the notes on

Part I. and Part. II., will be found a full explanation with regard to the method of learning, which I think it advisable for the student to pursue.

To avoid all loss of time in searching for paradigms, I have thrown them into a body at the end of the work; which will greatly facilitate the labor of the student. The index at the close of the volume, I have made so full as to render easy the finding of any thing important which the work contains.

The labor which I have bestowed on the present edition, will at least be regarded, I would hope, as furnishing some evidence that my desire is strong to improve the work as much as lies in my power. Every work of this nature is of course merely progressive, even when the most strenuous efforts and the best intentions are directed toward it. That teachers and learners may find some progress toward a more improved method of representing the grammatical phenomena of the Hebrew language, and more convenience for use, in this edition, is sincerely hoped for by

THE AUTHOR.

Andover : Theol. Seminary.
Sept. 1831.

PART I.

ORTHOGRAPHY AND ORTHOEPY.

I. ANCIENT HEBREW ALPHABET.

Form	Represented by	Sounded as	Names in Hebrew.	Represented by	Names sounded as	Signification of Names.
א	ʼ	ʼ	אָלֶף	Ālĕph	Aw′-lĕf	ox.
ב	bh, b	v, b	בֵּית	Bēth	Baith	house.
ג	gh, g	g	גִּימֶל	Gīmĕl	Geé-mĕl	camel.
ד	dh, d	th in that, d	דָּלֶת	Dālĕth	Daw′-lĕth	door.
ה	h	h	הֵא	Hē	Hay	hollow.
ו	v	v	וָו	Vāv	Vawv	hook.
ז	z	z	זַיִן	Zayĭn	Zâ-yin	armour.
ח	hh	hh	חֵית	Hhēth	Hhaith	travelling-scrip
ט	t	t	טֵית	Tēt	Tait	serpent.
י	y	y	יוֹד	Yōdh	Yoadh	hand.
כ	kh, k	kh, k	כַּף	Kăph	Kăf	hollow-hand.
ל	l	l	לָמֶד	Lāmĕdh	Law′-mĕdh	ox-goad.
מ	m	m	מֵם	Mēm	Maim	water.
נ	n	n	נוּן	Nūn	Noon	fish.
ס	s	s	סָמֶךְ	Sāmĕkh	Saw′-mĕkh	prop.
ע	ʻ	"	עַיִן	ʻAyĭn	A-yĭn	eye.
פ	ph, p	f, p	פֵּא	Pē	Pay	mouth.
צ	ts	ts	צָדֵי	Tsādhē	Tsaw-dhéy	screech-locust.
ק	q	q	קוֹף	Qōph	Qoaf	ear.
ר	r	r	רֵישׁ	Rēsh	Raish	head.
שׁ	s, sh	s, sh	שִׁין	Shīn	Sheen	tooth.
ת	th, t	th, t	תָו	Tāv	Tawv	cross.

2

No. II. LATER HEB. ALPHABET.   No. III. ORIENTAL ALPHABETS.

Forms.	Rep. by	Sounded as	Names.	Arabic alphabet.	Syriac alphabet.	Hebrew coin-letter.	Samar. alphab.	Heb.
א	א	'	āleph	ا	ܐ	F Ψ ⩜	⩜	א
ב	bh	v	Bēth	بَ	ܒ	9 ⏉	⨯	ב
בּ	b	b				⏉	⨯	ג
ג	gh	g	Gīmĕl	ج	ܓ	⊢	⩜	ד
גּ	g	g				⊢ ⊨	⨯	ה
ד	dh	{th in that}	Dālĕth	ذ	ܕ	⩜ ⩜ ⩜	⨯	ו
דּ	d	d		ج			⨯	ז
ה	h	h	Hē	ه	ܗ	⊟ ◇	⨯	ח
ו	v	v	Vāv	و	ܘ	⩜ ⩜	⩜	ט
ז	z	z	Zayĭn	ز	ܙ	⩜	⩜	י
ח	hh	hh	Hhēth	خ ح	ܚ	⩜ ⩜	⩜	כ
ט	t	t	Tēt	ط ظ	ܛ	⩜ ⩜	⩜	ל
י	y	y	Yōdh	ي	ܝ	⩜	⩜	מ
ך, כ	kh	kh,'h	Kăph	ك	ܟ	O O	O	נ
ךּ, כּ	k	k						ס
ל	l	l	Lāmĕdh	ل	ܠ	⩜	⩜	ע
ם, מ	m	m	Mēm	م	ܡ	⩜ ⩜	⩜	פ
ן, נ	n	n	Nūn	ن	ܢ	P P q q	P q	צ
ס	s	s	Sāmĕkh		ܣ	W ⨯	⩜	ק
ע	'	"	'ayĭn	ع غ	ܥ			ר
ף, פ	ph	ph, f	Pē	ف	ܦ	X	⩜	ש
ףּ, פּ	p	p						ת
ץ, צ	ts	ts	Tsādhē	ص ض	ܨ			
ק	q	q	Qōph	ق	ܩ			
ר	r	r	Rēsh	ر	ܪ			
שׂ	s	s	Sĭn	س	ܣ			
שׁ	sh	sh	Shīn	ش	ܫ			
ת	th	th	Tāv	ث	ܬ			
תּ	t	t		ت				

IV. TABLE OF THE VOWELS.

I. Class; *A* sound, corresponding vowel-letter, *Aleph*.

Names.		Form.	Sound.	Rep. by
קָמֶץ	Qāmĕts	מָא מָ מָט	= *a* in *all*	ā
פַּתַּח	Păttăhh *long*	מָ	= *a* in *father*	â
.....	Păttăhh *short*	מַ מַט	= *a* in {faring / man}	ă
סֶגוֹל	Sɛghōl *long*	מֵ מֵה מֵי	= *a* in *hate*	ê
.....	Sɛghōl *short*	מֶ מֶט	= *a* in {hated / climate}	ĕ

II. Class; *E* and *I* sound, corresponding vowel-letter, *Yodh*.

צֵירִי	Tsērī	מֵ מֵי מֵט	= *ey* in *they*	ē
סֶגוֹל	Sɛghōl *long*	מֶ מֶה מֶי	= *ey* in *purvey*	ê
.....	Sɛghōl *short*	מֶ מֶט	= *e* in {preying / men}	ĕ
חִירֶק	Hhīrĕq *long*	מִ מִי	= *i* in *machine*	ī
.....	Hhīrĕq *short*	מִ מִט	= *i* in {estimate / pin}	ĭ

III. Class; *O* and *U* sound, corresponding vowel-letter, *Vav*.

חוֹלֶם	Hhōlĕm	מֹ מוֹ מֹט	= *o* in *go*	ō
קָמֶץ חֲטֶף	{Qāmĕts Hhā-tēph *short*.}	מָ מָט	= *o* in {holiness / not}	ŏ
שׁוּרֶק	Shūrĕq	מוּ מוּט	= *oo* in *moon*	ū
קִבּוּץ	Qĭbbūts {vicarious and *long*}	מֻ מֻט	= *oo* in *moon*	ū
.....	Qĭbbūts *long*	מֻ	= *ue* in *rue*	û
.....	Qĭbbūts *short*	מֻט	= *u* in *full*	ŭ

IV. [Half-vowels] Shɛvā, simple and composite.

שְׁוָה	Shɛvā (simple)	מְ	= *e* in *begin*	ɛ
חֲטֶף פַּתַּח	Hhātēph Păttăhh	חֲ	= *a* in *litany*	a
חֲטֶף סֶגוֹל	Hhātēph Sɛghōl	אֱ	= *e* in *begin*	e
חֲטֶף קָמֶץ	Hhātēph Qāmĕts	חֳ	= *o* in *ivory*	o

Remarks on the Alphabet.

§ 1. *The ancient number of letters* was only 22; which is clear from the *alphabetic* Psalms, viz. Ps. 25. 34. 37. 111. 112. 119. 145; also from *alphabetic* compositions in Prov. 31: 10 seq. Lam. I—IV. But in Ps. 25. 34. 145, one letter is omitted; in Ps. 37. צ is repeated, and ע omitted. All the other Shemitish alphabets, (and the ancient Greek one also), had originally the same number of letters, viz. 22.

Note. The present *square* form of the Hebrew letters, is not the most ancient one; as is evident from inscriptions on Hebrew coins, stamped in the time of the Maccabees, which have characters such as are designated in alphabet No. III. The present square letter is evidently derived from the Aramaean forms of letters, and probably originated some time *after* the birth of Christ. This Kopp has recently shewn, in a satisfactory manner, in his *Bilder und Schriften der Vorzeit*, II. p. 95 seq., particularly p. 156 seq.

§ 2. *The usual arrangement of the letters* is fully settled by the same alphabetic compositions, in the Hebrew Scriptures. Most of the arrangement seems to have been originally accidental; yet not all. For example, the Liquids, ל, מ, נ, are ranged together. Za-yĭn (ז) *shield*, and Hhêth (ח) probably *travelling-scrip*, are associated. So Yôdh (י) *hand*, and Käph (כ) *hollow-hand;* Mêm (מ) *water*, and Nūn (נ) *fish;* also ע̆a-yĭn (ע) *eye*, Pē (פ) *mouth*, Qôph (ק) *ear*, Rêsh (ר) *head*, and Shīn (ש) *tooth*. In Lam. I—IV. ע stands ranged after פ; which shews that the arrangement was not uniform in all cases, at the time when this book was written.

§ 3. *The age of the alphabetic names* seems to mount higher than that of the Hebrew, or of any of the present Shemitish languages. Some of the forms of these names are like the Aramaean, e. g. מֵם, רֵישׁ, בֵּית; two seem to be of appropriate Hebrew stamp, viz. זַיִן, עַיִן; but אָלֶף, גִּימֶל, דָּלֶת, לָמֶד, סָמֶךְ, with וָו, and שִׁין (instead of שֵׁין), are manifestly *exotics*, derived from a kindred language which is now no more, but which, as the more simple forms of the words shew, was probably older than the time of Moses.

§ 4. *The significance of the names* is, in most cases (not all), sufficiently plain. The names are borrowed from natural objects; but the resemblance of the letters to them is not to be traced in many of the *present* Hebrew letters, which differ much from the form of the corresponding *ancient* ones. Alphabet No. 1. col. 7, shews the most probable original significations. For an admirable exhibition of the very ancient forms of Shemitish letters, Kopp's *Bilder und Schriften der Vorzeit*, II. 157, may be consulted.

§ 5. *The pronunciation of the names* is given in No. I. col. 6, as exactly as the English alphabet will permit. The vowels in col. 5 of the same, are sounded as directed in the table of the vowels under No. IV.

§ 6. *The later Hebrew alphabet*, as it now appears in all our pointed Hebrew books, consists of *twenty nine* letters,. as given in No. II. Six of these, as the alphabet shews, have two sounds each, but retain only the ancient single name ; one (שׁ *Sin* pronounced *Seen*) is furnished with a point over its *left* tooth, (*Shin* has one over the *right* tooth, שׁ), and also with a different name, in order to distinguish it. The modern Arabians have twenty eight letters, six of which are thus distinguished merely by a diacritical point; as is the case with the same number of letters, in the later Hebrew alphabet. Comp. Arab. alphabet in No. III.

§ 7. *The final forms* of five of the letters, appear in the short left-hand column of them, in the alphabet No. II. They are doubtless subsequent to the original forms; but when they were introduced is not known. When manuscripts were written continuously, i. e. without separating the words, (as they originally were), these final letters aided very much in making the proper divisions. Why more of them were not invented for this purpose, it is difficult to say. The practice of employing the *final forms* at the end of words, is universal, so far as they go. Conceit or mistake has excepted only some two or three cases ; e. g. מנ (for מִן), Job 38: 1. לְסָרְבָּה (for לְמַרְבָּה), Is. 9: 6. Neh. 2: 13.

§ 8. *The sounds of the letters* are given according to the usage of the most enlightened Hebrew scholars of the present time. There is a difference of opinion among the learned about some of the niceties of sound, in regard to several of them. But in respect to a language which has been dead for 2000 years, such questions can never be determined with satisfactory certainty. I add a few remarks on particular letters, which are of the more difficult class.

Aleph (א), all agree, was of a very slight sound. It easily coalesced with, or conformed to, other proximate sounds. I have chosen the *spiritus lenis* of the Greeks to represent it. *Practically* we do not sound it all, at least not perceptibly. In *theory*, it is a real consonant ; and the Hebrews doubtless sounded it, so as to make it perceptible in most cases.

Beth (ב), *bh*=v. So the modern Greeks sound their β.

Gimel (ג), when it is equivalent to *gh*, is represented in the alphabets as sounded like *g*. But the real sound is quite uncertain. The Arabians sound the same letter (ج) like our *j* ; just as in English, we sound *g* soft before *e* and *i*. I follow the general usage, and sound it *g* hard.

Daleth (ד), *dh*=*th* in *that ;* a sound which much perplexes Europeans of the continent ; but which is altogether easy and familiar to the English, and to the modern Greeks who so sound their δ.

§§ 8. 9. REMARKS ON THE ALPHABET.

He (ה) is a feeble *h*. Vav (ו) is a feeble *v*. The Arab sounds it like our *w;* which, more probably, was the Hebrew usage. I conform to general European usage.

Hheth (ח) *hh*, i. e. a strong aspirate. Yet not always so in *practice,* among the Hebrews; for at the *end* of words, it appears to have been very much softened. E. g. the Seventy represent חָרַח, by Θάῤῥα; and שֶׁבָח, by Σαλά. But they translate חַם, by Χάμ; and רָחֵל, by 'Ραχήλ. The Arabians have two gradations of sound for this letter.

Tet (ט) is a hard guttural kind of *t*, for which we have no due representative in English. The corresponding Greek letter is ϑ.

Kaph (כ), *kh*, a difficult sound. The Greeks have it in their χ. The usual practice sounds it like '*h*, i. e. makes a kind of guttural of it. *Kh* can be distinctly sounded by special effort; but what is gained by this, is not worth the trouble necessary to gain it. Common usage sounds בְּךָ, as *bɛ-hāw*. I would conform to this, as it is so much easier than to sound *kh* fully.

Samekh (ס) is sounded as the Greek σ, of which it is the undoubted prototype. It does not differ perceptibly from the letter שׂ, *Sin;* and the Hebrews have, in their orthography, written many words indifferently with either the one or the other, as פָּרַס and פָּרַשׂ, *to divide.*

The sound of Ayin (ע) is represented by ('), the double *spiritus asper* of the Greeks, for want of a better representative. Grammarians have represented it by *g, gh, hgh,* sounded gutturally; also by *hh, hhh,* and by the nasal *gn, ng, ngn.* The Arabians have two sounds for it; the deeper one is scarcely attainable by any European. The ancient Hebrews appear to have had two also; e. g. the Sept. render עֲמֹרָה Γόμοῤῥα, עַזָּה Γάζα; but עֵלִי 'Ηλί, עֲמָלֵק 'Αμαλήκ. That it sometimes had comparatively a feeble sound, is evident from its admitting of coalescence or contraction, as בַּל for בְּעַל; also from its commutation with א; see in the Hebrew Lexicon under א. Europeans generally neglect to sound it. Jerome calls it a *vowel;* see above, in 'Αμαλήκ, the ground of this. The vowel accompanying it should have a strong impetus or effect of the voice in pronouncing it.

Tsadhe (צ), *ts* hard. Qoph (ק), a deep guttural *k*, pronounced with impetus. Resh (ר), the rolling *r* of the French, or the Greek ῤ. Tav (ת), *t* soft.

§ 9. *Dilated letters* are a mere expedient to make out the adjustment of a line; for the Hebrews do not separate words at the end of lines. The usual ones are א, ה, ל, ם, ת, i. e. א, ה, ל, ם, ת.

§§ 10. 11. REMARKS ON THE ALPHABET.

[§ 10. *Unusual letters.* These are, (1) *Literae majusculae;* as וְכָבָה, Ps. 80: 16. (2) *Minusculae;* as בְּהִבָּרְאָם, Gen. 2: 4. (3) *Suspensae;* as מִיַּעַר, Ps. 80: 14. (4) *Inversae;* as בְּנָסֹעַ, Numb. 10: 5. The Rabbins find mysteries in these; the considerate critic will only find mistakes in copying.]

§ 11. *Similar letters.* These are numerous in the Hebrew alphabet. The student should carefully note them, at the outset. They are as follows;

1. Beth ב	כ Kaph	8. Zayin ז	ן Nun
2. Gimel ג	נ Nun	9. Hheth ח	ה He
3. Daleth ד	ך Kaph	10. Hheth ח	ת Tav
4. Daleth ד	ר Resh	11. Mem מ	ט Tet
5. Vav ו	י Yodh	12. Mem ם	ס Samekh
6. Vav ו	ן Nun	13. Tsadhe צ	ע Ayin
7. Zayin ז	ו Vav.		

Explanations.

(1) ב is distinguished from כ, by the right angle which its perpendicular side makes with the strokes at the top and bottom of the letter; כ is *round* at its corners instead of being angular. In some printed copies, כ is distinguished from ב only by the roundness of its corner at the bottom. (2) ג is distinguished from נ, by having the stroke at the bottom united to the perpendicular only by a small point; in נ, the bottom stroke is united without any variation of its magnitude. (3) ך *final* descends below the line; ד does not. (4) ד is distinguished from ר, by having a right angle at the top, at which part ר is round or obtuse. (5) ו decends to the bottom of the line; י does not. (6) ן *final* falls below the line; ו does not. (7) The top of ז is continued a little to the right of the perpendicular, while that of ו is not; the upright line of ז is small at the top, where it inclines to the right, while it is gibbous below; which is not the case with ו. (8) ז decends only to the line; ן *final* falls below it. (9) ח has no space between its left side and the top; ה exhibits a small chasm. (10) ח has a small dotted circle at the bottom of the perpendicular stroke on the left hand; ת has not this mark. (11) ט is open at the top; מ at the bottom. (12) ס is almost round; ם *final* is a square or parallelogram. (13) צ is angular on the right side of it, and the bottom is parallel with the line; ע turns to the left only. Final ץ, in its falling stroke, either turns a little to the right or descends perpendicularly.

§§ 12. 13. CLASSIFICATION OF THE LETTERS.

N. B. The learner will find it altogether the easiest method of making himself familiar with the distinctions between the Hebrew letters, and with the respective sounds of the letters, (as also of the vowels), to practice writing them down, calling each aloud by its name, and uttering the sound of it as often as he writes it. Let this practice be persisted in, until all the vowels and consonants can be recognized with facility and pronounced readily; their distinctions definitely described and drawn with the pen at pleasure; and their names familiarly recalled. In this way the student learns to *write* Hebrew letters and vowels, (which he should by all means do); and he fixes the names, forms, and sounds of all the written signs indelibly upon his memory.

[§ 12. *Classification of the letters.* This has been usually made, agreeably to the *organs* principally employed in pronouncing them, as follows; viz.

(*a*) Gutturals   א ה ח ע   technically called אֲהַחַע

(*b*) Labials   ב ו מ פ   בּוּמָף

(*c*) Dentals   ז ס צ ר שׁ (שׂ)   זַסְצְרַשׁ

(*d*) Linguals   ד ט ל נ ת   דַּטְלָנֶת

(*e*) Palatals   ג י כ ק   גִּיכֶק

Of these, the most important classes are the *Gutturals* and the *Labials*. But א is oftentimes not a Guttural; and ר is not unfrequently treated like one.]

§ 13. A much more important division than this, for *practical* purposes, is one which selects only those letters that are the subjects of some peculiarity. This is as follows, viz.

(*a*) *Aspirates ;* viz. ב, ג, ד, כ, פ, ת, technically called Begädh-kephäth, בְּגַד כְּפַת.

They are named *Aspirates*, because, when there is no point (Daghesh) in them, they are aspirated, i. e. associated with an *h*-sound; see alphabet No. II.

When they are destitute of this point or Daghesh, these letters are called, by the older grammarians, *molles* and *raphatae*; with it, *durae* and *dagessatae*.

(*b*) *Quiescents ;* viz. א, ה, ו, י, technically named Nehevï, אֱהֱוִי. The reason of this is, that the sound of these letters being in itself somewhat feeble, it often coalesces with the vowel sound which precedes; so that these letters are said *to quiesce*, i. e. to lose their separate, consonant sound, by falling into the preceding vowel.

(*c*) *Gutturals ;* viz. א, ה, ח, ע, or ä-h^ahhă, אֲהַחַע, as stated above.

Resh is sometimes to be added, and *Aleph* sometimes excepted; as stated in § 12.

(*d*) *Liquids ;* viz. ל, מ, נ, ר, of which ר is to be regarded only as a kind of half-liquid. Technically these may be called, limnăr, לִמְנַר.

The student should impress these classes, particularly the *three first*, deeply on his memory.

VOWELS.

§ 14. Originally the Hebrew alphabet consisted only of consonants. Some learned men have maintained the contrary, and averred that א, ו, י, were originally designed to be *vowels*. But the fact, that these letters constitute essential parts of the *triliteral* roots in Hebrew, and that they are susceptible of forming syllables by union with every sort of vowel sound, proves beyond all reasonable doubt that they are essentially *consonants*.

§ 15. But as the sound of א, ו, י, was feeble, and often in *practice* was made coalescent with the vowel which preceded them, it was natural, that in process of time they should come to be considered, in many cases, as representatives of the vowels with which they were customarily made to coalesce. Hence, in later Hebrew writings, we find א, ו, י, not unfrequently used in the room of vowels; more rarely in the early writings. But the still later Chaldaeo-Rabbinic Hebrew employs these three letters very often, merely for the purpose of designating vowels. For these reasons, these three letters are called *vowel-letters*, by recent grammarians, when they are spoken of in reference to the usage now in question. The older grammarians called them, with like reference, *matres lectionis*, i. e. authors or guides of [right] reading. In reference to another ground of classification, these same letters (together with ה) are called *Ehevi* (אֱהְוִי) or *Quiescents*, § 13. *b*.

[The most ancient Hebrew MSS. consisted of only the letters in the alphabet No. I., but in a very different shape from the present one; see § 1. Note. When the *diacritical* signs, i. e. small dots in or over a letter, which distinguish the later alphabet and increase the number of letters, together with all the vowel-points and accents, were first introduced, no historical documents, satisfactorily shew. But it is now generally agreed, that the introduction was a *gradual* one; and that, however early some few particular things in the general system may have been commenced, yet the *whole* system of diacritical signs, vowel-points, and accents, was not completed, so as to exist in its present form, until several centuries after the birth of Christ; pretty certainly not until after the fifth century. In regard to reading MSS. destitute of all this system of helps, there is no serious difficulty; at least none to any one who well understands the language. The same thing is habitually done, at the present day, by the Arabians, the Persians, and the Syrians, in their respective tongues; and in Hebrew, by the Jewish Rabbies, and all the learned in the Shemitish languages.]

§ 16. From what has just been said, the student will see why (in the Table No. IV.) א, ו, and י, are represented as *vowel-letters* corresponding to their respective classes of vowels. It is because these letters were occasionally employed (א more rarely) to designate more or less of the vowel-sounds, which are associated with them.

§ 17. In the same Table, in column 2d, the letters מ י ט ו ה א, are used merely to exhibit to the learner the manner in which the

§§ 18—24. VOWELS: QUALITY AND QUANTITY.

Hebrew vowels are written, in respect to the alphabetic letters with which they are associated, i. e. whether *above*, *below*, or *in* them.

§ 18. The student must free himself, at the outset, from the habit of giving *English* sounds to the English representatives of the Hebrew vowels, and be very careful always to sound these representatives as directed in the table.

§ 19. The ground of classification in the Table No. IV. is, that the vowels in these respective classes, not only have a natural relation to each other in respect to sound, but *for the most part are often commuted for each other*. Seldom does commutation take place, without the limits of the respective classes.

Quality and Quantity of the Vowels.

[§ 20. The division in respect to *quantity*, among the older grammarians, was as follows; viz. LONG—Qamets, Tseri, Hhireq magnum, Hholem, Shureq; SHORT—Pattahh, Seghol, Hhireq parvum, Qamets Hhateph, and Qibbuts. But all of these so called *short* vowels, are in fact often *long*, with the exception of Qamets Hhateph. Hence the student is greatly perplexed and misled, by such a division. A much better one is that proposed by the ancient Jewish grammarians, and lately adopted by the leading Hebrew grammarians in Germany; the basis of which is exhibited in Table IV. In like manner, the Arabic has only three classes of vowels.]

Ewald, in his recent Hebrew grammar (1827), has attempted to reduce the vowels to *two* classes; with much ingenuity, but not satisfactorily.

§ 21. The vowels may be distributed into different classes, both in respect to *quality* and *quantity*.

§ 22. (*a*) IN REGARD TO QUALITY, they may be considered as *pure* or *impure*.

The *quality* of vowels, with respect to the kinds of sound which they represent and the relations of those sounds to each other, is represented in Table No. IV. The quality of *purity* or *impurity* remains to be considered here.

§ 23. A *pure* vowel is one with which no consonant sound coalesces.

§ 24. An *impure* vowel is one with which a consonant sound coalesces.

E. g. in דָּבָר *dā-bhār* both vowels are pure; the first in דָּ, because no consonant follows; the second in בָר, because, although a consonant follows, it preserves its distinct sound, and does not coalesce with the vowel. On the contrary, in בָּא *bā* the א has no distinct sound, because it coalesces with the Qamets; and in בָּרֶךְ, (so written instead of בְּרִךְ, § 111. § 112), the Qamets contains a coalescent Resh, which is suppressed in the writing by omitting a Daghesh in the ר; in both which cases, Qamets is *impure*. And thus of all the other vowels, which admit a consonant to coalesce with them; see §§ 58. 59.

§ 25. (*b*) IN REGARD TO QUANTITY, vowels are divided into *long* and *short*.

This classification cannot always be made out by inspection, or according to the *appearance* merely of the vowels; for, as will be seen in the sequel, the appearance of some of them is often doubtful, or determines nothing in regard to quantity.

§ 26. The long vowels may be divided into two classes. (1) *Those long by nature*, i. e. always long. (2) *Those long by position*, i. e. long only when made so by a peculiar position. These last may be named (in regard to their appearance only) *doubtful*.

§ 27. *Long by nature* are Qamets, Tseri, Hhireq magnum, Hholem, and almost always Shureq.

Note. Hhireq is called *magnum*, when a Yodh quiescent, either expressed or implied, follows it. For the exceptions to Shureq, see § 31. Note 3.

§ 28. *Long by position* (short elsewhere) may be Pattahh, Seghol, Hhireq, and Qibbuts.

In this respect, these vowels correspond with the doubtful Greek vowels, *α, ι, υ*.

§ 29. THE VOWELS LONG BY NATURE, in regard to *quality*, are divided into two classes, viz. (1) Pure. (2) Impure.

§ 30. (1) *The pure vowels long by nature*, are Qamets, Tseri, and Hholem.

But these are pure only when they have no consonant coalescing with them, i. e. contain neither a Quiescent nor a Daghesh'd letter, § 53. § 23; e. g. דָּבָר *dā-bhār*, שֵׁן *shēn*, יִקְטֹל *yĭq-tōl*. Hhireq magnum and Shureq are always *impure*, i. e. Yodh or Vav, expressed or implied, always coalesces with them.

§ 31. (2) *The impure vowels long by nature* may be subdivided into *two* kinds, not differing in their essence, but only in the manner of their formation.

(*a*) Long vowels followed by a *quiescent* letter expressed or implied, and coalescing with them, § 53.

For distinction's sake these may be called QUIESCENT LONG VOWELS.

§§ 31. 32. VOWELS : QUALITY AND QUANTITY.

E. g. Qamets, as in בָּא *bā*; Tseri, as in בֵּין *bēn*, גֵּלֵה *gĕlē*; Hhireq magnum, as in נִיר *nīr*; Hholem, as in לֹו *lō*, קוֹל *qōl*; and Shureq, as in קוּם *qūm*. In all such cases, the Quiescent makes an addition to the *quantity* of the vowel, by coalescing with it. See § 55.

Note 1. *Appearance merely* will not determine whether a vowel long by nature is pure or impure; inasmuch as the quiescent letter which coalesces with it, is often omitted in the writing; e. g. קָם *qām* (impure) stands for קָאם *qām*, נִר *nīr* for נִיר, קֹל *qōl* for קוֹל, etc. see § 63. In a multitude of cases, the student can distinguish vowels of this kind, only when he comes to obtain a knowledge of etymology and of the analogies of the Hebrew language.

Note 2. *Vice versâ*, the Quiescents are sometimes inserted after vowels long by nature, without mixing with them and rendering them impure; in which case, they are merely a kind of *fulcrum* for the vowel; e. g. יִלְמוֹד *yĭl-mōdh* with Hholem pure, i. q. יִלְמֹד; סֹבֵיב *sō-bhēbh* with Tseri pure, i. q. סֹבֵב; see § 64, and comp. §§ 14—16, which exhibit the grounds of introducing such anomalies.

Note 3. There are a few cases also, in which Shureq appears to be *short*, i. e. to be the same as Qibbuts, even when it seems to coalesce with Vav; viz. when it stands before a daghesh'd letter, e. g. חוּקָּה *hhŭq-qā*, זוּגָּה *zŭn-nā*, מְעוּזִּי *mā-ŭz-zī*, etc. In Chaldee, Syriac, and Arabic, this is very common. But there are so few cases of this nature in Hebrew, that it seems probable they result from the use of a vowel-letter by transcribers, as the sign of a vowel; see §§ 14—16.

Note 4. Similar cases of Hhireq with Yodh, are also affirmed by most grammarians to exist. But the examples evidently do not justify this conclusion, as they only amount to different modes of orthography and pronunciation in respect to the same word; e. g. זִקְלָג *zĭq-lāgh* and זִיקְלָג *zī-qĕlāgh*, קִמֹשׁ *qĭm-mōsh* and קִימוֹשׁ *qī-mōsh*, פִּלֶּגֶשׁ *pĭl-lĕ-ghĕsh* and פִּילֶגֶשׁ *pī-lĕ-ghĕsh*, מֹרְגִים *mō-rĭg-gīm* and מוֹרִגִים *mō-rī-ghīm*; see § 64, respecting Yodh fulcrum.

§ 32. (*b*) Long vowels followed by a *daghesh'd* letter implied, but not expressed, excepting that the vowel is prolonged on account of the suppression; see § 58.

For distinction's sake, these may be called DAGHESH'D LONG VOWELS. The words *daghesh'd* and *quiescent*, thus applied to vowels, merely designate the particular way in which the vowels are lengthened; which is often a great convenience to teacher and learner. Of the actual or relative length of these different classes of vowels long by nature, whether pure or impure, quiescent or daghesh'd, we can determine nothing certain. In *theory*, the impure long vowels would seem to be the more protracted. Comp. §§ 24. 55. 58.

Note. Appearance merely will not distinguish these from the pure long vowels. A knowledge of forms and etymology is necessary.

§ 33. THE VOWELS LONG BY POSITION (§ 28) retain the same form as when short; they are made long only by their position before a daghesh'd letter suppressed in the writing; or before a Quiescent expressed or implied; see §§ 58. 55. Of course they are always IMPURE.

It is only from a knowledge of etymology and of the analogy of forms, that the student can be enabled, for the most part, to determine when these vowels are long.

Note. Pattahh, Hhireq, and Qibbuts (not vicarious) are made long only by the coalescence of an implied Daghesh'd letter; as בָּהֵל *bá-hēl*, for בַּהֵל *băh-hēl*; נִחַם *ni-hhăm*, for נִחַּם *nĭhh-hhăm*; רֻחַץ *rú-hhăts*, for רֻחַץ *rŭhh-hhăts*. For cases like לִקְרַאת, פֵּאָרָה, where Pattahh and Qibbuts apparently have a quiescent א, see § 118 with the notes, and also the Lexicon. Seghol may be made long, either by a Quiescent, as גִּי, צֵא, מֵה, *gê, tsê, mê;* or by the coalescense of a daghesh'd letter, as הֶהָרִים *hé-hā-rîm*, פֵּהָה *pé-hhā*, אֶחָיו *ê-hhāv*, where the Gutturals ה, ח, ה, exclude the Daghesh forte which belongs to them. See §§ 58. 111. 112. 54.

§ 34. THE SHORT VOWELS are Pattahh, Seghol, short Hhireq, Qamets Hhateph, and Qibbuts (not vicarious), when they are pure.

Note 1. The short vowels may stand either in a mixed syllable,* or in a simple one;† e. g. as דַּל *dăl*, בֶּן *bĕn*, מִקְנֶה *mĭq-nê*, חָכְמָה *hhŏkh-mā*, מֻקְטָר *mŭq-tār*, in mixed syllables; and מֶלֶךְ *mĕ-lĕk*, נַעַר *nă-ʼăr*, וַיִּגֶל *văy-yĭ-ghĕl*, אֹהֳלוֹ *ŏ-hºlō*, in simple syllables. This latter class is naturally pronounced somewhat longer than the other, as the stress of voice falls almost uniformly on these vowels when in a simple syllable.

Note 2. Some cases are dubious in respect to appearance; e. g. נֵר appears short, but is in fact i. q. נִיר. So in קָטֵל, Qibbuts appears short, but is i. q. קָטוּל, Qibbuts being *vicarious*. In like manner, appearances are frequently dubious in regard to simple syllables; e. g. נִחַם with a long impure daghesh'd Hhireq (§ 32), and וַיִּגֶל with a Hhireq pure and short; so בַּהֵל with an impure daghesh'd long Pattahh, but בַּיִת with a pure short one. If the student can discover whether the vowel is *pure* or not, he of course can determine the quantity. Experience only, with a knowledge of etymology and analogy, will enable him to do this; nor is it usually at all difficult, after a moderate progress in the language.

§ 35. The student will see, by Table No. IV., that Seghol is reck-

---

* A mixed syllable is one which ends in a vocal consonant.
† A simple syllable is one which ends in a vowel sound, either pure or impure.

oned both to the *first* and *second* class of vowels. The reason is, that it is often put in the place of Qamets and Pattahh, as well as exchanged with Tseri ; and so it is treated as belonging to both classes. Compare § 19.

Syllabication as affected by the Vowels.

§ 36. *A pure long vowel* may stand in a simple syllable; or in a mixed one when it is accented, and only then.

E. g. דָּבָר *dā-bhār*, שֵׁנָה *shē-nā*; שֵׁן *shēn*, יִקְטֹל *yiq-tōl*.

§ 37. So with *the quiescent long vowels*, § 31 *a*.

E. g. בָּא *bā*, קָאם *qām*; גֵּלֵה *gɛlē*, בֵּין *bēn*; לִי *lī*, נִיר *nīr*; לוֹ *lō*, קוֹל *qōl*; קוּמוּ *qū-mū*, קוּם *qūm*.

§ 38. *Daghesh'd vowels*, long by nature or position, can stand only in a simple syllable.

E. g. בָּרֵךְ *bā-rēkh*, נֵהֲל *nē-hăl*, בֹּרָךְ *bō-rǎkh*; בַּהֵל, נִחַם, רֶחַץ ; all with the first vowel impure and daghesh'd.

§ 39. *The short vowels* stand either in a mixed or simple syllable ; see § 34. Note. 1.

§ 41. *Qibbuts vicarious* is nothing more than a mere expedient for representing Shureq when the Vav falls out; and it may be in a simple, or in a mixed syllable.

E. g. קֻמוּ *qū-mū*, i. q. קוּמוּ; קָטֻל *qā-tǔl*, i. q. קָטוּל. In a mixed syllable it appears like Qibbuts short, and only a knowledge of the nature of Hebrew forms can determine the quantity.

GENERAL REMARKS. No theory of the Hebrew vowels has ever yet been broached, which is not liable to some objections. Almost all beginners complain of this part of Hebrew Grammar as complicated and difficult. It is somewhat so ; and yet far less so than the vowels in our own mother tongue, or in the Greek language. The relation of *long* and *short*, with respect to Hebrew vowels, is for us more a matter of *theory*, than of *practice*. In this light, however, it is very important to the student, who, without understanding this theory well, cannot analyze with satisfaction or success great numbers of changes in the forms of Hebrew words. Hebrew grammars in general have not at all recognized the fact, that both *Quiescents* and *suppressed daghesh'd letters* coalesce with the preceding vowel and lengthen it and make it impure, on principles which are in all important respects substantially the same. The principle at the basis of every possible case of this nature is very simple, viz. *that a consonant suppressed in sound, finds its equivalent in the preceding vowel by augmenting its length.* That *Quiescents* and *Gutturals* are, in general, the only classes of letters which are subject to the law of suppression, belongs to the nature of the language. The development of facts respecting these phenomena, belongs to grammar. But whether a long vowel (Qamets for example) was any longer when it included a Quiescent, than when it included a daghesh'd letter, (e. g. בָּא, בָּרֵךְ); or whether Qamets in בָּרֵךְ was any longer than Pattahh impure and long in בַּהֵל ; and many other questions of the like nature, we have no means of determining, nor is it necessary to determine them. If a student understands well the distinction between *pure* and *impure* vowels, and between *long* and *short* ones, he need not trouble himself to inquire how long the Hebrews dwelt on the sounds of the one or the other. If he complains that the system is *complicated*, he will remember that this belongs to the language; it is not to be charged upon a grammar which does no more than to state *facts* as they are.

SHEVA.

§ 42. The Hebrews never amalgamated two or more consonant-sounds together, (as we do in *plan, stripe, shrink*, etc.), except at the *end* of a word; and even then very rarely, and never to the extent of more than two letters. In a multitude of cases they even supplied a furtive vowel in the final syllable of words, in order to shun the amalgamation of two consonants; e. g. for סֵפֶר *sēphr*, they wrote and read סֵפֶר *sĕ-phĕr*. Still they admit, in a few cases, such forms as קָטַלְתְּ *qā-tălt*.

§ 43. When two consonants *begin* a syllable they are not combined in one sound, but a very short half-vowel is supplied, after the first letter, in order to smooth the transition to the second letter. This is called Shɛva, שְׁוָה.

Note. Instead of saying *brā, brē*, by one impetus of voice as we do, the Hebrews pronounced *bᵉrā, bᵉrē*, i. e. with a very short vowel-sound between the two consonants.

§ 44. Shevas usually mark either the beginning or the end of syllables.

Note. The only exception is a Sheva on the *penult* letter of a word, whose final syllable ends with two consonants, as קָטַלְתְּ *qā-tălt*.

§ 45. All syllables *beginning* with two consonants, have a Sheva (either simple or composite) under the first of them. All syllables *ending* with one or two vocal consonants, take a Sheva simple either expressed or implied under them.

§ 46. All Shevas at the *beginning* of syllables are *vocal*, i. e. sounded; all Shevas at the *end* are *silent*. Hence result the following rules; viz.

Sheva Vocal.

(*a*) All the *composite* Shevas; because they are always placed at the beginning of a syllable. (*b*) Simple Sheva after a simple syllable; as לְמְדָה *lā-mɛdhā*. (*c*) After another Sheva; as יִלְמְדוּ *yĭl-mɛdhū*. But if the second Sheva be at the *end* of a word, it is not vocal; as לָמַדְתְּ *lā-mădht*; see *i* below. (*d*) Under a letter at the beginning of a word, as לְמֹד *lɛmōdh*. (*e*) Under a letter with Daghesh forte expressed; as לִמְּדוּ

lĭm-mɛdhū=לִמְמְדוּ, § 71. (*f*) Under a letter in which a Daghesh forte is implied; as הַלְלוּ (=הַלְּלוּ) *hăl-lɛlū* or perhaps *hâ-lɛlū*, not הַלְלוּ *hăl-lū*.
[Note. The common maxim of grammarians in regard to the case *f*, is, that "Sheva is always vocal when under a letter which is immediately repeated." This is evidently incorrect; e. g. הַרְרֵי *hăr-rē* (not hăr-rɛrē), לִבְבֵי *lĭbh-bhē* (not lĭb-bɛbhē), and so חַלְלֵי (plur. const. of חָלָל) is *hhăl-lē*, not hhăl-lɛlē. On the contrary, הַלְלוּ reads *hăl-lɛlū*, because it belongs to a Daghesh'd form of the verb הָלַל, and the Daghesh is omitted merely from the frequent usage of rejecting it from a letter when it would be immediately followed by a vocal Sheva; see § 73. Note 3. Some knowledge of Hebrew forms is necessary, in order to distinguish such cases.]

Sheva Silent.

(*g*) After a short vowel in a mixed syllable; as יִלְמֹד *yĭl-mōdh*.
(*h*) After long vowel in a mixed tone syllable; as תִּלְמֹדְנָה *tĭl-mōdh-nā*.
(*i*) Two Shevas at the end of a word are both silent; לָמַדְתְּ *lā-mădht*.

§ 47. The *form* of the Shevas is exhibited fully by Table IV. No. IV. The *composite* Shevas are so called, because each is made by a union of Sheva with one of the short vowels; as is evident from inspection.

§ 48. *The quantity of the Shevas* is, at least in *theory*, the same; i. e. none of them are considered as a proper vowel.

E. g. פְּקֹד *pɛqōdh*, זֲהָב *zᵃhăbh*, אֱלֵי *ᵉlē*, חֳלִי *hhᵒlī*, are all considered as *monosyllabic*. What *practical* difference between the length of these sounds existed among the Hebrews, cannot now be determined.

§ 49. *The composite Shevas* belong *appropriately* to the Gutturals, and are used under them instead of simple Sheva.

No definite rules can be given as to the kind of Sheva under the respective Gutturals; usage varying them, in different words having the same letters, and in different positions. In general, ה, ח, ע, at the beginning of words take (ֲ); but א takes (ֱ).

§ 50. Gutturals (and other letters) which take a composite Sheva, always *begin* a syllable. *A Guttural which* ENDS *a syllable, must, like the other consonants, take Sheva simple;* for there is no other *silent* Sheva. E. g. שָׁמַעְתִּי *shā-măᵥ-tī*, יֶחְדַּל *yĕhh-dăl*, יֶהְגֶּה *yĕh-gê*, יֶאְסֹר *yĕʾ-sōr*.

§ 51. The composite Shevas (ֳ) and (ֱ) occur, not unfrequently, under most of the other consonants besides Gutturals; e. g. זֲהָב *zᵃhăbh*, קֳדָשִׁים *qᵒdhā-shīm*, etc. But (ֱ) is limited to Gutturals.

Note. No uniform rules can be given for the former cases. The *general* principle seems plainly to be, *a design to mark the letter as hav-*

§§ 52. 53. COALESCENCE OF VOWELS AND QUIESCENTS. 25

ing a real vocal *Sheva*, and consequently to advertise the reader, that the preceding vowel is not to attach the letter to which the Sheva belongs to itself; e. g. וּזְהַב *ū-zᵃhăbh*, not *ūz-hăbh;* הֲבָרְכָה *hă-bhᵃrā-khā*, not *hăbh-rā-khā;* תִּמְלֹךְ *ti-mᵃlōkh*, not *tĭm-lōkh*. There can scarcely be a doubt, that all such Shevas as these are designed only to designate some peculiar niceties practised in *oral* enunciation. They cannot be considered as belonging to the *essential* forms of words; nor can they be reduced to rule.]

§ 52. It is a general principle, that all moveable consonants,* not immediately followed by a vowel, must have a Sheva of some kind, either express or implied.

At the end of words in general, Sheva is not usually *expressed* but only *implied;* e. g. קָם *qām*, the same as קָֽם. The exceptions to this rule are, (1) In a final Kaph; as סָמַךְ. (2) When the final syllable ends with two consonants; as לָמַדְתְּ *lā-mădht;* but here, in case the penult consonant is a Guttural, it takes a Pattahh furtive, § 233. Note.

Note 1. The Quiescents, when they coalesce with the preceding vowel, have no Sheva. Whenever these letters have a Sheva, they are to be regarded as *moveable* consonants.

Note. 2. When a word ends with two consonants, of which the first is a Quiescent, usage is various as to Sheva under the *final* letter; e. g. we find בָּאת and בָּאְתְּ.

General Remarks. There can be but little doubt, that the *composite* Shevas were more distinctly sounded than the *simple* ones. Hence their application to the Gutturals, which peculiarly needed more vowel aid to enounce them than other consonants. Hence too, their use in regard to other letters, for the sake of more distinct pronunciation; § 51. note. But all the niceties of living vernacular pronunciation are now lost, no more to be recalled. Present general usage is all that is aimed at in this grammar.

Coalescence of Vowels and Quiescents.

To such a *coalescence*, the preceding explanations have rendered it necessary to advert. It must now be more fully explained.

§ 53. The sound of the quiescent letters, א, ה, ו, י, being feeble, (specially at the end of a syllable), they always coalesce with a vowel-sound which precedes them, in case they have neither a vowel, nor a Sheva expressed or implied, of their own, and provided that such vowel-sound is homogeneous.†

---

* A moveable consonant is one which is sounded, and does not quiesce or coalesce.

† That vowel sound is called *homogeneous*, which is adapted to coalesce with the Quiescents respectively; that is called *heterogeneous*, which is not adapted to coalesce.

§§ 54—56. COALESCENCE OF VOWELS AND QUIESCENTS.

§ 54. The following table exhibits the coalescence of the respective Quiescents, with their *homogeneous* vowels.

Aleph (א)	quiesces in	Qamets	(ָ)	בָּא	bā.
	–	Tseri	(ֵ)	רֵאשׁ	rēsh.
	–	Seghol	(ֶ)	תִּמְצֶאנָה	tĭm-tsê-nā.
	–	Hholem	(ֹ)	יֹאמֵר	yō-mēr.
Yodh (י)	—	Tseri	(ֵ)	בֵּין	bēn.
	–	Seghol	(ֶ)	גֵּיא	gê.
	–	Hhireq	(ִ)	דִּין	dīn.
Vav (ו)	—	Hholem	(ֹ)	קוֹל	qōl.
	–	Shureq	(וּ)	קוּם	qūm.
He (ה)	—	Qamets	(ָ)	גָּלָה	gɛlā.
	–	Tseri	(ֵ)	גָּלֵה	gɛlē.
	–	Seghol	(ֶ)	גָּלֶה	gō-lê.
	–	Hholem	(ֹ)	גָּלֹה	gā-lō.

In English we have a multitude of cases similar to these; e. g. *low, show,* etc. with *w* quiescent; *say, day,* etc. with *y* quiescent. Almost every letter in our alphabet is, in some situations, quiescent before or after some other letter.

Note 1. There are some other cases, besides those presented in the Table, of which Quiescence has been affirmed by most grammarians; e. g. רִאשׁוֹן *ri-shōn,* לִקְרַאת *liq-rŭth,* פְּאֵרָה *pŭ-rā,* § 63. But א is *otiant* here, not quiescent; see § 118 with the Notes.

Note 2. Although the Hholem is written over the ו, as in וֹ; and the Shureq is written in it, as וּ; yet, in both cases, the vowels usually belong to the *preceding* consonant; e. g. in קוֹל to the ק, in קוּם to the ק. Cases like עָוֹן *ă-vōn* occur; but they are easily distinguished, because the letter preceding the ו has then a vowel of its own, independently of that connected with the ו.

§ 55. The sound of the Quiescents, in case of *coalescence,* is not lost, but united with the preceding vowel; so that it makes long vowels more protracted, and renders short ones long, § 31.

§ 56. The *Ehevi* (אהוי) retain their proper consonant power, i. e. do not quiesce, (1) Always at the beginning of a syllable; as אָמַר *ă-măr,* הֵם *hēm,* יָלַד *yā-lădh,* וְלֵד *vĕ-lĕdh.* (2) Always when they end a

§§ 57. 58. OTIUM OF THE EHEVI, ETC.

syllable, in case they have a simple Sheva under them, either expressed or implied; e. g. יֶאְסֹר‎ yĕă-sōr, נֶהְפָּךְ‎ nĕh-păkh, שָׁלַוְתִּי‎ shā-lăv-tī, חַי‎ hhăy, קָו‎ qăv. In the two last cases, the Sheva is *implied*, i. e. חַיְ=חַי‎, and קָו=קָוְ‎, see § 52. (3) Usually, when preceded by a *heterogeneous* vowel; e. g. תָּו‎ tāv, קָו‎ qăv, שָׁלֵו‎ shā-lēv, זִיו‎ zīv, חַי‎ hhăy, גּוֹי‎ gōy, גָּלוּי‎ gā-lŭy, קַיָם‎ qăy-yēm, קָוָם‎ qăv-văm, etc. In all cases of this kind, it is easy to judge whether the *Ehevi* quiesce, or are moveable, by the nature of the preceding vowel. See further on the Quiescents, § 115 seq.

Note 1. In the *middle* of a word, the *Ehevi* are *always* marked with a Sheva in case they are moveable; at the *end* of a word, as Sheva is not written (§ 52), one must judge from the nature of the vowel which precedes, whether the *Ehevi* are quiescent or not.

Note 3. All the *Ehevi*, in the *middle* of words, not unfrequently *resist coalescence*, i. e. remain moveable; ה‎ always, א‎ sometimes even when the vowel is adapted to coalescence. At the *end* of words, they generally (not all of them uniformly) coalesce, unless the preceding vowel is heterogeneous. Compare § 119. *b.* § 120. *b.* § 121. *b.*

Otium of the Ehevi.

§ 57. There are some cases, in which the *Ehevi* are neither moveable consonants, nor coalescent with preceding vowels. They are then said to be *otiant*, (*in otio, otiantur*).

This happens in the following cases; viz. (*a*) When preceded by silent Sheva; as חָטְא‎ hhēt, אָתְּ‎ ăt. (*b*) Preceded by a Quiescent; as הֵבִיאתָ‎ hē-bhē-thā, with א‎ otiant. (*c*) Followed by Daghesh forte; as מַה־זֶּה‎ măz-zé=מַזֶּה‎. (*d*) Yodh preceded by Qamets and followed by ו‎ with a Sheva implied, is *otiant;* as דְּבָרָיו‎ dĕbhā-rāv, where Sheva is implied under the final ו‎, § 52.

Note. In such cases the *otiant* letter is mostly (not always) retained, out of regard to orthography, and to indicate the etymology of the word. So in a multitude of cases in English, we have *otiant* vowels; as in *honour, hear, moan*, etc.

Coalescence of Daghesh'd letters omitted with Vowels.

§ 58. The Gutturals and Resh scarcely ever admit Daghesh, i. e. reduplication, § 71. § 111. In cases where by analogy they ought to be doubled, but are not, the letter omitted by excluding the Daghesh, coalesces with the preceding vowel and lengthens it, § 32.

E. g. הָאָרֶץ‎ hā-ă-rĕts, instead of הָאָרֶץ‎ hăă-ă-rĕts; יֵאָמֵר‎ yē-ăă mēr, instead of יֵאָמֵר‎ yĭă-ă-mēr; בָּהֵל‎ bă-hēl, with Pattahh long and impure (§ 33), instead of בַּהֵל băh-hēl; בִּהֵל bĭ-hēl with Hhireq long and impure (§ 32), instead of בִּהֵל bĭh-hēl; אַחִים ăă-hhĭm with Pattahh long and impure (§ 33), instead of אַחִים ăhh-hhĭm; נִחָם nĭ-hhăm with Hhireq long and impure (§ 32), instead of נִחָם nĭhh-hhăm; בַּעֵר bă-עēr (§ 32), instead of בַּעֵר bă-עēr; מֵעִים mē-עĭm, instead of מִעִים mĭ-עĭm; בֵּרֵךְ bē-rēkh, instead of בִּרֵךְ bĭr-rēkh; בָּרֵךְ bā-rēkh, instead of בַּרֵךְ băr-rēkh, etc. Com. § 111. § 112.

Note. In regard to this usage, it is plain that an excluded daghesh'd letter lengthens the quantity of the preceding vowel; for in some cases this is expressed by using a vowel long by nature instead of a short one, as בָּרֵךְ for בַּרֵךְ. When in other cases the *form* of a doubtful vowel remains, the *quantity* of it is of course *long*, § 33.

To give reasons why a doubtful vowel is at one time used, and at another a vowel long by nature before the Gutturals excluding Daghesh, is out of our power. We can only notice and record the facts; but in respect to the grounds of them, we can merely say, Sic voluit usus.

§ 59. Some other letters occasionally omit Daghesh, with a similar effect, for the most part, on the preceding vowel.

E. g. וַיְהִי vă-yɛhī, instead of וַיְהִי văy-yɛhī. But it is doubtful how such cases as יְקָחוּ (for יִקְחוּ) were read; i. e. whether they were pronounced yĭ-qɛhhu or yĭq-hhu. The probability is, that there was a variety of pronunciation; for some of them are marked with a Methegh (§ 85), as וַיְהִי (for וַיְהִי); some with composite Sheva, as לֲקָחָה lŭ-qohhā (for לְקָחָה); both of which show that the first syllable is to be read as a simple one, vă-yɛhī, lŭ-qohhā; and so of others like them. But some words have neither of these marks, e. g. יְקָחוּ (for יִקְחוּ); and in such cases, they are probably to be read as יְקָחוּ yĭq-hhŭ, etc. The omission of Daghesh, in all such instances, seems to have respect only to the *niceties* of pronunciation in regard to a few words, which the Punctators strove to express. It does not belong to the essential form of words.

ORTHOGRAPHY OF THE VOWELS.

§ 60. By inspecting Table No. IV., it will be seen that the two first classes of vowels are all written *under* the consonants. Of the third class, Qibbuts also is written *under* them; but Hholem is written *over*, and Shureq *in* them. Qamets, however, is written in the bosom of a *final* Kaph; e. g. ךָ khā.

§ 61. The proper place of a vowel is under or over the *middle*, or (as they are now printed) the *right* side, of a consonant. Shureq is always written after the consonant to which it belongs, i. e. in the bosom of the following ו. Hholem is commonly written over the right side of the let-

§§ 62—64. ORTHOGRAPHY OF THE VOWELS.   29

ter next following that to which it belongs, as תֹּם *tōm*, קוֹל *qōl;* but sometimes necessity prevents this, e. g. in קָדְשׁ, where the type will not admit such a disposition of the Hholem. Hholem following א is commonly written over its left side, as אֹכֶל; unless followed by ו, as אוֹכֵל.

§ 62. The diacritical point over שׁ and שׂ often coincides with *Hholem;* in which case it serves the double purpose of marking the vowel and of distinguishing the letter. (1) שׁ beginning a syllable, if followed by a consonant having a vowel of its own, is read *sō;* e. g. שֹׂנֵה *sō-nê.* (2) שׁ following a consonant that has no vowel, contains a Hholem for that consonant, and also marks *sh;* e. g. מֹשֶׁה *mō-shê.* On the other hand, (3) שׁ with two points, *beginning* a syllable, is read *shō;* e. g. שֹׁמֵר *shō-mēr.* (4) שׂ with two points, *ending* a syllable, is read *ōs;* e. g. יִרְפֹּשׂ *yĭr-pōs.*

§ 62. Vav (ו) with a Hholem *over* it and a vowel *under* it, is joined as a moveable consonant with the vowel under it; e. g. לֹוֶה *lō-vê*, יְהֹוָה *yɛhō-vā*, the Hholem belonging to the preceding letter.

§ 63. *Vowels in connection with the Quiescents,* exhibit various modes of orthography which require explanation. As the Ehevi or Quiescents drop their distinct consonant-sound in case of coalescence (§ 53), and the words with vowel-points are sounded in the same manner whether the Quiescents are omitted or inserted; so, in practice, they are often omitted.

Note. Words in which the Quiescents are inserted, are said to be written *fully;* those in which they are omitted, to be written *defectively.* In both cases, the pronunciation and quantity of the vowels remain the same; as the following examples will shew.

Written fully.	Written defectively.	Read.
מִלֵּאתִי	מִלֵּתִי	*mă-lē-thĭ.*
נִיר	נִר	*nīr.*
קוֹל	קֹל	*qōl.*
קָמוּס	קָמֻס	*qă-mŭs.*

§ 64. There are some cases, in which Vav and Yodh (particularly the former) are inserted, when they are not proper Quiescents, and have no influence on the sound or nature of the vowel. In all these cases, they are mere orthographic *Fulcra.*

E. g. יְלָמוּד, the same as יְלָמֹד *yĭl-mōdh;* סֹבֵיב, the same as סֹבֵב *sō-bhēbh;* חוּקֵק, the same as חֻקֵק *hhŭq-qē;* comp. § 31. Notes 2. 3. In all probability, such forms sprung from the practice of employing Vav and Yodh as vowel-letters, § 15. How to distinguish such cases from those where ו and י are employed as true Quiescents, etymology only can teach; and with a knowledge of this, it is very easy.

§ 65. No certain rule can be given for the insertion or omission of Quiescents, when there is a real coalescence. More generally, when two syllables are immediately connected, in both of which there is a Quiescent, the first syllable omits it; e. g. צַדִּיק, צַדְּקִים. But instances of a contrary usage also exist; e. g. קוֹלוֹת=קֹלֹת; and sometimes both Quiescents are omitted, as שָׁלְשִׁם for שָׁלִישִׁים; so נִר for נִיר, etc. Even the same word is variously written; e. g. הֲקִימוֹתִי, הֲקְמוֹתִי, הֲקִמֹתִי, הֲקְמֹתִי, all pronounced $h^a q\bar{\imath}$-$m\bar{o}$-$th\bar{\imath}$.

Orthography of Qamets Hhateph.

From Table No. IV. it appears, that Qamets Hhateph (short *o*) has the same form with Qamets, viz. (ָ). It is important to point out how they may be distinguished.

I. Qamets Hhateph in a mixed syllable.

§ 66. (*a*) The figure (ָ) followed by simple Sheva without any Methegh between, is short *o*, if in a syllable not accented.

E. g. חָכְמָה *hhŏkh-mā*, not *hhā-khɛmā*. But with a Methegh it reads thus, חָֽכְמָה *hhā-khɛmā*. With an accent it reads as Qamets; e. g. מָ֫וְתָה *māv-tā*, שָׁ֫וְא *shāv*, לָ֫יְלָה *lāy-lā*.

Note. There are some few cases, where Methegh does not distinguish Qamets from short *o*; e. g. דָּרְבֹנוֹת *dŏr-bhō-nōth*, not *dhā-rɛbho-nōth*; so קָרְבָּן *qŏr-bān*, not *qā-rɛbhăn*; שָׁמְרָה *shŏm-rā*, not *shā-mɛrā*. But in these and the like cases, manuscripts and editions vary as to the Methegh; and etymology only can settle the true pronunciation.

(*b*) When followed by a letter with Daghesh forte, in a syllable not accented, (ָ) is short *o*.

E. g. בָּתִּים *bŏt-tīm*, חָנֵּנִי *hhŏn-nē-ni*. If the syllable is accented, it is read as long *a*; e. g. יָמָּה *yăm-mā*, לָמָּה *lăm-mā*, etc.

Note 1. An *euphonic* Daghesh (§ 75 seq.) at the *beginning* of a word does not make short *ŏ* of the (ָ) belonging to the last syllable of the preceding word; it remains long *ā* still; e. g. שָׁכְנָתָּ בּוֹ, read *shā-khăn-tāb-bō*. But this is merely a euphonic matter, and is contrary to the laws of the language in general.

Note 2. A Methegh after (ָ) does not *always* denote long *ā*; e. g. בָּתֵּיכֶם *bŏt-tē-khĕm*, not *bā-tē-khĕm*. See the the note under *a* above.

§§ 67—69. PATTAHH FURTIVE.

(c) The figure (ָ) in a final mixed syllable unaccented, is short *o*.

E. g. unaccented, as וַיָּ֫קָם *văy-yă-qŏm*. With accent, as הָאָדָ֫ם *hă-ă-dhām*, it is long *a*.

Remark. All the cases, *a, b, c,* are virtually one and the same, i. e. they are all cases of (ָ) in a *mixed unaccented* syllable; e. g. חָכְמָה *hhŏkh-mā,* בָּתִּים=בְּתִּים *bŏt-tīm,* וַיָּ֫קָם=וַיִּ֫קָם *văy-yă-qŏm,* all virtually the same as the case exhibited under the letter *a* above.

II. Qamets Hhateph in a simple syllable.

§ 67. The figure (ָ) is short *o* in a simple syllable, (*a*) When Qamets Hhateph, i. e. short *o* immediately follows.

E. g. פָּעָלְךָ *pŏ-ŏl-khā,* קָטְבְךָ *qŏ-tŏbh-khā.* But here (the reverse of § 66. *a*) a Methegh always stands after the first short *o*.

Note. But there are cases here, where etymology only can distinguish; e. g. קָטָ֫נִּי *qā-tōn-nī* (with Methegh according to § 87. *e*), not *qŏ-tōn-nī,* for the root is קָטֹן *qā-tōn.*

(*b*) When the composite Sheva, Hhateph Qamets (ֳ) immediately follows.

E. g. פָּעֳלוֹ *pŏ-ŏ°lō,* בְּחֳרִי *bŏ-hh°rī.* Methegh always stands after the (ָ) here also.

Note. Here also etymology alone can determine the reading in some cases. E. g. הָאֳנִיָּה *hă-ă°nīy-yā,* because הָ is the article (§ 162. § 152. *a.* 2); בָּאֳנִיָּה *bā-ă°nīy-yā,* because בָּ has the article included in it (§ 152. note); בְּאֳנִיָּה *bŏ-ă°nīy-yā,* because בְּ is the simple preposition בְּ, § 139.

§ 68. The nouns שָׁרָשִׁים *shŏ-rā-shīm* (from שֹׁרֶשׁ), and קָדָשִׁים *qŏ-dhā-shīm* (from קֹדֶשׁ), are altogether anomalous in their reading.

PATTAHH FURTIVE.

§ 69. This is a short Pattahh, employed for the sake of ease and euphony, when a word has either of the Gutturals, ה, ח, ע, at the end of its final syllable, preceded by a long vowel not of the *A* class.

E. g. גָּבוֹהַּ *gā-bho^ah,* רוּחַ *rū^ahh,* רֵעַ *rē^aʿ.* In order to pronounce these, lay the stress of the voice on the proper vowel, and just touch the Pattahh; somewhat as *ă* in the English words, *trial, vial,* etc. The furtive Pattahh is sounded *before* the final consonant. As it is merely a *euphonic* help, and belongs not to the essential form of the word; so it falls away, as soon as the syllable in which it stands changes its relative position; e. g. רוּחַ *rŭᵃhh*, plur. רוּחוֹת *rŭ-hhōth*.

Note. Aleph never takes Pattahh furtive.

DAGHESH.

§ 70. Dāghĕsh is a point in the bosom of a letter, and serves two purposes; (1) To double a letter. (2) To remove its aspiration.

§ 71. When Daghesh serves to double the letter in which it is written, it is called *Daghesh forte*. When it only removes the aspiration, it is called *Daghesh lene*.

Note. There is a kind of Daghesh that doubles a letter, (and may therefore be ranked under the head of Daghesh *forte)*, which is designed merely to regulate some peculiar mode of pronouncing certain words, and belongs not to the general analogy of the language. It is called *Daghesh euphonic* when we wish to distinguish it from Daghesh forte in general.

I. DAGHESH FORTE.

§ 72. *Daghesh forte distinguished from Daghesh lene.* The former is never written in the *final* letter of a word, unless such letter has a vowel; nor in the *first* letter, (although Daghesh euphonic usually appears here); and it is always *immediately preceded by a vowel-sound*.

Note. This last circumstance separates it entirely from Daghesh *lene;* which is *preceded immediately by a silent Sheva*, or if by a vowel, it is in a preceding word, which word has a *disjunctive* accent; see under § 93.

§ 73. *Orthography of Daghesh forte.* When the same letter is to be repeated, and the first one takes a *silent* Sheva, it is the usual practice to designate it by the point Daghesh forte; e. g. קְטַטֵל=קִטֵּל *qĭt-tēl.*

Note 1. Still there are many cases of a different orthography, which may be called *plenary*. E. g. צִלְלוֹ *tsĭl-lō*, instead of צִלּוֹ; יְשָׁדְדֵם for יְשַׁדֵּם *yĕshŏd-dēm*, etc.; particularly in derived forms of words, as קָלַת (not קִבַּת) from קָלְלָה, etc., in which cases Daghesh forte is not used.

Note 2. If the *first* of the two letters must have a Sheva *vocal*, Daghesh forte is excluded; e. g. עֹלֲלִים *ŏ-lĕlīm*, not עֹלִּים *ŏl-līm*.

Note 3. Practice not unfrequently omits Daghesh forte, when it would

§§ 74—76. DAGHESH EUPHONIC.

be immediately followed by a *vocal* Sheva, in case it were inserted; e. g. יִקְחוּ *yĭq-hhu̇*, instead of יִקְּחוּ *yĭq-qɛhhu̇*. Particularly is Daghesh omitted in such cases, if another letter of the same kind immediately follows; as הָלְלוּ *hâ-lɛlu̇* (not *hăl-lu̇*) because the word stands for הַלְּלוּ; which can be known, however, only by etymology. Comp. § 46. *f*. Note.

Note 4. Shureq is written in the same manner as Daghesh *forte*, in the letter וּ; e. g. וּ. But it is easily distinguished. When the *preceding* letter has no vowel, the point stands for Shureq; when it has one, it stands for Daghesh *forte*; e. g. קוּם is read *qu̇m*, but קוּם is sounded *qĭv-văm*.

§ 74. *Division of Daghesh forte.* (*a*) It is *compensative*, i. e. merely supplying a letter omitted in the writing.

E. g. נָתַנּוּ *nă-thăn-nu̇* for נָתַנְנוּ, יִגַּשׁ *yĭg-găsh* for יִנְגַּשׁ (§ 107. *a*) where נ is assimilated.

(*b*) *Characteristic*, i. e. distinguishing the particular form of a word.

E. g. קִטֵּל, the form of the conjugation *Piel*, in distinction from the form in Kal, viz. קָטַל.

Note. In אַתְּ *ăt*, probably for אַנְתְּ; שְׁתַּיִם *shɛta-yĭm*, for שְׁנְתַיִם; and such cases as כָּרַתְּ *kā-răt*, for כָּרַתְתְּ; the Daghesh in the Tav is properly *compensative*, although in a peculiar way.

Daghesh Euphonic.

So I name all those kinds of Daghesh forte which are merely *occasional*, and have respect only to *modes of reading* that are peculiar, in some particular cases.

[§ 75. Daghesh euphonic is of three kinds. (*a*) *Daghesh conjunctive.* So the first species of euphonic Daghesh may be named. It is frequently inserted in the *initial* consonant of a word, when it is preceded by a vowel *unaccented*. E. g. קָרִיתִי לִּי *qā-ri-thāl-li*, מַה־זֶּה *măz-zê*=מַזֶּה, יֶחֱסֶה־בּוֹ *yĕ-hhᵉsêb-bō*. The vowels Qamets, Pattahh, and Seghol, are almost the only ones employed before Daghesh *conjunctive*. Sometimes examples are found, like צְאוּ קוּמּוּ *qu̇-mu̇ts-tsɛ*אu̇.. Daghesh conjunctive is frequent, especially in the Psalms. It is rarely found after words with an accent on the *ultimate*; and where it is so, the reading is doubtful.

§ 76. (*b*) *Daghesh affectuosum.* This is a euphonic Daghesh, sometimes inserted in the *penult* letter of a word, when the tone falls on the penult syllable of the same; e. g. הָדְלּוּ *hhă-dhêl-lu̇*, instead of הָדְלוּ *hhă-dhɛlu̇*; יֵחַתּוּ *yē-hhăt-tu̇*, instead of יֵחַתּוּ. It were better to call this *Daghesh accented.* The object of it seems to be, to create a penult syllable on which the voice can rest, without the intervention of a Sheva before the final syllable.

§ 77. (c) *Daghesh acuting.* This appears in some cases where a letter would by analogy have a Sheva *silent;* and it both doubles the letter, and makes Sheva *vocal;* e. g. אֶבְרָךָ *ăĕk-kɛrĕ-hā,* instead of אֶכְרָךָ *ăĕkh-rĕ-hā.*]

Remark. In all cases of *euphonic Daghesh,* the manner of reading only is concerned; not the essential forms of words. The Daghesh of this kind is merely an attempt to preserve some niceties of pronunciation.

II. DAGHESH LENE.

§ 78. *Daghesh lene* belongs only to the Aspirates (בְּגַד כְּפַת *Bɛghădh kɛphăth),* and is a sign that they are to be pronounced without any aspiration, i. e. without an *h*-sound. E. g. ב is *bh,* but בּ=*b*; כּ=*kh,* כּ=*k,* etc. See alphabet No. II.

Note 1. Daghesh forte also appears in the Aspirates, as often as in other letters. But it is easily distinguished from Daghesh *lene;* for Daghesh *forte* is always preceded by a vowel belonging to the letter immediately before it; while the preceding letter has a silent Sheva under it, in case the Daghesh is *lene;* or if such preceding letter have a proper vowel, this vowel has a *disjunctive* accent upon it and belongs to a preceding word, § 92.

Note 2. Daghesh *forte* in an Aspirate, not only doubles it, but also (by usage in pronunciation) removes the aspiration; e. g. אַפִּי *ăp-pī,* not *ăph-pī,* although when written out in full, it would seem to be the latter, as אַפְפִי. Ease of enunciation demands the doubling of the letter without the aspiration.

General rules for the insertion of Daghesh lene.

§ 79. (1) It is inserted in all Aspirates standing at the commencement of a chapter or verse.

E. g. Gen. 1: 1, in בְּרֵאשִׁית the Beth takes Daghesh lene; so at the beginning of a verse, Gen. 3: 5, כִּי *kī* (not כִי *khī),* etc.

(2) In all cases, after a *silent* Sheva either expressed or implied.

E. g. in פָּקַדְתָּ, Tav has a Daghesh lene after a silent Sheva expressed; in עַל פְּנֵי, Pe has one after a Sheva *implied* under the ל, § 52.

(3) When preceded by a vowel (either pure or impure) at the end of a word having a *disjunctive* accent, an Aspirate at the beginning of the word that follows, takes a *Daghesh lene.*

E. g. Ps. 1: 3, וְהָיָה כְּעֵץ, where the Kaph must be aspirated, were it not that the disjunctive accent (*Rebhi*ᵅ) is on the preceding syllable יָהּ. And so of all the other Disjunctives; see the accents, § 92 seq.

General rules for the rejection of Daghesh lene.

§ 80. It is rejected when the Aspirates stand next after a *vocal* Sheva, or after a vowel either pure or impure, whether this vowel be within the same word, or at the end of a preceding one which has no *disjunctive* accent upon it.

E. g. Gen. 1: 2, וְהָיְתָה תֹהוּ, where the Tav in וְהָיְתָה follows a *vocal* Sheva (יְ *yɛ*); and in תֹהוּ *thō-hŭ* (not *tō-hŭ*), the ה follows a vowel with a quiescent letter, and that vowel is associated with a *conjunctive* accent (Merka), consequently ת remains aspirated. So after a composite Sheva; e. g. עֲבֹד *yᵃbhōdh* (not *yᵃbōdh*), because such Sheva is always *vocal*, § 46. *a*.

Note. In cases where a mere Pattahh furtive precedes an Aspirate, it sakes Daghesh lene; e. g. לָקַחַת *lā-qaᵃhht*, so written instead of לָקְחַת, § 233. Note.

General Exceptions.

Etymology and special usage have made many exceptions to these *general* rules.

[§ 81. (1) An Aspirate in the middle of a word, which is *derived by inflection* from a form of the same word that excluded Daghesh lene, also excludes it.

E. g. רִדְפוּ *rĭdh-phŭ* (not רִדְּפוּ) because the ground-form is רְדֹף, where the Pe, being immediately preceded by a Hholem, cannot take a Daghesh lene, § 80. So מַלְכֵי *măl-khē*, ground-form מְלָכִים, in which כ is preceded by a vowel; יַעֲזְבוּ *yă-ăz-bhŭ*, ground-form יַעֲזֹב, where ב, having a vowel before it, cannot receive Daghesh lene; Infinitive mode בְּגֹד *bɛghŏdh*, and with suffix בִּגְדוֹ *bĭgh-dhō*, because ד in the ground-form has a vowel before it.

(2) Loose prefixes (which in fact are separate words) do not affect the insertion or omission of Daghesh lene, in respect to the second letter of any word when it is an Aspirate.

E. g. כְּתָב with the preposition בְּ prefixed, is written בִּכְתָב *bĭkh-thābh* (not בְּכְתָב); כְּפִיר with כְּ prefixed, בִּכְפִיר *kĭkh-phĭr* (not בְּכְפִיר); גְּבוּל with לְ, לִגְבוּל *lĭgh-bhŭl* (not לְגְבוּל), etc.

Note 1. The Infinitive mode with such a loose prefix, varies in its usage. E. g. סָפַד, Infin. סְפֹד, with prefix לְ, לִסְפֹד *lĭs-pōdh*; and such is the *more common* usage. But we find also נָפַל, Infin. נְפֹל, with pre-

fix בְּ, בִּנְפֹל *bĭn-phōl*; with כְּ, כִּנְפֹל *kĭn-phōl*; but with לְ, לִנְפֹל *lĭn-pol*.
Usage therefore is variable in regard to this mode.

Note 2. But when the prefix is *closely* united to a word, so as to constitute (as it were) an essential part of the word itself, then the general rule (§ 79. 2) is followed; e. g. יִסְפֹּד *yĭs-podh* (not יִסְפֹד), Fut. of Kal from the root סָפַד *sā-phădh*; or (if you please) from the Infinitive form, סְפֹד *sɛphōdh*. So in Hiphil, הִשְׁפִּיל *hĭs-pīl* (not הִשְׁפִיל), from שָׁפֵל. In all such cases, the prefix is considered and treated as an *essential formative* part of the word.]

Particular Exceptions.

[§ 82. (1) *Rejection of Daghesh lene*. (*a*) The suffix pronouns, ךָ, כֶם, בֶן, reject it. (*b*) Generally, an Aspirate preceding the final syllable וּת; as מַלְכוּת, עַבְדוּת, יַלְדוּת, etc.; but not always, as תַּרְבּוּת *tăr-būth*. (*c*) The various forms of בֶּגֶד; e. g. בִּגְדוֹ, בִּגְדִי, etc.

(2) *Admission of it contrary to the general rules*. (*d*) Some words beginning with two Aspirates, viz. בב, בפ, כב, e. g. Jer. 3: 25, נִשְׁכְּבָה בְּבָשְׁתֵּנוּ; Ex. 14: 17, וְאִכָּבְדָה בְּפַרְעֹה; Is. 10: 19, כְּכַרְכְּמִישׁ לֹא: but in all such cases, manuscripts and editions differ; some extending the rule, so as to begin with Daghesh lene in most cases where a word commences with two Aspirates; others scarcely observing such a rule at all; e. g. Michaelis' Hebrew Bible. (*e*) A few words which usage only has excepted from the general rule; e. g. עֹמְדִים from עָמְדֵי, רֹשְׁפֵי from רְשָׁפִים. (*f*) An apparent exception is an Aspirate after יְהוָה, which takes Daghesh lene. But the Hebrews read this word אֲדֹנָי *a"dō-nāy*, which ends in the consonant *y* having a silent Sheva.]

Remark. The detail of Daghesh lene, as to some *few* words and forms, is not regulated by any established usage; the Masora, the Rabbins, manuscripts, and editions, differing in respect to some particulars. But as nothing important in grammar depends on the insertion or omission of Daghesh, in such cases, the student need not be perplexed, if he occasionally meet with instances not conformed to the general principles. Mistakes in printing and transcribing have occasioned some of these anomalies; and conceit has increased the number.

RAPHE.

§ 83. Rāphê (רָפֶה) means *soft*. It is a small parallel stroke, of the same form as Pattahh, put *over* Aspirates, to show that they retain their aspiration; e. g. כָבְדָה *khā-bhɛdhā*; and so it is directly the opposite of Daghesh lene.

The printed editions of the Hebrew Scriptures have long ceased to use this sign, (which indeed is quite superfluous), with the exception of a very few solitary cases; e. g. Judg. 16: 16, 28. Num. 32: 42, in Van der Hooght. In ancient manuscripts it was very common;

§§ 84—87. MAPPIQ.—METHEGH.

and it was sometimes employed, moreover, to shew that Daghesh forte was omitted; sometimes, that Mappiq did not belong to ה; and sometimes, to note that א and ה at the end of words were quiescent.

MAPPIQ.

§ 84. Măppīq (מַפִּיק) is a point in the bosom of a final ה, (which is almost always quiescent), denoting that it is moveable.

E. g. יָה yăh (יָה would read yā); גָּבָהּ gā-bhăh (גבה must be written גָּבָה and read gā-bhā).

Note. Mappiq is now used only in final ה; but in some Hebrew manuscripts it is found in the other Quiescents, denoting that they are moveable.

METHEGH.

§ 85. Mĕthĕgh (מֶתֶג) is a small perpendicular mark (׀), preceding the tone-syllable more or less according to the various purposes for which it is employed, and denoting a secondary or half-accent, analogous to that on the first syllable of our English words un˙dertáke, nòminátion, etc.

The word *Methegh (fraenum, retinaculum)* denotes, when technically employed, a holding in or restraint of the voice, viz. in reading, *(decora suspensio vocis)*; which of course gives a kind of half tone or accent to the syllable. It does not, like the other accents, relate to the connection of words with each other, but only to the manner of reading the syllable on which it is placed; and is therefore of comparatively little importance to us.

Note. The mark (׀) on the last or penult syllable of a verse, is always the accent Silluq (§ 93), not Methegh.

[§ 86. Manuscripts and editions differ widely as to the frequency of using Methegh; the Spanish manuscripts exhibiting it very sparingly, the German ones very frequently. The Codex Cassel. scarcely has it at all. In regard to many cases, the Jewish grammarians themselves are not agreed about the use of it. Consequently there is much discrepancy respecting it in our best Hebrew bibles.]

Uniform or general use of Methegh.

[§ 87. IT IS UNIFORMLY EMPLOYED, (a) Before all the composite Shevas, when they are preceded by a vowel, (and technically called in this case מַאֲרִיךְ mă-a^arīkh); e. g. יַעֲמֹד, יַחֲלֹף, הָעֳמַד, זְעָקָה, אֹהֳלוֹ, etc. (b) *Almost uniformly* in such cases, after the composite Sheva has fallen away by inflection, etc.; e. g. יַעֲמֹד, by inflection יַעַמְדוּ, preserving the Methegh; (or this case may be ranked with *e* below). (c) After a

§ 87. METHEGH.

long vowel next before the tone syllable, and followed by Sheva vocal ; e. g. גְּבֻלְךָ, תּוֹלְדוֹת, תִּירְאִי, תֵּלְדִי, חָיְתָה with Qibbuts vicarious. (d) The verbs הָיָה and חָיָה, when they take formative or other prefixes with a short vowel, employ Methegh after such vowel ; e. g. לִהְיוֹת וִהְיוּ, Imp. with ו, Gen. 12: 2, יְחִיֶה, etc. ; nearly without exception, in good editions. In principle, this may be classed with h below.

VERY GENERALLY EMPLOYED, (e) On the second syllable before the tone, where it is a simple one ; as הָאָדָם, יוֹנָתָן. (f) But if this be a mixed syllable, then on the *third* before the tone, provided it be simple ; e. g. וּמְחָלְבֵהֶן, וָאֶגְתֹּר. (g) After a short vowel made long by position (§ 33), before a letter which excludes a Daghesh forte either necessarily or arbitrarily ; as בְּהָלוֹת, וַיְבָרֶךְ, לַמְנַצֵּחַ, בַּחוּרִים, הֶחָכָם בְּסְעָרָה, 2 K. 2: 11. etc. But this is sometimes neglected, as הַחֹשֶׁךְ ; specially when Yodh with Sheva follows the vowel made long by omitting the Daghesh, e. e. וַיְבָרֶךְ, וַיְכַלּוּ, &c. ; and commonly so, in regard to Hhireq, as Piel נִחַל, נַחֵל, etc. without Methegh.]

The qualifying terms, *almost uniformly, very generally*, will of course advertise the student that he is not to expect *uniformity* in the cases ranged under them.

Occasional use of Methegh.

[(h) After a short vowel in a mixed syllable (not made by Daghesh forte), especially after Pattahh and short Hhireq, Methegh is placed, sometimes on the first, and sometimes on the second syllable before the tone ; e. g. on the *first*, as תִּדְשָׁא, עֲרָבוֹת, יַחְדִּלוּ, לְנַרְעֲבָם, סֻכְּבֵי, Is. 10: 34, נִדְרִי. Ps. 76: 12, וַיִּזְבְּחוּ, וּמִכְנָסֵי ; with other short vowels, וִהְיָה (d above), יֶחְגֶּה, שָׁמְרָה shŏmrā, קָרְבָּן qŏrbān, דָּרְבָּן dŏrban, עָמָדְךָ ʿᵃmŏdhkha, etc. ; on the *second*, as הִשְׁתַּחֲווּ, וַיִּתְפָּרְקוּ, מְתֵיהַדָּרִים, etc. The cases with other vowels than Pattahh or short Hhireq, are rare. (i) On the first syllable of a polysyllabic word, when this syllable ends with a daghesh'd letter ; e. g. בְּתֵיכֶם, וַיִּשְׁחָטוּ, הַקְּדֵשִׁים, מִסְפַּרְךָ, etc. ; especially when the first letter is Vav conversive, Mem prefix, or He article.]

Rare use of Methegh.

[(j) Very seldom, after a vocal Sheva under the first letter ; as וָאֵת, דְּבַה, שָׂאוּ ; more rarely still, even before Sheva initial, as וָאֵת, Est. 9: 7—9, ten times. In these cases it is called Methegh *initial ;* the older Jewish grammarians named it גַּעְיָא, *mugitus ;* a name afterwards extended to Methegh generally.]

Methegh before Maqqeph.

[(l) The general principle is the same as if the two words joined by Maqqeph were one, (they being read as one) ; so that the above rules

generally apply; e. g. מֵעַל־בִּי, e; וְרָאָה־לּוֹ, h; כִּי־עִמּוֹ, e; בְּתוֹךְ־
הָאָרֶץ, e, etc. (m) In many cases long monosyllables before Maqqeph
take a Methegh (often otherwise), although a tone-syllable follows immediately, e. g. בֵית־אֵל, הֲלֹא־זֶה; and even when it does not, and the
monosyllable is a mixed one, as שׁוּב־אָדָם, etc., contrary to e. Short
vowels before Maqqeph commonly reject Methegh; as עַד־בֵּית, etc.]

Such are the numerous and very indefinite (not to say contradictory) principles for the use of
Methegh. No wonder that no two editions or manuscripts agree in regard to it. Some of the
very words employed here as examples, are differently marked in different editions.

Note 1. The conjunction ו (and) does not generally receive Methegh.

Note 2. Several Metheghs may appear on the same word, if the different rules for writing it should require them; e. g. צַאֲצָאֵיהֶם, for the
Methegh on צ, see e above; for that on צ, see a.

Note 3. Instead of Methegh, the *conjunctive* accents (especially
Munahh, Qadma, and Merka, § 93) are frequently used, when a word
has a *distinctive* accent upon it; e. g. וְלִמוֹעֲדִים with Munahh under מ,
instead of וְלִמוֹעֲדִים with Methegh; and so in very many cases.

MAQQEPH.

§ 88. Măqqēph (מַקֵּף), somewhat like our hyphen,
connects two words together, and makes them as one in
respect to interpunction and reading.

E. g. אֲחֻסָּה־בּוֹ, אֶת־הַשָּׁמַיִם. Usually either the former or latter
word, in cases of this nature, is *short;* as in the examples produced.

§ 89. The word before Maqqeph throws off its tonic
accent; and a long vowel in its final syllable is for the
most part shortened, if pure.

E. g. עַל־הָאָרֶץ, where עַל has no accent, Gen. 1: 15. For the reason why the long vowels before Maqqeph (which removes the tone) are
shortened, see § 36. § 129. *a*. But here, the punctators were not uniform;
for we have לֵב־דָּוִד *lēbh-Dāvidh* (not לֵב־דָּוִד), and without Methegh
too, in 1 Sam. 24: 6; but also לֵב־אִישׁ *lēbh-*אish, 2 K. 12: 5; and thus
in other cases.

Note 1. Mappeph sometimes appears between several words in succession, as אֶת־כָּל־אֲשֶׁר־לוֹ. Mostly it is employed only between
words closely connected in sense, e. g. between prepositions and their
nouns, words in regimen, etc.; but its use is not confined to these, and
is very arbitrary in many cases, about which manuscripts and editions,
and also Jewish grammarians and critics, disagree. In some few cases
it stands after a polysyllabic word; as הִתְהַלֶּךְ־נֹחַ, Gen. 6: 9.

Note 2. Maqqeph might itself well be called a *conjunctive* accent *sui generis*, as it in most cases plainly supplies the place of a usual Conjunctive. E. g. the famous Jewish critics, Ben Asher and Ben Naphthali, disagree, in a multitude of cases, whether a Maqqeph or a Conjunctive is to be put on certain words. It differs from other Conjunctives only in this, viz. that it usually causes the preceding long mutable vowel to be shortened. In like manner, Pesiq, inserted *between* words, is reckoned a *disjunctive* accent.

RULES FOR READING HEBREW.

§ 90. The principal difficulty is, to know where to begin and end a syllable. The following rules may aid the beginner.

1. Every syllable must begin with a moveable letter.

Note. Vav with Shureq (וּ) in the beginning of words is the only exception, and is sounded *ŭ*=*oo* in English. In אָמַר *ā-mǎr*, עָנֻד *ǎ-mǎdh*, etc. the א and ע are moveable, although *we* do not sound them, because we know not what sound to give them.

2. No syllable can have more than two moveable letters *before* its vowel; and none admits more than one *after* its vowel, except a final syllable which may have two.

3. Every vowel stands in a *simple* syllable, when followed by a letter which has a vowel belonging to it.

4. Every *short* vowel in a *mixed* syllable, is followed by a simple Sheva expressed or implied, or by a Daghesh forte; e. g. בַּרְזֶל *bǎr-zěl*, in which the first syllable has a Sheva expressed, the second a Sheva implied; so לִמְּדֵּ *lĭm-mĕdh*=לִמְמֵד.

5. Every *long* vowel makes a *mixed* syllable, when followed by a simple Sheva expressed or implied, or by an implied Daghesh forte, *provided* such vowel be in *a tone-syllable*. E. g. קָם *qām*; יִקְטֹלְנָה *yĭq-tōl-nā*, where the Hholem is in a mixed tone-syllable; יָמָּה *yām-mā*=לְיָמְמָה; אֵת *ēth*, where Sheva is implied under the ת.

6. A *long* vowel, not in a tone-syllable, makes a *simple* syllable, though followed by a Sheva; e. g. קָטְלָה *qā-tɛlā*, בְּגָדִים *bō-gɛdhīm*; but not always so before a Maqqeph, as לֶב־דָּוִד *lēbh-Dā-vidh*.

7. Every vowel followed by a real Quiescent makes a *simple* syllable, provided the letter next after the Quiescent have a vowel belonging to it, or the Quiescent stands at the end of a word. E. g. in רֵאשִׁית *rē-shīth*, רֵא is a simple syllable, because the שׁ which comes next after it has a vowel of its own; in בָּרָא *bā-rā*, רָא is a final simple syllable.

§ 91. READING OF THE HEBREW. 41

8. Every vowel followed by a real Quiescent makes a *mixed* syllable, if the next succeeding moveable letter is destitute of a vowel. E. g. in רֵאשִׁית *rē-shīth*; שִׁית is a mixed syllable because ה has no vowel of its own. But such syllables must always be tone-syllables; excepting the very few cases where quiescent ו is irregularly used in short syllables, § 31. Note 3.

9. Short vowels make a simple syllable, when the next succeeding letter has a vowel of its own.

10. Every composite Sheva, and every simple Sheva vocal, stands of course at the beginning of a syllable, § 46.

11. The vowels long by position, i. e. the doubtful vowels having a daghesh'd letter in them, always stand in a simple syllable.

Exemplification of reading Hebrew.

§ 91. (1) Gen. 1: 1. בְּרֵאשִׁית *bɛrē-shīth;* בְּ with Daghesh lene 79.*1; with a Sheva under it 45, and with a Sheva *vocal* 46. — רֵ *rē*, with a quiescent long vowel 31, quiescent in Aleph 54 א. — שִׁית *shīth*, with the like vowel followed by quiescent Yodh 54 י; ה without any Sheva expressed, having one implied 52; also without a Daghesh lene 80. — שִׁית is a mixed syllable 90. 8.

(2) בָּרָא *bā-rā;* בָּ with Daghesh lene 79. 2, בָּ a simple syllable 90. 3. — רָא *rā*, vowel protracted 31. *a*, א quiescent 54.

(3) אֱלֹהִים *ɛlō-hīm;* אֱ with composite Sheva 49, which is moveable 46. *a*. —ֹל *lō*, simple syllable 90. 3. — הִים *hīm*, with Yodh quiescent 54, and Hhireq protracted 31. *a*, and in a mixed syllable 90. 8.

(4) אֵת *ēth* 90. 5. — הַשָּׁמַיִם *hāsh-shā-mă-yim* ; הַשׁ *hăsh*, this syllable comprising the *sh* which is made by the Daghesh forte in the שׁ 71 and 73, also 90. 4. — שָׁ *shā* 90. 3. — מַ *mă*, with Pattahh pure and short 34, also with accent upon it 100. *b*, and in a simple syllable 90. 9. — יִם *yĭm*, with short Hhireq 141 and 100. *a*, mixed short syllable 90. 4.

(5) וְאֵת *vɛēth;* Vav moveable 56. 1, אֵת as above in No. 4.

(6) הָאָרֶץ *hā-ʾā-rɛts;* הָ 90. 3. — אָ 90. 3, and with א moveable 56. 1. — רֶץ *rɛts*, with short Seghol 34, and in a mixed syllable 90. 4.

(7) VERSE 2. וְהָאָרֶץ *vɛhā-ʾā-rɛts;* וְ *vɛ* in No. 5.

(8) הָיְתָה *hā-yɛthā ;* הָ with Qamets long 66. *a*. — יְ *yɛ*, Yodh moveable 56. 1. — תָה *thā*, ת without Daghesh lene 80, and followed by ה quiescent 54 ה.

(9) תֹהוּ *thō-hū;* ת without Daghesh lene 80. — הוּ *hū* with ה moveable 56. 1, and with ו quiescent 54 ו.

† Note. In this exemplification, the first number in any reference stands for a section (§) in the Grammar; others following this, stand for the subdivisions under the section.

(10) וּבְהוּ *vā-bhō-hŭ;* וְ *vā* 56. 1, simple syllable 90. 3. — בְ *bhō,* ב without Daghesh lene 80, simple syllable 90. 3.

(11) וְחִכֶּךָ *vɛhhō-shĕkh;* וְ *vɛ* 56. 1.— חֹ *hhō,* Hholem in a pure syllable; the point over the right tooth of the Shin stands as well for the vowel Hholem as to mark *sh* 62. 2; read as a simple syllable *hhō* 90. 3. — שֶׁךְ *shĕkh,* short Seghol and mixed syllable, see in No. 6; Sheva in the final Kaph, 52. 1.

(12) עַל *ăl* 90. 4.— פְּנֵי *pɛnē;* Pe with Daghesh lene 79. 2, Sheva vocal 46. *d.* — נֵי *nē* 54 י.

(13) תְּהוֹם *thɛhōm;* ת without Daghesh lene 80.— הוֹם *hhōm* 90. 8.

(14) וְרוּחַ *vɛrū*ᵃ*hh;* וְ *vɛ* in No. 5. — רוּחַ *rū*ᵃ*hh,* with Pattahh furtive 69.

(15) אֱלֹהִים *ĕlō-hīm,* No. 3. מְרַחֶפֶת *mɛrâ-hhĕ-phĕth;* רַ with Pattahh long 33 and 90. 11.— חֶ *hhĕ,* with Seghol pure and short 34, and accented 100. *a.*

(16) עַל־פְּנֵי *ăl pɛnē,* No. 12. הַמָּיִם *hăm-mā-yĭm,* the Daghesh forte in Mem attaches to the first syllable *hăm,* 90. 4. — מָיִם *mā-yĭm* 90. 3. — יִם *yĭm,* with short *ĭ* 328.

(17) VERSE 3. *Văy-yō-mĕr* אֱלֹהִים *yɛhī,* אוֹר (with א moveable 56. 1, although we do not sound it); *vâ-yɛhī* אוֹר, (in *vá* the Pattahh has a Daghesh implied in it, and is to be regarded as long 59).

(18) VERSE 4. וַיַּרְא *văy-yăr* (with א *otiant* at the end 57. *a*) *ĕlō-hīm ĕth hā-*אוֹר *kī-tōbh, văy-yăbh-dēl ĕlō-hīm bēn hā-*אוֹר *ū-bhēn* (*ŭ* 90. 1. Note) *hâ-hhō-shĕkh* (הַ *há* 59).

(19) VERSE 5. *Văy-yĭq-rā* אֱלֹהִים *lā-*אוֹר *yōm, vɛlâ-hhō-shĕkh* (לַ *lá* 59) *qā-rā lāy-lā* (לָ֫י *lāy* 66. *a.* under e. g.) *vâ-yɛhī* (*vá* in No. 17) *yĕ-rĕbh vâ-yɛhī bhō-qĕr yōm* אֵ*ê-hhādh* (אֵ *ê* 58).

ACCENTS.

§ 92. The other small marks of various forms accompanying the Hebrew text, are *accents.** They are divided into two great classes; viz. (*a*) Such as separate words, or parts of sentences, from each other; which are called DISJUNCTIVES. (*b*) Such as serve to shew that words are to be closely connected, either in the reading or in the sense; which are called CONJUNCTIVES.

---

* Usually called *tonic* accents, in order to distinguish them from Methegh which is called the *euphonic* accent.

§ 93. ACCENTS.

[§ 93. The following table exhibits the forms, names, and classification of the accents. Some of them are used both in poetry and prose; and such have no mark prefixed. Others are peculiar to prose, and these have (†) prefixed. Others are peculiar to poetry, and these have (*) prefixed. *Poetry* means (according to the accentuators) only the books of Job, Psalms, and Proverbs, called technically אֱמֶת, these being the three initials of the Hebrew names of these books.

Note. The reader will observe, that the parallel blank line within the parentheses which stand next after the numbers, is intended to represent the line of Hebrew letters; and consequently the position of the accents in relation to this, is also marked.

I. DISJUNCTIVES.

(1) *Pause-accents, or Disjunctives of the first class.*

1. (:֖—) *Silluq*, סִלּוּק, i. e. stop, pause. In connection with the two large points that always follow it, it is named סִלּוּק בְּסוֹף פָּסוּק, *pause at the end of a verse.* Elsewhere this same mark stands for Methegh, § 85. Note.

2. (֑—) *Athnahh*, אַתְנָח, i. e. respiration.

* 3. (֤—) *Merka Mahpakh*, מֵרְכָא מַהְפָּךְ, a composite accent, see Nos. 23. 25.

(2) *Occasional Pause-accents, or Disjunctives of the second class.*

† 4. (֖—) *Tiphhha*, תִּפְחָה (posterius), i. e. palm of the hand, from the shape. It is also named תַּרְחָא *retardation*, and (when next before Silluq and Athnahh) מַאְיְלָא *strong*. In poetry, it is merely a Conjunctive; see No. 30.

* 5. (֖—) *Tiphhha* (anterius); *praepositive*, § 95. a.

† 6. (֔—) *Zaqeph Qaton*, זָקֵף קָטוֹן, i. e. elevator minor.

† 7. (֕—) *Zaqeph Gadhol*, זָקֵף גָּדוֹל, i. e. elevator major.

† 8. (֒—) *Segholta*, סְגֹלְתָּא, i.e. cluster of grapes; *postpositive*, § 95.a.

(3) *Lesser Disjunctives, or Disjunctives of the third Class.*

† 9. (֛—) *Tebhir*, תְּבִיר, i. e. interruption.

10. (֗—) *Rebhi*ᵃ, רְבִיעַ, i. e. resting upon or lying over.

* 11. (֗—) *Rebhi*ᵃ *Geresh*, a composite accent, with the Geresh *praepositive*, comp. Nos. 10, 15; also § 95. a.

† 12. (֙—) *Pashta*, פַּשְׁטָא, i. e. expansion (of the voice); *postpositive*, § 95. a.

13. (֮—) *Zarqa*, זַרְקָא, i. e. dispersion; *postpositive*. In poetry (when not postpositive) it is a mere Conjunctive; see No. 31, also § 95. a.

§ 93. ACCENTS.

† 14. (־֚) *Yethibh,* יְתִיב, i. e. sitting; *praepositive.* It is also called שֹׁפָר מוּקְדָם *tuba anterior,* and שֹׁפָר מֻשְׁפָּל *tuba inferior;* see § 95. *a.*

* 15. (־֜) *Geresh,* גֶּרֶשׁ, i. e. expulsion. Also called טֶרֶס *shield* (Arabic تُرْس *clypeus*), and אַזְלָא *retention* (أَزَلَ *cohibuit*).

† 16. (־֞) *Garshăyim,* גֵּרְשַׁיִם, i. e. double Geresh. Also called טְרָסִין, טְרָסַיִם, dual and plural of טֶרֶס *shield.*

† 17. (־֛) *Telisha Gedhola,* תְּלִישָׁה גְדוֹלָה, i. e. evulsio major; also תַּרְסָא; *praepositive,* § 95. *a.*

† 18. (־֟) *Qarne Phara,* קַרְנֵי פָרָה, i. e. the two horns of a heifer, (from the shape).

19. (־֡) *Pazer,* פָּזֵר, i. e. disperser. Also פָּזֵר גָּדוֹל.

20. (׀) *Pesiq,* פְּסִיק, i. e. cessation, written in the line between words, and placed (as here) perpendicularly. Also called פִּסְקָא, *separation.* Always preceded by a Conjunctive on the word after which it is placed.

II. CONJUNCTIVES.

21. (־ֽ) *Munahh,* מֻנָּח, i. e. joined. Also שֹׁפָר יָשָׁר *tuba recta,* and שֹׁפָר הֹלֵךְ *tuba ambulans.* In poetry both *superius* and *inferius.* On an ultimate syllable, and followed by Athnahh, Zarqa, or Zaqeph Qaton, it is called עִלּוּי, *Illŭy,* i. e. ascent. When placed at the beginning of a word, and followed by Zaqeph Qaton, it is named מְכַרְבֵּל *mekharbel, sieve,* i. e. agitation (of the voice).

22. (־֨) *Qadhma,* קַדְמָא, i. e. before.

23. (־֥) *Merka,* מֵרְכָא (apoc. of מַאֲרְכָא) i. e. prolonging; also מֵרִיךְ, מַאֲרִיךְ id.

† 24. (־֦) *Merka Kehphula,* מֵרְכָא כְפוּלָה, i. e. Merka doubled. Also תְּרֵין חוּטְרִין, *two rods.*

25. (־֤) *Mahpakh,* מַהְפַּךְ, i. e. inversion. Also שֹׁפָר מְהֻפָּךְ, *crooked trumpet,* שֹׁפָר הָפוּךְ *inverted trumpet.* In poetry, *superius* or *inferius;* in prose, *inferius.*

26. (־֓) *Shalsheleth,* שַׁלְשֶׁלֶת, i. e. chain.

† 27. (־֧) *Darga,* דַּרְגָּה, i. e. steps, gradation.

† 28. (־֩) *Telisha Qetanna,* תְּלִישָׁה קְטַנָּה, i. e. evulsio minor. Also תְּלִשָׁה *(eradicator?) postpositive,* § 95. *a.*

29. (‍ָ—) *Yerahh*, יֶרַח, i. e. moon. Also יֶרַח בֶּן־יוֹמוֹ, *the moon a day old*, עֲגֻלָּה *round*, גַּלְגַּל *wheel*.

* 30. (֡—) *Tiphhha* (posterius), in poetry a Conjunctive; comp. no. 4.

* 31. (—֘) *Zarqa*, in poetry a Conjunctive, when it is *not* postpositive; see No. 13.]

§ 94. The accents are said to be subservient to three purposes; viz. (1) To mark the tone-syllable. (2) To serve as signs of interpunction. (3) To regulate the reading, or rather, the *cantillating* of the Scriptures.

§ 95. (1) *To mark the tone-syllable*, is what they generally do. But the cases of exception are very numerous.

[(*a*) Eight of them are always confined to the same position, let the tone be where it may; e. g. Segholta, Pashta, Zarqa (No. 13), and Telisha Qetanna, must always be put over the *last* letter of a word, and are therefore called POSTPOSITIVE ; while Tiphhha *anterius*, Yethibh, Telisha Gedhola, and Geresh in the composite accent *Rebhi^a Geresh* (No. 11), belong only to the *first* letter of a word, and are therefore called PRAEPOSITIVE; see the Table. Of course these accents sometimes fall in with the tone-syllable; but oftentimes the reverse of this happens.

<small>The student therefore can never depend on them as universal guides, in respect to the *tone* of words. He must resort to the *general principles* which regulate the tone, in all doubtful cases.</small>

(*b*) Many words have *two* accents on them. In this case, if both accents are of the *same* form, the *first* marks the tone; e. g. הֹוִי , with the tone on the *penult*. If the accents are of *different* forms, then the *last* (left hand one) marks the tone-syllable, i. e. if it belong to those accents which always mark the tone; e. g. וּבְמֹעֲדִים , where דִים֑_ is acuted. Here is one *Conjunctive* and one *Disjunctive* upon the word ; but sometimes there are two *Disjunctives*, as קָֽרְבוּ֘ , Lev. 10: 4 ; and sometimes even two on the same monosyllable, as חָֽי֑ , Gen. 5: 29. Very often, two *Conjunctives* are put upon one and the same word, as גְּדֻלוֹת , Ps. 96 : 4.

<small>All this shews the utter improbability that the accents were originally invented for the purpose of marking the tone. The numerous cases of *double* accentuation, and of *praepositive* and *postpositive* accents that do not coincide with the tone syllable, prove that the marking of it by the accents in general, is a *secondary*, and not a *primary* object of these signs. If this be maintained, are we to say that one and the same syllable has *two* tones at the same time ? For so we must conclude from this principle, and from the occurrence of such examples as חָֽי֑ . But if the *cantillation* is marked by the accents (§ 97), then two accents may both be regarded and expressed, when on the same syllable; but not on any other ground.]</small>

§ 96. (2) *Accents as signs of interpunction*. This is the use most commonly assigned to them as the principal one. In many cases they accord well with the divisions of sense. In the poetical books, the pause-accents are useful in marking the end of στίχοι; and for the most part, they do this with accuracy. But in all parts of the Bible there is a multitude of cases, where the accents make pauses in utter disagreement with the sense; so obviously is this the case, that the Punctators cannot be supposed, by any one, to have been ignorant of it. E. g. in Gen. 1: 1, we have אֱלֹהִים, i. e. a pause-accent (Athnahh) of the largest kind, like our colon, placed between a verb with its subject, and the Acc. case which the verb governs; and so, in many hundreds of instances. This serves to shew, that the use of the accents by way of *interpunction* is only secondary.

[Note. The *pause-accents* are supposed to mark the greater divisions of the sense, (like our colon and semicolon); the *Disjunctives* of the second class, subdivide these; and those of the third class make a division of these parts into minuter portions still, (like our comma, and as it were like a half-comma); so that a verse is broken up into very small portions, of one, two, or three words, each; rarely of more. But all this arrangement of accents has its regular order, for the most part; for there is a prescribed *consecution* of the accents, each Disjunctive having its appropriate place when admitted by the nature and length of a verse, and its respective Conjunctives (shewing what words are to be joined together) being regularly attached to it, i. e. preceding it. The manner and order of this *consecution*, belongs properly to a treatise on the accents. The student who wishes to become acquainted with it, may find it represented at great length in Boston's *Tractatus Stigmologicus*, Wasmuth's *Institt. Accentuum*, Abicht *de Accentibus*; and in the second edition of this Grammar, in the Appendix, he will find an abridged exhibition of the whole system, on which much time and pains have been bestowed.]

§ 97. *Accents as signs of cantillation.* The Jews do not read, but *cantillate* the Scriptures; as the Moslems do their Koran. The accents direct this. The Koran too has marks for such a purpose. This appears to me plainly to have been the *original* design of the accents, viz. to guide the *recitativo*. Now as this was regulated, more or less, by the *tones* of words and by the *sense* of a passage, so the accentuation very often (and more usually) accords with these objects; but still, in a multitude of cases it has no direct reference to them.

For an exhibition in musical notes of the *recitativo* power of the accents, see Jablonskii Praef. ad *Bib. Heb.* § 24, and Bartoloccii *Bibliotheca Rabbin.* IV. p. 341.

§ 98. The *proper* place of an accent (neither praepositive nor postpositive), is over or under *the left side* of the letter which begins a syllable. The imperfection of types sometimes prevents the *printed* books from following this rule.

Remark. The student should *gradually* make himself acquainted with the accents, so as to distinguish and to name them. The Conjunctives often shew what words should be *connected* in sense; the Disjunctives, which should be *separated*. They serve, therefore, as an index of the construction which the Accentuators put upon the Hebrew text. In a very great number of cases, the pause-accents (and sometimes all the others) affect the forms of words, by their influence on the vowels; so that the student should by no means supersede so much attention to them, as will enable him readily to distinguish their nature and office, so far as they have an influence on the tone, or interpunction, or on the vowel-system. One must often be in the dark on these subjects, who is not familiar in some degree with the power of the accents.

TONE-SYLLABLE.

§ 99. THE GENERAL RULE is, that *the tone is on the last syllable.**

To this there are many exceptions. In Syriac and Arabic, the *penult* is more generally accented.

Note. Technically an Oxytone, i. e. a word with the tone on the ultimate, is called מִלְרַע *Mĭlrăʿ (from below)*; a word with the tone on the *penult*, is called מִלְעֵיל *Mĭlʿēl (from above)*.

Exceptions.

Several classes of words have the tone on the PENULT, viz.

§ 100. (*a*) All Segholate forms, i. e. those which have a furtive vowel in their final syllable, § 359.

[This vowel is almost universally Seghol, Pattahh, or short Hhireq, § 34. In a few cases, Shureq and Hhireq with Yodh appear to be *furtive*, and consequently employed as short vowels; e. g. in תֹּהוּ and בֹּהוּ, which stand for תֹּהֶו and בֹּהֶו; פְּרִי for פֶּרְי, § 120. *b*. In proper names ending with יָהוּ, the *penult* syllable is accented, as מִיכָיְהוּ *Micaiah*; so also in וַיִּשְׁתַּחוּ, where the ו is *quasi* furtive, § 120. *b*.]

(*b*) All duals are penacuted; and plurals of the same form with duals.

E. g. dual, רַגְלַיִם; plurals like the dual, מַיִם, שָׁמַיִם; in all which cases the final Hhireq is short.

[(*c*) Apocopated futures in verbs לה״, which take a furtive vowel; as יִגֶל, יִגְל, § 283. 3. γ. § 288.

(*d*) All the forms of regular verbs, which receive formative syllabic suffixes *beginning* with a consonant; excepting those which have תֶּם and תֶּן, § 194. § 197.

Exceptions to this rule may be found, but they are either the result of error in copyists or printers, or the accent has been moved from its proper place by some of the causes described in § 101.

(*e*) In Hiphil of regular verbs, all the persons are *penacuted* which have Yodh characteristic between the two last radicals. The other persons follow the rule in *d*.

(*f*) In Kal, Niphal, Hiphil, and Hophal of verbs ע״ע,

---

* Words with the tone on the *ultimate*, are not marked in this grammar with the accent, except for special purposes. The reader will understand, therefore, that a word without a tone-accent noted, is after this to be regarded as having the tone on the *ultimate*. From this remark, however, the Hebrew that is exhibited in the *syntax* is to be excepted, where the *penult* tone syllables are not marked, except for special purposes.

§ 100. TONE-SYLLABLE.

the tone rests on the *penult* in all the persons which have formative suffixes *beginning* with a vowel, i. e. wherever הָ ,וּ ,ִי, is added to the root. See Par. XII.

But sometimes the tone is *Milra;* as רַבּוּ, Imper. רְאִי. Such exceptions are limited chiefly to Kal.

Note. In all the persons of these verbs which have formative syllabic suffixes *beginning* with a consonant, (excepting the suffixes כֶּם and כֶּן), the tone rests on the epenthetic וֹ or ִי ֵ (§ 259) which is inserted between the verb and the formative suffix. To this rule there are a few exceptions; as דַּלֹּתִי, etc., where the tone is on the *ultimate*.

N. B. Poel, Poal, and Hithpoel of those verbs are *regularly* accented; i. e. they have their tone like the corresponding conjugations in a regular verb.

(*g*) In Kal, Niphal, and Hiphil of verbs עֹל, the tone rests on the *penult*, in those persons which have formative suffixes *beginning with a vowel,* i. e. the suff. הָ ,וּ ,ִי .

In a few cases, the tone here is on the last syllable; as שֹׁמּוּ, Imper. שֻׁבִּי. This is very rare, except in Kal. Comp. above under *f;* see Par. XIII.

Note. As in the rule *f* (Note) above, all the persons of these verbs which have an epenthetic וֹ or ִי ֵ (§ 268. *c*) before formative suffixes *beginning* with a consonant, (excepting the suffixes כֶּם and כֶּן), have the tone on the epenthetic syllable, i. e. on the *penult*.

N. B. All the other parts of the verbs עֹל are regularly accented, viz. Hophal, Poel, Polal, Hithpoel, and those persons in Kal which have formative syllabic suffixes beginning with consonants and not preceded by an epenthetic syllable (וֹ or ִי ֵ); as קָמְתֶּם etc. So participles of these verbs, in the fem. and plural, are regularly accented. Comp. under *f*.

(*h*) The paragogic endings הָ and הָ, when suffixed to verbs, affect the tone in the same manner as the *formative* suffixes הָ ,וּ, and ִי.

Of course they draw down the tone upon the *ultimate*, in all cases except such as are noted above, under *e, f*, and *g*, where it is *penacute* with these paragogics. E. g. *Milra*, זָמְרָה for זָמַר, Imp. Piel of זָמַר; דְּעָה for דַּע, Imp. of יָדַע. *Milel*, אָסְבָה for אָסֹב, 1 pers. Fut. of סָבַב; נָרְפָּה for נָרֹם, from רָמַם; נְקוּמָה for נָקוּם, from קוּם.

Note. הָ and הָ paragogic are rarely added to any persons, except those which end with a radical letter of the verb; and this mostly in the Fut. tense. In the Praeter, only the 3d pers. feminine, in a very few cases, receives a paragogic הָ or הָ, (all other apparent cases of paragoge in the Praeter being quite doubtful); and this 3d pers. feminine retains, like a paragogic noun, the accent on the *penult*, contrary to *h*

§§ 100. 101. SHIFTING OF THE TONE-SYLLABLE.

above. E. g. הֶחְבֵּאָתָה, Josh. 6:17; נִפְלְאָתָה, 2 Sam. 1:26, with Pattahh under א, where we might expect Qamets.

(*i*) Nouns, pronouns, adverbs, and (in a few cases) participles, are *penacuted*, when they have הָ◌ or הֶ◌ paragogic or local.

E. g. לָ֫מָּה, הֵ֫מָּה, שָׁ֫מָּה, בַּ֫עְרָה masc. In a few instances, the accent in such cases is found on the *ultimate*.

Note. Yodh paragogic always draws down the accent upon itself, unless there are special causes to counteract this.

(*j*) Verbs, nouns, etc. are *penacuted*, with the following suffix-pronouns; viz. ־֫נִי ־֫נִי ־֫נִי ־֫הוּ ־֫הוּ ־֫הוּ ־ָ֫הּ ־ֶ֫הָ ־ֵ֫נוּ ־ֶ֫נוּ ־ֵ֫נוּ ־ָ֫מוֹ and some others; also with ךָ֫ ־ָ֫ם ־ָ֫ן shortened from ךָ֫ ־ָ֫ם ־ָ֫ן; which latter suffixes are *Milra* or acuted on the *ultimate*.

The suffix-pronoun ךָ, preceded by a Sheva vocal, is *Milra;* preceded by a vowel, *Milel;* e. g. דְּבָרְךָ, but דְּבָרֶ֫יךָ.

(*k*) Nun epenthetic always makes the tone *penult;* e. g. יְסֻֽרַנִי, קְחֶ֫נָּה. Nun paragogic always brings it to the final syllable; as תְּמוּתוּ, but with Nun, תְּמוּתוּ֫ן.

(*l*) Pause-accents frequently, (sometimes other accents), occasion the tone to stand upon the *penult*, when its regular place would be on the ultimate; and *vice versa*.

E. g. וַיֹּ֫אמַר, וַיָּ֫מָת; נָ֫תְנוּ, נָ֫תְנוּ. This properly belongs to the next head; but it is well here to advertise the student, that there is a class of *penacuted* words, which are made so as it were *accidentally*, their proper accent being on the ultimate.]

Shifting of the tone-syllable.

[§ 101. The rules in § 99. § 100, constitute the *regular* and *usual* principles of accentuation. But the tone-syllable is often shifted from its natural place; e. g.

(*a*) *Vav* prefixed to the Praeter of verbs, commonly makes the word *Milra*.

E. g. וְהִכְבִּידָה, הִכְבִּ֫ידָה, Hiph.; וְאָכְלָ֫ה, אָכְלָ֫ה; וְשָׁבַרְתִּ֫י, שָׁבַ֫רְתִּי. So too in verbs עַ and עוֹ, § 100. *f. g*, and also in *h*.

§ 101. SHIFTING OF THE TONE-SYLLABLE.

EXCEPTIONS. (1) *Always*, the first pers. plur. of verbs; as וְאָמַ֫רְנוּ. (2) *Generally*, verbs whose third radical is a Quiescent; as וַיִּרְאַ֫תְּ, וּבָ֫אתָ וּבָנִ֫יתָ. (3) Verbs with a pause-accent on the penult. (4) When a tone-syllable immediately follows, the tone is then commonly (not always) thrown back; as וְשִׁלַּ֫חְתִּי דָבָ֫ר.

Note. Besides these exceptions, there are other *occasional* instances of exception to the rule in *a* above, which either want of consistency, or inaccuracy in transcribers, has occasioned.

(*b*) *Vav conversive* prefixed to the Future, commonly (not always) makes the word *Milel*.

E. g. וַיֹּ֫אמֶר, יֹאמַ֫ר. In such cases, the verb must end with a radical letter, and its *penult* syllable be *simple*; otherwise the change in question is excluded.

Note 1. Apocopated verbs with a *furtive* final vowel, are all accented on the *penult* in the Future. See § 283. 2. γ. § 288.

Note 2. Futures with Vav conversive remain *Milra*, (*a*) In the first pers. sing.; as וָאֹמַ֫ר. (*b*) In verbs לֹא; as וַיִּירָ֫א. (*c*) With a pause-accent on the final syllable.

(*c*) The particle אַל (*not*) before the Future, usually (not always) makes it *Milel*.

E. g. אַל־תּ֫וֹכַח *do not reprove*, אַל־תֹּ֫סֶף *you must not add*, with the tone on the penult. But here practice is not uniform, as the accent is sometimes on the ultimate.

Verbs הֹל preceded by אַל, commonly suffer both apocope and retraction of the accent.

(*d*) A word regularly *Milra*, if immediately followed by a tone-syllable, more usually becomes *Milel*.

E. g. ח֫וֹסֵי בוֹ, regularly accented ח֫וֹסֵי; בָּ֫גְדָה אוֹר, standing alone, נָגְדָ֫ה. But as the penult syllable is often *not adapted* to receive an accent, and as the change of tone would, in some cases, have a tendency to obscure the sense in reading, the usage in question is *often* neglected.

(*e*) The Imp. and Fut. apocopated, with an optative or hortative sense, *commonly* (not always) throw back the accent.

E. g. הִשָּׁ֫מֶר *keep thyself*, for הִשָּׁמֵ֫ר; יֵ֫רֶא *let him see*, for יִרְאֶ֫ה; יַ֫רְדְּ for יַרְדֶּ֫ה. The Future always does this, when it has a *furtive* vowel.

N. B. Pause accents frequently occasion the tone to be shifted both forwards and backwards; see above, § 100. *l.*]

CRITICAL MARKS, AND MASORETIC NOTES.

[§ 102. In the common editions of the Bible with Masoretic notes, etc. a small circle over any word, e. g. הוֹצִאָ, shews that the margin is to be consulted, either for a different reading (as Gen. 8:17, היצא in the case above), or for *literae majores* or *minores*, *Pisqa*, *puncta extraordinaria*, etc. The mark (*) over words in Van der Hooght, etc. refers to a marginal note.]

[§ 103. *Qerī* and *Kethībh*. There are a considerable number of marginal readings (about 1000) in our common Hebrew Bibles, most of which are quite ancient. Some of them correct grammatical anomalies, some are euphemisms, and some propose a different word. They are probably the result of an ancient recension of Hebrew manuscripts. The marginal word is called קְרִי *Qerī*, which means *read;* i. e. this word is to be read instead of the word in the text to which it relates and which is called כְּתִיב *Kethībh*, i. e. *written* or *text*. The vowel-points under the Kethibh belong to the Qeri, which is printed without points. If a word is omitted in the text, the vowel-points stand in the place with a small circle over them, while the letters belonging to them are printed in the margin; as in Judg. 20: 13. This is called קְרִי וְלֹא כְתִיב, *read but not written.* If a word is superfluous in the text, it is left unpointed; as in Ezek. 48: 16. This is called כְּתִיב וְלֹא קְרִי, *written but not read.*]

[§ 104. *Literae majores et minores* distinguish themselves, § 10. *Pīsqā* (פִּסְקָא) means *separation*, i. e. a space left in the text in the middle of a verse; as in Gen. 35: 22.

Puncta extraordinaria are marked thus, וַיִּשָּׁקֵהוּ. See Gen. 18: 9. 33: 44, where are examples of points over the letters which are *extraordinaria*.

· The Rabbins regard these as designating some mysterious significations of the words over which they are placed. Probably the original design of them was, to denote that the reading was suspicious. The number of words over which they are found is only fifteen. For a full account of all the marginal and other notes in the Masoretic editions of the Hebrew Bible, see the preface to Van der Hooght's Hebrew Bible, §§ 23—25.]

PART II.

CHANGES AND PECULIARITIES OF CONSONANTS AND VOWELS.

CHANGES OF CONSONANTS.

[§ 105. It is a principle occasionally developed in the Hebrew language, that *letters of the same organ are easily commuted.* E. g. גֵּו, גַּב, גַּף, all mean *back;* and the like in a number of cases, in the different classes of letters mentioned in § 12. But changes of this nature belong to *lexicography,* as they do not affect the grammatical forms of words.]

§ 106. The changes which affect the consonants, may be ranked under (*a*) *Assimilation.* (*b*) *Casting away.* (*c*) *Addition.* (*d*) *Transposition.*

§ 107. (*a*) *Assimilation.* Several consonants are occasionally assimilated; viz.

[(1) *In the first syllable of words;* viz. (*a*) *Nun* most frequently of all; e. g. מִזֶּה for מִנְזֶה *from this,* יִגַּשׁ for יִנְגַּשׁ. This is very common in verbs פ"ן (§ 252), but not universal. (*b*) *Lamedh* rarely; probably in the article הַ in all cases (§ 163), as הַשָּׁמַיִם for הַל שָׁמַיִם, etc. Also in the verb לָקַח; as Fut. יִקַּח, for יִלְקַח. (*c*) *Resh* very seldom; in אַשֶּׁר, as שֶׁיִּיְרוּ instead of אֲשֶׁר יִרְיוּ, *who will be;* כַּסָּא for כָּרְסָא, which is the form of the word in Syriac and Arabic. (*d*) *Tav,* in the praeformative הִת (in Hithpael), often assimilates itself to the first radical of the verb; e. g. הִדַּבֵּר for הִתְדַּבֵּר, etc. see § 187. *b.* 2. 3. (*e*) *Mem* only in a few foreign words; as לַפִּיד for לַמְפִּיד, in Greek λαμπάδες. (*f*) *Yodh* in some verbs פ"י, § 251.

(2) *In the last syllables of words.* In all the cases under No. 1, the assimilation, as we have seen, is indicated by a Daghesh forte in the following letter. But assimilation occasionally happens at the end of words, where a Daghesh forte cannot be written, § 72. This takes place, in cases where a *furtive* vowel would stand in the final syllable of the word in its full form; e. g. בַּת for בֶּנֶת, אַף for אָנֶף, בַּנְת for בָּנֶנֶת, etc. So also לַת for לָהַת, אַחַת for אֲחֶדֶת, מְשָׁחַת for מָשְׁחֶתֶת, מְשָׁרֶת for מְשָׁרֶתֶת

Note. A long vowel in such cases of assimilation and contraction (as תֵּת for תֶּנֶת), is rather unusual. The other examples here exhibit only Pattahh.

§§ 108—110. CHANGES OF CONSONANTS. 53

Remark. All languages have a practical tendency toward shortening words, and assimilating some of the letters. E. g. in Greek συλλαμβάνω instead of συνλαμβάνω; and so at the end of words, ὀδούς for ὀδόνς (Gen. ὀδόντος), Κλημῐς for Κλημῐνς (Gen. Κλημῐντος). In Latin, *illustris* for *inlustris*, etc.]

§ 108. (*b*) *Consonants cast away or dropped.* Instances of this nature occur ; viz.

[(*a*) *At the beginning of words*, by APHAERESIS, when a Sheva is under the letter. E. g. (1) *Aleph*; as בַּ֫חְנוּ for אֲבַ֫חְנוּ, and so not unfrequently. (2) *Yodh*; as בֵּד for יֵ֫לֶד, בּוּל for יְבוּל. (3) *Mem*; as קַח for מְקַח. (4) *Nun*; as תֵּן for נְתֵן. It is doubtful whether any letter which has a proper vowel, suffers *aphaeresis*. It seems to be limited to cases where Sheva is used under it.

(*b*) *In the middle of words*, by SYNCOPE. This happens, when a Sheva precedes the letter dropped. In case of syncope, the vowel of the letter syncopated takes the place of this Sheva; e. g. מַפַּת for מְאַפֵּת, קָרִים for קֹרְאִים; יַעֲמֵד for יְהַעֲמֵד, לַמֶּ֫לֶךְ for לְהַמֶּ֫לֶךְ; עִיר for עֲוִיר, כִּי for פְּנִי; גָּלוּ for גָּלְיוּ; בַּל for בְּעַל, etc. Syncope of א is pretty frequent; of ה, very common; of ו and י, more seldom, except in verbs לה; of ע very rare; see § 118 seq.

(*c*) *At the end of words*, by APOCOPE. (1) *Mem* and *Nun* at the end of all plural nouns, etc. in the construct state, § 332. (2) Perhaps Nun at the end of some proper names ; as מִגְדּוֹ for מִגְדּוֹן. (3) ה final is often dropped when words receive suffixes, etc.

Note. The omission or dropping of the *Quiescents* as such, which often happens, is treated of in §§ 63—65.]

§ 109. (*c*) *Consonants added.* This sometimes happens;—

[(*a*) *At the beginning of words*, by PROSTHESIS ; e. g. תְּמוֹל and אֶתְמוֹל; אַכְזָר, כְּזָר; (so Greek χθές, ἐχθές). (*b*) *In the middle of words*, by EPENTHESIS ; e. g. sing. אָמָה, plur. אֲמָהוֹת; אֶתְקֶנְךָ for אֶתְקָקְךָ. (*c*) *At the end of words*, by PARAGOGE ; as יִקְטְלוּן, יִקְטְלוּ. Also ה֫ and ה֫ are frequently added ; so י֫ and וֹ sometimes, to participles and nouns. See § 125. *b. c. d.*]

§ 110. (*d*) *The grammatical transposition* of letters is limited principally to the conjugation Hithpael, when it begins with a sibilant letter ; § 187. *a*.

[In lexicography, there are a considerable number of transpositions; e. g. כֶּ֫שֶׂב and כֶּ֫בֶשׂ, *a lamb*; פָּצָה and פָּרַץ, *to break*; עַלְוָה and עַוְלָה, *wickedness*, etc. Such transpositions are most frequent, between the Sibilants and Resh.

Note. The exchange of a letter for one of a corresponding class which may fill its place, is not an unfrequent thing in lexicography;

as עָלַז and עָלֵץ, *to exult;* סָגַר and סָכַר, *to shut up.* But these changes belong not to grammar. In Hithpael only, is the transposition in question a *grammatical* one, § 187.]

PECULIARITIES OF THE GUTTURALS AND RESH.

§ 111. The Gutturals are never doubled in pronunciation; and Resh in this respect is usually like them. Hence *Daghesh forte* (which is a sign of reduplication) is not admissible in the Gutturals, nor usually in Resh.

A few cases only occur of Daghesh forte in Resh; as שָׁרֵךְ, כָּרַת, מָרַת, etc.

§ 112. As a compensation for *Daghesh forte* excluded from the Gutturals and Resh, the preceding vowel is lengthened, § 58. comp. also § 59.

E. g. בֵּרֵךְ instead of בִּרֵךְ, מֵעִם instead of מִעִם, בָּרֵךְ instead of בַּרֵךְ, etc. But ה and ח commonly take daghesh'd Pattahh before them, § 33; as בַּהֵל instead of בֵּהֵל; אַחִים instead of אֵחִים.

[Note. In a great number of cases, Pattahh long is employed as a *compensative* vowel; almost always before ה and ח, when the *A* sound is required. In other cases, daghesh'd Hhireq is sometimes adopted instead of Tseri; e. g. בִּעֵר (not בֵּעֵר) instead of בֵּעֵר *bī'-ēr;* so נָאֵץ (not נֵאֵץ) for נִאֵץ; also Qibbuts long and impure instead of Hholem, as נִחָמָה (not נֹחָמָה) instead of נֶחָמָה. It follows that the student must not always expect a vowel long in *appearance* before the Gutturals; because daghesh'd Pattahh and daghesh'd Hhireq are frequently used instead of Qamets and Tseri. The use of daghesh'd Qibbuts instead of Hholem is unfrequent.]

§ 113. The Gutturals are prone to take the *A* sound before them; usually in a *final* syllable, and not unfrequently in a *penult* one.

E. g. שְׁמַע (Imp.) instead of שְׁמַע, זְרַע instead of זְרַע. In a *penult* syllable; נַעַר instead of נֵעֶר, יַחְמֹד instead of יְחְמֹד.

[Note 1. In almost all cases, where the *final* syllable has a Guttural at the end, and has also a *mutable* vowel, that vowel is exchanged for *Pattahh;* as Kal Imp. שְׁמַע instead of שְׁמַע; Piel, שִׁמַּע instead of שִׁמֵּעַ, etc.

Note 2. In case the *final* syllable with a Guttural has a long vowel, which is *immutable*, Pattahh furtive is put under the Guttural, as הוֹשִׁמִיעַ, גְּבוֹהַּ, etc. See § 69.

Note 3. Resh never takes a Pattahh furtive, like the Gutturals.

§ 114. Instead of simple Sheva vocal, the Gutturals take a composite Sheva; comp. § 49.

E. g. אֶלְּךָ, חֲפָךְ, חֲלִי. Sheva simple stands under the Gutturals, at the *end* of a mixed syllable and after a short vowel, when a *silent* Sheva is required; as יָדַעְתִּי, אֶחְבֹּל, see § 50.

PECULIARITIES OF QUIESCENTS.

In treating of the *vowels*, it was necessary to notice the *quiescent* and *otiant* power of the letters א ה ו י *(Ehevi)*, §§ 53—57, so far as might serve to illustrate the nature of the vowel sounds in which the *Ehevi* quiesce. Some more particular notice of the various phases and powers of these letters, is demanded and is proper here.

Principles which regulate Quiescence.

§ 115. The letters א, ו, י *(Evi)* quiesce, when a *homogeneous* vowel precedes them (§ 53), and according to the analogy of other consonants they would stand at the *end* of a mixed syllable, and take a simple Sheva silent either expressed or implied, § 56. 2.

E. g. מָצָא instead of מָצָא=מָצְא, בִּיהוּדָה instead of בְּיְהוּדָה, יֵיטַב instead of יְיְטַב, הוּשַׁב instead of הְוְשַׁב.

Note. If the preceding vowel be naturally *heterogeneous*, yet in many cases it does not exclude *quiescence*. But a peculiar expedient is adopted in order to effect this; see § 117. 1. Comp. with this, § 56. 3.

Such is the *general* rule for cases of *quiescence*, subject however to many exceptions. But quiescence is not limited to this case only; for,

§ 116. Quiescence *sometimes* happens, when the *Evi* would (by analogy) have a *vowel;* specially when they would take a *furtive* one; § 119. *c.* 2. § 120. *c.*

E. g. קוֹם instead of קָוֹם, קוּם instead of קָווּם, נִמְצֵאת instead of נִמְצָאֵת, רֹאשׁ instead of רְאֹשׁ, גְּלוֹת instead of גְּלֹוֶת, שְׁבִית instead of שְׁבְיַת; and so often, when the vowel preceding the *furtive* one is homogeneous. But usage only can enable the learner to distinguish such cases.

§ 117. The general rule demands that the preceding vowel should be *homogeneous*, as a condition of quiescence; but quiescence is often effected, in cases when such pre-

§ 118. PECULIARITIES OF QUIESCENTS.

ceding vowel would be naturally *heterogeneous;* and this, in two different ways.

(1) The vowel may conform to the Quiescent, in order to become homogeneous.

E. g. for הִוְשִׁיב (which would be the regular analogous form), is substituted הוֹשִׁיב, i. e. the heterogeneous short Hhireq in the syllable הִוְ, conforms to, or becomes homogeneous with, the Vav in הוֹ. So גָּלִיתָ for גָּלַיְתָ, עוֹלָה for עַוְלָה, etc.

(2) The Quiescent may conform to the vowel.

E. g. קָאם for קָם, גָּלָה for גָּלַי, שָׁלַו for שָׁלַו, etc.

Practice only can teach the student when the cases which come within those rules take place.

Special usage in regard to א, ה, ו, י.

§ 118. The letters א, ו, י, and likewise ה, having a vowel of their own, and being preceded by a consonant with Sheva, oftentimes remit their vowel to the place of the preceding Sheva, and become *otiant*, or *quiescent*.

E. g. פֵּארָה, בֵּאר for בְּאֵר, רִאישׁוֹן for רְאשׁוֹן, רֵאשִׁים for רְאשִׁים; בֵּוי for בְּוִי, עֵיר for עֲוִי, קֵים for קְוִם (*bevō*), בֵּוא for בְּוֹא; פֵּארָה for פְּארָה; גֵּלוּ (with Yodh omitted) for גְּלָיוּ, כֵּיתְרוֹן for כִּיתְרוֹן, אֵימָה for אֲיָמה, אֵיבָה for אֲיֵבָה, etc. So in respect to ה; e. g. בַּמֶּלֶךְ for לַהַמֶּלֶךְ, לַהַקְטִיל for לְהַקְטִיל, etc., see Note 3 below.

[Note 1. This has been named *Syriasm;* but improperly, since it appears so very often in Hebrew (taking all the cases together) as to shew that it is a property of the dialect, and not the result of error in Syraizing transcribers. Usage only can determine the cases in which it is admitted.

Note 2. Such cases, also, have been represented by all the grammarians as *quiescence*, in respect to א. That they are not so, but cases of *otium*, is plain from the following examples; viz. לִקְרֹאת (instead of לִקְרָאת), but with a sing. suffix לִקְרָאתוֹ, with a plural one לִקְרָאתָכֶם. So מְלֶאכָה (instead of מְלָאכָה), construct state מְלֶאכֶת, with suffix מְלַאכְתֶּךָ. Aleph then has no effect on the *mutability* or *quantity* of the vowel which precedes it, in such cases; consequently it is *otiant*. Instances of Vav, Yodh, and He, do not occur in the same way as those above of Aleph; but such cases as בֵּי for בְּוִי, עֵיר for עֲוִי; יִגְלוּ for יִגְלֵיוּ, תִּגְלִי for תִּגְלְיִי, בַּמֶּלֶךְ for בְּהַמֶּלֶךְ, לְהָמֶלֶךְ, etc. shew that Vav, Yodh, and He do become *otiant* or *quiescent*, and in the like way with א. Yodh and Vav are usually retained in such words as אֵימָה (for אֲיֵמָה), בּוֹא (for בְּוֹא); and in these cases they *appear* to be *quiescent*. The principle is ex-

§ 119. PECULIARITIES OF QUIESCENTS.

tensive in regard to *Vav* and *Yodh* in the so called verbs לֹה, which are properly לֹו and לֹי; and it will account for a great part of the abridged forms of these verbs; see § 281.

Note 3. א, ו, י, ה, being *otiant* or *quiescent*, are frequently omitted in writing; e. g. מַלְּאָּה for מְאַלְּאָה, יָהֵל for יָאֵהֵל; בֹּא for בּוֹא *bevō*, שָׁלוּ for שָׁלֲווּ; בִּי for בְּוִי, יִגְלוּ for יִגְלֲווּ, לַקְטִיל for לְהַקְטִיל, etc.; see § 57.

§ 63. Vav and Yodh are *usually* dropped when otiant, and He *always* in the middle of a word.]

Peculiarities of Aleph.

[§ 119. These are so many, that they need a separate statement.

(*a*) *Aleph* is sometimes, (1) A Guttural; as in יֶאְסֹף. (2) A Quiescent; as in וַיֹּאמֶר, מָצָא. (3) It is sometimes treated as a common moveable consonant; as in בֶּלֶא, plur. כְּלָאִים, בְּאָשָׁה *bŏ*a-*shā*. Usage only can determine all the respective cases of these different powers.

(*b*) *Aleph at the end of a word* has no guttural power (comp. § 69), but is either quiescent, otiant, or employed like other consonants; e. g. quiescent, as in מָצָא; otiant, as in הִמְצִיא, וַיַּרְא, see § 57. *b. a*; or it retains a common consonant power, as in Segholates, e. g. בֶּלֶא plur. כְּלָאִים, סֹבֵא with suffix סָבְאָם *sŏbh*-א*ām*.

(*c*) *Aleph in the middle of a word.* (1) Like other Gutturals, it takes a composite Sheva where they take one. But in some cases it drops the Sheva, and quiesces in the preceding vowel and lengthens it; e. g. לֵאמֹר instead of לֶאֱמֹר, לֵאלֹהִים instead of לֶאֱלֹהִים, נָאיָה instead of נַאֲיָה, אָהֵב for אֱאֱהַב, etc. comp. § 152. *c.* 2. These may be called *cases of contraction.* In לַיהוָה the points are not appropriate; for the Jews read לַאדֹנָי=לַאדֹנָי, as the Pattahh seems to be long. The word, however, is *sui generis* in respect to form. (2) But where other Gutturals take a Sheva silent (§ 114. Note), Aleph usually becomes *quiescent*, e. g. מְצָאתִי; but with another Guttural, שָׂמַחְתִּי. (3) Aleph *penult*, in words that would regularly be Segholates and where א would have a *furtive* vowel, more usually (not always) rejects such vowel, and quiesces in the preceding vowel (if homogeneous) and lengthens it; e. g. נִמְצָאת for נִמְצֶאת, רֹאשׁ for רֹאֶשׁ; § 116. (4) Aleph sometimes remits its vowel to the preceding letter with Sheva, and becomes *otiant*; § 118.

(*d Aleph at the beginning of a word.* (1) If it have a proper vowel, it is regular. (2) If it should regularly have a composite Sheva, in some few cases (after the manner of the Syriac) it employs a long vowel instead of it; e. g. אָמוּן instead of אֱמוּן, אָסָרֶם, אָסְרֵם for אֶאֱסְרֵם, אֹהָלֶיךָ for אָהֳלֶיךָ. The student should remember, that this happens only at the *beginning* of words.]

Peculiarities of Vav and Yodh.

[§ 120. (*a*) *At the end of syllables and words*, Vav and Yodh, in case they would regularly have a *silent* Sheva and are preceded by *homogeneous* vowels, uniformly *quiesce*, § 115. (*b*) They quiesce at the end of words, also, when analogically they would be preceded by a *silent* Sheva, or by a *furtive* vowel; e. g. פְּרִי instead of פְּרְיִ or פֶּרְיִ, יְהִי for יְהְיִ or יֶהְיִ, בֹּהוּ instead of בֹּהְוּ, יִשְׁתַּחוּ for יִשְׁתַּחְוְ with Pattahh furtive. To this principle there are a few exceptions in respect to *Vav*; e. g. קָצוּ.

Note. With א the case is different; e. g. חֵטְא (instead of חֵטְאָ) with א *otiant*; on the other hand, בְּלָא with א moveable like other consonants.

(*c*) *Vav* and *Yodh penult*, which would regularly take a *furtive* vowel, reject it, and quiesce in a preceding homogeneous vowel; e. g. גְּלוֹת instead of גְּלֹוְת *gelō-vĕth*, רְעוּת instead of רְעֹוְת *reʿō-vĕth*, שְׁבִית instead of שְׁבְיִת; comp. § 119. *c*. 3.]

Peculiarities of He.

[§ 121. (*a*) *At the beginning and in the middle of words*, when retained, it is always a moveable consonant. *Apparent* exceptions are some compound proper names (as פְּדָהצוּר with quiescent ה), which depend only on the transcriber. (*b*) *At the end of words*, it is nearly always quiescent; as גָּלָה *gā-lā*, § 54. When moveable, it is marked with *Mappiq*; as גָּבַהּ *gā-bhăh*, § 84. (*c*) Like א, it is capable of having a *furtive* homogeneous vowel before it without quiescence, e. g. גָּבַהּ, קָצַהּ, בָּסַהּ, etc.; for it must in such cases be considered as moveable; comp. א in § 119. *b*, in בְּלֵא, etc. (*d*) *He is frequently made otiant*, at the end of a word, by a Daghesh forte euphonic; e. g. מַה־זֶּה = מַזֶּה, מַה־טּוֹב *măt-tōbh*, עֹשֵׂה פְּרִי *ʿō-sĕp-perī*. But this belongs merely to *modes of reading*, and not to the grammatical forms of the language.]

Commutation, Apocope, and Paragoge of Quiescents.

§ 122. COMMUTATION. This naturally results from the fact, that the same vowels are homogeneous with different Quiescents. (1) At the end of words. E. g.

אָ	is put for	הָ	as	קָרְדָא	for קָרְדָה
אָ	...	הָ	..	מִקְנָא	.. מִקְנָה
אָ	...	הָ	..	יִשְׁנָא	.. יִשְׁנָה
אָ	...	הָ	..	פֹּא	.. פֹּה
הָ	...	אָ	..	מִקְשָׁה	.. מִקְשָׁא
הָ	...	אָ	..	פֶּרָה	.. פֶּרָא
ִי	...	אִ	..	רוֹשׁ	.. רֹאשׁ
ִי	...	הִ	..	עָשׂוֹ	.. עָשֹׂה
ָי	...	אָ	..	רִים	.. רָאם
ִי	...	אִ	..	רִישׁוֹן	.. רִאשׁוֹן

§§ 124—127. CHANGES OF THE VOWELS. 59

(2) Sometimes in the middle of words; as צְבָאִים for צְבָיִים, קָם for קוּם, חַיָּב for חָיָב, etc.

§ 124. APOCOPE. Not only are Quiescents frequently *omitted* in writing words (§ 63), but *apocope* in certain cases is even a law of the language.

[(*a*) In verbs לֹה, in the apoc. Fut. and Imper., and when they have suffixes; § 283. 3. γ. § 313.

(*b*) In nouns with suffixes or increase, derived from the same class of verbs; § 378. *b*.]

§ 125. PARAGOGE. The Quiescents (with a vowel preceding them) often constitute a *paragogic* ending.

[(*a*) Aleph is sometimes paragogic, after the syllables ־ָ, ־ֹו, ־וּ; e. g. הָלְכוּ=הָלְכוּא, רְבוּ=רְבוּא, נְקִי=נְקִיא *they go*. This last form with א paragogic, is a usual one in Arabic.

(*b*) Also ה ־ָ ה ־ֶ ה ־ִי ; e. g. אָקְטֹל, אָקְטְלָה; הֵן, הֵנָּה; עֶשֶׂר, עֲשָׂרָה.

(*c*) More seldom וֹ ; e. g. pronoun suffix ־ָם, parag. ־ָמוֹ; so the noun חַיַּת, parag. חַיְתוֹ.

(*d*) Rarely ־ִי, as מָקִים, מְקִימִי; but *Yodh* is often inserted between two words united to form a proper name; e. g. גַּבְרִיאֵל, *man* of *God*, united גַּבְרִיאֵל *Gabriel*, i. e. man of God.]

Note. Several pronouns are of the same form and sound as some of these paragogic letters. In such cases, the connection of the word with the context must determine whether such doubtful forms are pronouns or paragogic letters.

CHANGES OF THE VOWELS.

§ 126. The changes which words in the Hebrew undergo, in order to designate their various relations and significations, are effected partly by a change in the vowels, and partly by a change in the consonants. The laws which regulate the *vowel-changes*, are the subject of our present consideration.

Vowels Mutable and Immutable.

§ 127. GENERAL PRINCIPLE. Pure vowels are mutable; impure ones immutable. See § 23. seq.

[EXCEPTIONS. *Long impure vowels are sometimes exchanged*, (1) For each other; as מָנוֹס, plur. מְנוּסִים, where וֹ is exchanged for וּ. (2) For long pure ones; as Imp. 2d pers. masc. קוּם, 2d pers. plur. fem. קֹמְנָה, with Hholem pure; Niph. Fut. 3d masc. sing. יָקוֹם with Hholem impure and protracted, 3d plur. fem. תִּקְמְנָה, with Hholem pure and mutable; Hiph. Imper. 2d pers. plur. masc. הִקְטִילוּ, plur. fem. הִקְטֹלְנָה with Tseri pure. (3) For short pure ones; as גָּדוֹל, const. גְּדָל *gĕdhŏl;* חָכְמָה, constr. חָכְמַת. (4) For Shevas; e. g. גָּלָה, fem. גָּלְתָה. *All long* PURE *vowels are from their very nature mutable.*

<small>All these changes, excepting No. 1 and the first instance in No. 3, are very frequent in Hebrew. The laws of declension, in such cases, supersede the usual laws of the vowels, applicable to other cases; so that one can call no vowel in Hebrew *absolutely* immutable; all being liable in certain cases to change. But *when* and *where* this happens, can be learned only by practice. Nor can one avoid the conclusion above, by saying that the different persons, genders, etc., require *in themselves* different vowels, as pure, impure, etc.; for these changes are in the *usual* course of declension, conjugation, regimen, etc., which occasion almost all the vowel changes in the language.</small>

Note 1. The *composite* Shevas, in a like way, are frequently exchanged for each other, in the course of declension; e. g. נֶעֱלַם (part.) fem. נֶעֱלָמָה; יֶאֱסֹר, with suffix יַאַסְרֵ־נִי. The *A* sound appears to be shorter than the *E* sound.

Note 2. The vowels that are properly and usually *mutable*, are these; viz. Qamets, Tseri, and Hholem, long and pure; Pattahh, Seghol, Hhireq, Qamets Hhateph, and Qibbuts, short and pure. The other vowels are immutable in the sense above defined, i. e. they remain immutable, unless a particular form of a word becomes more imperious than the usual laws of the vowel-changes.]

<small>Gesenius says, that the *quiescent long* vowels are immutable always and in all circumstances, Hebrew Grammar 9 edit. § 16. Surely there are a multitude of exceptions to this rule, as the cases above presented show. He also states, that short vowels before a Daghesh forte are immutable; but he must have overlooked such instances as אָפָה, in pause אָתָה, etc.</small>

General principles of Vowel-changes.

§ 128. (*a*) The changes of vowels for each other, are very generally (not always) limited to the respective classes to which they belong, § 19. § 40.

Note. A few seeming exceptions appear; e. g. בַּד plur. מִדִּים; מוֹרָג plur. מוֹרִגִים. So Hiph. הִקְטִיל, 2 pers. הִקְטַלְתָּ. Every language has some such anomalies. Practice only can teach how to distinguish them.

(*b*) Each long mutable vowel has one or more corresponding short ones, for which it may be exchanged; and *vice versa*. E. g.

Long pure Vowels.	Corresponding short ones.
Qamets (ָ)	Pattahh . . . . (ַ)
Tseri (ֵ)	{ Pattahh (sometimes)(ַ) { Seghol . . . . (ֶ) { Hhireq . . . . (ִ)
Hholem (ֹ)	{ Qibbuts . . . (ֻ) { Qamets Hhateph (ָ)

§§ 129. 130. CHANGES OF THE VOWELS.

Long mutable Vowels exchanged for corresponding short ones.

[§ 129. (a) When they are in a mixed syllable on which the tone rested, and from which the tone, for some special cause, has been removed either forward or backward.

(b) *Forwards*; e. g. יָד, יַדְלֶם; יֵשׁ, יֶשְׁלֶם, בֵּן, בִּנְךָ; יִקְטֹל, יִקְטָלְךָ yĭq-tŏl-khā; יָסֹבּוּ, תְּחַבֶּינָה; before Maqqeph, as כֹּל, כָּל־אֲשֶׁר köl nᵃshĕr, § 89. (2) *Backwards*, i. e. towards the right hand; as וַיֵּלֶךְ, וַיֵּלֶךְ; יָקָם, וַיָּקָם văy-yă-qŏm; בִּקְשָׁתָם, בְּקָשָׁתָם. The reason of such changes is, that long vowels cannot stand in mixed syllables unless they are tone-syllables, § 36. Of course, when the tone is removed they must be *shortened*.

Note. A few solitary cases are found of *apparent* exception to this principle; e. g. 1 Sam. 17: 35, וַהֲמִיתִּיו. But the first *Yodh* here is merely a *fulcrum*, § 64; the word is read vă-hᵃmĭt-tĭv, with the first ĭ short.

(b) When they are in a mixed syllable, which the construct state requires to be shortened.

E. g. דָּבָר *word*, but דְּבַר יְהוָה *the word of Jehovah;* where the original syllable בָר is shortened to בַר; see § 342. b.

(c) Long vowels before a Daghesh forte latent in a final letter (not a Guttural), when a change is required, for the most part are exchanged for an *appropriate* short vowel.

E. g. (a) Tseri goes into Hhireq parvum; as אִם (with Daghesh forte implied in the מ), אִמִּי. (b) Hholem into Qibbuts short; as חֹק, חֻקָּה, but sometimes into *Qamets Hhateph*, as עֹז, עָזִּי öz-zĭ.

Note. If the tone remains, the vowel continues long in such cases; e. g. שָׁמָּה shăm-mā, הֵמָּה hēm-mā.

(d) A pause accent falling on final Tseri, not unfrequently changes it into Pattahh; see § 145.]

Short Vowels in mixed syllables made long.

§ 130. (a) This happens, when the form of the word is so changed, that they come to stand in a *simple* syllable.

E. g. שַׂד, שָׂדִי; הַב, הָבָה; קָטַל, קָטְלוּ. So of course before a Quiescent; as מָצָא instead of מַצָא, גָּלָה instead of גַּלָה = גַּלְיִ.

[(b) When a Daghesh forte is omitted in writing, a short

vowel placed before it becomes long either by nature or by position; § 112. § 58. § 59. § 33.

E. g. בָּרַךְ instead of בְּרַךְ, בָּרֵךְ instead of בְּרֵךְ, בֹּרַךְ instead of בֻּרַךְ, long by nature; בָּהֵל for בַּהֵל, נָחַם for נַחַם, etc. long by position.

Note 1. Daghesh forte *implied* in a letter at the end of a word, (it cannot be *written* in such a case, § 72), *usually* prolongs the vowel which precedes; e. g. יָגֵל instead of יְגַל, אָם instead of אַם, יִתְאָו for יִתְאַוּ, *yĭth-ăvv*; but sometimes the vowel remains short, as יְגַל for יָגֵל, סַב, יְגַל (not סָב) for סָבַב.

Note 2. In the case *b* above, the syllable with the short vowel becoming a *simple* one by the coalescence of the implied daghesh'd letter, the vowel must of course be lengthened, according to the rule *a* above. Before ה and ח, the vowel Pattahh usually remains in such cases, and is long, § 33.

(*c*) The *article*, prefixed to a few words, lengthens the short vowel in them.

E. g. הָאָרֶץ, אֶרֶץ; הַפָּר, פַּר; הַצָּר, צַר; הָהָר, הַר; הָעָם, עַם. Usage only can distinguish such cases; and they are not numerous.]

[§ 131. A pause-accent falling on Pattahh or Seghol pure, commonly (not always) lengthens them.

E. g. הָבָל, הֶבֶל; מָיִם, מַיִם. Occasionally other accents do the same; see § 149.]

Falling away of the Vowels.

§ 132. Vowels are said *to fall away*, when they are dropped and a Sheva takes their place.

E. g. דָּבָר, דְּבָרוֹ, where the vowel under the ד in the first word, falls away in the second.

Note. *Apocope* of vowels is dropping them at the end of a word; as וַיִּבֶן, יִבְנֶה, where the Seghol of the first word is dropped.

Falling away by change of Tone-syllable.

§ 133. (*a*) When the tone is moved forward ONE *syllable*, i. e. moved toward the left hand, the penult vowel of the ground-form* falls away, if pure and mutable.

E. g. עָנָב, עֲנָבִי; דָּבָר, דְּבָרִי. If the tone is not shifted, the vowel remains; e. g. יָסֹב, יְסֹבִּי.

---

* The *ground-form* is the *primary* one, in number, gender, or tense, to which it belongs; the original, from which the others are derived.

(b) *If the tone is moved forward* TWO *syllables*, both the ultimate and ‚penult vowels, when mutable, fall away.

E. g. דָּבָר, דִּבְרֵיכֶם; זָקֵן, זִקְנֵיהֶם, זִקְנֵיכֶם; where both vowels of the ground-form vanish. In regard to the short Hhireq which takes the place of one of them, see § 137. In regard to Sheva being inserted when the vowel is dropped, see § 52.

Falling away on account of Regimen.

[§ 134. Regimen or the construct state (§ 332) often occasions the penult, or both the ultimate and penult, vowels to fall away, if pure and mutable.

Note 1. (*a*) Regimen in the *singular*, usually causes the *penult* mutable vowel to fall away; as דָּבָר, in reg. דְּבַר יְהוָֹה, where the first vowel falls away and the last is shortened. The suffix state has the like effect on the *penult* vowel, e. g. דְּבָרִי. (*b*) The *plural* regimen causes both the ultimate and penult vowels to be dropped; e. g. דִּבְרֵי יְהוָֹה. In like manner *grave* suffixes affect both vowels; e. g. דִּבְרֵיכֶם. Comp. § 342. *b. c.*

Note 2. Vowels must be *pure*, in order to fall away. Even when they are so, usage does not always treat them in the same manner; e. g. שֵׁם is in reg. שֵׁם, but בֵּן in reg. makes בֶּן, the first retaining the long vowel, and the second shortening it. But in a suffix both drop it; e. g. שְׁמִי, בְּנִי.

Note 3. In Segholate forms (Dec. VI. of nouns), the final vowel is merely *furtive*; so that, those nouns being monosyllabic in theory, regimen makes no change in their vowels. See Paradigm of Dec. VI.]

Falling away on account of Accession.

[§ 135. (*a*) Where the ground-form of a word receives an accession at the *end* beginning with a *vowel*, which requires its *ultimate* and *penult* consonants to be united in the same syllable with such accession, then the *final* vowel of the ground-form falls away, if mutable.

This happens most frequently in verbs; e. g. קָטַל, fem. קָטְלָה, יִקְטֹל, plur. יִקְטְלוּ; כָּבֵד, fem. כָּבְדָה; part. pres. קֹטֵל, fem. קֹטְלָה, plur. קֹטְלִים; in Piel, מְלַמֵּד, fem. מְלַמְּדָה; so also in nouns of Dec. VII., as אֹיֵב, plur. אֹיְבִים.

(*b*) Where only the *final* consonant is united with an accessory vowel, and the penult consonant must have a Sheva *silent*, the final vowel of the ground-form falls away.

E. g. Imp. fem. קִטְלִי (not קְטֹלִי), ground-form קְטֹל; קִטְלוּ (not קְטֹלוּ), ground-form קְטֹל.

Note 1. If only the final letter of the ground-form is to be united with the *accessory* vowel, and the penult letter must retain a *vowel* instead of having a Sheva, then such vowel cannot fall away; e. g. דָּבָר, with suffix דְּבָרִי; כּוֹכָב, plur. כּוֹכָבִים.

Note 2. Usage only will enable the student readily to distinguish the cases where the rule is to be applied. We can see no reason, *a priori*, why the Hebrews might not have said דְּבָרוֹ as well as דְּבָרוֹ, (especially since they say קְטֹלוּ etc.); except that in this way, the *suffix-forms* are distinguished from those of simple declension which mark person and number.]

Rise of New Vowels.

§ 136. We have seen that two successive vowels may fall away (§ 133. *b.* § 134), on account of the tone being removed, or of regimen. In such cases an impossible syllable would arise, i. e. one with three consonants before a vowel, § 42; consequently a *new* vowel must be inserted in order to avoid this.

E. g. דָּבָר, constr. plur. דִּבְרֵי *dbhrē*. But this is inadmissible; see § 42. So אֲנָשִׁים, constr. אַנְשֵׁי (with one composite Sheva), which would be an impossible syllable. A vowel must therefore be *supplied*.

§ 137. In case the vowels falling away leave two *simple* Shevas, the usual supplied vowel is *short Hhireq*.

E. g. דָּבָר, plur. constr. דִּבְרֵי instead of דְּבְרֵי.

§ 138. But if one of the two letters that have been deprived of their vowels, is a Guttural, then *Pattahh* or *Seghol* must be the supplied vowel.

E. g. אֲנָשִׁים, constr. אַנְשֵׁי instead of אֲנְשֵׁי; חֲלָקִים, constr. חֶלְקֵי.

[§ 139. If an accessory letter with a Sheva, be prefixed to a Guttural having a composite Sheva, such accessory letter takes a *supplied* short vowel which is homogeneous with the composite Sheva.

E. g. עֲבֹד, but with prefix לְ, לַעֲבֹד; אֱכֹל, לֶאֱכֹל; חֱלִי, בָּחֳלִי *bŏ-hhŏlī*. But the Fut. of the verbs הָיָה and חָיָה makes יִהְיֶה, יִחְיֶה; and analogous to this is the pointing of the prefixes, as לִהְיוֹת, contrary to the analogy of other guttural forms.]

[§ 140. When in varying the forms of words it so happens, that analogically two Shevas would come under two

§§ 141. 142. FURTIVE VOWELS.—EUPHONIC CHANGES.

successive letters, and the *first* of these would be a *composite* Sheva; then the corresponding short vowel is substituted for such composite Sheva.

E. g. נֶהְפְּכָה instead of נֶהֶפְכָה, which would make an impossible syllable. So פָּעֳלָךְ *pŏ-ŏl-khā* instead of פָּעָלָךְ; יַעֲמְדוּ instead of יַעְמְדוּ. The ground of this is, that from their nature two Shevas cannot stand together unless the first be *silent* and the second *vocal*, except at the end of a word. But in the case above, the first is vocal, i. e. it is a composite Sheva, § 46. *a*; of course the expedient of a new vowel must be adopted, in order to avoid an impossible syllable.]

Rise of furtive Vowels.

§ 141. As the Hebrews rarely admit two consonants after a vowel in the same syllable (§ 42); so, in order to avoid this, they supply a *furtive* vowel in most cases where such a concurrence would otherwise take place. This vowel is commonly *Seghol short ;* but under words having a penult Guttural, it is *Pattahh short ;* with a penult Yodh, it is *short Hhireq.*

E. g. עֶלֶךְ instead of מַלְךְ, סֵפֶר for סִפְרְ, נַעַר for נַעְרְ, בַּיִת for בַּיְתְ. See on Dec. VI. § 359, also § 283. 3. *γ*. on Segholate forms of verbs.

[Note 1. The 2 pers. fem. sing. Praet. in verbs Lamedh Guttural, takes Pattahh *furtive* ; e. g. שָׁמַעַתְּ instead of שָׁמְעַתְּ, in order to ease the pronunciation, § 69.

Note 2. All words having a *furtive* vowel are *Milel*, i. e. accented on the *penult*. In this way they are distinguished from the few forms that resemble them in the final vowel, but are accented on the ultimate ; e. g. בְּבֶל, בַּרְזֶל, etc. Comp. § 100. *a*.]

Euphonic changes of the Vowels.

[§ 142. These are various. (*a*) A Guttural with Qamets seldom admits a Qamets or Pattahh immediately before it, but exchanges it for a Seghol ; e. g. הֶהָרִים instead of הָהָרִים, אֶחָיו for אָחָיו; פֶּחָה for פָּחָה, מֶה־אָנֹכִי for מָה־אָנֹכִי, etc.

Note. The rule is not uniform. Such cases occur, as הָאָרֶץ, הָהָר, הָעָם, etc. The word וְעָד is anomalous, being put for וְעֵד or וָעֵד. The practice required by the rule, is occasionally extended to cases where the Gutturals are not present; as צַד־מֶה כְּבוֹדִי, where מֶה stands for מָה; also to Gutturals not pointed with Qamets, as הֶחֳדָשִׁים for הַחֳדָשִׁים, *hā-hŏdhā-shīm.*

9

§§ 142—145. VOWELS CHANGED BY ACCENTS.

(b) In mixed syllables losing their tone, Seghol in some cases takes the place of Pattahh; e. g. יָד, יָדְכֶם for יַדְכֶם; אֲכָלְךָ for אֲכָלְךָ. The reason of this is, that Pattahh is better adapted to a mixed syllable *with* the tone; Seghol, to one *without* it. Consequently,

(c) In a tone-syllable, we sometimes find Pattahh instead of Seghol; e. g. זָקֵן, const. זְקַן not זְקֶן. See Dec. V. of nouns, Parad.

(d) A furtive vowel at the end of words causes the preceding vowel, if mutable, to conform. E. g. *Qamets*, as חוֹתֶמֶת instead of חוֹתָמֶת; *Pattahh*, as מֶלֶךְ for מַלֵּךְ; *Tseri*, as גְּבֶרֶת for גְּבֵרֶת. So in verbs, וַיִּגֶל for וַיִּגַל, חֶרֶף for חָרַף. In Gutturals, מוֹדַעַת for מוֹדֵעַת, etc.

(e) Anomalous changes of the vowels occasionally occur; probably to mark the *peculiar* pronunciation of certain words. E. g. (1) Long vowels are put for short ones before the composite Shevas; as הַעֲלָה for הֶעֱלָה, הָעֲלָה for הַעֲלָה, and perhaps תְּהֲלַךְ for תֵּהֲלַךְ. (2) Short vowels for long ones; as אֲחֵרוּ for אַחֲרֵי, אַחֲרֵי, יַחֲמוּ for יֵחַמוּ. (3) Long vowels are put for short ones arising out of composite Shevas; as תֵּאָהֲבוּ for תֶּאֱהָבוּ, תֵּאָכְלֵהוּ for תַּאֲכִילֵהוּ.]

N. B. All these cases under e are very unfrequent; and it is difficult to decide whether they should be attributed to mere accidental euphony, to negligence in transcribing, or to a principle of the language.

Vowels changed by Accents.

§ 143. Pause accents, and sometimes others (§ 149), not only occasion a shifting of the tone-syllable of words (§ 100. *l*), but very frequently occasion a change in the quantity of vowels; usually *lengthening* short vowels, but sometimes *shortening* long ones.

§ 144. (1) *They lengthen short vowels;* changing Pattahh, and Seghol when used for Pattahh (§ 142. *d*), into *Qamets*, and Qamets Hhateph into Hholem.

E. g. מַיִם, מָיִם; קָטַל, קָטָל; מֶלֶךְ (for מַלֵּךְ § 142. *d*), מָלֶךְ. So where they shift the tone also; as עַתָּה, אַתָּה; עַתָּה, עָתָּה. So וַיָּמָת *văy-yā-mŏth*, וַיָּמֹת.

Note. The *praepositive* and *postpositive* accents (§ 95) may affect vowels without standing on them, in the same manner as other accents which are placed on them; e. g. מָלָךְ (instead of מָלַךְ) with Tiphha *anterius*, Ps. 97:1; יִשְׁכָּבוּ (instead of יִשְׁכְּבוּ) with Segholta on the ultimate; see § 146.

[§ 145. (2) *They shorten the long vowels.* Verbs in pause* frequently exchange Tseri ultimate for Pattahh.

E. g. יֵלֵךְ, יֵלַךְ; יִגְמֹל, יִגְמַל; קָמֵל, קָמַל; הֵפֵר, הֵפַר. So with

---
* A word or syllable is said to be in *pause*, when a pause-accent rests upon it.

§§ 146—149. VOWELS CHANGED BY ACCENTS. 67

verbs taking suffixes; as אֲמִילֶם, אֲמִילָם; יְחִיתֶן, יְחִיתָן. But the cases are numerous in which Tseri remains in such examples. The whole thing seems to be merely *arbitrary* euphony.]

[§ 146. A pause-accent on a word, which by declension has dropped the final vowel of the ground-form (§ 135), restores that final vowel, and also lengthens the same if it be short.

This takes place, (*a*) When such accent falls on the *restored* vowel; as יָרְאָה, יָרֵאָה, ground-form יָרֵא; טָמְנוּ, טָמֵנוּ, ground-form טָמֵן; יִקְטְלוּ, יָקְטְלוּ, ground-form יִקְטֹל; יִשְׁמְעוּ, יִשְׁמָעוּ, ground-form יִשְׁמַע. (*b*) When it falls on the succeeding syllable; as יִרְקֹדוּן instead of יִרְקְדוּן, Joel 2:5; יִדְחָקוּן instead of יִדְחֲקוּן, Joel 2:8; הֵלְכוּן instead of הֲלְכוּן, Joel 2:7.]

N. B. Both of these usages are very often neglected, and the natural accentuation remains.

[§ 147. Pause accents, when they fall on those persons of verbs לה״ (properly לי״ § 280) which drop a letter and a vowel, sometimes restore the letter as well as the vowel dropped, and affect the vowel as stated in § 146.

E. g. בָּעָה = בָּעָה, from בְּעָיוּ, בְּעוּ; נְטַי = נָטָה, ground-form נְטָיוּ, נְטוּ. בַּעַר, § 280. Note.]

[§ 148. Where no vowel has been dropped, a pause-accent sometimes occasions changes; viz.

(*a*) Falling on *simple* Sheva penult, it puts Seghol in its place; e. g. מַלְכְּךָ, מַלְכֶּךָ; שְׁכֶם, שֶׁכֶם.

(*b*) Falling on a composite Sheva penult, it substitutes the corresponding long vowel.

E. g. אֲנִי, אָנִי; חֲלִי, חָלִי; cases with Hhateph Seghol do not occur. But the practice is not entirely uniform; e. g. עֲדִי, עֶדְי; חֲצִי, חֵצִי.]

§ 149. GENERAL REMARKS. The effect of pause-accents is not uniform. In a great number of cases, no change is occasioned by them. On the other hand, most of the *disjunctive* accents, and even several of the *conjunctives*, not unfrequently produce the same effect in prolonging syllables as the pause-accents. For example; (*a*) *Disjunctives*; יִרְבְּנוּ, בְּעִרְךָ, בְּעוּ; שָׁמְעָה, שִׁמְעָה; טָמְנוּ, טָמֵנוּ; רָבָשׁוּ, רָבֻשׁוּ, יִרְבְּנוּ Ps. 5:12, etc. (*b*) *Conjunctives*; as תִּדְהֲתָלוּ, תִּדְהֲתָלוּ; גֻּשׁוּ, גֻּשׁוּ; בִּרְכָתְךָ, בִּרְכָתֶךָ, חֲסָיָה, חָסָיָה, etc. The entire want of any *regular* system in regard to the influence of the accents over the vowels, shews very clearly that such influence belongs only to the *occasion-*

al method of reading certain passages or words, and not to the *essential* mutations of the language itself.

Vowels changed by accession and transposition.

[§ 150. Forms of verbs ending in ו, receiving an accessory pronoun beginning with a consonant and not having the tone upon it, drop the first vowel of the ground-form if it be mutable, and restore the second which had been dropped by declension, and (if it be short) lengthen it.

E. g. עָזַב, plur. עָזְבוּ, with suffix עֲזָבוּנִי; so יִמְצָאוּ, יִמְצָאוּנִי; שְׁמָעוּנִי, שְׁמָעוּ.]

[§ 151. *Transposition is only occasional and euphonic*. It belongs not to the rules of the language. Instances of it are such as the following, viz. יַחְדָּו for יַחְדָּו, רָחְבָּה for בְּהֲשַׁמָּה, בְּהַשַּׁמָּה for בְּהַשַּׁמָּה, etc.]

Vowels changed by position.

[§ 152. The *prefixes* to words, consisting of one letter, vary their vowels according to their position and the nature of the words to which they are attached.

(*a*) THE ARTICLE הַ (for הַל § 16) has, (1) Usually, Pattahh followed by Daghesh forte; e. g. הַנָּחָשׁ=הַל נָחָשׁ. (2) Before the Gutturals א, ע, and also ר, it takes Qamets; as הָאִישׁ, הָעַיִן, הָרֹאשׁ. (3) Before ה and ח, Pattahh long is the more usual vowel; as הַחֹשֶׁךְ, הַהֵלֶךְ. (4) Before all the Gutturals, when they have a Qamets under them, the article usually takes Seghol; see § 142. *a*. (5) The Daghesh after the article is not only omitted before the Gutturals and Resh (§ 111), but usually omitted, also, before words beginning with מְ and יְ having a simple Sheva; e. g. הַיְאֹר for הַיְאֹר, הַמְכַסֶּה for הַמְכַסֶּה.

Note. When the article is preceded by the particles, בְּ, כְּ, לְ, it usually suffers *syncope* (§ 108. *b*), and gives up its vowel to the particles; as בַּשַּׁבָּלִים for בְּהַשַּׁבָּלִים, כְּעָם for כְּהָעָם, לֶחָרִים for לְהֶחָרִים. On the contrary, it sometimes resists syncope; as לְהָעָם, etc.

(*b*) THE PARTICLES בְּ, כְּ, לְ, are appropriately pointed with Sheva simple. But, (1) Before the *composite* Shevas they take the corresponding short vowel; e. g. בַּחֲרוֹן, לָחֳלִי *lŏ-hhŏli*, etc. (2) Before accented syllables they usually take Qamets; as לָמוּת, לָגֶשֶׁת, לָכֶם. But this is confined chiefly to forms of the Inf. mode not in regimen; to pronouns; and to tone-syllables at the end of a verse, or of a disjunctive clause. In other cases, the usual punctuation is Sheva. (3) Before simple Sheva they take short Hhireq; comp. § 137.

§ 152. VOWELS CHANGED BY POSITION. 69

(c) The Conjunction וְ is appropriately pointed with a Sheva simple. But, (1) Before Gutturals with a composite Shevà, it takes the corresponding short vowel; as יַעֲבֹד. (2) Before א which would regularly have a composite Sheva, it *sometimes* takes a corresponding contracted vowel in which א quiesces, as וֵאלֹהִים for וֶאֱלֹהִים; comp. § 119. c. 1. (3) Before a *tone-syllable* it frequently takes Qamets; as וָפָ֫חַת, דּוֹר וָדוֹר. The usual cases of this nature are before a *disjunctive* accent; before a *conjunctive* one, וְ retains Sheva. (4) Before Sheva vocal, either simple or composite, standing under a letter not a Guttural, also before ב, מ, פ, it takes Shureq; as וּלְכֹל, וּזָהָב, וּצְעָקְךָ, וּבַ֫יִת, וּפַרְעֹה, וּמֶ֫לֶךְ. (5) Before Yodh which analogically would have a Sheva, it takes long Hhireq and makes the Yodh quiescent (comp. § 53); as וִימֵי, וִיהִי. (6) Before the verbs הָיָה and חָיָה, it sometimes takes short Hhireq or Seghol; as וֶהְיֵה, וִחְיוּ, וִהְיִיתֶם.

(d) The Interrogative הֲ changes its usual punctuation; (1) Before Sheva simple, where it takes Pattahh; as הַבְזוּנָה. (2) Before Gutturals with Qamets, it takes Seghol; as הֶחָכָם, *is he wise?* comp. § 142. a. (3) Before Gutturals without Qamets, it takes Pattahh, and sometimes Qamets; as הַאֵלֵךְ, *shall I go?* הָאַתֶּם *vos ne?* (4) It sometimes imitates the punctuation of the article before a letter with a Sheva; e. g. הַכְּתֹ֫נֶת *an tunica?* הַדְּרָכַי *viaene meae?* And even before a letter with a vowel it sometimes does the same, although very rarely; as הַיֵּיטַב *an bonum erit?*]

PART III.

GRAMMATICAL STRUCTURE AND FORMS OF WORDS.

§ 153. *Radical Words.* The Hebrew and its cognate languages, in their present state, exhibit a surprising degree of regularity and uniformity in the construction and sound of the radical words. This circumstance forms a broad line of distinction between them and all the western languages. Almost all radical words, which with few exceptions are verbs, consist of only three letters usually forming two syllables; as מָלַךְ *he reigned,* אֶרֶץ *the earth.* From such triliteral roots are derived the various forms of nouns and verbs, which are used to express case, number, gender, person, tense, etc., and the different forms of nouns, adjectives, particles, etc. From this *general* principle of derivation (which was commonly represented by the older grammarians as *universal*), are to be excepted, perhaps, a few nouns which constitute the names of familiar objects; e. g. אָב *father,* אֵם *mother,* יָד *hand,* etc. A few particles and primitive pronouns also appear to be *biliteral* in their root, and not derived from a *triliteral* word.

§ 154. *Conformity to the general principle.* So extensively, in Hebrew, is the principle of inflection grounded on derivation from a triliteral root, that nouns which are primitive and biliteral, conform to the common laws in their declension; i. e. they are treated as though they were derived from triliteral roots. Thus אֵם by inflection becomes אִמְּי =אַמְמִי, as if derived from אָמַם; although אֵם seems to be a primitive.

§ 155. *Biliteral roots.* From some appearances in the Hebrew language, it is probable that originally it contained a greater number of biliteral roots, than at present; and that its triliteral forms were, in many instances, constituted by doubling the second radical of the root, or adding to it one of the vowel-letters, or the semi-vowel Nun: e. g. יָטַב and טוֹב *to be good,* common root טב; נָפַח and פּוּחַ *to blow,* common root פח; דָּכָה, דָּכָא, דּוּךְ, דָּכַךְ, *to thrust down,* common root דך.

In like manner, there is a considerable number of triliteral words in the Hebrew and its cognate dialects, in which two of the radicals are the same, while the third is quite different, and yet the meaning of each word which exhibits the same two radicals, remains the same in all: e. g. the verb signifying *to lick,* is either לָעַע, לָעַב, לָעַט, לָעַס, לָעַף, לָצַץ, or לָקַק; the letters לע being uniform in all.

But if biliteral roots were originally more numerous than at present, they had conformed to the common laws of the language at least as early as any of the written Hebrew now extant; since the written language every where presents the *triliteral* forms, as principally constituting the radical words.

§ 156. *Quadriliteral and quinqueliteral roots* are very rare in the Hebrew; such as כַּרְמֶל *a fruitful field,* כִּרְסֵם *to devour,* שַׁלְאֲנַן *to be quiet.* Those which exist, are formed by the addition or insertion of a letter or letters, to lengthen the triliteral root; in the same manner as triliterals are formed from biliterals, as described above in § 155.

§ 157. The parts of speech in Hebrew are, *the article, pronoun, verb* (including the *participle,*) *noun, adjective, adverb, preposition, conjunction,* and *interjection;* which will be treated of in their order.

§ 158. *The proportional number of roots* in the various parts of speech in the Hebrew, may be thus arranged. (*a*) The verb is altogether most frequently primitive. (*b*) Only a small number of nouns are primitive. (*c*) The original pronouns, personal, demonstrative, etc. are all primitive. (*d*) Particles are some of them primitive, and some are derived from other parts of speech. The Hebrew has very few particles.

Grammatical structure of words.

§ 159. There are two ways in which case, number, gender, person, tense, etc. may be expressed in any language : (1) By the inflection of the original words or ground forms. (2) By affixing other words or particles, which serve to express relation. The Hebrews, as the sequel will shew, made use of both these methods.

§ 160. *Composite words,* i. e. compound verbs, nouns, etc., which the Greek, Latin, and other western languages exhibit, are not usual in the Hebrew. Words properly *composite* are scarcely ever found in Hebrew, except in proper names; where, however, they frequently occur.

§ 161. The Hebrew also differs from the languages of the West, in the mode of writing many of its particles, and the oblique cases of personal pronouns. These, instead of standing by themselves, are commonly united with the verbs, nouns, etc., to which they belong, or on which they depend, so as to form with them but one word.

THE ARTICLE.

§ 162. The Hebrew has but one article, viz. הַל, commonly written הַ with a Daghesh forte after it. It corresponds in a good degree, but not universally, with the definite article *the* in English.

§ 163. In writing, the Lamedh of the article הַל is always assimilated to the first letter of the noun to which it is prefixed, and expressed by a Daghesh *forte* in that letter, or by some equivalent.

E. g. הַמָּטָר *the rain*, instead of הַל מָטָר; הָאָדָם *the man*, instead of הַל אָדָם, etc., § 107. 1. *b*. § 112. For the various pointing of the article, see § 152. *a*.

Note. That the original form of the article was הַל, seems probable from the form of the Arabic article אַל, whose ל is frequently assimilated in the same manner as the Hebrew. The only difference is, that in the Hebrew the assimilation, or some equivalent for it, is *universal;* in Arabic, it is usual only before the *solar* letters.

PRONOUNS.

I. *Pronouns personal.*

§ 164. The Hebrew is rich in personal pronouns; not only distinguishing the masc. and fem. of the 2d and 3d persons, when they stand as the subjects of verbs, but possessing forms appropriate to the oblique cases which follow verbs, nouns, or particles.

Nominative case or Ground-form of all the personal Pronouns.

	Singular.		Plural.	
com. *I*,	אָנֹכִי אֲנִי	*we*,	אֲנַחְנוּ	אָנוּ נַחְנוּ
mas. *thou*,	אַתָּה אַתְּ	*ye*,	אַתֶּם	
fem. *thou*,	אַתִּי אַתְּ	*ye*,	אַתֵּן (אַתֵּנָה)	
mas. *he* (*it*)	הוּא	*they*,	הֵם	הֵמָּה
fem. *she* (*it*)	הוּא הִיא (hī)	*they*,	הֵן	הֵנָּה

Notes.

[§ 165. (*a*) In *pause*, the pronouns assume the forms, אָתָּ, אָתָּה, אָנִי, etc., § 144. (*b*) The א in הוּא, הִיא (הוּא *hī*), is *paragogic* § 125. *a*,

§§ 166—168. PRONOUNS. 73

and *otiant* § 57. (c) The form בַּחְנוּ occurs only six times; אֲנוּ, only in Jer. 42: 6. (d) In אַתֵּנָה (in some Codd. אַתֵּנָה), הֵנָּה, הֵנָּה, the הָ‎ is *paragogic*, § 125. b. (e) The forms אַתָּה, אַתְּ, אַתִּי (ăt), אַתֶּם, אַתֶּן (אַתֵּן), are probably for אַנְתָּה, אַנְתְּ, אַנְתִּי, אַנְתֶּם, אַנְתֶּן, § 107. a; for the full forms, i. e. those with נ, are found in Syriac and Arabic. (f) הוּא (hī) is anomalous, (the older form of the pronoun was הוּא, which was both masc. and fem.); the marginal reading or Keri (§ 103) always supplying the form הִיא (הָיא), as a correction. It is found only in the Pentateuch.

N. B. The ground-forms of the pronouns above, though generally designating only the Nominative case, do sometimes stand in other cases, § 468.]

§ 166. The *oblique* cases of personal pronouns in Hebrew, are represented by fragments of primitive pronouns suffixed to verbs, nouns, and particles, so as to make one word, instead of being written separately as in the western languages.

For an account of these *pronominal suffixes*, as appended to the above mentioned classes of words respectively, see for verbs § 309 seq., for nouns § 336, for adverbs § 405, for prepositions § 408, and for interjections § 410, Note.

II. *Pronouns demonstrative.*

§ 167. Of these there are but few in the Hebrew, viz.

	Singular.			Plural.	
Masc. זֶה	fem. זֹאת	com. זוּ	*this*	Com. אֵלֶּה	*these*
הַלָּזֶה	(זֹה) זוּ	הַלָּז	*this*		אֵל *these*

The *usual* forms are those in the first line; those in the second, are *unusual*. For זֹאת, the form הַלֵּזוּ is once employed, Ezek. 36: 35.

Note. The pronouns of the 3d person, i. e. הֵן, הֵם, הִיא, הוּא, are also frequently employed as *demonstratives;* in which case they usually prefix the article, as בַּיּוֹם הַהוּא, *on that day.*

III. *Pronouns relative.*

§ 168. The only proper one is אֲשֶׁר, *who, which, what,* of every gender and number.

[Note. This pronoun is contracted mostly in the later Hebrew, by dropping the א (§ 108. a), and assimilating the ר (§ 107. c); as שֶׁלֹּא instead of אֲשֶׁר לֹו. The שׁ (the *apocopate* form) has various vowels,

10

according to the nature of the word which follows; e. g. שֶׁ, שֶׁ followed by a Daghesh, שַׁ, שֶׁ, as שֶׁהֵם Ecc. 3: 18. In this last case, there is no compensation for the ר which is cast away.]

§ 169. The *demonstratives* זֶה and זוּ, are occasionally employed as *relatives*.

IV. *Pronouns Interrogative.*

§ 170. These are two; viz. מִי *who*, and מָה (מַה, מֶה) *what*.

Note. Before a Daghesh *euphonic* the form מַה is used, as מַה־לְּךָ; also before ע, ה, ה, not having Qamets; before a Guttural with Qamets, מֶה, as מֶה אָנֹכִי § 142. *a*; but sometimes מָה also before such Gutturals, as in Ex. 12: 26, מָה הָעֲבוֹדָה.

VERBS.

§ 171. CLASSIFICATION. They are distributed into (*a*) *Primitive*, i. e. underived from any other words; e. g. מָלַךְ *to reign*,* יָשַׁב *to sit*, and so of most of the Hebrew verbs. (*b*) *Derivative*, i. e. such as come from primitives by the accession of formative letters. Such are all the conjugations of verbs excepting the first or *Kal*. (*c*) *Denominative*, i. e. those which are formed from nouns *(de nomine)*; e. g. אָהַל *to live in a tent*, from אֹהֶל *a tent*.

<small>Note. These divisions concern the *origin* of verbs, but not the mode of inflection. A great number of verbs is comprehended in the class *b*, while very few belong to the class *c*.</small>

§ 172. INFLECTION. In respect to *inflection*, verbs are divided into *regular* and *irregular*. Regular verbs are those which are analagous in their inflection, and preserve through all their changes their original *triliteral* root. Verbs irregular are either pluriliteral, or those which drop or assimilate one or more of their radical letters.

§ 173. CONJUGATION. (*a*) The term *conjugation*, in grammars of the Greek, Latin, and some modern languages, is employed to denote different classes of verbs, which are distinguished from each other by certain peculiar characteristics of form or inflection, which are therefore said to belong to the first, second, third, etc. conjugation. In this sense, the Hebrew might be said to have several conjugations; but this word is not so used by Hebrew grammarians.

(*b*) In the Hebrew grammar, the word *conjugation* is applied to *dif-*

<small>* Literally, *he reigned*. The Infinitive in English is used in this work, merely for the sake of brevity, in preference to the third person of the past tense, which would exactly correspond to the Hebrew root.</small>

§§ 174, 175. VERBS; PECULIAR CONJUGATIONS.

ferent forms of the same verb, and corresponds in some degree with the term *voice* in Greek grammar, although it is employed in a much more extensive sense. The passive and middle voices, in Greek, exhibit the original idea of the verb under certain modifications, or with some additional shades of meaning. So the property of all the conjugations in Hebrew is, *to vary the primary meaning of the verb, by uniting with it an accessory signification*. The Hebrews were thus enabled to express, by means of their conjugations, all those various modifications and relations of verbs, which, in most other languages, are expressed either by composite verbs, or by several words.

Note. The most convenient arrangement is, to make as many conjugations as there are forms of verbs, original and derived. These are presented to view in the following section.

Usual Conjugations.

	ACTIVE.		PASSIVE AND REFLEXIVE.	
	Name.	Form.	Name.	Form.
§ 174.	1. Kal	קָטַל	2. Niphal	נִקְטַל
	3. Piel	קִטֵּל	4. Pual	{ קֻטַּל / קֻטָּל
	5. Hiphil	הִקְטִיל	6. Hophal	{ הָקְטַל / הֻקְטַל
	7. Hithpael	הִתְקַטֵּל		

Peculiar Conjugations.

§ 175. (*a*) 1 Poel סוֹבֵב. 2 Poal סוֹבַב. 3. Hithpoel הִסְתּוֹבֵב, without a sibilant letter, הִתְגּוֹלֵל from גָּלַל.

These conjugations are found in the class of verbs named *Ayin doubled* (עע), and very rarely appear in any other. They take the place of Piel, Pual, and Hithpael, as these appear in regular verbs; see § 262.

(*b*) 1 Polel קוֹמֵם. 2 Polal קוֹמַם. 3 Hithpolel הִתְקוֹמֵם.

In verbs *Ayin Vav* (עוּ § 269) these forms are the common substitutes for the regular Piel, Pual, and Hithpael.

Note. Although the appearance of the two classes, *a* and *b*, is the same, yet the mode of formation is very different; e. g. סוֹבֵב, etc. comes from the root סָבַב, and is formed *by inserting ו between the two first radicals*; while קוֹמֵם, etc. comes from קוּם, and is formed *by doubling the last radical*. Most of the lexicons and grammars name the class *b*, Pilel, Pulal, etc., because, in regular verbs, the shape of these conjugations would be like קִטְלֵל, קֻטְלַל, etc. But as these conjugations scarcely have an existence in regular verbs, (and have not even a similar corresponding one in the Arabic, excepting the very rare and peculiar conj. IX. and XI.), so it is much better, for the sake of perspicuity, to name them as I have done here. *A potiori nomen fit*, is a good rule in making out artificial denominations of this nature.

Unusual Conjugations.

[§ 176. Most of these are of very rare occurrence; and several of them occur not more than two or three times, in the whole Scriptures. They are as follows; viz.

(1) *Hothpaal* or *Huthpaal*, הִתְקַטֵּל, הָתְקַטַּל, both passive forms of Hithpael; comp. Pual in § 174. They are of very rare occurrence.

(2) *Pilel* active and *Pulal* passive, קָטְלַל, קָטְלֵל (comp. § 175. *b*. Note), occurring only in five or six cases, in regular verbs.

(3) *Pilpel* active and *Polpal* passive, formed out of verbs עע and עי, by repeating the first and last radicals; e. g. from גָּלַל comes גִּלְגֵּל, גָּלְגַּל; from בּוּל, כִּלְכֵּל and כִּלְכַּל. These are equivalent to the forms from the same verbs, described in § 175. *a*. *b*.

(4) A form *Tiphel* seems to have been in existence; e. g. תַּחֲרָה from חָרָה, תִּרְגַּל a denominative (§ 171. *c*) from רֶגֶל. Once we have a *Peoel* form; e. g. in הַצּוֹעֵר, in all respects a ἅπαξ λεγόμενον in Hebrew.

Note. Other conjugations are made by some grammarians; but they are disputed ones, and it is of little or no importance to the student to insert them here, as his lexicon will give him the requisite information.]

[§ 177. PLURILITERAL VERBS, i. e. verbs whose root consists of more than *three* letters, take the following forms; viz. שַׁאֲנַן, פֵּרֶשׁ, כִּרְסֵם, active; חֲמַרְמַר, רִטְפַּשׁ, כִּרְבֵּל, passive.]

§ 178. No one verb in Hebrew exhibits all the conjugations above mentioned; and very few exhibit even all the *usual* ones in § 174. Neither is the active or passive meaning *always* attached to the forms under which it is ranged; as will be seen in the sequel. *Predominant* usage directs the classification of the respective conjugations.

§ 179. The names of all the *derived* conjugations are borrowed from the various forms of the verb פָּעַל, which the old grammarians used in constructing paradigms; and are merely the modes of pronouncing those several forms. The first conjugation is called קַל *Qăl*, or (as it is usually written) *Kăl*, i. e. *light*; because it is not, like the derived forms, increased by the addition of any letter to the root. The other names are formed thus; נִפְעַל *Niph-yăl*; פִּעֵל *Pi-yēl*, Daghesh forte being excluded by the Guttural; פֻּעַל *Pŭ-yăl*, Daghesh being excluded; הִפְעִיל *Hiph-yil*; הָפְעַל *Hŏph-yăl*; הִתְפַּעֵל *Hith-pă-yēl*, Daghesh excluded; and so of the unusual conjugations.

§ 180. The third person singular of the Praeter tense in Kal, is regarded as the root of all verbs; one class (verbs עוּ) excepted, whose root is the triliteral Infinitive, e. g. קוּם.

Form and Signification of the usual Conjugations.

§ 181. (*a*) KAL is generally *active;* but it may be either *transitive* or *intransitive.*

(*b*) The root, which is the third person singular masculine, has three different forms, distinguished by the final vowels, Pattahh, Tseri, and Hholem.

E. g. פָּקַד *to visit,* זָקֵן *to be old,* and יָגֹר *to fear.*

Note 1. The form with final Pattahh is generally *active* and *transitive;* but sometimes it is *intransitive,* as גָּדַל *to be great.* The other two forms are usually *intransitive,* but sometimes otherwise.

Note 2. Some verbs in Kal have a *passive* meaning; e. g. שָׁבַן, *to inhabit* and *to be inhabited;* עָלָה, *to elevate* and *to be elevated.*

§ 182. (*a*) FORM OF NIPHAL. It is formed by prefixing Nun to the ground-form of the verb, and dropping the first vowel of the same: e. g. קָטַל, נִקְטַל.

Note. The real prefix seems to be הִן, (in Arabic it is אַן). In the Infinitive this develops itself; e. g. הִנְקְטַל=הִקָּטֵל, Nun being *assimilated* in the first form, § 107. *a.* The appropriate pointing of the prefix Nun, in the Praeter, would be Sheva (נְ); but short Hhireq is necessarily substituted for it, inasmuch as the vowel under the first radical falls away, § 137, or an equivalent vowel in case the first radical is a Guttural, § 138.

(*b*) SIGNIFICATIONS OF NIPHAL. (1) It is *passive* of Kal, when Kal is transitive. (2) *Passive* of Piel, or of Hiphil, when they are transitive and Kal is intransitive. (3) It is often a *reflexive* form, corresponding to the middle voice of the Greeks; as הִשָּׁמֵר *watch thyself,* נִשְׁאַל *he asked for himself.* Such are the *usual* meanings; but,

(4) It also has an *intransitive* sense, and often expresses passion or affection; as נֶחֱלָה, *he was sick,* in Kal חָלָה with the same sense; נֶאֱנַח *to sigh.* (5) To show one's self as doing a thing, or as suffering it to be done; e. g. נִכְבַּד *to show one's self honourable,* נֻגַּע (=נִנְגַּע) *to exhibit one's self as smitten,* נֶעְתַּר *to suffer one's self to be entreated.* (6) To express reciprocal action; as נִשְׁפַּט *to contend,* viz. with another; נִלְחַם *to fight,* viz. with an enemy; נוֹדַע *to confer with,* viz. another. (7) Sometimes simply as Kal; e. g. נִשְׁבַּע, *juravit.*

Note. It is often used in such a connection that it must be translated by a corresponding verb having *can, may, must, ought, could, would, should,* etc. before it; e. g. Gen. 6: 21. 16: 10. 20: 9, etc.

§ 183. (a) FORM OF PIEL. This is characterized by a doubling of the middle radical; as קָטֵּל.

Note. In case the middle radical is a Guttural, and cannot take a Daghesh forte, the preceding vowel is prolonged as a compensation (§ 111. § 112); e. g. בֵּרֵךְ for בֵּרַךְ, etc.

(b) SIGNIFICATIONS OF PIEL. (1) It is *causative* of Kal; e. g. אָבַד to perish, אִבֵּד to cause to perish. This is the predominant meaning.

(2) To let any thing or person be or do thus and so; to regard or exhibit it or him, as being or doing thus and so; e. g. חִיָּה to let one live; צִדֵּק, to show or pronounce one to be just; טִמֵּא, to pronounce one unclean. (3) It is *intensive* of Kal; e. g. שָׁאַל to ask, שִׁאֵל to beg; שָׁבַר to break, שִׁבֵּר to dash in pieces. (4) It has a *privative* sense; e. g. נָכַר to know, נִכֵּר to misapprehend; Hiph. הִשְׁרִישׁ to take root, Piel. שֵׁרֵשׁ to root out. (5) It often agrees in signification with Kal *transitive*; seldom has it an *intransitive* meaning. (6) Sometimes it has a reflexive sense; e. g. Gen. 41: 14, וַיְגַלַּח and he shaved himself.

§ 184. PUAL. This is simply the *passive* of Piel, and is characterized by a Daghesh in the middle radical, (or a compensation for it when it is excluded), and by Qibbuts short or Qamets Hhateph in the first syllable; e. g. קֻטַּל, or קָטָּל *qŏttāl*.

§ 185. (a) FORM OF HIPHIL. It prefixes He, and inserts Yodh before the two last radicals; e. g. קָטַל, Hiph. הִקְטִיל.

(b) SIGNIFICATION OF HIPHIL. (1) It is causative of Kal; as קָדַשׁ to be holy, הִקְדִּישׁ to make holy. This is the *usual* meaning.

(2) Not unfrequently is Hiphil used in the same sense (transitive and intransitive) as Kal; e. g. הִשְׁחִית to corrupt, הִשְׁקִים to be quiet, הִלְבִּין to be white.

Note. Seldom are the Piel and Hiphil of the same verb both used in a *causative* sense. When both are employed, it is generally with some shade of difference in their signification; e. g. כִּבֵּד to honour, הִכְבִּיר to render powerful.

§ 186. HOPHAL. This is characterized by ה prefixed to the root, followed by the vowel Qamets Hhateph or short Qibbuts; e. g. הָקְטַל, or הֻקְטַל.

It is usually the *passive* of Hiphil; but it occasionally has an intransitive meaning, as Fut. Hoph. יוּכַל *he shall be able*, from יָכֹל; sometimes an active one, as הֶעֱבַדְתָּם, serve them, Ex. 20: 5. Deut. 5: 9. 13: 13; which, however, is capable of being rendered, *that we may not be caused to serve*, etc.

§ 187. (a) FORM OF HITHPAEL. It prefixes הִת to the Inf. form of Piel; e. g. Inf. Pi. קַטֵּל, Hith. הִתְקַטֵּל.

[(b) The characteristic הִת undergoes several mutations, when it comes before the Sibilants, or the cognate letters. E. g.

(1) Before a Sibilant, the ת changes places with it; as in the following examples, viz.

	Kal		Hithpa.		instead of	
ס	סָבַל	—	הִסְתַּבֵּל	—	הִתְסַבֵּל	
שׁ	שָׂגַב	—	הִשְׂתַּגֵּב	—	הִתְשַׂגֵּב	
שׁ	שָׁמַר	—	הִשְׁתַּמֵּר	—	הִתְשַׁמֵּר	
צ	צָדַק	—	הִצְטַדֵּק	—	הִתְצַדֵּק	

In the latter case (צ) the ת is not only transposed, but changed into its cognate ט. This case, however, is very unfrequent in Hebrew, though common in the cognate languages.

(2) Before a cognate letter the ת is more commonly *assimilated*; e.g.

	instead of		from	
הִדַּבֵּר	—	הִתְדַּבֵּר	—	דָּבַר
הִטַּהֵר	—	הִתְטַהֵר	—	טָהַר
הִתַּמָּם	—	הִתְתַּמָּם	—	תָּמַם

(3) The same usage of assimilation is *occasionally* extended to some other letters; e. g.

	as		instead of		from	
ז	as	הִזַּכּוּ	—	הִתְזַכּוּ	—	זָכָה
כ	as	הִכַּסֶּה	—	הִתְכַּסֶּה	—	כָּסָה
נ	as	הִנַּבֵּא	—	הִתְנַבֵּא	—	נָבָא
ר	as	אָרוֹמֵם	—	אֶתְרוֹמֵם	—	רוּם (§ 112)
שׁ	as	תְּשׁוֹמֵם	—	תִּתְשׁוֹמֵם	—	שָׁמַם]

(c) SIGNIFICATIONS OF HITHPAEL. (1) It is *reflexive* of Piel; as קִדֵּשׁ *to sanctify*, הִתְקַדֵּשׁ *he sanctified himself*. (2) It signifies to make one's self be or do, or to exhibit one's self as being or doing, that which the verb in its ground-form signifies; e. g. הִתְחַכֵּם *to show one's self cunning*, from חָכַם *to be wise*; הִתְגַּדֵּל *to behave one's self proudly*, from גָּדַל *to be great*; הִתְחַלָּה *to represent one's self as sick*, from חָלָה *to be sick*. Also with some slight modifications, as הִתְחַכֵּם *to think one's self wise*, from חָכַם *to be wise*; הִתְחַפֵּשׂ *to make one's self to be sought*, i. e. *to conceal one's self*, from חָפַשׂ *to seek*; הִתְחַנֵּן *to ask favor for one's self*, properly *to make one gracious*, from חָנַן *to be gracious*. These are the leading significations.

(3) It is sometimes the passive of Piel; as פָּקַד *to number*, הִתְפָּקַד *to be numbered*. (4) It is also intransitive; as הִתְאַנַּף *to be angry*. (5) It is not unfrequently active and transitive; as הִשְׁתַּמֵּר *to keep or observe*, viz. laws, statutes, etc.

Signification of the unusual Conjugations.

[§ 188. Poel, Poal, and Hithpoel, are merely substitutes for the daghesh'd conjugations (§ 175 a); as are also Polel, Polal and Hithpolel (§ 175. b); and likewise Pilel and Pulal (§ 176. 2).

Note. When the regular Piel, Pual, etc. of verbs עע and עו are employed, together with the forms just mentioned, there is generally some slight distinction of meaning between them, such as is described in § 185. b. Note.]

[§ 189. Pilpal and Polpal are only another form for Piel and Pual, § 176. 3,]

[§ 190. Hothpaal and Huthpaal agree in meaning with Hithpael, when it is used in a *passive* sense.

Note. The other unfrequent conjugations have generally an *intensive* signification. The pluriliteral verbs are few, and of various significations.]

MODE, TENSE, ETC.

§ 191. The *modes* and *tenses* of verbs are very limited in Hebrew. The modes are the Indicative, the Imperative, and the Infinitive; the tenses are the Praeter and Future.

§ 192. The *number, person*, and *gender* of verbs, are expressed with unusual fulness and accuracy.

§ 193. The *ground-forms* of all verbs are (1) *The Praeter*, 3d pers. sing. masc.; which is the ground-form of the past tense and the present participle. (2) *The Infinitive construct;* which is generally regarded as the ground-form of the Future and Imperative.

Note. But in verbs with Future Pattahh, the Infinitive construct takes *Hholem* regularly; which seems to be at variance with this principle; at least it is an exception (a large one too) to the maxim just laid down, see § 212. 2. § 230, respecting the Inf. const. as a ground-form. However, out of Kal the Inf. may well be taken as the ground-form of the Future and Imperative in all the conjugations; and even the participles in Piel, Pual, Hiphil, Hophal, and Hithpael, are derived from the Infinitive form in the same conjugations.

§ 194. *The Praeter* is declined by adding to the root (the 3d pers. sing. masc.) fragments of pronouns, in order to designate person and gender; e. g.

§§ 195—197. VERBS; FORMATION OF PRAETER, ETC.

		Singular.				
3 mas.	קָטַל	ground-form.				
3 fem.	קָטְלָה	by adding הָ		. . . .	fragment of	הִיא .
2 mas.	קָטַלְתָּ	—	תָּ	תָּה	— —	אַתָּה .
2 fem.	קָטַלְתְּ	—	תְּ	תִּי	— —	אַתְּ אַתִּי .
1 com.	קָטַלְתִּי	—	תִּי	תּ	prob. from obs.	אִתִּי .
		Plural.				
3 com.	קָטְלוּ	—	וּ	וּא	derivation unknown.	
2 mas.	קְטַלְתֶּם	—	תֶּם		fragment of	אַתֶּם .
2 fem.	קְטַלְתֶּן	—	תֶּן	תֶּנָה	— —	אַתֶּן .
1 com.	קָטַלְנוּ	—	נוּ		— —	אֲנוּ .

§ 195. *The Inf. construct* in Kal (the ground-form of the Fut. and Imp. mood) has, like the Praeter Kal (§ 181. b), three forms; viz. קְטֹל, שְׁכַב, נְתֹן. The Inf. in the *derived* conjugations, takes the vowels peculiar to such conjugations respectively.

Note. Besides these endings, the Inf. of regular verbs, specially in Kal, sometimes takes the form of a fem. noun, § 212. 3; and in some irregular ones, the fem. form in Kal is almost the only one in use, e. g. in verbs Pe Yodh, etc.

§ 196. *The Infinite absolute* takes Qamets in the first syllable, and Hholem impure in the last; e. g. קָטוֹל.

Note. This form is preserved even in most of the irregular verbs. In verbs עוּ, however, we have קוֹם for קוּם. The *derived* conjugations preserve, for the most part, the final Hholem impure; e. g. Niph. הִקָּטֹל, Piel קַטֵּל, Hoph. קָטֵל. Hiphil has Tseri; as הַקְטִיל or הַקְטֵל. The variations will be noted under the respective classes of verbs.

§ 197. *The Future tense* is declined by prefixing fragments of pronouns to the ground-form, i. e. the Inf. construct; and also by suffixing them, in some cases, in order to mark the gender, or number, or both.

Compare the Praeter (§ 194), which is declined by the aid of formative *suffixes* only. The following table exhibits the probable derivation of most of the Fut. formative prefixes and suffixes.

§§ 198—201. VERBS; FORMATION OF THE FUTURE.

Singular.

Inf. const.	קְטֹל	ground-form.		
3 masc.	יִקְטֹל	by prefixing	— י	{ prob. from הוּא, י for י to begin a word.
3 fem.	תִּקְטֹל	. . . .	— ת	deriv. uncertain.
2 masc.	תִּקְטֹל	. . . .	— ת	from אַתָּה.
2 fem.	תִּקְטְלִי	by suff. and pref., ־ִי — ת		{ pref. from אַתְּ; suff. from היא to mark the fem.
1 com.	אֶקְטֹל	by prefixing	— א	from אֲנִי.

Plural.

3 masc.	יִקְטְלוּ	by suff. and pref., ו — י		deriv. of ו uncertain.
3 fem.	תִּקְטֹלְנָה	. . . .	נָה — ת	{ deriv. of ת uncertain; נָה from הֵפָּה.
2 mas.	תִּקְטְלוּ	. . . .	ו — ת	pref. from אַתֶּם.
2 fem.	תִּקְטֹלְנָה	. . . .	נָה — ת	{ prefix from אַתֶּן; נָה from הֵפָּה.
1 com.	נִקְטֹל	by prefixing	— נ	from אֲנוּ.

[§ 198. The *praeformative affixes* to the Fut. would appropriately have a Sheva for their vowel-pointing, (as in Piel and Pual they have), but this receives various modifications, according to the pointing of the letter which follows; §§ 136—139.]

[§ 199. In the derived conjugations, Niphal, Hiphil, Hophal, and Hithpael, the *praeformatives* of the Fut. usually expel the characteristics of the conjugation, and transfer their vowel points to themselves, § 118; e. g.

Fut Niphal	יִקָּטֵל	instead of	יִהְקָטֵל	from Inf.	הִקָּטֵל
— —	in verbs עו	יִקּוֹם	—	יִהְקוֹם	—	הִקּוֹם
— Hiphil	יַקְטִיל	—	יְהַקְטִיל	—	הַקְטִיל
— —	in verbs עו	יָקִים	—	יְהָקִים	—	הָקִים
— Hophal	יָקְטַל	—	יְהָקְטַל	—	הָקְטַל
— —	in verbs עו	יוּקַם	—	יְהוּקַם	—	הוּקַם
— Hithpael	יִתְקַטֵּל	—	יְהִתְקַטֵּל	—	וְהִתְקַטֵּל

§ 200. The *final vowel of the Fut.* may be (like that of the Praeter and Inf.) either Hholem, Pattahh, or Tseri.

E. g. *Hholem;* which is by far the most usual form, as יִקְטֹל. *Pattahh;* which is common in *intransitive* verbs having a Praeter with Tseri, and also in verbs with a Guttural in the final syllable, and some others, as יִכְבַּד, יִשְׁמַע, יִמְצָא=יִמְצָא, יִגְמַל=יִגְמַל, יִגְמַל, etc. *Tseri;* as יֹאמַר, יֵשֵׁב, יִתֵּן=יִתֵּן, etc.

§ 201. The *Imperative* follows the same analogy as the Future, taking the same vowels in its final syllable, and for the like reasons. It is declined by means of *suffix*-fragments, like those in the Praeter and Future.

Note. The Imp. has only the *second* persons. When an Imp. sense for the 1st and 3d persons was needed, the Hebrews employed those persons respectively of the Fut. tense.

§ 202. *The participles* in Kal are both *active* and *passive;* in the other conjugations there is but one form, which follows the respective conjugations with regard to its meaning.

E. g. Kal, כּוֹתֵב *scribens*, כָּתוּב *scriptum*. But in verbs with final Tseri and Hholem, the part. present retains the form of the Praeter, as Praet. מָלֵא, part. מָלֵא; Praet. יָגֹר, part. יָגֹר; so in verbs עוֹ, Praet. קָם, part. קָם. In Niphal the same principle prevails, with a slight variation; as Niph. נִקְטַל, part. נִקְטָל, i. e. with final Pattahh prolonged.

Note 1. *Intransitive verbs* usually have but one form of the participle in Kal; which may have either an *active* or *passive* meaning, as the case requires.

Note 2. Beyond Niphal, all the participles are derived from the Inf. form of their respective conjugations, by prefixing מ, and dropping the characteristic ה where it occurs; e. g. Piel מְקַטֵּל, Pual מְקֻטָּל, Hiphil מַקְטִיל, Hophal מָקְטָל, Hithpael מִתְקַטֵּל. In the *passive* forms, the final Pattahh of the ground-form is prolonged, i. e. it becomes Qamets. Any departures from this principle will be noticed where they occur.

Note 3. Particples are declined in the same manner as adjectives, having sing. and plur. forms of the masc. and fem. gender.

Subjunctive and Optative Moods.

§ 203. The Hebrew has neither of these in separate, regularly defined forms, as in Greek; but it employs in the room of them, and to a certain extent, *peculiar forms of the Fut. tense.*

Note. In the Arabic, the usage of the Fut. in this way, is far more defined and general than in the Hebrew. In Syriac and Chaldee, the usage does not at all appear. The Hebrew use is a kind of medium between the two, as it is somewhat frequent, and yet far from being general.

§ 204. The Future is varied, for the purpose of expressing an *optative* or *conditional* sense, by paragoge and apocope.

(*a*) *By paragoge*, viz. of ָה and sometimes ֶה; e. g. Fut. אֲדַבֵּר, with paragoge אֲדַבְּרָה; so אֹמַר, with paragoge אֹמְרָה.

(*b*) *By a kind of apocope;* which generally consists in rendering shorter the final long vowel; and in some cases, in casting away the final letter and vowel; e. g. יַקְטִיל, apoc. יַקְטֵל; יָמוּת, apoc. יָמֹת with Hholem pure, (which is shorter than וּ); יִגְלֶה, apoc. יִגֶל.

§ 205. *The paragogic Future* is, for the most part, confined to the 1st person, singular and plural; the 2d and 3d persons rarely exhibiting it. It is employed in all the conjugations except the *passive* ones, and is used,

(*a*) As an *Optative*; e. g. אָמוּתָה *let me die*. (*b*) To express excitement, urging, assurance, strong determination; as אֵלְכָה *I must go*, אָעִירָה *let me rise up*, אֲדַבְּרָה *I am resolved to speak*, נֵלְכָה *let us go*, etc. (*c*) After the particles לְמַעַן, וְ (*that*), it expresses the latter part of *conditional* sentences; as לְמַעַן אֲסַפְּרָה, *so that I may declare;* וְנֹאכֵלָה, *that we may eat.* (*d*) In some cases, it is used in this last (conditional) sense, where the particle is omitted.

Note 1. Examples of paragoge in respect to the *third* and *second* persons of verbs, may be found in Is. 5: 19. Ezek. 23: 20. Ps. 20: 4.

Note 2. Vav conversive (§ 208) frequently occasions the *paragogic* form of the verb in the first person to be adopted, particularly in the later Hebrew; but not with any speciality of meaning; as וָאֹמְרָה *and I said*, Gen. 41: 11 וַנַּחַלְמָה *and we dreamed;* comp. § 206. Note 1.

§ 206. *The apocopate Future*, on the other hand, is mostly confined to the 2d and 3d persons, rarely making its appearance in the first; e. g.

Reg. verb Hiph.	יַקְטִיל	apoc. יַקְטֵל		תַּקְטִיל apoc. תַּקְטֵל.	
Verbs עוּ Kal	יָמוּת	— יָמֹת		תָּמוּת — תָּמֹת.	
Hiph.	יָמִית	— יָמֵת		תָּמִית — תָּמֵת.	
Verbs לה Kal	יִגְלֶה	— (יִגְל) יִגֶל		תִּגְלֶה — (תִּגְל) תִּגֶל.	
Piel	יְגַלֶּה	— (יְגַל) יְגַל		תְּגַלֶּה — (תְּגַל) תְּגַל.	
Hiph.	יַגְלֶה	— (וְיַגְל) יַגֶל		תַּגְלֶה — (תַּגְל) תַּגֶל.	

This Future is employed, (*a*) To express command, wish, prohibition; e. g. יַכְרֵת, *let him destroy;* אַל תַּסְתֵּר, *hide not.* (*b*) After וְ in a conditional sentence; as וְיַגֵּד, *that he may tell.* (*c*) After the particles of negation, אַל, לֹא; as לֹא תוֹסֵף, *thou shalt not add;* אַל תּוֹתַר, *thou shalt not be preferred.*

[Note 1. Vav conversive (§ 208) connects itself very often with such apocopate forms, but frequently without any speciality of meaning; e. g. וַיַּבְדֵּל, *and he divided.* Comp. § 205. Note; also § 101. *b.*

Note 2. The apoc. Future is confined to conjugations and forms, such as the table above exhibits. All Futures do by no means admit it.

Note 3. The apocopate Futures, in poetry and in the later He-

§§ 207—209. VERBS; FUTURE AND PRAETER WITH VAV. 85

brew, are not always of *special* significancy, but are often employed as the common ones.]

§ 207. The Imperative, like the Future, has both paragogic and apocopate forms, which give intensity to the meaning.

E. g. *Paragogic;* as שְׁמֹר, שָׁמְרָה; קוּמָה, קוּם; סַפֵּר, סַפְּרָה. *Apocopate;* as הַקְטֵל (for הַקְטִיל); so גַּלֵּה, apoc. גַּל; מוּל, apoc. מֹל; קְרָאנָה apoc. of קְרָאןָ, שְׁמַעְנָה apoc. of שְׁמַעַן.

Future with Vav conversive.

§ 208. Vav with Pattahh prefixed to the Fut. tense, and followed by a Daghesh forte, is called *Vav conversive;* because its usual effect is to convert such Future into a Praeter, in respect to meaning.

E. g. אָמַר *he said,* also וַיֹּאמֶר *he said,* or *and he said.* If the praeformative letter of the Fut. be א, the Daghesh is omitted and the vowel is lengthened; as וָאֶקְטֹל, § 112. If the praeformative letter of the verb have a Sheva simple, Daghesh forte is usually omitted after the Vav; e. g. וַיְקַטֵּל, § 73. Note 3.

[Note 1. *Vav conversive* is often connected with the paragogic first pers. Fut., § 205. Note; also with the apocopate 2d and 3d pers. Fut., § 206. Note 1; in many cases without giving an *Optative* or *Subjunctive* meaning to them.

Note 2. *Vav conversive* commonly (not always) makes the Future *Milel,* and consequently shortens the final vowel if it be long, § 101. *b.*

Note 3. *Vav conversive* is probably a fragment of the verb הָוָה *to be.* The first letter is dropped (as it commonly is in Syriac), and the fragment וָה is united to the Future by assimilating the ה, (as in מַה־זֶּה=מָזֶּה); so that הָוָה יִקְטֹל=וַיִּקְטֹל *it was* [that] *he killed,* i. e. he killed. So the Arabians make their Imperfect, only they write out the verb of existence in full; and so the Syrians, except that they employ the *participle* of the verb of existence.]

Note 4. When Vav is *not* conversive, and is prefixed to the Fut., it has a different punctuation from the above; e. g. in Gen. 1: 6, וִיהִי, with Vav conversive וַיְהִי; וְיִקְטֹל, with Vav conversive וַיִּקְטֹל.]

Praeter with Vav.

§ 209. Vav prefixed to the Praeter is merely a conjunction. But it often gives to the Praeter the sense of a Future, because it connects it with a preceding Future or Imperative.

Note. As Vav conversive prefixed to the Future, retracts the tone (§ 208. Note 2); so, on the contrary, Vav joined to the Praeter usually throws the tone forward, as וְשָׁבַרְתִּ֫י, שָׁבַ֫רְתִּי, § 101. *a*.

§ 210. *General remark on the tenses.* The tenses in Hebrew are real *Aorists*, capable of every variety of meaning as to designation of time. See this fully developed in the Syntax, § 503. § 504.

Occasional peculiarities in the forms of Verbs.

[§ 211. The peculiarities now to be noted are not confined to any one conjugation or class of verbs, but apply more or less to all the different conjugations and classes of them.

(*a*) Paragogic letters are often suffixed to some of the forms; e. g.

(1) *Nun*, to persons ending in ו or ־ִי; as יִרְקְדוּן instead of יִרְקְדוּ, תִּדְבָּקִין instead of תִּדְבְּקִי; rarely to the Praeter, as יְדָעוּן instead of יָדְעוּ; see § 109. *c*. § 146. *b*. (2) (*a*) ־ָה, usually to the Fut. and Imp. active, § 204. § 205. § 207; rarely in the Praeter, as בְּגַדְתָה for בָּגַדְתָּ; Niph. Praet. fem. נִפְלָאָה, with ־ָה parag. נִפְלָאָ֫תָה; Hiph. fem. הֶחְבִּאָ֫תָה, with parag. הֶחְבִּיאָה. (*b*) Sometimes ־ָה is used instead of ־ֶה; e. g. 1 Sam. 28: 15, וַֽאֶקְרָאָה. (3) *Aleph* paragogic or otiant, rarely; as הֲלָכוּא, הֲלָכוּ the same; so יַעֲשׂוּא for יַעֲשׂוּ, § 125. *a*. (4) Participles sometimes take *He* or *Yodh* paragogic, especially the latter, when they are in regimen; as הַֽמַּשְׁפִּילִי לִרְאוֹת. (5) Sometimes the Inf. mood takes it; as לְהוֹשִׁיבִי. (6) Also the Praeter 2d pers. fem., as קָטַלְתִּי.

(*b*) Forms with Quiescents are sometimes *defectively* written, § 63.

E. g. אָמַר for אָמְרוּ, יָזְנֶה for יָזְנוּ (comp. § 122. 1); but this usage is rare. Oftener ה is written for ־ָה; as תִּגְּשַׁן for תִּגְּשֶׁ֑נָה. Sometimes ־ְתִ for ־ְתִי; as יָדַעְתְ for יָדַ֫עְתִי, עָשִׂית for עָשִׂיתִי. So אָרַב for אָרְבָּה, etc.

(*c*) The prepositions בְּ, כְּ, לְ, prefixed to the Inf. of Niphal, often (not always), expel the ה characteristic, and stand in its place; as בְּהִקָּטֵל for בְּהִקָּטֵל; comp. § 199.

(*d*) *Mem praeformative* in participles is sometimes (rarely) omitted; as לֻקָּח for מְלֻקָּח, בְּתִקוֹמֵם for בְּמִתְקוֹמֵם, etc.]

REGULAR VERBS TRANSITIVE.*

NOTES ON PARADIGM I.

The student is first of all to commit paradigm I. of the Verbs. The following notes will serve to explain variations and anomalies. The paradigms are, for convenience' sake, thrown together at the end of the Grammar.

N. B. The learner will be careful to note, that the tone is on the *ultimate* in all cases where it is not marked with an accent over the penult. Particular care, at the outset, will enable him always to accent the verbs rightly, without any trouble.

Kal.

[§ 212. (1) *Praeter.* The unusual forms are 3 fem. sing. in הָ ,
e. g. אָזְלַת from אָזַל; also 2 pers. masc. בְּגַדְתָּה for בָּגַדְתָּ (ה parag.),
§ 211. 2; הֲלַכְתִּי for הָלַכְתְּ 2 pers. sing. fem. (Yodh parag.), § 211. 6.

(2) The example רָכַב exhibits the Fut. with Pattahh, (familiarly called Fut. *A*); but there are very few verbs with such a Future, unless the last syllable has a Guttural in it, or the verb belongs to the classes with final Tseri or Hholem in the Praeter; § 181. *b*. The Inf. of רָכַב is רְכֹב; and so in other cases of the like nature; which seems not to agree with the idea of its being the ground-form of such Futures and Imperatives as take *Pattahh;* § 193. 2.

(3) *Less usual forms of the Infinitive.* Besides the usual forms in the paradigm, there are, (*a*) Inf. absolute קָטֹל, Vav omitted; Inf. construct קְטוֹל, Vav *fulcrum* only, also קְטֹל. (*b*) The Inf. has *feminine* forms also, though rarely; e. g. like קָטְלָה, קִטְלָה, קָטְלָה; (מִקְטַל, like the Chaldee, is doubtful).

Note. The Hholem in the Inf. absolute is impure and immutable; but in the Inf. const. it is pure and mutable. Hence it is shortened before Maqqeph; as קְטָל־ *qetöl.* Before suffixes it is both shortened and transposed; see the Inf. with suffixes in Par. XXII.

(4) *Less usual forms of the Future.* These are יִקְטוֹל (Vav *fulcrum*), rarely as יִקְטַל except in verbs with a Guttural in the final syllable, or verbs intransitive having a Praeter with Tseri; still more seldom as יִקְטוּלוּ. First pers. parag. as אֶקְטְלָה very rare. In pause יִרְכְּבוּ, יִרְכְּבוּ, § 146; with ן parag. the latter form (יִרְכַּב) becomes יִרְכָּבוּן. Three times the 3d plur. fem. has a praeformative י instead of ת; e. g. יַעֲמֹדְנָה instead of תַּעֲמֹדְנָה, Dan. 8: 22, also the like forms in Gen. 30: 38. 1 Sam. 6: 12.

(5) *Imperative;* קְטוֹל (Vav *fulcrum*), sometimes as קְטַל. Paragogic, קָטְלָה, קִטְלָה, rarely as קְטָלָה, קָטְלָה. Imp. 2d pers. fem. sing. seldom as קִטְלִי, קְסָמִי, 1 Sam. 28: 8. Second pers. masc. plur. (seldom) קְטֻלוּ; in pause, sometimes as קְטֹלוּ, קְטוֹלוּ. The Hholem here

---

* Some of the verbs here treated of are *intransitive* also; but *in general* it is otherwise. *A potiori nomen fit.*

is pure; as it is also in the Inf. and Future. A kind of apocopate form is not unfrequent of the 2 pers. fem. plural; e. g. שְׁמַעַן with final furtive Pattahh, instead of שְׁמַעְנָה.

Note 1. As the Hholem in the Future, Inf., and Imper., is *pure*, whether written without a Vav or with one, it is of course shortened when the accent is thrown off; e. g. before Maqqeph, יִקְטָל־ *qiq-tŏl*, so before a suffix, יִקְטָלְכֶם; Inf. and Imp. קְטָל־ *qetŏl*.

Note 2. Some verbs have both Fut. *O* and *A*; e. g. such as שָׁבַת, חָפֵץ, נָדַר, טָרַף, etc. (see Lex.), without any difference in their meaning. Others have Fut. *O* and *A*, with a difference in their signification; e. g. קָצַר, חָרַשׁ, חָלַשׁ, גָּזַר, etc. (see lexicon).

(6) *Participles active*. Frequently written קֹטֵל, although the Hholem is *impure*, § 63; very seldom as קוֹטֵל, קוֹטִיל, or קְטִיל. With Yodh parag., קְטִלִי, fem. קְטָלָתִי (from the fem. form קְטָלָה). Participles are declined as adjectives, having masc. and fem. as well as sing. and plural forms; see parad. XXI.

(7) *Participles passive*. Sometimes written קָטֻל (§ 41), seldom as קָטִיל. The sense is not uniformly *passive*, but sometimes *active*; often so in neuter and intransitive verbs; as is the case also in Syriac.]

Niphal.

[§ 213. (1) The *Praeter* has no variations from the paradigm. (2) Inf. abs. אִדָּרֵשׁ for הִדָּרֵשׁ, Ezek. 14: 3; הִנָּדֹף for הִנָּדֵף, Ps. 68: 3.

(3) The final Tseri, in the forms of the Inf. const., Fut., and Imp., is *pure*, and of course shortened when the accent is thrown off; e. g. הִשָּׁמֵר, יִכָּבֵד, Inf. הִסָּתֵר־. A *disjunctive* accent often changes the Tseri to Pattahh; as וַיִּגָּמַל, § 129. *d*. § 145. The plur. fem. 2d and 3d persons more usually have Pattahh, even without a *disjunctive* accent, or the presence of a Guttural; as תֵּאָכַלְנָה, Jer. 24: 2; so that as to the forms with TSERI, as in the paradigm, it is somewhat doubtful whether they are the predominant ones.

(4) *Future* 1st pers. sing. often takes Hhireq under the praeformative; e. g. as אִקָּטֵל, אִדָּרֵשׁ, etc.]

Piel.

[§ 214. (1) *Praeter* sometimes with Seghol, as דִּבֶּר; oftener with Pattahh, as לִמַּד, specially before a Maqqeph, as מִלַּט־הוּא. (2) *Infinitive* fem. forms rather frequent, as זַמְּרָה; with suff., as צַדְּקָתְךָ. (3) *Imperative A*, as פַּלֵּג. (4) *Participle* sometimes without מְ, as שַׁבֵּת for מְשַׁבֵּת, Ecc. 4: 2. § 108. *a*. 3. The plur. fem. Future has sometimes Pattahh instead of Tseri, e. g. תְּקַטַּלְנָה instead of תְּקַטֵּלְנָה; comp. § 213. 3.

Note 1. The final Tseri throughout Piel is *pure*; and of course it should be shortened whenever it loses the accent; e. g. קַדֶּשׁ־לִי. Nun parag. usually retains it, as יְהַלֵּכוּן.

Note 2. *Daghesh forte* in the middle radical, is not unfrequently omitted in writing, when the middle radical has a Sheva; as יְבַקְשׁוּ for יְבַקְּשׁוּ, § 73. Note 3.]

Pual.

[§ 215. (1) *Praeter* very rarely as קוּטַל, a mere orthographic variation. Once לֻקָּחָה for לֻקְחָה. (2) *Participle* sometimes omits מְ; as לֻקָּח for מְלֻקָּח, מֹרָט for מְמֹרָט, etc. § 108. *a*. 3.]

Note. Daghesh is sometimes omitted in writing here, as in Piel; see Note 2 above.

Hiphil.

[§ 216. (1) *Praeter* sometimes with Seghol under the ה, as הִכְלַמְנוּ instead of הִכְלַמְנוּ. Rarely א is put for ה, as אַגְאַלְתִּי (Is. 63:3) 1st pers. sing. for הִגְאַלְתִּי.

(2) *Infinitive absolute* frequently as הַקְטֵל, (once אַשְׁכֵּם Jer. 25:3, Chaldee form א for ה), or הַקְטִיל. (3) *Inf. construct* seldom as הַקְטֵל. With preposition, as לְהַקְטִיל and לַקְטִיל, § 108. *b*. In a few instances the praeformative has *Hhireq*; as הִרְגִּיז, like the Praeter.

(4) *Future apocopate* יַקְטֵל, and specially with וְ as וַיַּקְטֵל, having a Tseri pure and mutable, § 206. This of course is shortened, when it loses the accent. A peculiar anomaly of the 3d pers. plur. here, is וַיִּדְבְּקוּ, וַיִּדְרְכוּ, 1 Sam. 14:22. 31:2. Jer. 9:2. This is the Aramaean form.

(5) *Imperative* takes the apocopate form with Tseri, in the 2d pers. sing. masc. and 2d plur. fem.; but it sometimes has the form הַקְטִיל here; and with parag. ־ָה, and with suffix pronouns, it always follows this model; e. g. הַקְטִילָה, הַקְטִילֵהוּ.

(6) The apoc. form of the Part. (מַקְטֵל) in the singular, is doubtful. But plural forms derived from such a singular, sometimes occur; e. g. מַחְלָמִים as from מַחְלָם, Jer. 28:8, מַעְזְרִים as from מַעְזֵר, 2 Chron. 28:23.

Remarks. We see that in the Praeter the ־ִי is held fast, not being exchanged, in the persons where it is used at all, for any other vowel; but in the Inf., Fut., and Imp., the apoc. forms, and those with וְ prefixed, or preceded by אַל, take Tseri instead of ־ִי, which Tseri is for the most part pure and mutable. Instead of this, Pattahh is employed when the final syllable of the verb has a Guttural in it, § 236. § 230. § 206.]

Note. See respecting the tone-syllable in this conjugation, § 100.

Hophal.

[§ 217. Some verbs have both forms, i. e. as הָקְטַל and הֻקְטַל; some the one *exclusively*, and some the other. No actual case of the Inf. *construct* occurs in this conjugation.

In a very few cases, the ה characteristic of the conjugation remains after the praeformative, e. g. מְהִקְצָעוֹת for מֻקְצָעוֹת ; so in Hiph. יְהוֹדָה for יוֹדָה, verb להֹ. Instances of Hoph. Inf. abs. occur in Ezek. 16 : 4 (bis). Josh. 9 : 24.]

Hithpael.

[§ 218. (1) The end syllable with *Pattahh* is frequent here, which of course makes Qamets in pause ; as הִתְקַדָּשׁ, הִתְקַדֶּשׁ‎. (2) In the second and first persons of the Praeter (where the usual vowel between the second and third radical is *Pattahh*, as in the paradigm), if the tone is thrown off from this penult syllable, it occasionally takes *Hhireq* instead of Pattahh ; as וְהִתְקַדִּשְׁתִּי, וְהִתְקַדִּשְׁתֶּם, (3) Maqqeph shortens the forms with Tseri, as this vowel is here pure and mutable; e. g. הִתְהַלֶּךְ־נֹחַ. (4) *Nun parag.* usually retains and prolongs the Pattahh, when that vowel is used; as הִתְהַלָּכוּן. (5) *Daghesh forte* in the middle radical is sometimes omitted here, as in Piel and Pual; e. g. יִתְפָּקְדוּ (for יִתְפַּקְּדוּ), Judg. 20 : 15, the Pattahh being prolonged as a compensation.

(6) *The passive of Hithpael*, i. e. HOTHPAEL, sometimes occurs ; e. g. הָתְפָּקְדוּ, Num. 1: 47. 2 : 23 ; so הֻטַּמָּא (for הִתְטַמָּא), הֻכַּבֵּס (for הִתְכַּבֵּס), with Qibbuts instead of Qamets Hhateph ; comp. § 184.]

Special Forms.

[§ 219. Besides the conjugations of the regular verbs here noted, Poel and Poal, and Pilel and Pulal, sometimes occur ; but they are exceedingly rare. E. g. of the former, are שׁוֹרֵשׁ and שֹׁרֵשׁ, part. מְשֻׁפָּט Job 9 : 15, מְלוֹשְׁנִי (for so it should be pointed) Ps. 101: 5, יוֹדַעְתִּי 1 Sam. 21 : 3 ; of the latter, אֻמְלַל, צָמְתָה, נִפְלָל.]

REGULAR VERBS INTRANSITIVE.
NOTES ON PARADIGM II.

§ 220. The 3d pers. sing. Praeter is the principal one which exhibits a departure from the forms of the regular transitive verb; as will be seen by inspection of the paradigms.

§ 221. Verbs final Hholem (of which there are not half a score), generally retain the Hholem in the derived forms ; יְגֹרְתִּי from יָגֹר, יָכֹלְתִּי from יָכֹל ; but not always, as שְׁכָלְתִּי *shā-khāl-ti* from שָׁכֹל. As the Hholem in these verbs is pure, so it is shortened when it loses the accent ; as וַיִּגְרָהּ *veyā-ghŏr-tā*.

§ 222. In the same manner, those few verbs which retain Tseri in the *derived* forms, shorten it either into Hhireq or Seghol when the tone is removed ; e. g. יָלֵד, יְלִדְתִּיךָ ; שָׁאֵל, שְׁאֵלְתָּם.

§§ 223—225. VERBS WITH GUTTURALS.

[Note 1. All the futures are with *Pattahh*, unless the Praeter has two forms, *A* and *E* ; as שָׁכַן and שָׁכֵן, Fut. only יִשְׁכֹּן, as in the paradigm.

Note 2. In *pause* the Tseri of verbs intransitive most frequently makes its appearance ; e. g. דָּבֵקוּ, and so often. In a number of cases, a pause-accent makes the Tseri appear, which elsewhere does not appear ; as שָׁבָן, שָׁכֵן only in pause.

Note 3. Out of Kal the intransitive verbs conform to the model of the transitive ones, and need no separate paradigms. The whole number of them is very small ; and the cases of departure in inflection from the model of Par. I., are comparatively very few.

Note 4. The verbs called *intransitive*, are in some cases *transitive*. As before, *a potiori nomen fit.*]

VERBS WITH GUTTURALS.

§ 223. We have seen (§ 179) that the verb פָּעַל, (the example for paradigms in the old grammars), is employed to give *technical* designations to the various forms of verbs. Accordingly, as פ is the first letter in this verb, ע the second, and ל the third ; so verbs with Gutturals may be denominated פ *guttural*, ע *guttural*, ל *guttural*, whose first, or second, or third *radical* letter is a Guttural.

Verbs Pe Guttural ; Par. III. IV.

§ 224. Where other verbs would take a simple Sheva under the first radical, these *more usually* have a *composite* Sheva. This may be called *the smooth enunciation*.

E. g. חֲזַק, אֱסֹף, עֲמֹד, יֶחֱזַק, יֶאֱסֹף, יַעֲמֹד, etc.

Note. The praeformative letters must have the short vowel which corresponds with the composite Shevas, in such cases ; see § 139. This extends to the letters formative of conjugation, as well as of tense ; e. g. Niph. נֶעֱמַד, Hiph. הֶעֱמִיד, Hoph. הָעֳמַד, etc.

Note 2. When the final vowel is Hholem, the preceding vowels are generally (ֱ) ; but when it is Pattahh, they are usually (ֲ) ; e. g. יֶחֱזַק, יַעֲמֹד. Yet such forms as יֶהֱרֹס do sometimes occur.

Note 3. As (ֱ) seems to be shorter than (ֲ), so the first is sometimes put for the second, where a more rapid enunciation is required ; e. g. הֶעֱמַדְתִּי, but with וְ, וְהַעֲמַדְתִּי.

§ 225. But not unfrequently the Guttural retains Sheva simple ; and then the vowel under the praeformative, etc. is the same as it would be in case a composite Sheva had been employed. This may be called *the rough enunciation*.

נֶחְפַּךְ, יַעֲזֹר, יַעֲזוֹר, נֶחְפַּךְ, יֶחְבַּשׁ, instead of יֶאֱסֹר, יַעֲזוֹר, יֶחְבָּשׁ. Only the verbs הָיָה and חָיָה make such forms in Pe Guttural as יִחְיֶה and יֶחֱיֶה.

§ 226. When, in the course of inflection, a simple Sheva comes immediately to follow a composite Sheva under the Guttural, the Guttural assumes the corresponding short vowel; see § 140.

E. g. יַעַמְדוּ, not יַעֲמְדוּ, which would make an impossible syllable, § 42. § 140. So יֶאֶסְפוּ, not יֶאֱסְפוּ; הָעָמְדִי, not הָעֲמְדִי.

§ 227. Where the first radical would regularly be doubled, (as in the Inf. Fut. and Imp. of Niphal), but this is prevented by its being a Guttural (§ 111), the preceding vowel is lengthened (§ 112), as the paradigm shews.

Note. In this respect verbs Pe Resh agree with verbs Pe Guttural, § 111; e. g. תֵּרָמֵס instead of תִּרָּמֵס.

Notes on the Paradigm.

[§ 228. (a) KAL. (1) *Inf. construct*, receiving prefix-prepositions with a Sheva, causes them to be pointed as the *praeformatives* in the Future are; e. g. לַעֲמֹד, לֶאֱכֹל, also לֶאְכֹל. Inf. fem. like אַשְׁמָה, חֶמְלָה, חָזְקָה.

(2) *The Future* has two forms; as will be seen in the paradigm. Aleph here, whether a *radical*, or a *praeformative* of the first pers. sing., takes the Seghol vowels in preference to the others. The two forms ֶ ֱ and ֶ ְ are not unfrequently interchanged in the Fut. of the same verbs; and sometimes the singular has one form, and the plural another, just as adjunct words may require the pronunciation to be more or less rapid; e. g. יֶאֱסֹף, plur. יַאַסְפוּ. The reason of their exchange for each other, in many cases, is not apparent to us. It depended, probably, on the niceties of *vivâ voce* enunciation.

The Futures with the rough enunciation, i. e. with Sheva simple, are as יַחְדַּל, יַחְגֹּר, having Pattahh in the first syllable when the last is *O*, and Seghol when the last is *A;* so as to avoid the repetition of two Pattahhs. The declension of these forms is otherwise regular, as in Par. I.; excepting that where the *final* Pattahh falls away, the praeformative may take, and sometimes does take, Pattahh; as יַחְסַר, plur. יַחְסְרוּ.

(3) *Imperative* with א, as אֱסֹף, אֱחֹז. With ה parag., as אָסְפָה. Imp. fem. sing. חָשְׁפִּי, אֲחָזִי Ruth 3: 15, a peculiar form.

(*b*) NIPHAL. The common vowel of the first syllable is of the Se-

§§ 228—232. VERBS AYIN GUTTURAL.

ghol class; e. g. נֶעֱמַד, or (according to the *rough* enunciation) נֶחְשַׁב. But in the Inf. absolute with Hholem final, it is Pattahh (comp. *a.* 2, above), as נַהֲפוֹךְ, נַעֲתוֹר; very seldom with Pattahh in other cases, yet sometimes so, as נַחְבָּאת, Gen. 31: 27. Vav prefixed commonly occasions Pattahh; comp. §224. Note 3. The increased Part. forms also receive it; as נַעֲלָמִים, נַעֲלָמָה, נֶעְלָם. In Est. 8: 8, we find נַחְתּוֹם, a Part. *sui generis.*

(*c*) HIPHIL. (1) Sometimes with the rough enunciation, as הֶחְסִיר. Peculiar is הֶעְלָה, § 142. *e.* 1. Vav prefixed changes the composite Sheva to the *A* class; e. g. וְהֶחֱרַמְתִּי, i. e. it hastens the pronunciation of the first part of the word, because the tone is thrown forward; comp. § 224 Note 3. (2) *Inf. abs.* and *constr.* are sometimes interchanged in their usage; e. g. הַעֲבִיר (Josh. 7: 7) for Inf. absolute הַעֲבֵר; לַעְשֵׂר, Inf. abs. (Deut. 26: 12) for Inf. const. לַעְשִׂיר. (3) *Future* with rough enunciation יַעְסִיר; and so the Part. מַחְסִיר. מֵזִין is for מַאֲזִין, § 119. *c.* 1.

(*d*) HOPHAL. With rough enunciation, הָהְפַּךְ; also (rarely) הָעְלָה, § 142. *e.* 1; הָחְתַּל, Inf. abs. *sui generis*, Ezek. 16: 4.

Note. The Daghesh'd conjugations (i. e. Piel, Pual, and Hithpael) are *regular*, because they can never have a Sheva under their first *radical.*]

Verbs Ayin Guttural; Par. V.

§ 229. Where other verbs have Sheva simple under the *middle* radical, these take a composite Sheva, § 49.

§ 230. Final syllables in the ground-forms of any of the conjugations, having Hholem or Tseri in them, may exchange these for Pattahh. In Kal this is usual; in the other conjugations, less common. But the Inf. const. in Kal takes Hholem.

E. g. Fut. יִזְעַק, rarely as יִרְהַם; Piel נָחַם, נָהַג; Hiphil Imp. הַרְחַק, etc. Verbs Ayin Resh sometimes imitate this.

§ 231. As the conjugations Piel, Pual, Hithpael, cannot admit a Daghesh in the middle radical, they prolong the preceding vowel in cases where analogy would require one. Verbs Ayin Resh imitate them in this; § 111. § 112.

Notes on Paradigm V.

[§ 232. (*a*) KAL. (1) *Inf. fem.* as שָׁחֲטָה, אַהֲבָה; also as רָחֳקָה, זְעָקָה § 142. *c.* 1. (2) *Future* anomalous יִצְחַק, § 142. *c.* 1.

(b) PIEL. *Praeter* with middle א, takes either Tseri or Hhireq long before it; as נָאֵן, מֵאֵן. Middle ה prefixes long Hhireq; as כִּהֵן. Middle ח and ע, long Hhireq and rarely Tseri; as כִּחֵשׁ, אַחֵר, בִּעֵר, רֵעָה. Resh demands Tseri; as בֵּרַךְ.

The *Future* Inf., Imp., and Part., with middle א and ר, *usually* require Qamets before them; as בָּרַךְ, יְפָאֵר. But ה, ח, ע, most commonly prefix Pattahh; as יְנַעֵר, יְרַחֵם יְנַהֵג, etc.

(c) PUAL. Here compensation is usually made for Daghesh excluded, by Hholem, e. g. יְגֹאַל, בֹּרַךְ; sometimes by Qibbuts impure and long, as רֻחַם, רֻחַץ.

(d) HITHPAEL. Here the vowel before the Guttural is varied, just as in the fut. Piel; see above under *b*. The accent affects Pattahh here in a peculiar way; e. g. הִתְנֶחָמְתִּי, instead of הִתְנַחַמְתִּי, which is explained by § 142. *a*, and § 144. מִתְנָאֵץ=מִנֹּאֵץ (§ 187. *b*. 3) is an instance of *Hithpoel*.]

Verbs Lamedh Guttural; Par. VI.

§ 233. Where by analogy the Guttural must have a Sheva, the vowel-points are regular.

Note. The 2 pers. sing. fem. takes a furtive Pattahh under the Guttural; e. g. שָׁמַעַתְּ instead of שָׁמַעְתְּ, § 52. 2. If the Pattahh under ע here was a proper vowel, the pointing would be שָׁמֵעַת, i. e. with ה *Raphē*. Punctuation like נְגַעְנוּךָ is very rare.

§ 234. Where the Guttural is preceded by וֹ, וּ, יִ֫, immutable, it takes a Pattahh furtive, § 69.

E. g. in the Inf. absolute and in the Part. pass. of Kal; in Hiph. throughout, where יִ֫ is usually retained. The Inf. const. in Kal commonly follows the same usage, as שְׁמֹעַ; compare (§ 230) a similar punctuation as it respects the Hholem.

§ 235. In Kal, the Fut. and Imp. nearly always take Pattahh; also the fem. Part. Segholate; as שֹׁמַעַת.

Note. The Imp. appears to have Hholem sometimes; e. g. טְבֹחַ, Gen. 43: 16.

§ 236. All the forms with pure final *Tseri* may retain it, and put a Pattahh *furtive* under the Guttural; or they may substitute a real Pattahh in their stead, e. g. שֹׁמֵעַ or שֹׁמַע.

Note 1. The *prolonged* forms, i. e. such as the Inf. abs., the forms with a pause-accent, etc., retain Tseri. The *apocopate* forms take Pattahh.

Note 2. Verbs לֹ"ה frequently imitate this class of guttural verbs, as to their final vowel.

IRREGULAR VERBS.

§ 237. Under this class are included all those, in which any of the radical letters are *dropped*, or *assimilated*, or in which they become *quiescent*.

§ 238. These may be most conveniently distributed into (*a*) Those which are irregular פּ֞, i. e. in the first radical (§ 223). (*b*) Those which are irregular ע֞, i. e. in their second radical. (*c*) Those which are irregular ל֞, i. e. in their third radical. (*d*) Those which are irregular פּ֞ and ל֞, i. e. in their first and third radical.

I. CLASS OF IRREGULAR VERBS.

§ 239. These consist of verbs פָֿא, פִֿי, and פֻֿן, i. e. whose first radical is either א, י, or נ.

VERBS PE ALEPH; PAR. VII.

§ 240. In most cases, verbs with א for their first radical belong to the class Pe Guttural, א being treated as a Guttural. The verbs belonging to the class now in question, are those in which א as first radical is *quiescent*.

[Note. Of these there are only *five*, viz. אָמַר, אָכַל, אָבָה, אָבַד, אָפָה. *Three* more, viz. אָסַף, אָחַז, אָהַב, sometimes exhibit a *quiescent* א, and sometimes a *guttural* one; e. g. יֵאָחֵז, יֶאֱחֹז. For other explanations, see under paradigm VII.]

Notes on the Paradigm.

[§ 241. (*a*) KAL. (1) *The Future* drops א quiescent of the root in the 1st pers. sing., and retains only the א praeformative which designates the first person; e. g. אֹמַר instead of אֹאמַר, thus avoiding the occurrence of two Alephs. (2) In a very few cases, the first syllable takes a *Tseri* instead of a Hholem; as יֵאָתֶה (not יֹאתֶה); in אָהַב the Fut. has both forms, e. g. 1st pers. sing. אֹהַב and אֱהַב. The last syllable in these verbs usually exhibits Tseri, specially when it has a *disjunctive* accent; with a *conjunctive* one, Pattahh is very common in the same syllable; e. g. יֹאכֵל, יֹאכַל.

Note. Quiescent א here is not unfrequently omitted in writing; as יֹסֶף for יֹאסֵף, יֹמְרוּ for יֹאמְרוּ, etc; see § 63.

(3) *Inf. construct* from אָמַר, אָמֹר‎ for לֶאֱמֹר‎, § 119. *c.* 1. *Imperative* once אֱפוּ‎ for אֵפוּ‎, see § 119. *d.* 2.

(*b*) *Derived conjugations.* (1) NIPHAL once as נֹאחַז‎. (2) PIEL admits contraction; as מַלֵּף‎ for מְאַלֵּף‎, תָּזֵר‎ for תְּאַזֵּר‎; see § 118. Note 3. (3) HIPHIL also admits contraction, in a little different manner; e. g. הָכִיל‎ for הַאֲכִיל‎. *Future*, וַיֹּאצֶל‎ (with accent retracted § 129) instead of וַיַּאֲצֵל‎, מֵזִין‎ for מַאֲזִין‎; see § 119. *c.* 1. Fut. once with Hholem, as אֹבִידָה‎, Jer. 40: 8. *Imperative*, הֵתָיוּ‎ for הַאֲתָיוּ‎, § 119. *c.* 1. (4) HOPHAL, (וּ) יוּכְלוּ‎ for א § 122. 2.) for יֵאָכְלוּ‎, like the contractions in § 119. *c.* 1.]

VERBS PE YODH; PAR. VIII—X.

§ 242. These may be divided into *three* classes; viz. (1) Such as have (originally) a Vav for the first radical; e. g. וָלַד‎=יָלַד‎. (2) Those whose first radical is properly Yodh; as יָטַב‎. (3) Such as follow the analogy of verds Pe Nun, in assimilating the first radical in the Future, etc.

First Class of verbs Pe Yodh; Par. VIII.

§ 243. (*a*) In Kal Inf., Fut., and Imp., the Yodh is for the most part dropped; the Praeter and Part. are regular.

(*b*) In Niphal, Hiphil, and Hophal, the original ו appears; but it is *quiescent*, except in the Inf., Fut., and Imp. Niphal, where it is moveable.

§ 244. The Inf., Fut., and Imp. of Kal exhibit two forms; viz. one with *final Tseri*, and another with *final Pattahh*.

(*a*) *The forms with final Tseri* take Tseri in the first syllable also, and more generally omit the Yodh; as שֵׁב‎, etc. in Par. VIII.

[Note. The Fut. sometimes (rarely) retains the Yodh in the writing of these verbs; as 1st. pers. sing. Fut. parag. אֵילְכָה‎ (from יָלַךְ‎), יִיקַר‎ (from יָקַר‎), with final Pattahh because of the Resh. With a Guttural in the final syllable, Pattahh of course takes the place of Tseri; as יֵדַע‎, not יֵדֵע‎. In the Inf. const. and Imp., Yodh disappears almost throughout, in the forms with final Tseri.]

(*b*) *The forms with final Pattahh* more usually retain the Yodh in Inf., Imp., and Fut. of Kal, and the Fut. takes Hhireq prolonged in the first syllable; as יָשֹׁן‎, יָרַשׁ‎, יִירַשׁ‎; see in Par. VIII.

§§ 245—247. IRREG. VERBS; PE YODH, I. CLASS.

[Note 1. Yodh quiescent is sometimes omitted here in writing; as יִבֵשׁ for יִיבַשׁ, Ps. 102: 5, § 63. So יִרְאוּ for יִירְאוּ.
Note 2. The Inf. construct of the masc. form, is not analogical here. It takes Hholem; as יְבֹשׁ, יְשֹׁן. One would naturally expect Pattahh.]

§ 245. *The derived conjugations* of both these species of verbs are alike; the model is exhibited in the paradigm.

[§ 246. Some verbs פִּ"י take both the forms above noted;
E. g. יָצַק, Imp. צַק and יִצֹק; יָקַר, Fut. יִיקַר, also יֵיקַר or יִקַר. The lexicons note such.]

Notes on the Paradigm.

[§ 247. KAL. (*a*) The Inf. of the class Fut. Tseri has more usually the fem. Segholate ending, as in the paradigm. With a Guttural, Pattahh of course is used; e. g. דַּעַת (not דֶּעֶת) from יָדַע, § 113. But sometimes the apocopate masc. form is used; as דֵּע from יָדַע. Another fem. form of the Inf. is as לֵדָה from יָלַד. The suffix Inf. fem. is as רִדְתִּי, רֶדֶת from יָרַד; so יָשַׁב (שַׁבְתִּי) שִׁבְתִּי, שֶׁבֶת, etc.
(*b*) The Inf. of the class Fut. Pattahh is regular; see § 244. *b.*
Note 2. The feminine forms are as יְבֹלֶת, from יָבַל; יִרְאָה from יָרֵא. A form with Vav *fulcrum*, יְשׁוֹן.
(*c*) *The Future which has Tseri final*, is pure, so that it may be shortened; as it is in וַיֵּשֶׁב, with tone retracted, § 129. With ה parag., as יְדַע, יֵדְעָה. Altogether anomalous is the Fut. יִירַע.
(*d*) *The Imperative*; (1) Where the Future is Tseri, commonly takes a *paragogic* letter; as לְכָה, רְדָה (לְךָ), from רֵד, לֵךְ masc. forms; so with ה‍ָ parag., as דְּעָה, masc. דַּע, § 125. *b.* (2) The Imp. of the verbs Fut. Pattahh regularly retains its Yodh radical.
(*e*) NIPHAL. (1) *Future* sometimes retains the Yodh, instead of exchanging it for the original ו; e. g. יִירְאֶה, יִיָּחֵל with retracted tone, § 129.
Note. It is peculiar also, that the first pers. sing. here retains Hhireq (like the other persons) in its first syllable, as אִוָּרֵשׁ, אִוָּסֵר, etc.; not אֶוָּשֵׁב, etc., as in most other analogous cases.
(2) Part. plur. const. נוּגֵי (instead of נוֹגֵי) from יָגָה; also נוֹקֵשׁ with Tseri, instead of נוֹקַשׁ, from יָקֹשׁ.
(*f*) PIEL. The Fut. here, preceded by Vav conversive, drops the first of its Yodhs, and writes it by a Daghesh in the second; e. g. וַיְיַבֵּשׁ instead of וַיְיַבֵּשׁ, וַיְיַדּוּ for וַיְיַדּוּ, etc.
(*g*) HIPHIL. (1) *The Future* with retracted tone, as וַיּוֹלֶד. Sometimes the characteristic ה is retained in the Future, as יְהוֹשִׁיעַ

for יוֹשִׁיעַ; so יְהוֹדָה, יְהוֹסִף, from יָסַף, יָדָה; comp. § 199. (2) *The Imperative* sometimes retains its Vav moveable; as הַוְצֵא for הוֹצֵא, Gen. 8:17; so הַוְשֵׁר for הוֹשֵׁר, Ps. 5:9.

(h) HITHPAEL sometimes retains the original Vav, and uses it as moveable, e. g. הִתְנַבֵּחַ, הִתְוַדָּה, הִתְוַדַּע.]

Second Class of Verbs Pe Yodh; Par. IX.

§ 248. These are such as have a Yodh originally for their first radical; which they retain in Hiphil, and thus distinguish themselves from the other class described.

See remarks in Par. IX.

Note. Only seven verbs belong to this class; viz. יָמַר, יָלַל, יָטַב, יָנַק, יָסַר, יָשַׁר, הֵימִין Hiph.

§ 249. *The Future Kal* here is sometimes with Pattahh, and sometimes with Tseri; mostly written fully, but sometimes defectively.

E. g. יִיטַב, as in the paradigm; but also, וַיִּיצֶר, יִיצֶר; וַיִּיקֶץ, יִיקֶץ. Of course this class of verbs agrees with the preceding one, as to the final vowel in the Fut. of Kal. No Inf. form occurs here.

Notes on the Paradigm.

[§ 250. HIPHIL, as the paradigm shews, may be written either *plené* or *defectivé*. (1) *The Future* sometimes exhibits *moveable* Yodh, instead of Yodh quiescent; יְיַשְּׁרוּ, Prov. 4:25; אֲיָסִירֵם, Hos. 7:2. Comp. § 247. *g.* 2. *h.*

Note. Two Futures are altogether anomalous; e. g. יְיֵטִיב, Job. 24. 21; also יְיֵלִיל. The like to this, is יְיֵדַע in Kal Future, Ps. 138:6. § 247. *c.*

(2) *Imperative* once retains a moveable Yodh in the Qeri, הַיְשֵׁר, Ps. 5:9. So the Part. of Hiphil, as מַיְמִינִים 1 Chron 12:2.]

Third Class of Verbs Pe Yodh; Par. X.

§ 251. The peculiarity of these verbs is, that they assimilate their Yodh in Kal Fut., Niph., Hiph., and Hophal.

[Note 1. Only four verbs belong wholly here; viz. יָצַת, יָצַג, יָנַח, יָצַע. Five others partake partly of the peculiarities of these verbs, and partly of the other classes, viz. יָסַד, יָצַק, יָצַר, יָסַר, יָשַׁר.

Note 2. Simonis and Eichhorn derive all the *peculiar* forms of this class of verbs, from roots פֶּ׳ן. The question is one of etymology. It matters not for the student, which way it is decided. I follow the lexicon of Gesenius, for convenience' sake rather than from conviction. The fulness of the paradigm supersedes the necessity of additional notes.]

Verbs Pe Nun; Par. XI.

§ 252. The peculiarity of these verbs is, (a) That whenever נ (their first radical) would analogically take a Sheva, in the course of declension, etc., it more usually becomes assimilated to the letter which follows, and is expressed by a *Daghesh forte.*

(b) That in the Inf. and Imp. of Kal, the Nun is sometimes dropped, in the manner of verbs Pe Yodh.

[In this case, the Imper. more commonly takes the parag. form, as גְּשָׁה, גַּשׁ; תֵּן, תְּנָה. The Inf. commonly has a Segholate form, in cases of aphaeresis, i. e. where the first radical is dropped; as גֶּשֶׁת in the paradigm. *But abridged forms in these verbs either of the Inf. or Imp., are not frequent at all.* These Inf. and Imp. modes more generally preserve the radical נ, even when the Fut. assimilates it; e. g. Inf. and Imp. נְקֹם, Fut. יִקֹּם; Inf. and Imp. נְתֹץ, Fut. יִתֹּץ.]

§ 253. Verbs whose second radical is a proper Quiescent or a Guttural, exclude the *peculiarities* of verbs פֶ״ן.

The reason is, that the Daghesh (compensative of Nun) cannot be inserted in either of these classes of letters; and therefore usage commonly preserved the Nun before them. But in Niphal Praeter, where a Guttural is the second radical, and Nun would be repeated if it were preserved, it is dropped, as נָחַם, not נִנְחַם, the vowel in the first syllable being prolonged as usual, § 112. Note. The verb נָחַת more usually drops נ in the Fut. of Kal; as יֵחַת, but also תִּנְחַת 2d person. In other respects, the verbs just named are *regular* in respect to Nun.

Notes on the Paradigm.

[254. (a) KAL. (1) Inf. const. like גֶּשֶׁת, occurs only in six verbs. Once שׂוֹא from נָשָׂא, Ps. 89: 10. The reg. form נְגֹעַ, נְצֹר, נְקֹם, is *most frequent.* Some verbs have both forms; as נְטֹעַ and טַעַת I find no example of reg. Inf. with final Pattahh. Fem. form with suffix, as גַּשְׁתּוֹ, גִּשְׁתּוֹ.

(2) *Future Hholem* is more frequent than Fut. Pattahh in these verbs. Fut. Tseri only in נָתַן. Some verbs have both Fut. O and A, as נָדַר, נָדַר. Some at one time retain נ, and at another omit it, in different examples of the Fut.; as נָדַף, נָצַר, etc.

(3) *Imperative,* like the Inf., seldom drops the radical נ, § 252. b. The abridged forms are like גַּשׁ, גַּשׁ (before Maqqeph גֶּשׁ־), גְּשׁוּ; תֵּן from נָתַן.

(b) NIPHAL. (1) Praeter appears like Piel, because it drops the נ

of the root, and inserts a Daghesh or prolongs the vowel; as נָשָׂא, Piel and Niph. נִשָּׂא; נָהַם, Pi. and Niph. נִהַם, § 253. Once with Hholem, as נְמוֹל. (2) *Infinitive abs.* sometimes as נָגוֹף, הִנָּדֹף Ps. 68: 3, הִנָּתוֹן Jer. 32: 4. (3) *Participle* once as נִדְחָה, with suffix ךָ.

(*c*) HIPHIL very rarely retains the נ; as הִנְתִּיךָ, לַנְפִּל. So in Hophal, הָנְתְּקָה. The usual vowel in Hophal is *short* Qibbuts, as in the paradigm.

Note. The verb לָקַח imitates פן in Kal; see lexicon. The verb נָתַן assimilates its final ן also, before suffixes beginning with ת or נ; as נַתְנוּ instead of נָתְנוּ, נָתַתִּי, etc. The Inf. is תֵּת for תֶּנֶת (§ 107. 2), with suff. תִּתִּי, Tseri being shortened, § 129. *a*.]

Remark. The great variety of usage in verbs of this class, shews that the sound of נ was quite variable, and the letter less prominent and distinct than most of the consonants. The *predominant* usage in Kal, is *regular;* in Niph. Hiph. Hophal, *irregular*. Gesenius states the contrary of this, as to Kal, even in the latest edition of his Hebrew grammar, p. 106; but a minute examination of all these verbs will shew that he is mistaken. The daghesh'd conjugations are regular throughout; so that no paradigm is needed.

II. CLASS OF IRREGULAR VERBS,

(Verbs irregular עׇ.*)*

§ 255. These comprehend such as are defective in respect to their middle radical; i. e. such whose middle radical either falls out, or becomes quiescent.

VERBS AYIN DOUBLED (עע); PAR. XII.

§ 256. This class comprises all those whose second and third radicals are the same letter, and which often (not always) drop the second radical in the course of inflection; as סָבַב, Praet. סַב, Inf. סֹב.

These verbs might well be named *contracted verbs*, (not very unlike the Greek τιμάω, τιμῶ, φιλέω, φιλῶ, etc.); for a great part of their irregularity arises from *contraction*. But dispute about *names* would not be important.

First law of contraction.

§ 257. This is, that the second radical is dropped, and with it the points of the preceding letter (whether a pro-

§§ 258—260. IRREG. VERBS; AYIN DOUBLED. 101

per vowel or a Sheva), and the vowel belonging to the second radical is then transferred to the first radical. E. g. סָבַב ,סַב ; סָבַב, סֹב ; יִסְבֹּב ,יָסֹב, etc. The alterations occasioned in the formative praefixes, etc., by this, will be considered in the sequel.

N. B. All the forms which have an impure vowel in them, or a Daghesh forte in the middle radical, are incapable of contraction ; e. g. סֹבֵב ,סָבוֹב ,סָבוּב ,סוֹבֵב, etc.

§ 258. Any accession to the end of a contracted form, (by declension or in any other manner), causes the second radical to reappear by a Daghesh forte, but does not restore to the first radical its original vowel.

E. g. סָבַב, contr. סַב, with accession סַבּוּ săb-bŭ (not סָבְבוּ), סַבּוֹתִי, יָסֹבּוּ, סֹבִּי, etc. In all such cases, the middle radical, having lost its vowel, is written by a Daghesh in the last radical, and joined in a syllable with the *preceding* vowel.

§ 259. In order to render more audible the doubling of the final letter of the root, the epenthetic syllables וֹ and יִ_ (with the tone) are inserted before suffixes *beginning with a consonant*.

In the Praeter וֹ, as סַבּוֹתָ, סַבּוֹנוּ; in the Fut. and Imp. יִ_, as סַבֶּינָה, תְּסֻבֶּינָה. The Arabian, while he *writes* the words fully regular in these cases, *pronounces* them like the Hebrew.

§ 260. The praeformatives of tense and conjugation, instead of the *short* vowel of regular verbs, in their contracted forms usually assume long *pure* vowels, § 130.

Hophal only has an *impure* vowel following its characteristic; e. g. הוּסַב instead of הֻסְבַּב.

Note. In most cases, the *original* ground-forms, from which the *contracted* forms seem evidently to be derived, are somewhat different from those of the regular verbs; e. g. Kal Fut. יָסֹב appears to come from a full Fut. יַסְבֹּב (like the Arabic Future); so that when ס is thrown, by contraction, into the second syllable, and Pattahh under the Yodh praeformative comes to stand in a simple syllable, it of course becomes long, i. e. it goes into Qamets, § 130. So in Niph., where we have נָסַב apparently for נַסְבַּב, and in the Fut. יִסַּב for יִסָּבֵב; in Hiph., הֵסֵב from הִסְבֵּב, etc. But in some few cases, the contracted forms appear to come from *regular* original ones; as Fut. יָמַר, apparently from יִמְרַר; so Niph. נָחַל as from נִחְלַל; Inf. הָחֵל, as from הִחְלֵל, etc.

Second law of Contraction.

§ 261. This is, to insert a Daghesh in the *first* radical after praeformatives, to give those praeformatives the regular short vowel, and then to omit the doubling of the last radical when the word receives an accession at the end. The epenthetic וֹ and יְ are also omitted in this case.

E. g. Kal Fut. יִסֹּב, etc.; Hiph. יָתֵם (from תֵּמַם) instead of יָתֵם; Hoph. יֻכַּת (from כֻּתַּת) instead of יוּכַת.

Note. In Kal Fut. this is not uncommon; in other conjugations it is rare. In Chaldee, this is the reigning method of contraction.

§ 262. The conjugations Poel, Poal, Hithpoel *usually* take the place of the regular daghesh'd conjugations here, but not always; and sometimes both exist together, either as synonymous, or with shades of difference, § 188. § 175. *a*.

§ 263. Verbs ע״ע with the second and third radicals *guttural*, lengthen the preceding vowel in cases where Daghesh forte should be inserted but is excluded by the Guttural, § 112.

E. g. שָׁחַח, contracted שַׁח, 3d pers. fem. שָׁחָה, 1st pers. שַׁחוֹתִי. So מָרַר, 3d. fem. מָרָה (not מַרָּה), מָרוֹתִי (not מַרּוֹתִי), etc.

Note 1. The tone syllables in the usual contracted forms are peculiar. See an account of them in § 100. *f*.

Note 2. The student must not fail to note, that in Kal verbs ע״ע often retain the *regular* form; specially in the Praeter, and sometimes in the Infinitive. In most other cases, they generally follow the models in the paradigm; with more anomalies, however, than most other classes of verbs, as the sequel will shew. An instance of conformity to both models in the Fut. is חָנַן, Fut. יָחֹן and יְחֻנַּן; so רָנַן, Hiph. הִרְנִין regular.

Notes on the Paradigm.

[§ 264. (*a*) KAL. (1) *The Praeter* of verbs final Hholem conforms to the law of contraction in § 257; e. g. רָמֹם, 3 plur. רֹמּוּ; and so רֹבּוּ, etc. Once, תַּמְנוּ=תַּמּוֹנוּ, Ps. 64: 7; comp. § 266.

(2) *Infinitive const.* sometimes with Pattahh; as שַׁךְ, גַּל. Inf. fem. רֹעָה from רָעַע. The Inf., in a considerable number of cases, is writ-

§ 264. IRREG. VERBS; AYIN DOUBLED. 103

ten with a Vav fulcrum, § 64; e. g. גּוֹל, דּוֹם, צוּר. So Imp., even when it has a Daghesh, as דֹּלְמִי, קוֹשׁ. Rarely has the Inf. a Shureq, as בּוּר, Ecc. 9: 1.

In the suffix state, or before Maqqeph, the Inf. having a pure Hholem shortens it; as קׁ, חֹק, חֻקִּי; תֹּם, תָּם־ *töm*.

(3) *The Future* usually has Hholem pure; but sometimes it appears with Vav fulcrum (§ 64); as יָעוּז for יָעֹז. This Hholem is shortened by losing the tone: as יָחֹן, יְהָגֹּה, Ps. 67: 2, or יְחָגֻּה, Is. 27: 11; וַיִּסֹּב.

The Fut. with Pattahh also occurs, which gives a Tseri to the praeformative; as יֵמַר, יֵקַל, יֵחַם, אֵיתַם 1st pers. with Yodh fulcrum (§ 64) from תָּמַם.

The Fut. also has Shureq in a few cases; as יָרוּן, יָרוּץ. So the second kind of contracted Future; as תִּתֻּם (= תִּתּוּם) instead of תִּתֹּם, from תָּמַם.

4. *Imperative* also has Pattahh sometimes, as גַּל; with ה parag. as כַּנֵּה; with a Resh, as אָרָה. It also has Vav fulcrum, as דּוֹם, Josh. 10: 12, (No. 3 above.) The Imp. with Hholem pure of course shortens this vowel when the tone is removed; as סָלּוּהָ, רָבִּי.]

Niphal.

[(b) (1) *Praeter* sometimes with Tseri, as נֵקַל; also with Hholem, as נָגֹלּוּ, Is. 34: 4. The praeformative has sometimes other vowels besides Qamets; e. g. נַחַן from חָנַן, נָחַל from חָלַל; נִחַת from חָתַת; where the vowel under נ is long, because the Dag. forte is omitted in the second radical; which conforms to the *second* mode of contraction described above, § 261; comp. § 260. Note, at the end; also § 111. § 112. According to these forms, we find נְחַלְתָּ (from חָלַל), Ezek. 22: 16; נְחַנֹּתִי (from חָנַן), Jer. 22: 23.

(2) *Infinitive abs.* with Hholem; as הִבּוֹז, הִבּוֹק. *Inf. const.* with Tseri; as הֵחֵל, הִמַּם, § 261. § 112.

(3) *Future* with Hholem as יִדֹּם; with Resh, תֵּרוֹץ 2d pers., יֵרֹמּוּ 3d pers. plur., from רָמַם.

(4) *Imp.* with Hholem; as הֵרֹמּוּ. (5) *Part.* with Tseri, as נָמֵס.]

Hiphil.

[(c) This conj. has a *pure* Tseri throughout, in both syllables; which is therefore liable to change, as is usual with all pure vowels; e. g. הֵסֵב, Hiph., 2 pers. הֲסִבּוֹתָ, etc.

(1) It should be noted here, that Hiphil not only takes a PATTAHH *final*, in case it has a Guttural or a Resh in the last syllable, as הֵשַׁח, הֵמַר; and in pause, as הֵתַן, § 145; but also (not unfrequently) without either of these reasons; as הֵדַק, הֵסַבּוּ, Part. מֵצַל.

(2) *Praeter* once הֵזִיל=הֵזֵל, § 261. *Sui generis* is הֲפִתִּיתָ for הֲפִתּוֹתָ, Prov. 24: 28; unless it may come from פָּתָה, which is more probable. (3) *Future* with tone retracted, וַיָּסָב, etc.

(d) HOPHAL has no special anomalies except the manner in which the praeform. is pointed, הוּסַב for הֻסְבַב.]

§ 265. *Resemblance between verbs* עָ״עָ *and* עֹ״ו. This is great. Hophal is the same in both; and the praeformatives take, in the same way, a long pure vowel. Besides these general resemblances, there are many particular instances, in which verbs עָ״עָ exhibit the same appearance as verbs עֹ״ו.

E. g. Inf. בּוּר from בָּרַר, בְּחוּקִי (instead of בְּחֻקִּי) from חָקַק. Fut. יָשׁוּד, יָרוּץ, יָרוּד, etc. Hiph. Inf. הֵתִימְךָ (for הֲתִמְּךָ) from תָּמַם. Fut. יָשִׁים, from שָׁמַם; יְחִיתַן (for יְחִתֵּן) from חָתַת. It may be justly doubted, however, whether the root is not עֹ״ו in all such cases, § 298.

§ 299. I merely conform to the lexicons, in this arrangement.

[§ 266. PECULIAR ANOMALY. Verbs עָ״עָ, with the *first* form of contraction (§§ 257—260), sometimes omit the usual Daghesh forte in the increased forms (§ 258), and also the vowel which precedes it.

E. g. Fut. נָבְלָה for נָבֹלָּה, יָזְמוּ for יָזֹמּוּ; Inf. לַחְמָם for לְחָמָּם; Niph. נָבְקָה for נָבֹקָּה, Is. 19: 3; Fut. נִדְמָה for נִדַּמָּה, Jer. 8: 14. But these anomalies are by no means frequent.]

Note. The conjs. Poel, Poal, and Hithpoel, with their substitutes, Pilpel, Pulpal, and Hithpalpal, are declined regularly; the final Tseri in them being pure, and subject to changes as usual.

Remark 1. Of the whole number of verbs Ayin doubled (124), 26 have only Piel etc. forms; 20 have only Poel etc. form; 10 have only Pilpel etc. forms; 11 have both Piel etc. and Poel etc.; 2 have Piel etc. with Pilpal etc.; and 3, Poel etc. with Pilpel etc. The other 52 supply no examples of any of these conjugations. It appears, therefore, that the *regular* form in Piel, is as frequent as any other.

Remark 2. The lexicons are very irregular in designating the conjugations Poel, Poal, etc. The student must accommodate the designation to the actual form. The Hholem in these conjugations is sometimes omitted in writing, § 63.

Remark 3. Almost all the anomalies perplexing to the student, arise from the peculiarities noted in § 261 and § 266. But those in § 261 are altogether of the most frequent occurrence. If the student thoroughly possesses himself of the *second* mode of contraction there exhibited, he will meet with but few cases which will trouble him.

Verbs Ayin Vav; Par. XIII.

§ 267. This class comprises all those whose *second* radical is Vav, and whose root throughout becomes *monosyllabic* by contraction.

This species of verbs might also be justly called *contracted*, so that verbs עָעֽ may be named the *first* class of *contracts*, and verbs עֽו the *second*.

§ 268. The laws of contraction are essentially the same here as in verbs עָעֽ; the principal differences are occasioned merely by the nature of Vav as a Quiescent.

(*a*) The *last* vowel of the full form is transferred to the first radical, and takes the place of its appropriate punctuation which falls out; comp. § 257.

E. g. Uncontracted קָוַם, contracted קָאַם = קָם; the original ו conforms to the heterogeneous vowel (§ 117. 2), i. e. ו becomes א in order to conform to the Pattahh of the root, which Pattahh then coalesces with the substituted א and therefore becomes *Qamets*. So Praeter *E* and *O*; e. g. מָוֵת, contr. מִיַת = מֵת, Vav conforming to the final vowel Tseri (§ 117. 2); בֱוֹשׁ *bă-vōsh*, contr. בּוֹשׁ *bōsh*. In Hiph. Fut. יָקְוִים, contr. יָקִים, the Vav, after conforming to the vowel i. e. after becoming Yodh, falling out as superfluous before another Yodh in Hiphil, and the Pattahh under the praeformative being of course lengthened by coming to be placed in a simple syllable, § 130. In Hoph. הוּקַם, there seems to be a transposition of the Vav to the first syllable, as if הֻוְקַם were put for הֻקְוַם. But see and comp. Hoph. of verbs עָעֽ, § 260. Note. § 264. *d*.

Note. All the forms where Vav takes a Daghesh forte, and also where it is immediately followed by ה as a third radical, are incapable of contraction; e. g. עֻוֵּר, קִוָּה, etc.

(*b*) The praeformatives all take long *pure* vowels, in the contracted forms; the kind of vowel being determined by the original uncontracted forms, which appear to have differed from the common regular forms; like those in verbs עָעֽ, § 260 with the Note.

E. g. Kal. Fut. יָקוּם, as if from יַקְווּם (comp. the Arabic Fut. יַקְטֻל); Part. קָם, as if from קָוֵם, an old Part. form; Imp. and Inf. קוּם, as if from קְוֻם. So in Niph. נָקוֹם, as if from נַקְווֹם; Hiph. הֵקִים, as from הַקְוִים, etc.

(c) In like manner as verbs עָ"ע (§ 259), these verbs in some cases insert וֹ and י ֵ with the tone, in the Praeter and Future, before suffixes *beginning with a consonant.*

E. g. Niph. Praeter, נְקוּמוֹתָ‍ ,נְקוּמוֹתֶם; Hiph. הֲקִימוֹת; Kal Fut. תְּקוּמֶינָה. So far as the principle extends, it is developed in the same manner as in verbs עָ"ע. But in verbs עוּ it extends only to the Praeter of Niph. and Hiphil as to the epenthetic וֹ, and only to the Fut. of Kal as to י ֶ; while in verbs עָ"ע it extends throughout the four contracted conjugations, Kal, Niphal, Hiphil, and Hophal.

(d) The tone-syllable in these verbs is throughout analogous to that in verbs עָ"ע; see § 100. g.

§ 269. Piel, Pual, and Hithpael are here very rare; instead of them, Polel, Polal, and Hithpolel are employed, § 175. b. § 188.

Examples of Piel are קִנֵּה, עִוֵּר. Most instances of Piel assume Yodh; as קַיֵּם, חִיֵּב, for קוֹם, הוּב, etc. In regard to the difference between סוֹבֵב in verbs עָ"ע, and קוֹמֵם here, see § 175. b. Note.

Remark 1. The 2d and 1st persons in Kal praeter are peculiar, inasmuch as they take a *short* vowel in their contraction. So it is also in the corresponding Arabic and Syriac. Hophal also takes a short vowel in the contracted root. Both these cases conform, indeed, to the general principle § 268. *a;* but they differ from the manner of contraction in Kal Praet. 3d persons, and in Niphal throughout.

Remark 2. The anomalous vowels in different tenses and conjugations, may be easily accounted for on the principles developed in § 117. E. g. in the Fut. יָקוּם (instead of יָקוֹם which we might expect), the vowel conforms to the Vav with the *Ŭ* sound. It might indeed take the *O* sound equally well, for ought that we can see; but its present form distinguishes it more clearly from the Fut. of verbs עָ"ע. So in Niph. Praet., נָקוֹם (instead of נָקַם), the vowel having conformed to the Vav, § 117. 1. So also in the Inf., Fut., etc. of Niph.; the Hholem arises from the conformity just described. In Hiphil the Vav of the root conforms to the vowel (Hhireq), i. e. the Vav becomes Yodh, and then falls out before the Yodh characteristic of the conjugation.

Notes on the Paradigm.

[§ 270. (*a*) KAL. (1) *Praeter* rarely as קָאם, Hos. 10: 14. Fem. 3d pers. once with ת, as שָׁבַת (like the Chald., Syr., and Arab.) for שָׁבָה, Ezek. 46: 17. In Mal. 3: 20, פִּשְׁתֶּם comes from פּוּשׁ = פָּוַשׁ, comp. § 181. *b*. Very seldom is the 3d person with Pattahh; e. g. בַּז, מַח, as if from בָּזַז, מָחַח.

The parad. exhibits a verb *final Tseri*. The final ת of מֵת, (and of other verbs ending with ת), before a suffix beginning with ת, is desig-

§ 271. IRREG. VERBS; AYIN VAV. 107

nated by a Daghesh in the suffix letter, instead of being fully written, § 293.

Verbs *final Hholem* are also found among the class עוּ. They retain the ו in the 3d. pers. Praeter, because it is homogeneous, and the third person is protracted; e. g. בּוֹשׁ, אוֹר. But in the other persons (which are shorter), they usually omit the Vav; e. g. בּשׁ, בּוֹשָׁה, בּשְׁנוּ, בּשְׁתֶּן, בּשְׁתֶּם, בּוֹשׁוּ—בּשְׁתִּי, בּשְׁתָּ, בּשְׁתְּ. Inf., Imp., Part. also, בּוֹשׁ.

(2) *Infinitive const.* sometimes with Hholem instead of Shureq; as טוֹב, בּוֹא, מוֹת, etc. The Vav is sometimes omitted, as לָבֹא, etc. § 63.

(3) *Future* sometimes with *O* instead of *U;* as יָבוֹא, יָבוֹשׁ, יָחוֹט, יָקוֹט. Forms *defectively* written, are יָקֹט, יָקֹם, etc. Fem. plur. sometimes without the epenthetic ־ֶי, as תָּשֹׁבְנָה, or תָּשֹׁבְן, instead of תְּשֻׁבֶינָה.

Future apoc. as יָקֹם, with Hholem pure and mutable; e. g. וַיָּקָם *vǎy-yā-qŏm*, תָּשֹׁב־נָא *tā-shŏbh-nā*. It is sometimes written as יָקוֹם (Vav *fulcrum*); sometimes it appears with *Qibbuts*, as יָקֻם. With a Guttural or Resh, the apoc. Fut. usually takes Pattahh; as וַיָּנַח, וַיָּסַר.

(4) *Imperative* also is sometimes *defectively* written, as מֻת, קֻם, etc. § 63. *Paragogic* forms; שֻׁבָה, קוּמָה, etc. *Imp. apoc.* as מֹל, like the Fut. with *O* pure.

(5) *Participle* with *O*, as בּוֹשִׁים; with *E*, as מֵת, לֵנִים, § 202. With א retained, as שֹׁאט, שֹׁאטִים=שָׁטִים.]

Niphal.

[(b) (1) *Praeter* rarely with Tseri penult, as נֵעוֹר. Out of the 3d pers., Hholem is usually exchanged for Shureq (§ 127. Exc. 1), as being equally homogeneous with the Vav and somewhat shorter, and to be shorter is required because the accent is thrown forward upon the epenth. וֹ. Hholem rarely remains; as נְפֹצֹתֶם.

(2) *Infinitive const.* rarely with *U;* as הִדּוֹשׁ. (3) *Participle* also has rarely *U;* נְבוֹכִים=נְבֻכִים for נְבֻכִים.]

Hiphil.

[(c) (1) *Praeter* written defectively is rare; הֵעִיד=הֵעַד. Sometimes the epenth. וֹ is omitted; as הֲנִפֹתִי=הֲנִיפוֹתִי, וְהַטַּלְתִּי=וַהֲטִילוֹתִי; הֲבֵאתִי, הֲבִיאוֹתִי, instead of הֲמִיתוֹתִי=הֲמִתִּי. So also, not unfrequently in the 2d and 1st pers., the forms are contracted; e. g. הֲמִתִּי for הֲמִיתוֹתִי, הֲמִתֶּם for הֲמִיתוֹתָם, etc. Sometimes Tseri is used instead of Hhireq; as הֲרֵמֹת, הֲשֵׁבוֹת, הֲקֵמֹנוּ, etc. Hhateph Seghol sometimes stands under the praeform. instead of Hhateph Pattahh; as הֱטִיבוֹת.

§ 271. IRREG. VERBS; AYIN VAV.

Peculiar is הָרֵעַ הָרֵעַ, הָרֵעַ, and הָפֵר, as if from roots עֵע; see lexicon. Once הֵסִית (from סוּת), like verbs עֵע in the second form of contraction, § 261. The praeform. הַ (in the derivates of עוּד) takes Pattahh instead of a comp. Sheva; e. g. הַעִידוֹתִ, הָעֵדוֹת, הַעִידוֹת.

(2) *Infinitive* fem. once הֲנָפָה, apoc. form of masc. הָנִיף. *Infinitive abs.* once הָעֵד because of the Guttural. (3) *Future* רָלִינוּ; comp. forms in § 261, which this imitates. The plural fem. is תְּקֻמְנָה (instead of תְּקִימְנָה), because a mixed syllable with Yodh and Hhireq long cannot be penultimate, even if an accent supports it. *Future apoc.* shortens the Tseri whenever it loses the tone; e. g. וַיָּקָם, וַיָּסַל, וַתָּרַע ; אַל־תֵּלֶן. With a Guttural or Resh; as וַתָּרַע, וַיָּסַל.

(4) *Imperative* once with Tseri; as הָשֵׁיב, 2 K. 8: 6. (5) *Participle* rarely as מֵסִית, מֵלִין, (for מְלִינִים, מֵסִית), imitating verbs עֵע; see § 261.]

Other Conjugations.

[(d) HOPHAL is sometimes written with *Qibbuts vicarious*; as הֻפַר, יֻמְתוּ, instead of הוּפַר, יוּמְתוּ, § 41.

(e) POLEL, POLAL, and HITHPOLEL are declined, in all respects, like Poel etc. in verbs עֵע, i. e. like Piel, Pual, etc. in regular verbs, as the former stand in the place of the latter. Polal occurs in only *four* verbs.

(f) HITHPOLEL, like Hithp. in reg. verbs (§ 218), often takes Pattahh in the final syllable; which in pause becomes Qamets, as הִתְבּוֹנָן. Once the מ of the praeform. is omitted in the Part., as בְּתִקוֹמֵם for בְּמִתְקוֹמֵם, Ps. 139: 21.

(g) PILPEL etc. are declined like Polel etc. Pilpel is found in only five verbs; Polpal only in כּוּל; and Hithpalpal only in חוּל.]

§ 271. *General remarks on verbs* עוּ. (a) The great similarity of them to verbs עֵע is very manifest, from § 268. *a. b. c. d;* and indeed, from many of the forms produced under § 270, specially under § 270. *c.* 1. It might indeed be doubted whether more less of these forms, so much like עֵע, have not a root belonging to that species of verbs. The resemblances in the general principles of contraction, are too manifest to escape notice.

[(b) The number of verbs עוּ is about 141. Of these 13 are לה, and incapable of contraction, § 268. *a.* Note; 6 resist contraction, viz. רָוַח, צוּחַ, עָנַת, חָוַר, גָּוַע, and שָׁוַע; the rest are contracted. *Five* only have the conj. Piel.]

Verbs Ayin Yodh. Par. XIV.

§ 272. These are such as have a Yodh originally for their middle radical, and which retain it in more or less of the forms in Kal.

273. Out of Kal, verbs עִי֫ in all respects are like those עִ֫וֹ.

Notes on the Paradigm.

[§ 274. Kal. (1) *Praeter* has Yodh only in three verbs, viz. בִּין, דִּיג, רִיב; and where this is retained, the epenth. י is inserted before the formative suffixes beginning with a consonant, as the paradigm shews. All the other cases of the Praeter conform to that of verbs עוֹ.
(2) *The Future* in all respects resembles Hiphil, in regard to form. So the apoc. form also; e. g. יָבֵן, וַיָּבֶן; יָשֵׂם, וַיָּשֶׂם. (3) *Participle* in one case is regular, viz. אוֹיֵב, from אָיַב.
Note. Very few verbs are exclusively עִי֫; most being also עוֹ in Kal. The older grammarians and lexicographers admitted no class עִי֫, but ranked such forms as בִּינוּ under Hiphil, with an *aphaeresis* of the ה. But as this is without other example, and as the kindred languages exhibit verbs עִי֫, this class is now generally admitted.]

III. CLASS OF IRREGULAR VERBS.

§ 275. This comprehends those, whose third radical becomes quiescent, or disappears.

Verbs Lamedh Aleph. Par. XV.

§ 276. Aleph at the end of words is usually *quiescent*, § 119. *b*. Throughout verbs לֹא֫, Aleph is *quiescent* or *otiant* when it *ends* a word or a syllable.

§ 277. The general laws of quiescence are, (*a*) In the Praeter of all the *derived* conjugations, before formative suffixes beginning with a *consonant*, א quiesces in Tseri. (*b*) In the Fut. and Imp. of all the conjugations, before formative suffixes beginning with a *consonant*, א quiesces in Seghol. (*c*) In all other cases, it quiesces (when at

110   §§ 278, 279. IRREG. VERBS ; LAMEDH ALEPH.

the end of a word or syllable) in the regular vowel ; excepting that whenever it meets with Pattahh, it lengthens it into Qamets.

E. g. מְצָאתָ, מְצָאנוּ, מְצָאנָה, תִּמְצָאנָה, הֲמְצָאנָה, etc. In Kal the Fut. יִמְצָא with Pattahh becomes יִמְצָא, by reason of א quiescent ; in Niph. we have נִמְצָא instead of נִמְצָא ; Pual, מֻצָּא instead of מֻצָּא, etc. § 115.

Note. *But the vowels made long by such quiescence, do not remain immutable.* The laws of declension supersede the laws of quiescence ; and Qamets, etc. (made by quiescence) fall away like any mutable pure vowels ; e. g. מָצָא, fem. מָצְאָה ; Fut. יִמְצָא, 2d fem. תִּמְצְאִי, etc. See § 127. Exc. 4. So Piel מִצֵּא, fem. מִצְּאָה, etc.

Notes on the Paradigm.

[§ 278. (*a*) KAL. (1) *Praeter of verbs final Tseri* usually retain the Tseri here ; as יָרֵא, יָרֵאתָ, יְרֵאתֶם, etc. The 3d pers. sing. fem. sometimes takes ת (like the Aramaean) ; as קָרָאת, Is. 7: 14. Sometimes these verbs are written *defectively* ; as מָצָתִי for מָצָאתִי, § 63.

(2) *Infinitive fem.* יִרְאָה, חֶטְאָה ; also with ת, as מְלֹאת=מְלֹאָה, קְרֹאות (with ו fulcrum merely)=קְרֹאת ; see § 119. c. 3. *Infinitive masc.* sometimes as הָטוֹ=הָטוֹא, § 63.

(3) *Imperative* יִרְאוּ ye-rū=יִרְאוּ, see § 118. In plur. fem., קְרֶאןָ apoc. for קְרֶאנָה ; צֶאינָה for צֶאנָה (from יָצָא) is *sui generis*, Cant. 3: 11 ; comp. § 118. Or is the root צָאָה ?

(4) *Participle fem.* מֹצֵאת for מֹצֵאת, יוֹצֵאת for יוֹצֵאת, § 119. c. 3. With suff. בֹּרְאָם, for בֹּרְאָם, § 118.

(*b*) NIPHAL. (1) *Praeter fem.* נִפְלָאת ; see under *a*. 1. above. Forms *defective*, נִטְמֵתֶם for נִטְמָאתֶם. (2) *Infinitive abs.* נִקְרֹא. (3) *Participle* sometimes as נִמְצָאִים, seemingly from נִמְצָא.

(*c*) PIEL. Inf. sometimes as מַלֹּאת, מַלֹּאוֹת ; comp. *a*. 2. above.

(*d*) HIPHIL. Praeter *defective,* as הֶחֱטִיא=הֶחֱטִי ; Inf. also הַחֲטִי, Jer. 32: 35.]

Interchange of forms between verbs לא and לה.

§ 279. In the Chaldee and Syriac, these two species of verbs fall under one and the same category, and have the same forms throughout. In Hebrew, there is plainly an incipient tendency toward this idiom, which develops itself in the frequent interchanges of these verbs for each other, in regard to vowels, or consonants, or both. E. g. verbs לא imitate verbs לה :

§§ 280—282. IRREG. VERBS; LAMEDH HE. 111

(1) As to vowels.			(2) As to consonants.		
[KAL	כָּלָאתִי	for כָּלָאתִי '	KAL. Imp.	רְפָה	for רְפָא
Part.	מֹצֵא	for מֹצָא		נְסֹה	for נְסֹא
PIEL	מִלֵּא	for מִלָּא	Fut.	תִּרְפֶּינָה	for תִּרְפֶּאנָה
	רִפֵּאתִי	for רִפֵּאתִי	NIPH.	נֶחְבָּה	for נֶחְבָּא
Fut.	יְגַמֶּה	for יְגַמֵּא		נִבֵּית	for נִבֵּאת
Inf.	מַלֹּאת	for מַלֵּא	Inf. const.	הַרְפֵּה	for הַרְפֵּא
HITH.	הִנַּבֵּאת	for הִתְנַבֵּא	PIEL.	יְמַלֵּה	for יְמַלֵּא

(3) *As to both vowels and consonants.* KAL. מָלוּ for צָמְאָה, צָמָת for מָלְאוּ, see § 118. Part. act. יֹצֶה for יֹצְאָה, § 118. צִבְיָה for צִבְאָיָה, § 118. Pass. נָשׂוּי for נָשׂוּא, Ps. 32: 1.
NIPH. נִטְמֵינוּ for נִטְמֵאנוּ. נִרְפְּתָה for נִרְפְּאָה. Fut. יִמָּצוּ for יִמָּצְאוּ, § 118.
PIEL. יְרַפּוּ for יְרַפְּאוּ, § 118.
HIPH. הִמְצִיתִיךָ for הִמְצֵאתִיךָ. Part. מַקְנֶה for מַקְנִיא.
HITH. הִתְנַבִּית for הִתְנַבֵּאת. הִתְנַבּוֹת for הִתְנַבֵּא.

Compare with these resemblances to verbs לה, the similarities of those verbs to לא, in § 290. See on the general principle of such interchanges, § 122.]

VERBS LAMEDH HE. PAR. XVI.

§ 280. These comprise verbs originally with a final Yodh or a final Vav; both of which coming at the end of a word after a heterogeneous vowel (Pattahh), conform to the vowel, i. e. become ה and quiesce in it, § 117. 2.

Note. Verbs originally לו are few; e. g. as שָׁלָה for שָׁלַוְ, 1st pers. Praet. שָׁלַוְתִּי; most verbs לה are originally לי. Only the *derivate* forms develope the original root; e. g. נָקִי from נָקָה = נָקִי; קָצוּ from קָצֶה = קָצוּ. Verbs with ה Mappiq are verbs which originally have a final ה, and belong to the class of ל Gutturals.

§ 281. The final radical in these verbs either quiesces, or becomes otiant and falls out, both in conjugation and declension, every where with only two exceptions.

These are, (1) *Praeter* 3d pers. fem., where the final radical is exchanged for ת; as נִגְלְתָה, גָּלְתָה, etc. (2) *Participle pass.;* as גָּלוּי *gā-lūy*, where the Yodh remains a proper consonant.

§ 282. The rules of quiescence, and the form of the quiescent letter, differ in different persons and tenses. They are as follows:

(a) The *Praeter* 3d masc. sing. in all the conjugations, requires ה quiescent in Qamets; see paradigm.

(b) The other forms without accession at the end, take הָ throughout; excepting the Imp. 2 masc. sing. which has הֵ, and the Inf. abs. which has הֹ.

(c) Before sufformatives beginning with a *consonant*, (1) The *Praeter* of Kal has יָ. (2) The *Praeter* of all the derived conjugations, has יִ. (3) The Fut. and Imp. throughout have יֶ; see paradigm.

(d) Before sufformatives beginning with a *vowel*, the Quiescent falls away.

E. g. גָּלוּ instead of גָּלְיוּ‎, גָּלְיִ for גָּלְיִי, etc. § 118. But a pause-accent restores the Quiescent and prolongs the original vowel which preceded it; e. g. יִגְלָיוּ instead of יִגְלוּ or יִגְלְיוּ, § 147.

Note. The falling away of the Quiescent here, throughout, depends on the principle stated in § 118 with the Note.

Notes on the Paradigm.

[§ 283. (a) KAL. (1) *Praeter* sometimes has the Chaldee form, as עָשָׂת for עָשְׂתָה, comp. § 278. a. 1. With Vav moveable once, שָׁלַוְתִּי, Job. 3:26. Forms written *defectively* are rather unusal; as בָּנִתִי for בָּנִיתִי.

(2) *Infinitive* abs. sometimes drops the ה, and takes the form גָּלֹו for גָּלֹה, etc. Twice it takes ת; as שָׁתוֹת‎, רָאוֹת. *Infinitive constr.* (rarely) as קְנֹה, עֲשׂה. Fem. form. רְאָה (רָאֹה), retaining the Vav, Ezek. 28:17. Once הֱיֵה, in Ezek. 21:15.

Note. The usual Inf. constr., as גְּלוֹת, is a fem. Segholate form, and is merely a contraction of גְּלֹיֶת; see § 120. c. Comp. fem. Infinitives, § 212. 3.

(3) *Future.* (α) תֶּזְנֶה, תֹּאבֶה, תָּבֹא, תִּזְנִי, תִּהְיֶה, (instead of תִּזְנֶה, תֹּאבֶה, תִּהְיֶה), are mere imitations of the Chaldee pointing in the Fut. of these verbs, and are probably errors of transcribers.

(β) *The Yodh quiescent of the root* is sometimes omitted before suffixes, as תַּעֲשֶׂנָה for תַּעֲשֶׂינָה; and sometimes it becomes *otiant* by reason of a Dag. euphonic, as תִּרְאֶיּנָה; and even falls out here also, as תַּעֲנֶנָה.]

Apocopate Future of Kal.

[(γ) This is common to all the conjugations of this verb. It is formed by dropping the final ה with the preceding vowel. It then appears, (1) Usually with a furtive vowel under the first radical. (2) Without one. E. g.

§ 283. IRREG. VERBS; LAMEDH HE. 113

	(1) Forms with a furtive vowel.			(2) Third pers. without a furt. vowel.		
	full form.	apoc. form.		full form.	apoc. form.	
Sing. 3	יִגְלֶה	(יֶשְׁלְ) וַיִּגֶל	a	יִבְכֶּה	(תֵּבְךְּ), יֵבְךְ	i
— 2	תִּגְלֶה	וַתִּגֶל	b	יֶהֱיֶה	יְהִי, יֶהִי, (אֱהִי)	j
— 1	אֶגְלֶה	וָאֶגֶל	c	יֶחֱיֶה	יְחִי, יֶחִי, (תְּחִי)	k
(Plural) 1	נִפְנֶה	וַנִּפֶן	d	....	יְדַ	l
ע gutt. 3	יִשְׁעֶה	וַיִּשַׁע	e	יִפְתֶּה	וַיִּפְתְּ Job 31: 27.	m
— 2	תִּתְעֶה	וַתַּתַע	f	יִרְאֶה	וַיֵּרָא, א in otio (§ 57. a)	n
ה gutt. 3	יַעֲשֶׂה	וַיַּעַשׂ	g	יִרְדֶּה	וַיֵּרֶד, יֵרֶד Ps. 72: 8.	o
3	יֶחֱרֶה	וַיִּחַר	h	יִשְׁבֶּה	וַיֵּשְׁב	p

Note 1. *The Segholate forms* in verbs differ in one respect from those of nouns, etc.; inasmuch as verbs take short Hhireq for a *penult* vowel; whereas nouns, etc., allow only of Seghol, Tseri, Pattahh, Qamets (in a few cases), and Hholem, all pure. In the above table, *a, e,* and *h* have short Hhireq for a penult vowel.

Note 2. In the apoc. forms of the 2d and 1st persons sing. and plural, the Hhireq is prolonged into Tseri, so *b, c, d;* not וַתִּגֶל, וָאֶגֶל, etc. On the other hand, the third person very rarely has a Tseri in the penult, like יֵשְׁלְ from שָׁלָה, under *a.*

Note 3. When the second radical is a Guttural, the apoc. forms assume the usual Pattahh in the final syllable; as in *e* and *f,* § 113. When the first radical is a Guttural, both vowels more usually are Pattahh, as in *g*; but ה and ח may take Hhireq, as in *h*.

Note 4. The nude apoc. forms in No. 2, without furtive vowels, are not frequent; yet they occur sufficiently often to be distinctly acknowledged. In *form* they resemble such nouns as קֶשֶׁט, גֶּרֶךְ, etc. The learner will observe, that the Hhireq under the praeform. is occasionally prolonged, and so becomes Tseri; e. g. in *i*. In *l*, the Pattahh in יְדַ *(yĭ-hhăd?)* is only *furtive*, as the Daghesh lene in ד shews.

Note 5. In the forms under *j, k,* the *Segholate* shape accommodates itself to the words which have a final Yodh; e. g. יְהִי instead of יֶהִי or יֶהִי, etc. See the ground of this, in § 120. *b*. So also יְהוּ (written once יְהוּא § 125. *a.*), from הָיָה.

Note 5. All the apoc. forms of the Future more usually have a ו conversive before them; but some occur without it; and ו does *not* always occasion apocope, e. g. וַיַּעֲנֶה 2 K. 1: 10, וַיִּבְכֶּה 2 K. 6: 23.

Remark. The student will observe, that none of the Segholates in Kal have the common form of two Seghols, like מֶלֶךְ. In this respect the forms of Kal are distinct from those of Hiphil, which adopts the double Seghol wherever the nature of the word permits.

(4) *Imperative.* For the forms גְּלִי, גְּלוּ, instead of גְּלָיִו, גְּלָיִ, see § 118 with Notes 1. 2. 3.

15

(5) *The active Part. fem.* is גּוֹלָה (for גּוֹלְיָה § 118). Sometimes it assumes the form גָּלְיָה, plur. גָּלְיוֹת, as if from גָּלְיִי, of the form תֹּמְךְ, § 212. 6.

(6) *The passive Part.* rarely as עָשׂוּ for עָשׂוּי, צָפוּ for צָפוּי. In Kethib, נְטוּלוֹת *nĕtŭ-vōth*, Qeri, נְטוּיוֹת.]

Restoration of the Yodh Radical.

[§ 284. In the forms where Yodh radical is dropped, it is occasionally restored, either by a pause-accent, by Nun parag., or by the emphasis required upon the word. See § 147 for pause-accent. With *Nun*, יִרְבּוּ, יִרְבְּיוּן and יִרְבְּיוּן. Emphasis חָסָיָה Ps. 57: 2. Imp. בְּעָיוּ, Is. 21: 12. With ה parag. also, Fut. אֶחֱמָיָה.

Note. From these cases of restored and prolonged vowels, it is clear, that the Fut. and Imp. of verbs לה have, in the real ground-form, a final Pattahh, since the restored vowel goes into Qamets; § 146.]

Niphal.

[§ 285. (1) *Praeter* sometimes with Hhireq before י; as נִקְיָת from נָקָה, נִגְלֵינוּ. In pause נְטִיִּ from נָטָה.

(2) *Infinitive abs.* rarely as נִגְלֹה. *Infinitive const.* very rarely as הֵרָאֹה, Judg. 13: 21.

(3) *The Future apoc.* merely drops the final ה with the preceding vowel.]

Piel.

[§ 286. (1) *Praeter* sometimes with Hhireq before י, as גִּלִּיתָ. (2) The apoc. forms in this conj. not only drop their final ה with its vowel, but also the Daghesh forte from the middle radical (see par.), because this letter now becomes a *final* one, § 72. The preceding vowel is sometimes prolonged, as וַיְתִי = וַיְתָוֶּה.

(3) With Yodh restored; Imp. דַּלְיוּ (for דַּלְיוּ, § 73. Note 3). Fut. with suff. תְּדַבְּמֵיוּנִי.]

Hiphil.

[§ 287. (1) *Praeter* sometimes with Hhireq; as הִגְלֵיתִי, הוֹרֵינוּ. Sing. fem. 3d pers. sometimes as הִגְלָת; comp. § 283. a. 1. In some cases the ה prefix takes Seghol; as הֶגְלָה, הֶרְאָה. Also the Chaldee, הֶחֱלִי for הֶחֱלָה; comp. § 283. 3. a.

(2) *Infinitive abs.* once as הַרְבָה. *Infinitive const.* once הַקְצוֹת for הַקְצוֹת, Lev. 14: 43. (3) *Future* 3d pers. plur. once הִמְסִיו *him-siv*, like the Chaldee רָמִיו, etc. Once תֶּמְחִי for תַּמְחֶה, Jer. 18: 23.]

[§ 288. FUTURES APOCOPATE. Like those in Kal, they are divided into two kinds. (1) With a furtive vowel; e. g. וַיִּגֶל, וַיַּחַת, וַיַּעַל. Here the penult vowel is Seghol, or Pattahh when the first radical is a

Guttural. The usual forms of noun-Segholates are here prevalent, in distinction from those in Kal; Remark, p. 113.

(2) With nude apocope; as יָרַדְהּ, יָרְדְּ, יֵרֶדּ; יִפְתֶּה, יִפְתּ, etc.

Note. The Imper. follows the analogy of No. 1; e. g. with a furtive vowel, always as חֶרֶב, חֹרֶף, instead of חַרְפָּה, חַרְבָּה, etc. With a Guttural, as הַעַל for הַעֲלֵה, etc.]

[§ 289. PECULIAR ANOMALIES. Such are the endings in (‥) in the Infin., and Future; e. g. Inf. Kal, חְיֹה to be; Piel. עֻנֹּה opprimendo; Hoph. הֻפְּדֵה. In Kal Fut. תֹּבֹא, תִּהְיֶה for תֹּאבֶה; Piel, תְּגֻלֵּה. In Syr. and Chaldee, the Fut. ends in ־א or ־י in these verbs.]

[§ 290. IMITATIONS OF VERBS לֹא; comp. § 279. (a) Imitation in respect to consonants; e. g. רָצִיתִי for רָצָאתִי; נָשֹׁא Inf. abs. for נָשׂוֹ, Imp. הֱוֵא. So רְשֶׁנָא, חֲלָא, for יִשְׁנֶה, חֲלֵה; שְׁנָא for שְׁנֵה Piel; יְשֻׁנֶּא for יְשֻׁנֶּה, Ecc. 8:1. (b) As to vowels; e. g. תִּכְלֶה for תָּכְלָה, אֶשְׁעָה for אֶשְׁעֶה; Piel Inf. עַנֵּה for עַנּוֹת, Fut. תִּגְלֶה for תִּגְלָה; Part. Niph. נַחְלָה for נַחְלֶה.]

§ 291. *General remark on the usage described in* § 279, § 290. The number of these anomalies will be increased or diminished very much, according to the principles assumed by the lexicographer. If he constitute roots both in לֹא and in לֹה, with the same meaning, then the anomalies are reduced to a very small number. If he make but one root, then they are multiplied. I observe that Gesenius, (very rightly in my apprehension), in his latest works, increases the number of the roots and thus diminishes the anomalies.

[§ 292. *Pilel* appears only twice, viz. in נַאֲיָה (contract. נָאיָה § 119. c. 1) from נָאָה; and in מְטַחֲוֵי Part. const. plur., from טָחָה, Pilel טַחֲוָה.

Hithpalel appears only in שָׁחָה, Hith. הִשְׁתַּחֲוָה, Fut. apoc. יִשְׁתַּחוּ instead of יִשְׁתַּחֲו, § 120. *b.* Inf. with ה parag. הִשְׁתַּחֲוָיָה, 2 K. 5: 18.]

VERBS LAMEDH TAV.

[§ 293. These are not strictly irregular; but in all the persons which receive a suffix beginning with ת, the ת final of the root is inserted by a Daghesh forte in the suffix letter; e. g. כָּרַת, כָּרַתָּ, כָּרַתִּי, כְּרַתֶּם, etc. So also, מֵת *he died*, מַתָּ, מַתִּי, etc. as in the paradigm.]

VERBS DOUBLY ANOMALOUS.

§ 294. These are such as have two radicals (usually the first and third) which may be dropped, or assimilated, or may become quiescent; as נָשָׂא, יָרָה, יָצָא, אָתָה, נָטָה etc.

§§ 295. 296. IRREG. VERBS; DOUBLY ANOMALOUS.

Note. Very few cases occur like בוֹא, where two irregular letters come together. Two cases only occur of verbs irregular פ and ע; e. g. נָדַד, and נָסַס; for which see lexicon. The verbs כּוּר and נוּעַ, are regular as to the *Nun*, § 253.

§ 295. In regard to the *first* radical, these verbs exhibit all the various phases of verbs irregular פ; and in regard to the *third* radical all the phases of verbs irregular ל; see Par. XVII—XX.

[§ 296. The following examples and notes on the paradigms just mentioned, exhibit all the forms of these verbs in which the student is likely to meet with any difficulty.

(*a*) Verbs פ״א and ל״ה.

אָלָה, Hiph. fut. apoc. וַיֹּאֶל 1 Sam. 14: 24, for וַיֹּאֲלֶה.

אָפָה, Imp. אֱפוּ Ex. 16: 23, by Syriasm for אֵפוּ (119. *d*. 2); Fut. with suff. וַתֹּאפֵהוּ 1 Sam. 28: 24, for וַתֹּאפֶהוּ.

אָתָה, Praet. in pause אָתָיוּ Jer. 3: 22; Imp. in pause, אֱתָיוּ for אֲתָיוּ (§ 119. *d*. 2. § 147); Fut. וַיֵּאתָא Deut. 33: 21, for וַיֶּאְתֶה, a change being made in both the final vowel and consonant; § 290. *a. b*; וַיֵּאָתוּ Is. 41: 25, for וַיֶּאֱתָה. Hiph. Imp. in pause, הֵתָיוּ for הֶאֱתָיוּ, § 119. *c*. 1. § 147.

(*b*) Verbs פ״י and ל״א.

יָצָא, Inf. fem. צֵאת for צָאֵת, § 119. *c*. 1. Imp. צֵא, § 243. *a*.

(*c*) Verbs פ״י and ל״ה, Par. XVII.

יָדָה, not found in Kal; Piel. Fut. וַיַּדּוּ Lam. 3: 53, for וַיְיַדּוּ. Hiph. Fut. with ה retained, יְהוֹדֶה Neh. 11: 17; 1st pers. with suffix אוֹדְךָ Ps. 35: 18, and in pause אוֹדֶךָּ Ps. 30: 13.

יָנָה, Fut. 1st pers. plur. with suff., יוֹנָם, Ps. 74: 8.

יָפָה, Fut. apoc. וַיִּיף, Ezek. 31: 7; *Popaal*, יְפֵיפִיתָ, Ps. 45: 3.

יָרָה, Fut. 1st pers. with suff. יִירָם, Num. 21: 30. Hiph. Fut. with suff. יֹרֵם, 2 K. 17: 27; תּוֹרְךָ Ps. 45: 8 etc.

(*d*) Verbs פ״ן and ל״א, Par. XVIII.

The paradigm exhibits in Kal and Niphal the forms of נָשָׂא; in Hiphil those of נָשָׁא, because the former does not occur in Hiphil.

Infinitive construct, שֵׂאת for שְׂאֵת, § 119. *c*. 1. Fut. תִּשֶּׁנָּה Ruth 1: 14, without Aleph. Hiph. Fut., יַשִּׁי, Ps. 55: 16, Kethib for יַשִּׂיא.

(*e*) Verbs פ״ן and ל״ה Par. XIX.

The three verbs נָכָה, נָטָה, נָזָה, are all of this form. Kal. Fut. apoc. with Vav, וַיֵּט and וַיַּט–; וַיִּז 2 K. 9: 33. Niphal of נָטָה Praet. 3 pers. plur. in pause, נִטָּיוּ, Num. 24: 6; Fut. 3 pers., יִנָּטֶה, Zech. 1: 16; 3 pers. plur. יִפָּשׂוּ, Jer. 6: 4. נָכָה, Praet. Niphal נִכָּה 2 Sam. 11: 15; נְכָאוּ, Job. 30: 8 (with א for ה § 290), or perhaps the root is נָכָא. Hiph. Fut. with suff, יַכּוֹ, 2 Sam. 14: 6; יַכֶּךָּ, Job 36: 18, etc.

§§ 297—300. PLURILIRERAL VERBS. 117

Fut. apoc. with Vav, וַיֵּט, וַיֵּךְ, etc. The Imp. also suffers apocope, and takes the forms בָּט, בָּךְ, which are of frequent occurrence.]

[§ 297. The verb בּוֹא has all the common inflections exhibited in paradigm XX. But it has many forms sui generis besides these; e. g. with suff., בָּאֲךָ, בָּאֲכָה; Fut. וַיָּבוֹא for וַיָּבֹא. Fem. 3d plur. תְּבֹאֶינָה, with epenth. ־ִי. Also תָּבֹאתָה Deut. 33: 16, for תָּבֹא; and תָּבֹאתִי 1 Sam. 25: 34, for תָּבֹאִי. Hiphil sometimes takes epenth. וֹ; as הֲבִיאוֹתָם, הֲבִיאוֹתִי, הֲבִיאוֹתָנִי. Defectively הֵבִי for הֵבִיא.

Note. The verbs נוּא and קוּא are used only in *Hiphil;* where they are declined like בּוֹא.]

RELATION OF IRREGULAR VERBS TO EACH OTHER.

§ 298. In the irregular verbs in general, only two of the radicals appear to be permanent and immutable. The other radical may be, and often actually is, supplied in different ways, according to the forms adopted by the different classes of irreg. verbs. E. g. from the biliteral דך, have been formed דָּכָה, דָּכָא, דּוּךְ, דָּכַךְ, all of the same meaning. So also יָצַב and נָצַב; צָרַר, צוּר, and יָצַר; קָרָא and קָרָה; טוּב and יָטַב; and so, more or less, of a large proportion of the irregular verbs, much larger than has yet been generally noticed. This principle reigns extensively, also, in the kindred Shemitish languages.

§ 299. In consequence of different forms having the same meaning, it happens in many cases that one form is employed only in some particular tense or conjugation, while another is employed exclusively in another. E. g. from הָלַךְ *ivit,* is derived the Praet. and Part.; while its equivalent יָלַךְ furnishes the Inf., Fut., and Imp. So חָקַק, as usual in Kal; but Pual חֻקַּק, and Hith. הִתְחַקֵּק, come from חָקָה.

Compare in Latin, *fero, tuli, latum;* Greek, φέρω, οἴσω, ἤνεγκα. It were to be wished that lexicographers would make a more extensive use of this obvious and widely extended principle in Hebrew etymology. It would greatly diminish the so called *anomalies* of the language.

PLURILITERAL VERBS.

[§ 300. These are properly very few; and they are declined like the conjs. Pilel and Pulal. The following list comprises the whole number that actually appear; viz.

(1) טִאטֵא, 1 pers. with suff. טֵאטֵאתִיהָ, Is. 14: 23. (2) כִּרְבֵּל, participle מְכֻרְבָּל, 1 Chr. 15: 27. (3) כִּרְסֵם, Fut. with suffix. יְכַרְסְמֶנָּה, Ps. 80: 14. (4) פַּרְשֵׁז, Job 26: 9. (5) רְטַפַּשׁ, Job 33: 25. (6) תַּחֲרָה, 2 pers. fut. תְּתַחֲרֶה, Jer. 12: 5; participle מִתַחֲרֶה, Jer. 22: 15. (7) A few other forms are noted in some of the lexicons, but in others they are more properly referred to the Pilel form, derived from a triliteral root; as Pilel 3 pers. fem. in pause רַעֲנָנָה, Job 15: 32. Cant. 1: 16, from רָעַן.]

PARTICIPLES.

301. Participles are treated as adjectives, i. e. they are declined as nouns; which is common in other languages. Participles in regard to case, tone-syllable, etc., follow the usages of nouns. Par. XXI. exhibits the various phases and declensions of their *absolute* state.

§ 302. All of them in the fem. may form Segholates, except the ground-form has an *immutable penult* vowel; e. g. קָמָה, מְסִבָּה, מְקִימָה, etc., are incapable of a Segholate form, because the *penult* vowels cannot be so changed as to conform to the laws of Segholates; see § 142. *d.* But in Hiphil the fem. Segholates are derived from an apoc. fem. form, like מַקְטִלָה, which resembles the apoc. Fut. יַקְטֵל.

VERBS WITH SUFFIX PRONOUNS.

§ 303. Pronouns following verbs and being governed by them, are attached to them and united in the same word. This is effected by taking the fragments or parts of the pronoun, with an appropriate vowel of union (where one is needed), and adjusting the form of the verb, when necessary, so as to receive it.

E. g. קְטָלַנִי instead of קָטַל אֲנִי, *he killed me;* קְטַלְתָּם instead of קָטַלְתָּ הֵם, *thou didst kill them.* Comp. Latin *eccum* for *ecce eum*, etc.

§ 304. Most of the suffix pronouns influence the tones of the verb, i. e. they move it *forward* or toward the left; and consequently they occasion more or less changes in the mutable vowels of verbs, usually (not always) according to the general principles of the vowel changes, § 126 seq. In some few cases, the *consonants* of the verb suffer a change in order to receive a suffix, § 311.

§ 305. As all the conjugations of verbs terminate in the same manner, they all receive suffixes in the like manner with Kal, with very little variation. But *neuter* verbs, and those which are *passive* or *reflexive*, do not from the nature of the case admit of suffixes, as they do not govern words after them;

Note. Verbs of the *first* and *second* persons do not receive suffixes of the same persons, because the *reflexive* forms of the verbs express the sense which would be thus conveyed.

§ 306. The Inf. mode and participles receive suffixes either in the manner of verbs or of nouns.

But not with the same meaning, as it respects the Inf. mode; for a noun-suffix appended to it, denotes the *subject* or *agent* of the verb; but a verbal suffix, the *object* of the action implied by the verb. E. g. Inf. פְּקֹד, with noun suffix פָּקְדִי *my punishment*, viz. that which I inflict; with a verbal suffix לְפָקְדֵנִי, *to punish me*.

§ 307. *Different forms of pronoun suffixes.* Most of the verbal-suffixes or fragments of primitive pronouns have at least three different forms, adapted to the different ending or tense of the verb to which they are appended.

(*a*) The most simple form of the suffixes is that in which they begin with a *consonant*. In this shape they are appended, through all the tenses and modes, to forms of verbs which end with a *vowel;* see Note below.

(*b*) To the simple form of the suffixes, i. e. to suffixes beginning with a consonant, is prefixed a vowel of the *A* class, viz. Qamets or Pattahh. In this shape they are appended to forms of verbs which end with a *consonant*, *usually in the Praeter only.*

(*c*) To the same forms are prefixed a vowel of the *E* class, viz. Tseri or Seghol. In this shape they are appended to forms of verbs in the Fut. and Imp. which end with a *consonant*.

Note. The vowel which is thus prefixed to the suffixes, serves to connect them more readily with the verb, and is therefore called the *union-vowel*. When the verb ends in a vowel, that vowel of course serves as a union-vowel.

§ 308. Between the suffix and the union-vowel there is sometimes inserted an epenthetic *Nun*, § 109. *b*, which is usually assimilated to the first letter of the suffix and expressed in it by a Daghesh forte. In poetry, the Nun is sometimes fully written. This class of suffixes is limited principally to the sing. number of the pronouns, and to the Fut. tense of verbs.

§§ 309. 310. VERBS WITH SUFFIX PRONOUNS.

[§ 309. The following table exhibits the suffixes as appended, (a) To verbs ending with a vowel in all the moods and tenses. (b) To those ending with a consonant in the Praeter. (c) To those ending with a consonant in the Fut. and Imperative. (d) It exhibits also those suffixes which receive an epenthetic Nun.

(a) Sing. common.	(b) Praeter.	(c) Future etc.
1. ־ִי	־ַ֫נִי in pause ־ֵ֫נִי	־ֵ֫נִי
2 m. ־ְךָ ־ֶ֫ךָ	ךָ in pause ־ֶ֫ךָ ־ָ֫ךְ	ךָ &c. ־ֶ֫ךָ
2 f. כִי ךְ	־ֵךְ ־ֶךְ ־ָךְ	־ֵךְ ־ֶ֫כִי ־ָךְ
3 m. ־ֹו ־ֵ֫הוּ	וֹ ־ֵ֫הוּ	וֹ ־ֵ֫הוּ
3 f. ־ָהּ	־ָ֫הָ ־ָהּ	־ֶ֫הָ
Pl. 1. ־ֵ֫נוּ	־ָ֫נוּ	־ֵ֫נוּ
2 m. כֶם	כֶם	כֶם
2 f. כֶן	כֶן	כֶן
3 m. ם poet. ־ָ֫מוֹ	־ָם ־ֵם poet. ־ָ֫מוֹ	־ֵם ־ָם poet. ־ֵ֫מוֹ
3. f. הֶן ן	־ַן ־ָן	־ַן

Future with epenthetic Nun.

(d)
Sing. 1. ־ֵ֫נִי ־ֶ֫נִּי for ־ֵ֫נִי &c. | Sing. 3m. ־ֶ֫נּוּ for ־ֵ֫הוּ, also נוּ
— 2 m. ־ֶ֫ךָּ ־ֶ֫כָּה for ־ֶ֫ךָ &c. | — 3 f. ־ֶ֫נָּה for ־ֶ֫הָ
| 1st Plur. ־ֶ֫נּוּ for ־ֵ֫נוּ]

Notes on the table of suffixes.

[§ 310. (1) In a very few instances, the Future has the suffixes ־ַ֫נִי כֶם like the Praeter; and vice versâ the Praeter very rarely takes suffixes like the Future, viz. ־ֵ֫נִי, and a few times פִ֫י ־ֵ֫.

(2) The original union-vowels would seem to be Qamets and Tseri; which shorten into Pattahh and Seghol when the tone is removed. Before the epenthetic Nun, the two latter only are found. So also in ־ֶ֫נִי, which in pause becomes ־ֵ֫נִי.

(3) The 2d pers. sing. fem. ־ֶךְ in b, occurs but seldom; the more common form in the Praeter is ־ֵךְ (without tone ־ָךְ), as in the Future. The form with paragogic Yodh (כִי ־ֵ֫) occurs often in the later Psalms.

§§ 310—312. VERBS WITH SUFFIX PRONOUNS. 121

(4) The suffixes בְּךָ, כֶם, never take a *union-vowel;* nor does the suffix ךָ or כָה, except in pause. The 3 pers. sing. fem. of the Praeter also takes suffixes either *with* or *without* a union-vowel; see below § 312. 2.

(5) The forms מוֹ ־ מוֹ ־ מוֹ ־ with a parag. וֹ, are common in poetry. The form מוֹ is found as a suffix once, Ex. 15: 5; so in Ethiopic. The form הֶם ־ occurs in Deut. 32: 26.

(6) Instead of the fem. suffix ן of the 3d pers. plural, the masc. form ם appears, specially after the sufformatives ה and יִ ־ ; perhaps in order that the fem. suffix may not be confounded with the parag. ן ; as וַיְגָרְשֻׁם, Ex. 2: 17, for וַיְגָרְשׁוּן; וַיַּאַסְרוּם, 1 Sam. 6: 10. Gen. 26: 15. Num. 17: 3, 4. Josh. 4: 8. Hos. 2: 14. Prov. 6: 21. But ן is used in Jer. 48: 7.

(7) The suffixes with epenth. Nun are occasionally found in the Imp., but rarely in the Praeter; see No 1. above. In Chaldee, an epenth. Nun is always found before the suff. of the Fut., Imp., and Infinitive.

(8) Wherever there is a union-vowel, it uniformly takes the tone. The suffixes כֶם and כֶן always draw down the tone upon themselves, removing it two places if necessary; and are on that account denominated *grave* suffixes. The others never move the tone more than one syllable, and are called *light* suffixes.

The suffix ךָ or כָה when appended to verbs ending in a *consonant,* usually takes the tone. The 3 pers. sing. fem. of the Praeter is excepted; see paradigm.

(9) Some of these suffix-forms of pronouns are derived from primitive forms which are still in use; as ם, ן, from הֵם, הֵן, etc. Others would seem to come from forms which are now obsolete in Hebrew; as ךָ from אַכָּה=אַנְכָה *thou,* like אָנֹכִי *I;* כֶם from אַכֶּם etc. The form ךָ still appears in Ethiopic, as a regular sufform. in the flexion of verbs.]

Note. Verbal-suffixes are also united, in all their forms, with certain adverbs and interjections; in which condition they are in the Nominative case.

§ 311. The changes in the *vowels* of the verb, occasioned by the suffix pronouns, are seen in the paradigm. In the *consonants,* the following changes take place; viz. Praet. 3 fem. הָ ־ becomes תָ ־ (תָ ־); the fem. תְּ (תִּי) becomes תִּי; 2 plur. masc. תֶם becomes תוּ; as the paradigm shews. The forms ending with נָה ־ receive ו in its room.

Notes on the Paradigm.

[§ 312. KAL, *Praeter third person masc. singular.* In קְטָלַנִי, as the tone is moved forward, the first vowel falls away, § 133; the second

16

§ 312. VERBS WITH SUFFIX PRONOUNS.

vowel of the original word is thrown into a simple syllable, and becomes long, § 130; but where the syllable remains mixed, Pattahh continues, as קְטָלְבֶם. In such a way, the student will easily account for most of the changes made in the original vowels of the verb. Verbs final Tseri retain it, when a long vowel is required in the last syllable of the verb; as לְבֵשָׁם.

(2) *Praeter* 3 *fem.* substitutes ת for the final ה, unites this (for the most part) in a syllable with the last radical of the verb, and always puts the tone upon the same syllable. It is only when a suffix begins with a *vowel*, (which occurs only in ךָ, ם, ן), that the final ת is taken away from this syllable (§ 90. 1), which of course prolongs the Pattahh, § 130. E. g. with suff. ךָ, קְטָלָתְךָ, where the Tseri of the suffix is shortened, in consequence of falling into a mixed syllable without the tone, § 129 *a*. So ם, ן, make, by the same rules, קְטָלָתַן, קְטָלָתַם.

Note. The suffix הוּ and הָ sometimes assimilate their ה to the final ת of the verb; e. g. גְּמָלַתְהוּ=גְּמָלַתּוּ, 1 Sam. 1: 24; אֲהָזַתָּה=אֲחָזָתְהָ, Jer. 49: 24.

(3) *Praeter* 2 *fem.* exhibits the form קְטַלְתִּי before a suffix, (as stated in § 311); and in this way it appears in the same manner as the 1st pers. sing. when it takes the suffix of the 3d pers. sing. and plural. The student will remark that here, and in the 2d pers. plural, a *union-vowel* is provided for the verb by adopting the forms קְטַלְתִּי, קְטַלְתּוּ.

(4) *The Infinitive* most usually takes suffixes in the manner of Segholate nouns, in Dec. VI; i. e. the final vowel is thrown back upon the first radical and shortened. If the verb be ע' *Guttural*, then the points are regulated by the usual principles, in § 114. § 128. See the examples in the paradigm. The variety of punctuation with the suffixes ךָ, כֶם, כֶן, may also be there seen.

The Infinitive of a verb Fut. Pattahh usually takes Hhireq under the first radical before suffixes; as בִּקְעָם in the paradigm; but sometimes Pattahh, as רַקְעֵךְ, פַּעֲמוֹ, etc. Verbs Pe Guttural sometimes take a Seghol in the first syllable; as חֲנֹתֹה, Ps. 102: 14.

The *Infinitive fem. Segholate* takes suffixes like nouns of Dec. XIII. Hhireq is the usual vowel in the first syllable; e. g. רִשְׁתִּי, רֶשֶׁת; but sometimes Pattahh, as שַׁבְתִּי, שֶׁבֶת.

(5) *Future suffixes* are provided with a union-vowel in most cases, where the verb ends with a consonant; in which cases the final Hholem or Tseri of the verb is dropped. But with suff. ךָ, כֶם, כֶן, these vowels are retained, and shortened because they lose the tone. On the other hand, verbs Future Pattahh retain this vowel, and prolong it before a union-vowel; as יְלַבְּשֵׁם from יִלְבַּשׁ.

§§ 313—316. VERBS WITH SUFFIXES—NOUNS.   123

(6) *Imperative* follows the analogy of the Future throughout; and this in regard to verbs final Pattahh, as well as others.

(7) *Participles* follow the manner of the nouns to whose declension they belong, in receiving suffixes.

(8) PIEL usually drops its final Tseri before a union-vowel, as in the paradigm; but before ךְ, כֶם, בֶן, it commonly shortens it into Seghol or short Hhireq, as קִבֶּצְךָ, פָּרְשְׁכֶם; rarely into Pattahh, as בֵּרַכְךָ, Deut. 2: 7. Pattahh final here remains, as רִחַצְךָ.

(9) POEL, POLEL, etc., imitate Piel in their suffixes.

(10) HIPHIL appends suffixes to its *full* forms, not to the apocopate ones. Very rarely is the final vowel of the verb dropped; as in יַעְשְׁרְכֻּ instead of יַעֲשִׁירְכֻּ.]

Verbs Lamedh He with suffixes.

[§ 313. Suffixes here cause the final letter and vowel to fall away. The union-vowel is then supplied, or omitted, as the nature of the case requires.

Note 1. *Praeter 3d sing. fem.* rejects the final הָ֫, and then follows the analogy in regular verbs as to the ת before the suffix.

Note 2. Suffixes beginning with a consonant sometimes cause the original Yodh to be restored; as הָיִיְהוּ, יְמַסִּימוֹ, יְמָאֵירֶהֶם, אֶפְאֵירֶהֶם, etc.]

NOUNS.

§ 314. *Derivation.* Most nouns in Hebrew are derived from verbs; and *in general they have for their ground-forms the Inf. mode or participles.* A comparatively small number of nouns are probably *primitive;* but these conform, in their inflection, to the usual laws which regulate those derived from verbs.

§ 315. *Declension* in Hebrew nouns differs much from declension in Greek and Latin. The plural and dual numbers are, indeed, distinguished by appropriate endings added to the ground-forms; but *case*, properly considered, is not marked by any peculiarity of inflection in the noun itself. For the most part, it is designated by prepositions and the construct state of the preceding noun, § 332. But the plural and dual endings, the suffixes, and whatever increases the original ground-forms of the noun, and shift the place of its tone, occasion a variety of changes in the vowel-points and in the forms of nouns, which may not unaptly be called *declensions.*

§ 316. *Classes of nouns in respect to origin.* Nouns, like verbs, are either *primitive* or *derivative.* Those of the latter class are divided into *verbals* or those derived from *verbs*, and *denominatives* or those derived from *nouns*. Three classes of nouns may therefore be reckoned.

(*a*) *Nouns primitive*; which are principally those that designate animals, plants, metals, numbers, members of the human and animal body, and some of the great objects of the natural world. But among the names of all these, are some of verbal derivation.

<small>Note. The *form* of *primitive* nouns is not distinguished from that of *derived* ones. They are treated, in their inflections, in the same manner as if they were *derived*. Only a knowledge of etymology, therefore, can enable the student to determine whether a noun is primitive or derivative; and in some cases it may be doubtful to the best etymologist, whether a noun belongs to the first, second, or third class above specified.</small>

(*b*) *Nouns derivative*; which are altogether the most numerous class. Very many of them appear to be derived either from participles, or from the Inf. mood. The former more commonly denote the subject or object of action or passion, (*nomen agentis* vel *patientis*); the latter denote action or passion, (*nomen actionis* vel *passionis*). The first class are named *concretes*, being used to designate some being or thing; the second *abstracts*, denoting simple action or passion. But to this principle there are very many exceptions.

(*c*) *Nouns denominative*; which are nouns derived from other nouns, either primitive or verbal. E. g. כֹּרֵם *a vine-dresser*, from the primitive כֶּרֶם *a vineyard*; קַדְמוֹן *eastern*, from the verbal קֶדֶם *the east*. The forms of these resemble those of the other classes.

[Note. *Denominatives* are usually formed, (1) By adding to verbals the masc. termination ־ִי, or the fem. ־ִיָּה; e. g. שֵׁשׁ *six*, שִׁשִּׁי *sixth*; מוֹאָבִי *a Moabite*, from מוֹאָב; יִשְׂרְאֵלִי *an Israelite*, from יִשְׂרָאֵל, etc. Several adjectives also are formed in this manner; as נָכְרִי, fem. נָכְרִיָּה *strange*, from נֵכָר *a stranger*; קַדְמֹנִי *first*, from קַדְמוֹן, etc.

(2) By adding ־ִית, which is usually of the fem. gender. E. g. רֹאשׁ *princeps*, רֵאשִׁית *principium*. Words of this form are sometimes defectively written, as צִצָה for צִיצִית, etc.

(3) Rarely by adding the terminations ־ָה, ־ֶה, ־ִי and ־ָן. E. g. אַרְיֵה *a lion*, from אֲרִי; אִשֶּׁה *fire-offering*, from אֵשׁ; כִּילַי *a deceiver*, from כִּיל; גִּנְזָךְ *a treasury*, from גָּנַז.]

[§ 317. *Nouns composite and proper.* Composite nouns are very rarely found in Hebrew, except in proper names. A few however occur, which are made up of two nouns, or of a noun and a particle. E. g. צַלְמָוֶת=צֵל מָוֶת *shade of death*; בְּלִיַּעַל *worthless*, from בְּלִי *not* and יַעַל *profit*.

<small>Note 1. Proper names, in their formation, follow the general analogy of verbals as given in § 316. *b.* Very many of them are *composite*,</small>

and consist usually of two nouns, or of a noun and a verb. E. g. בִּנְיָמִין *Benjamin*, or *son of my right hand*; יְהוֹיָקִים *Jehoiakim*, or *Jehovah will exalt*.

Note 2. To the first word in composite proper names a Yodh is usually added, as גַּבְרִיאֵל *Gabriel* or *man of God*, from גֶּבֶר and אֵל; sometimes a Vav, as שְׁמוּאֵל *Samuel* or *name of God*, from שֵׁם and אֵל. The name of God (אֵל or יְהֹוָה) forms the beginning or the termination of a great multitude of Hebrew proper names.]

Gender of Nouns.

§ 318. The Hebrew has only two genders, viz. the masculine and feminine. These are distinguished sometimes by the *form*, and sometimes by the *signification*, of words.

§ 319. I. *Gender distinguished by form.* (*a*) In general, nouns are *masculine* which end in one of the original radical letters of the word.

(*b*) The *feminine* is distinguished by adding to the masculine, either ה ָ , ת, ת ֶ or ת ַ .

E. g. מֶלֶךְ *a king*, מַלְכָּה *a queen*; חֹטֵא *a sinner* חַטָּאת *sin*, and עִבְרִי *a Hebrew man* עִבְרִית *a Hebrew woman*; קְטוֹר, fem. קְטֹרֶת *incense*; מוֹדָע, fem. מוֹדַעַת *acquaintance*. The fem. ת ַ is appropriate to words with Gutturals at the end, § 141.

[Note 1. The following terminations of the feminine actually occur, but they are rare; viz. (1) א ָ ; as שֵׂיָא, for שֵׂיָה, § 122. 1. (2) ת ֶ ; as זִמְרָת, poetic for זִמְרָה. (3) ת ַ with the proper vowel Pattahh, and with the tone on the ultimate; as בָּקְרַת *emerald*, קָאת *pelican* Ps. 102: 6.

Note 2. The endings ית ַ and וּת are also *feminine*. They are contracted forms, for the full fem. ת ַ יָ and ת ֶ וֶ, neither of which the language permits, § 120. *c.*]

§ 320. II. *Gender distinguished by signification.* (*a*) Nouns which designate objects such as the following, are *masculine*, although they have a feminine termination.

(1) Names of men; as יְהוּדָה *Judah*. (2) Offices of men; as פֶּחָה *a governor*. (3) Nations; as יְהוּדָה the nation of *Judah*. (4) Rivers; as אֲמָנָה *Amana*.

(*b*) Nouns which designate objects such as the following, are *feminine*, although they have a masc. termination.

(1) Names of women; as רָחֵל *Rachel*. (2) Office or relations of women; as אֵם *mother*. (3) Countries; as אַשּׁוּר *Assyria*. (4) Towns;

as צוּר *Tyre*. (5) Female beasts; as אָתוֹן *a she-ass*. (6) Members of the body by nature double; as אֹזֶן *the ear*.

Note 1. The same word may be masc. in one meaning, and fem. in another; as יְהוּדָה, *Judah* or *the Jews*, masc.; but יְהוּדָה, *the country of Judea*, fem.

Note 2. There are some nouns which are feminine, although destitute of any distinctive sign of this gender either in form or signification; as בְּאֵר *a well*; כִּכָּר *a talent*, etc. These can be learned only from practice.

§ 321. *Nouns of common gender.* A considerable number of nouns are of common gender. Such are generally the names of beasts, birds, metals, etc.

Note 1. These nouns are mostly masculine as to *form*. Some of them are more commonly employed as masc. nouns; others more frequently as feminine. These can be learned only from practice. What is of the *neuter* gender in the western languages, is generally designated in Hebrew by the fem.; as בַּת צוּר, *daughter of Tyre*, i. e. city of Tyre.

Note 2. Nouns of the dual number are universally of the common gender.

§ 322. *Gender of the plural.* In the plural, the appearance of nouns as to gender is in many cases dubious. A considerable number of masc. nouns form their plural as if they were feminine; while many feminine nouns have plurals of the masculine form, § 327. 1.

E. g. masc. אָב *a father*, plur. אָבוֹת. Fem. חִטָּה *wheat*, plur. חִטִּים etc.

Note. The *gender* of the plural, let the *form* be as it may, is, with few exceptions, regulated by that of the singular. Some words exhibit both the masc. and fem. *forms* of the plural, but the *gender* of both forms is the same, viz. it is the same as that of the singular.

Formation of fem. nouns from masc. ones.

[§ 323. The addition of fem. terminations (§ 319. *b*) to the masc. forms, usually occasions some change in the vowels of the masculine, because these terminations affect the tone-syllable of the ground-form. E. g. *(a)* 1. The ending הָ draws down the accent, and consequently causes the *penult* vowel of the masc. form, if mutable, to be dropped; § 133. (2) In nouns, etc., of the form of Dec. VII., the *final* vowel is dropped. (3) Such nouns as Dec. VIII., in case they have a long vowel, exchange it for a short one with Dag. forte, or in case this is excluded, substitute an equivalent for it, § 111. § 112. (4) Masc. Segho-

§§ 323. 324. NOUNS; FORMATION OF THE FEM. ETC. 127

lates receiving ה_ fem., assume the suffix-form in order to take it; see par. Dec. VI. (5) Nouns of declension IX. drop their final ה and its preceding vowel, in order to receive the fem. ה_. All these principles are apparent in the following table of formations, in which those nouns not accompanied by a common numeral mark, form the fem. by the mere addition of the fem. ה_ to the masculine; those marked 1, 2, 3, 4, 5, correspond in their formation to the rules given in 1, 2, etc. above. The Roman numerals mark the declensions to which the masc. nouns respectively belong.

Dec.	Masc.	Fem.	Dec.	Masc.	Fem.	Dec.	Masc.	Fem.
I.	סוּס	סוּסָה	VI.	מֶלֶךְ	(4) מַלְכָּה		עֵץ	עֵצָה
	תַּחְתּוֹן	תַּחְתּוֹנָה		גֶּבַע	(4) גִּבְעָה	VIII.	תָּם	(3) תַּמָּה
II.	מוֹצָא	מוֹצָאָה		אֹמֶר	(4) אָמְרָה		נֵץ	(3) נֵצָה
III.	גָּדוֹל	(1) גְּדוֹלָה		עֵגֶל	(4) עֶגְלָה		כֵּן	(3) כַּנָּה
	מָתוֹק	(1) מְתוּקָה		אֹכֶל	(4) אָכְלָה		חֹק	(3) חֻקָּה
	עָצוּם	(1) עֲצוּמָה		חֹזֶק	(4) חָזְקָה		בַּז	(3) בִּזָּה
	בָּרִיא	(1) בְּרִיאָה		עֹוֶל	(4) עַוְלָה		גַּן	(3) גַּנָּה
	מָקִים	(1) מְקִימָה		צַיִד	(4) צֵידָה		שַׂר	(3) שָׂרָה
IV.	נָקָם	(1) נְקָמָה	VII.	אֹרַח	(2) אֹרְחָה	IX.	יָפֶה	(5) יָפָה
V.	זָקֵן	(1) זְקֵנָה		מוֹקֵד	(2) מוֹקְדָה		מַרְאֶה	(5) מַרְאָה בַּרְאָה
	יָעֵן	יַעֲנָה (irreg.)		דֵּעַ	דֵּעָה			

Note. As nouns of Dec. V. not unfrequently imitate those of Dec. VI. in their const. form (see par.), so among the *feminines* derived from ground forms belonging here, are some that imitate the fem. of Dec. VI.; e. g. יָרֵךְ fem. יְרֵכָה, יָעֵל fem. יַעֲלָה. For the form מָתוֹק, fem. מְתוּקָה, under Dec. III., comp. § 127. Except. 1. § 270. *b*. 1.

(*b*) The ending ת makes no change in the original word; e. g. עִבְרִית, עִבְרִי; חַטָּאת, חַטָּא, etc.

(*c*) The Segholate endings, ת_, ה_, (1) Affect the *penult* vowel in the like manner with ה_; see above, *a*. (2) They change the ultimate *mutable* vowel, according to the rule in § 142. *d*. (3) If the final vowel be impure, they substitute a pure one in its room; e. g. אִישׁ, אֵשֶׁת; גְּבֶרֶת, גְּבִיר; נְחֹשֶׁת, נְחוּשָׁה; שְׁלֹשֶׁת, שָׁלוֹשׁ, etc.; § 127 Exceptions.

Note. The Fem. Segholate form is usually chosen for the *construct* state; while ה_ is more common in the *absolute* state. In the fem. Inf. and Part., the Segholate ending is the *usual* one. Nouns in Dec. VI. and IX. are not susceptible of fem. Segholate endings. Nouns in Dec. VIII. omit the Daghesh in the double letter, when they assume the Segholate form; e. g. שֵׁשׁ, שֵׁשֶׁת.]

Formation of the Plural.

§ 324. The Hebrew, like the Greek, has three numbers, the *singular, dual,* and *plural.* The plurals of masc.

and fem. nouns are usually, but not always, distinguished by appropriate forms.

§ 325. *Plural masculine.* The plural of masc. nouns is formed, (*a*) Usually by annexing to the singular, (1) ‎ִים. (2) ‎ִם simply, in some words ending in ‎ִי.

E. g. (1) סוּס, plur. סוּסִים. (2) נָכְרִי, נָכְרִים; also as לֵוִי, לְוִיִּם. But the plural ending, as might be expected, is sometimes written *defectively*; as תַּנִּינִים, also תַּנִּינִם, § 63.

(*b*) *The unusual forms of the plural,* are (1) ‎ִין; e. g. מֶלֶךְ, plur. מְלָכִין, Prov. 31: 3. (2) ‎ִי; e. g. חַלּוֹן, חַלּוֹנַי, Jer. 22: 14; גּוֹבַי Nah. 3: 17. (3) Perhaps ‎ִי; e. g. מִן, מֵי, Ps. 45: 9. The forms 1 and 2 coincide with the Chald. and Syr. plurals.

§ 326. *Plural feminine.* The plural of fem. nouns is formed, (*a*) By changing the terminations ‎ָה, ‎ַת, ‎ֶת of the fem. sing. into וֹת, and by corresponding vowel changes.

E. g. תּוֹרָה, plur. תּוֹרוֹת; אִגֶּרֶת, plur. אִגְּרוֹת; טַבַּעַת, plur. טַבָּעוֹת. The ת of the fem. ending sing. is, in a few cases, retained in the plural as if it were a radical; e. g. masc. דַּל, fem. דֶּלֶת, fem. plur. דְּלָתוֹת.

(*b*) By annexing וֹת simply to those feminines, which in the singular have a masc. form; as בְּאֵר, plur. בְּאֵרוֹת, § 320. Note 2.

(*c*) By changing ‎ִית into ‎ִיּוֹת, as עִבְרִית plural עִבְרִיּוֹת; and וּת into ‎ֻיּוֹת, as מַלְכוּת plur. מַלְכֻיּוֹת.

Note. The plurals under *c* appear to be derived from obsolete forms of the sing. in ‎ִיָּה and ‎ֻיָּה. Nouns of these classes sometimes also form their plural after the usual manner; as חֲנִית, plur. חֲנִיתִים and חֲנִיתוֹת; זְנוּת, plur. זְנוּתִים. The plural ending of the fem. form, also, is sometimes written *defectively*; as קְלֹת for קָלוֹת, etc.

HETEROCLITES.

[§ 327. Thus we may, in the manner of the grammarians, name those nouns which specially depart from *usual* analogy. They are of *five* classes. These are,

(1) Such as have a masc. singular, and yet have a plural of the fem. form and masc. gender, e. g. אָב, אָבוֹת, § 322 and the Note ; also such as have a fem. singular, and a plur. of the masc. form and fem. gender, e. g. לְבֵנָה, לְבֵנִים. (2) Such as have two forms of the plural, while the

§§ 328—331. NOUNS; FORMATION OF THE DUAL. 129

gender of both follows that of the singular, e. g. שָׁנָה fem. *a year*, plur. שָׁנִים and שָׁנוֹת fem., § 322. Note. (3) Some nouns have only a plur. form; e. g. פָּנִים, *the face*. (4) Some are found only in the singular; e. g. עוֹף *fowl*, טַף *children*, etc. These have a collective and plur. sense, as well as a sing. one. (5) Some words exhibit (like many in the Arabic) a *pluralis pluralium*, i. e. a plural formed by a second plural in addition to the first one; e. g. בָּמָה *a high place*, plur. בָּמוֹת, *pluralis pluralium* בָּמוֹתִים.]

Formation, use, etc. of the Dual.

§ 328. The dual is usually formed by adding the termination יִם ָ (יִן ָ) to the forms of the singular; e. g. (*a*) To masculines without change. (*b*) To feminines in הָ ָ, after changing the final ה into ת.

E. g. (*a*) יוֹם, יוֹמָיִם. (*b*) יַרְכָּה, יַרְכָתַיִם. In nouns of Dec. VI. the dual ending is appended to the suff. form, as רֶגֶל, רַגְלַיִם; see paradigm.

Note. The dual endings appear, in some few cases, to suffer contraction; e. g. דֹּתָן for דֹּתַיִן, יַרְכָּתָם for יַרְכָּתַיִם; יָדַי for יָדַיִם. These contracted forms are limited mostly to proper names.

§ 329. *Use of the dual.* It is used principally to designate such objects as are double either by nature or by custom.

[E. g. יָדַיִם *the two hands;* נַעֲלַיִם *a pair of shoes*, etc. The names of members of the human body which by nature are double, have also a plural as well as a dual form; but the dual is generally taken in a *literal*, and the plural in a *figurative* sense; as כַּפַּיִם *hands*, כַּפּוֹת *handles*.

Note 1. In a few instances the dual form stands, instead of the plural, for a greater number than two; e. g. שֵׁשׁ כְּנָפַיִם *six wings;* שָׁלֹשׁ שִׁנַּיִם *three teeth*. It hardly needs to be remarked, that the dual is of course essentially plural, requiring a plural verb, adjective, etc. In some cases it is difficult to show the reason of the dual form; as צָהֳרַיִם *mid-day*, etc. Perhaps it is intensive.

Note 2. The words שָׁמַיִם *heavens* and מַיִם *waters*, though apparently dual, are used as plurals.]

§ 330. *Gender of the dual.* It is of *common* gender; and it is found only among nouns, and not among adjectives or participles.

§ 331. The dual ending is sometimes annexed to the plural; e. g. חוֹמוֹת *walls*, dual חֹמֹתַיִם *two walls* etc. Comp. § 327. 5.

DECLENSION OF NOUNS.

Construct state.

§ 332. The Hebrew has no *cases*, in the sense in which we speak of cases in Latin and Greek. But when two nouns come together, the second of which is to be translated as a Genitive, this relation is indicated, contrary to the usual custom of other languages, by some change in the *first* noun (if it be susceptible of change) instead of the second. The first noun so situated, is said to be in *regimen* or in the *construct* state; while any noun not thus placed before a Genitive, is said to be in the *absolute* state.

<small>Two nouns in such a relation, are supposed to be uttered nearly as if they were one word; for which reason the first noun is usually contracted in the utterance, (if it be capable of contraction), so that the stress of voice may be transferred to the second.</small>

Changes of Consonants in declension of Nouns.

§ 333. The *consonants* of the ground-form or absolute state, are modified in *regimen* or the *construct* state as follows; viz.

(a) In all classes of masc. nouns sing. (not having a fem. form, § 320) the const. is like the abs. form as to its *consonants*.

(b) Feminines singular in הָ_ change this ending into תַ_; as יְרָאָה, const. יִרְאַת. Other feminines singular suffer no change of their consonants.

(c) The plur. ending יִם_ and the dual יִם_ become יֵ_; as סוּסִים, const. סוּסֵי; יָדַיִם, const. יְדֵי.

(d) Plurals in וֹת suffer no change in their consonants, in the construct state.

Remark. The *vowels* of words are also affected by regimen or construct state; see § 341 seq.

Suffix state.

§ 334. This is that form of nouns to which are appended or suffixed fragments of pronouns, equivalent in signification to our pronominal adjectives in English.

E. g. סוּס *a horse*, with suffix, סוּסוֹ *his horse*, etc. So קוֹל *voice*, קֹלוֹ *vox ejus*.

§§ 335. 336. NOUNS; SUFFIX STATE.

Note. Pronouns or fragments of pronouns thus suffixed, may be considered as equivalent in general to nouns in the Gen. case, and as putting the noun to which they are suffixed into a kind of regimen or const. state. Frequently the suff. state requires the same vowel-changes as the const. state, but not always; as may be seen by the paradigm of nouns, where both states are exhibited.

§ 335. Most of these suffixes (like those of verbs, § 304 seq.), cause the tone of the word to which they are appended to be moved forward, and of course produce a change in the vowel-points; see § 129 seq.

§ 336. Noun-suffixes (like those of verbs, § 307 seq.) have generally three different forms, adapted to the ending or number of the word to which they are appended.

(a) The most simple form of the suffixes is that in which they begin with a consonant, and are appended to nouns *singular* ending with a *vowel*.

(b) To this form of suffixes is prefixed a *union-vowel*, in which shape they are appended to nouns singular ending with a *consonant*.

(c) The third form of the suffixes is peculiar to nouns *plural*. Here *all* the suffixes take a union-vowel; and all of them, except that of the 1st person sing., insert a Yodh between the union-vowel and the suffix.

[The following table exhibits the suffixes as appended to the various forms of nouns; the first column (a) containing those which are attached to nouns *singular* ending with a *vowel*; the second (b) those which are attached to nouns *singular* ending with a *consonant*; the third (c) exhibiting the suffixes as they are attached to nouns *plural*. Several unusual forms of suffixes are subjoined.

Sing.	(a) Simple form.	(b) With un. vowel, etc.	(c) Suff. to nouns plural.
1. *my*	ִי	ִי	ַי
2 m. *thy*	ךָ, ךָֽ	ךָ ךְָ	ֶיךָ (ֶךָ)
2 f. *thy*	ךְ	ךְ ֵכִי	ַיִךְ ַיְכִי ֵךְ
3 m. *his*	וּ ֵהוּ	וֹ ֵהוּ	ָיו poet. ֵיהוּ
3 f. *her*	ָהּ	ָהּ ֶהָ	ֶיהָ
Pl. 1. *our*	ֵנוּ	ֵנוּ	ֵינוּ
2 m. *your*	כֶם	כֶם	ֵיכֶם
2 f. *your*	כֶן	כֶן	ֵיכֶן
3 m. *their*	הֶם	ָם poet. ֵימוֹ	ֵיהֶם poet. ֵימוֹ
3 f. *their*	הֶן הָן	ָן ֵנָה	ֵיהֶן

Notes.

Note 1. *Unusual suffixes to nouns singular.* SING. SUFF. 2 masc. בְכָה Ps. 139: 5, ־ֶכָה Ps. 10: 14.—2 fem. sing. ־ֵיךְ Ezek. 5: 12, ךְ־ Ezek. 23: 28, ־ֵכִי (for ךְ־) with ה־ parag. Nah. 2: 14, ־ְכִי Ps. 103: 3.—3 fem. ־ָהּ without Mappiq Num. 15: 28, ־ָא Ezek. 36: 5 for ־ָהּ. PLURAL. 1 pers. ־ָנוּ Ruth 3: 2. Job 22: 20.—2 fem. כֶנָה Ezek. 23: 48, 49.—3 masc. ־ֶהֶם 2 Sam. 23: 6.—3 fem. ־ְהֵנָה 1 K. 7: 37.

Note 2. *Unusual suffixes to nouns plural.* SING. SUFF. 3 masc. וֹהִי Ps. 116: 12, Chaldaic.—3 fem. ־ֶיהָא Ezek. 41: 15, for ־ֶיהָ. PLURAL. 2 fem. ־ְיבֶנָה Ezek. 13: 20.—3 masc. ־ְיהֵמָה Ezek. 40: 16.—3 fem. ־ְיהֶנָה Ezek. 1: 11 ; all with ה־ paragogic.

Note 3. The suff. ־ִי joined to a noun ending with י, usually coalesces with it; e. g. גּוֹי *a nation,* גּוֹיִי *my nation;* but sometimes as פְּרָיִי *my fruit.*

Note 4. The sing. forms 3 pers., ־הוּ, ־ָה, ־ָךְ are appended to nouns of Dec. IX. ־מוֹ is parag. for ־ָם , § 125. *c.*

Note 5. ANOMALIES. (1) Yodh in the plur. suff. is sometimes omitted in writing; as דְּרָכֶךָ for דְּרָכֶיךָ , חֶלְבְּהֶן for חֶלְבֵיהֶן, Gen. 4: 4. דְּבָרוּ for דְּבָרָיו, etc.   (2) Sometimes a sing. suff. is attached to a plur. noun; עֲדָתִי for עֵדֹתַי, Ps. 132: 12 ; מַכֹּתְךָ for מַכֹּתֶיךָ, Deut. 28: 59 ; אֲבוֹתָם for אֲבֹתֵיהֶם, etc.   (3) *Vice versâ,* plur. suffixes are sometimes appended to the singular; e. g. תְּחִלָּתֶיךָ for תְּחִלָּתְךָ, בְּנוֹתָיִךְ, *thy building,* for בְּנוֹתָךְ, Inf. noun from בָּנָה, Ezek. 16: 31. Nos. 2 and 3 are doubtless oversights of transcribers.

Remark. The suffixes כֶם, כֶן, הֶם, הֶן, are called *grave,* because they always bring down the *tone* upon them ; while other suffixes are called *light,* because they do not affect the tone uniformly in this manner. With nouns *singular,* they take no union-vowel. With nouns *plural* they have one, *but do not allow it to take the tone.* In all other cases, without exception, the union-vowel takes the tone upon itself. The sing. ךְ takes the tone when preceded by a consonant; and loses it when preceded by a vowel.]

§ 337. Feminines in ה־ָ, in order to receive suffixes, change the final ה־ָ into ת־ַ.

§ 338. Nouns *dual* take the suffixes of nouns plural.

§ 339. The plural and dual, in order to receive suffixes, drop the appropriate endings of the abs. state, and take the suffixes in their place.

E. g. דָּבָר, plur. דְּבָרִים, with suff. דְּבָרֶיךָ, where the ending ־ִים is dropped, and the suffix ־ֶיךָ taken in its room. So קֶרֶן, dual קַרְנַיִם, with suff. מַפַּיִנוּ, dropping ־ַיִם and taking ־ֵינוּ.

§§ 340—342. NOUNS; VOWEL CHANGES. 133

Notes on nouns with suffixes, Par. XXIV.

[§ 340. This paradigm shews the manner in which the suffixes are attached to masc. and fem. nouns. No. I. exhibits the usual suffixes, in connection with a masc. noun ending with a consonant. A fem. noun terminating in a consonant, receives suffixes in the same way. No. II. exhibits the manner in which suffixes are attached to nouns ending with a vowel or quiescent letter. The noun אָב in its abs. state ends, indeed, in a consonant, but it is in this respect irregular. The const. and suff. state has a Yodh, as if from a form אֲבִי ending with a Quiescent. The suffixes are of course of the simple form, i. e. *without* a union-vowel. The plur. of אָב is אָבוֹת; which takes suffixes like the plural of תּוֹרָה.

No. III. exhibits suffixes in connection with a fem. noun. For feminines in ה ָ and ת ַ with suffixes, see § 390 and Dec. XIII. in the paradigm of nouns.]

Changes of vowels in the declension of Nouns.

§ 341. As regimen and the suffix state usually either change the tone of words, or occasion contraction in the method of uttering them, it follows of course that the vowels must be affected by them. But in almost every case of this nature, only the *ultimate* and *penult* vowels are affected.

For the changes in the consonants, see § 333.

§ 342. VOWEL CHANGES. (*a*) When any accession *beginning with a vowel*, by means of declension or suffixes, moves the tone forward *one* place, the *penult* mutable vowel of the ground-form falls away; in nouns, etc. of the form of Dec. VII., the *ultimate* vowel falls away.

E. g. דָּבָר, plur. דְּבָרִים; with suff. דִּבְרֵי, דְּבָרֵנוּ; and so with all the suffixes which are either monosyllabic, or being dissyllabic have the tone on the *penult*. Examples of Dec. VII., where the *final* vowel falls away, are אוֹיֵב, אוֹיְבִים, אוֹיְבֵי, אוֹיְבֵנוּ, etc. See paradigm of nouns, Dec. VII.

Note 1. Nouns of Dec. VI. i. e. *Segholates*, inasmuch as their abs. form is an artificial one (§ 141), assume their original ground-form in order to receive suffixes, or to make the dual; e. g. abs. מֶלֶךְ, with suff. מַלְכִּי, dual מַלְכַּיִם.

(*b*) When the tone is moved forward *one* place, by a syllabic accession *beginning with a consonant*, and when the word is in the const. state. the penult vowel is dropped, and the ultimate one usually shortened.

E. g. (1) By syllabic accession, viz. the grave suffixes (§ 336. Rem.), as דָּבָר, דְּבַרְכֶם. (2) In the const. state; as דְּבַר אֱלֹהִים, *the word of God.* But in Dec. VI. the const. state remains unchanged, on account of the artificial form of the word (supra Note 1). In Dec. VII., words in the const. state for the most part (but not always) remain unchanged; see par. of Dec. VII.

Note 2. The suff. ךָ allows of two different forms in the noun to which it is appended; e. g. (1) It shortens the ultimate vowel; as שֵׁם *name*, שִׁמְךָ *thy name.* (2) It places it in a simple syllable, by combining the final letter of the root in a syllable with itself, and of course it then requires the previous vowel to be long; as דְּבָרְךָ *thy word.*

(c) When the tone is moved forward *two* places, and in the const. state of plur. nouns, both the *ultimate* and *penult* mutable vowels fall away.

E. g. (1) By plur. grave suffixes; as דִּבְרֵיכֶם. (2) By const. state; as דִּבְרֵי הָעָם *the words of the people.* For the mode of supplying *new* vowels, see § 137 seq.

§ 343. All fem. nouns having forms like masc. ones, are declined in the same manner. Besides the usual changes in the *penult* vowel (as in masc. nouns), feminines in הָ ֹ, (1) Before a suffix beginning with a *vowel*, merely change ה into ת. (2) Before a suff. beginning with a consonant they not only change the ה into ת, but also shorten the vowel immediately preceding the ת.

E. g. (1) שָׁנָה, with suff. שְׁנָתוֹ. (2) שְׁנַתְכֶם. Fem. plurals and Segholates follow the analogy of masc. nouns, as to their vowel changes.

General rule respecting plural suffixes.

§ 344. (1) In masc. nouns plural, *light* suffixes are attached to the absolute state abridged; *grave* suffixes (§ 336. Remark) to the construct state. (2) In fem. nouns plural, all the suffixes are attached to the construct state.

DECLENSION OF NOUNS MASCULINE.

First Declension.

§ 345. This comprehends all nouns, whether monosyllabic or pollysyllabic, *whose vowels are all immutable.*

E. g. עִיר, קָם, גֵּר, כְּתָב, אֱבִיוֹן, מַלְכוּת, etc. The single circumstance that the vowels are *immutable,* marks this declension; not the *kind* of vowels, nor the number of syllables. In many cases it is easy to decide whether the vowels are immutable, in others not. Thus in קוֹל, לְבוּשׁ, etc., the vowels are obviously immutable; but the vowels in כְּאֵב, פְּרָשׁ, etc., can be known to be immutable only from a lexicon, or from a knowledge of etymology.

[346. *Notes on the paradigm.* (1) As the vowels are immutable here, additions to the ground-form of course occasion no change. (2) Some few nouns are treated sometimes as belonging here, and at other times as being of Dec. II.; e. g. חָרָשׁ, const. חֲרַשׁ, Dec. II.; but plur. const. חָרָשֵׁי, Dec. I. The lexicons note such. (3) Some few nouns, having וֹ in the abs. state, exchange it for וּ in some of the derived forms; see Par. Dec. I. *c.* also § 127. Except. 1. § 270. *b.* 1. In the Par., *d* presents the manner in which nouns with a final Guttural and Pattahh furtive are declined.]

Second declension.

§ 347. This includes nouns *with final Qamets or Pattahh pure and mutable,* whether monosyllables, or polysyllables with preceding vowels immutable.

§ 348. *Changes.* In the const. state *singular,* before the grave suffixes, and sometimes before ךָ, final Qamets goes into Pattahh, § 342. *b.* In the *plural,* the final vowel falls away in the const. state, and before the grave suffixes, § 342. *c.*

Remarks. (*a*) The penult vowel in nouns of this Dec. being *immutable,* of course it is not affected by either regimen or suffixes. (*b*) Final Qamets is also immutable in many words, although it cannot be distinguished by the mere appearance; e. g. מוֹרָשׁ, plur. const. מוֹרָשֵׁי, etc., of Dec. I. Etymology and the lexicons determine such cases. (*c*) Some nouns with final Qamets mutable belong to Dec. VIII.; e. g. יָם, plur. יַמִּים, etc. The mode of declension, or of appending suffixes, etc., enables the student easily to distinguish cases of this nature.

[§ 349. *Notes on the paradigm.* (1) Under *a,* דְּמְכֶם (for דַּמְכֶם) is *sui generis.* So from יָד *hand,* we have both יֶדְכֶם and יָדְכֶם. (2) Cases like c and d (with final Pattahh) are rare. Only the forms of the *plural* determine the declension to which they belong. (3) Some participles in Niphal from verbs לֹא, seem at first view to belong here; but they drop their Qamets in the plural, e. g. נִטְמָאִים, instead of נְטֻמָּאִים; and such forms of participles as נִטְמָאִים probably have a ground-form like נִטְמָא.]

Third declension.

§ 350. This comprises all nouns which have *an immutable vowel in the final syllable, and Qamets or Tseri pure and mutable in the penult.*

§ 351. *Changes.* Out of the abs. state, the mutable vowel of the penult falls away.

Remarks. (a) Polysyllabic nouns, like כִּלָּיוֹן, etc., belong here, as well as dissyllabic ones. (b) In many cases, the penult vowel is *apparently* mutable, but *really* immutable; e. g. בְּרִיחַ = בָּרִיחַ, Dec. I. The lexicons, etymology, and declension, determine cases of this nature. Sometimes they are quite unexpected; as in גָּלוּת, חָזוּת, etc., with Qamets impure.

[§ 352. *Notes on the paradigm.* (1) Such nouns as the examples in *d* and *e*, more generally omit the Daghesh forte in the const. state, etc. as in the Par.; but they sometimes retain it, as the nouns in smaller print show. (2) The Seghol under ח in const. חֶזְיוֹן, is occasioned by the Guttural; so עֶשְׂרֹנִים, etc. But ע also takes Hhireq short, as const. עִצְּבוֹן. (3) As to exchanging Hholem for Shureq in *f*, see § 346. 3. § 127. 1. (4) In *g*, the Tseri under א in the sing. is immutable, only because it is a supposititious euphonic vowel, § 119. *d.* 2; the plur. is regular. The word, however, can scarcely be considered as really belonging to Dec. III. (5) In *h*, the short form in the const. state (גְּדָל- *gɛdhŏl*) is rare, § 127. 3. It is used only before a Maqqeph. (6) In such rare cases as מָדוֹן plur. מִדְיָנִים, it is probable that the ground-form of the plural is מִדְיָן; only the singular properly belongs to Dec. III. (7) A very few nouns fluctuate between Dec. I. and III.; e. g. סָרִיס, const. סְרִיס, as of Dec. III.; but plur. סָרִיסִים, as of Dec. I.]

Fourth declension.

§ 353. This includes *all dissyllabic nouns with Qamets pure in the ultimate, and Qamets or Tseri pure in the penult.*

§ 354. *Changes.* (a) Out of the ground-form the penult vowel always falls away. (b) In the const. sing., before the grave suffixes, and sometimes before ךָ, the *final*

Qamets shortens into Pattahh, § 342. b. (c) In the plur. const. and before the plur. grave suffixes, both the vowels of the ground-form fall away (§ 342. c), and then a new vowel, viz. Hhireq or Pattahh, is inserted, § 137. § 138.

[§ 355. *Notes on the paradigm.* (1) The vowels here as in other cases often present an ambiguous appearance. The lexicons will determine their nature. (2) The examples *c, d, e,* conform to the principles of pointing Gutturals, § 138. § 139. In *e,* however, the const. and suff. plur. conform to the analogy of other consonants, in the first vowel; as the Gutturals sometimes do. (3) So, on the contrary, other letters sometimes conform to the usage of Gutturals; e. g. const. and suff. plur. of כָּנָף in *f,* with a Pattahh for the first vowel. (4) Nouns of the form *g,* derivates of לֹא, belong in general to Dec. III., having the final אָ‎ immutable. But in some few cases, like צָבָא, the final Qamets is dropped in the const. and suff. plural; in which case they are of Dec. IV. (5) Cases like *h* and *i,* with a const. Segholate form, are not frequent in this declension; yet they occur often enough to demand a distinct recognition.]

Fifth declension.

§ 356. This comprehends dissyllabic nouns, *with Tseri pure in the ultimate and Qamets pure in the penult.*

§ 357. *Changes.* The vowel-changes follow the analogy of Dec. IV., even in the const. and suffix forms.

[§ 358. *Notes on the paradigm.* (1) This declension might have been ranked with Dec. IV.; but I conform to the present usage. (2) The Segholate forms of the sing. const. in *c* and *d,* are like those in *h, i,* of Dec. IV. (3) The assumption of Pattahh in the const. sing., and before the grave suffixes, etc., is *peculiar* to this declension, and can be accounted for only by the near relation of the vowels Pattahh and Seghol. (4) Derivates of לֹא (like מָלֵא) which apparently belong here, have a Tseri immutable and belong to Dec. III. The same is the case with a considerable number of other nouns and participials; e. g. יָנֵק, יָפֵחַ, יָשֵׁן, חָפֵץ, אָבֵל, שָׂבֵחַ, שָׂמֵחַ, etc., all of Dec. III., having their Tseri immutable. (5) A few words fluctuate between Dec. III. and Dec. V.; e. g. עֵקֶב, const. עֵקֶב, Dec. III.; but. plur. const. עִקְבֵי, Dec. V.]

Sixth declension.

§ 359. This comprises dissyllabic nouns, *which have the tone on the penult and a furtive vowel in the final syllable.*

In other words, this declension includes all Segholate nouns of two syllables; excepting a few nouns and Infinitives with the fem. Segholate endings הָ֫‎, הֶ֫‎, which belong to Dec. XII. The furtive vowel of the final syllable is Seghol, Pattahh, or short Hhireq, § 141.

Note. All Segholate forms are *factitious* and merely *euphonic*. They appear only in the abs. and const. states of the singular; for all nouns of this species, when they receive an accession, neglect the furtive vowel and develope their original state, which is a monosyllable ending with two consonants; as מֶ֫לֶךְ‎, original form מַלְךְ‎, with suff. מַלְכּוֹ‎, etc.

§ 360. *Changes.* (*a*) The const. sing. is generally the same as the absolute. (*b*) The suffixes of the singular are usually appended to the *original* form of the noun. (*c*) The plur. absolute assumes a form like that of nouns belonging to Dec. IV. (*d*) In the plur. const., and before the grave suffixes, the penult vowel of the plur. abs. is dropped, and the *original* vowel of the ground-form in the first syllable is restored.

Note. The plur. abs. of this declension is quite anomalous, and cannot be derived from either the original or factitious form of the singular, by any of the usual laws of declension.

§ 361. The *original* vowel of the monosyllabic ground-forms is *pure in all cases*, and mostly short. It is either of the *A, E,* or *O* class; as (1) מַלְךְ‎. (2) סִפְר, סֵפֶר‎. חֵלֶק‎. (3) קֹדֶשׁ, קֹדֶשׁ, קֹדְשׁ‎. In the *factitious* forms, the original vowel (if not of the *O* class) is mostly changed into Seghol by the influence of the furtive vowel, § 142. *d.*

§ 362. Segholate nouns may be divided into *three* classes, according to the original vowels of their ground-forms; and may be called Segholates of the *A, E,* or *O* class.

[§ 363. *Notes on the paradigm of the* A *class.* (1) All these having Pattahh under their first radical for their original vowel, assume it in the suff. state, § 360. *b.* (2) The examples *b, c,* shew the manner in which the Gutturals influence the form of these Segholates, § 141. (3) The const. form in *c,* viz. זָרַע‎ (like that of Dec. V.), is not usual.

(4) A few words belonging here, retain the *original* ground-form; e. g. גֵּיא, שָׁוְא, אֹרֶךְ‎ (not אֲרֶךְ‎), etc.]

[§ 364. *Notes on the* E *class.* (1) In such cases as *d, f, h*, we might naturally expect that the Tseri would be changed into Seghol, § 142. *d;* but Tseri often appears in the first syllable. (2) The examples *f, g*, exhibit the influence of ע Guttural; the example *h*, that of the final Guttural. Sometimes, however, Hhireq short is used in the const. and suff. plural of words Pe Guttural, like חִקְרֵי from חֵקֶר. (3) The student must not fail to note, that although such nouns as קֶבֶר, חֶלֶד, etc., exhibit in the abs. state the same appearance as those of the *A* class, viz. מֶלֶךְ; yet in the suff. state the difference in the *original* vowels is at once discerned; e. g. קִבְרִי, קֶבֶר, but מַלְכִּי, מֶלֶךְ, etc.
(4) *Original* forms are sometimes found here; as חֻטְא, נֵרְדְּ, etc. *Remark.* Some nouns, by usage, are treated as belonging both to the *A* and *E* classes; e. g. הֶדֶר, יֶלֶד, etc. see Lex.]

[§ 365. *Notes on the* O *class.* (1) The examples *i, j,* exhibit Qamets Hhateph (in the suff. state), which corresponds to the Hholem of the abs. state, and from which this Hholem is derived. (2) In *k*, the influence of ע Guttural is seen. For the form of the suff. state פָּעָלְכֶם *pŏ-ŏl-khĕm,* see § 140. Sometimes this form appears without a Guttural; e. g. קָטְבְךָ, from קֶטֶב, etc. (3) In *l,* a comp. Sheva is assumed under the first radical, in the plur. abs. and plur. light suff. state; an occurrence very rare among nouns of this class.
ANOMALIES. The nouns שֹׁרֶשׁ, קֹדֶשׁ, אֹהֶל, exhibit some anomalies in regard to their vowels; plur. שָׁרָשִׁים *shŏ-rā-shīm,* קָדָשִׁים *qŏ-dā-shīm,* אֹהָלִים, etc. Also בֹּצֶן, נֹגַהּ, נֹכַח, have anomalous plurals; see the Lex. on these words.
An *original* form here is קֹשְׁטְ.]

[§ 366. *Segholates of verbs* עוּ *and* עִי. (*a*) Those of the A class have two forms, viz. with middle ו (as in *m, n*), which out of the abs. state quiesces in Shureq or Hholem, as in the examples; or with middle י (as in *o, p*), which out of the abs. state quiesces in Tseri or Hhireq. The forms like תָּוֶךְ, מָוֶת, with Qamets for a penult vowel without the influence of an accent, are *sui generis*, and belong only to Segholates with middle ו in proper Hebrew nouns. Some of the forms, like עַיִר, have a regular plural.
(*b*) Those of the E class all belong to Dec. I., and quiesce in Tseri or Hhireq; as בִּין, דִּין, etc., the Segholate form not being admissible here.
(*c*) Those of the O class all quiesce in Hholem or Shureq in the *singular,* which belongs to Dec. I.; as *q, r.* But the plur. is occasionally regular; as in these examples. The form דוּד is equivalent to דָוֶד, and שׁוּר=שַׁוָּר.]

[§ 367. *Segholates derived from verbs* לֹה, imitate the Inf. Segholates. The root of verbs לֹה is properly לֹי or לֹו, § 280. Hence, as neither י nor ו at the end of a word will bear a furtive vowel before them (§ 120. *b*), so that we cannot write פֶּרֱי, בֹּהֱוּ, the form of the word is changed so as to accommodate the nature of the final י or ו, i. e. the Inf. Segholate form is chosen, and the final vowel becomes homogeneous with the Quiescent, § 117. 1. The examples *s—w* exhibit the modes of declining these peculiar nouns. They appear all of them to belong to the *E* or *O* class of Segholates. The paradigm exhibits the change which a pause-accent produces upon them. The examples *u, v, w*, exhibit the regular plurals which they occasionally form.

Note. The final quiescent י and ו here, do *not* make their vowel *immutable*. The general law of the vowel yields here to the law which respects the form of the noun in the suff. and plur. state. Forms like בֹּהֱוּ=בֹּהוּ, are not found in the suff. or plur. state, in our present Hebrew.]

[§ 368. *Infinitive Segholaies.* So I would choose to call such as are *monosyllabic* in their ground-form, with the vowel after the second radical; which is the established form of the Inf. construct, so often employed as a mere noun. The class of simple nouns with such forms as בְּאֵר, שֶׁכֶם, דְּבַשׁ, is not large; but the Inf. forms of this kind are very numerous, and the majority of them take a Hholem, as קְטֹל. The examples *x, y, z*, exhibit the mobes of declining *nouns* of this sort; *yy* and *zz*, the method of declining the const. Infinitives. See also in Par. XXII. the Inf. with suffixes, etc.

Note. The reason of classing these nouns and Inf. forms among the Segholates, is, that in the suff. state, etc., they conform altogether to the model of Segholates.]

[§ 369. *Anomalous plurals of Segholates.* Of these there are a number, which in the plur. absolute take in the first syllable the vowel appropriate to the plur. construct; e. g. עֲשָׂר, עֲשָׂרִים instead of עֲשָׂרִים; so שֶׁבַע, שְׁבָעִים; שְׁלַיִים, שְׁלָוִים; דְּלָיִו for דְּלָיָו. Forms like שִׁקְמִים for שִׁקְמִים; חֲבָנִים for חֲבָיִים, etc., sometimes occur.

Note. In the plur. construct, Daghesh forte *euphonic* is not unfrequent; as חַלְקֵי for חַלְקֵי, עִשְּׂבוֹת for עִשְׂבוֹת, § 77. Some other singularities of particular words are noticed in the lexicons.]

[§ 370. *Segholates with a paragogic* הָ. This is appended, like the light suffixes, to the original form of the word; e. g. אֶרֶץ, אַרְצָה; שֶׁכְמָה, שְׁכֶם; לַיְלָה, לָיִל; קָדְמָה, קֶדֶם, etc., the tone uniformly remaining on the penult.]

Seventh declension.

§ 371. This comprises *nouns with Tseri pure* (in a few cases with Hholem pure), *which are either monosyllabic, or have the preceding vowels immutable.*

§ 372. *Changes.* (*a*) The const. singular is generally like the absolute; in a few cases it exchanges final *Tseri* for *Pattahh*. (*b*) In case of accession, the final Tseri (and the Hholem also) *generally* falls away; except in the plur. abs. of monosyllabic words. (*c*) Before suffixes beginning with a consonant and taking the tone, the final Tseri is shortened into Hhireq, Pattahh, or Seghol, according to the nature of the word.

[§ 373. *Notes on the paradigm.* (1) This declension includes most of the *active* participles in their masc. forms, which are declined like *b, c*. The Part. of verbs ל Gutt., are declined like *d*. (2) The forms like *d, e*, with Pattahh final (instead of Tseri) in the const. state, are not confined to nouns ל Guttural, but appear in several other nouns; e. g. מִסְפָּד, const. מִסְפַּד. It is peculiar here, that a number of nouns which take a final Pattahh in regimen, throw away the preceding Pattahh in such a case, and take a Hhireq; e. g. מַפְתֵּחַ, מִפְתַּח מַרְבֵּץ, מִרְבַּץ, etc. Probably this is in order to avoid two Pattahhs in mixed syllables, in immediate succession. (4) The case *e* presents Seghol before the consonant-suffix כֶם. etc.; as in some few cases is the usage. (5) The final Tseri in this Dec. is not unfrequently retained, in the plur. absolute, as though it were immutable. Usually it is retained in monosyllabic words, as in the example *g*. Comp. § 358. 4.

(6) Some nouns, as בַּר, זָן, מַת (obs. root), lose their vowel in the suff. state and when they receive an accession, as if they belonged to this declension; e. g. בְּרִי, זָנִים, מְתִים.

(7) But few nouns which have final Hholem pure, are inflected in the manner of this declension; e. g. אֶשְׁכֹּל, plur. אֶשְׁכְּלוֹת; קָדְקֹד, suff. קָדְקֳדוֹ. Peculiar is plur. בָּמוֹת, *plur. pluralium* בָּמֳתֵי.]

Eighth declension.

§ 374. This includes all nouns *which insert Daghesh forte in the final letter of the ground-forms when they receive an accession.*

§ 375. *Changes.* (*a*) The construct state is generally

§ 376. NOUNS; DEC. VIII.

the same as the absolute ; but before Maqqeph, ultimate long vowels are shortened. (*b*) Any accession causes the Daghesh forte of the final letter to appear; and if such accession takes the accent, the final long vowel (when pure) of the ground-form is shortened. (*c*) Penultimate vowels, if mutable, conform to the rules in § 242 seq.

The following classes of words fall under this declension.

(*a*) Nouns derived from verbs עֵע ; as חֹק, עֹז, דַּל, חָן, etc.; and also the participles of these verbs in Niphal, Hiphil, and Hophal. (*b*) Other words in which the penult letter is dropped, or assimilated to the final one; as לֵב for לֵבָב ; Inf. תֵּת for תֶּנֶת, etc. (*c*) Some words which are primitive or are derived from a Pilel form of verbs; as גָּמָל, מָגֵן, etc.

[§ 376. *Notes on the paradigm.* (1) In *a, b, c,* the const. state is generally with Pattahh. In a few cases where the ground-form is as יָם, Qamets is retained. (2) In *c* the exchange of Pattahh for Hhireq in the suff. state, e. g. בַּד, מִדִּי, is peculiar, and is found in but few cases. (3) In *d* the Tseri sometimes goes into Pattahh ; כַּזּוּ, כֵּן; עִתִּי, עֵת, but with ה‍ָ parag. עַתָּה. In like manner Seghol goes into Hhireq short; as כַּרְמִלּוֹ, כַּרְמֶל. (4) In *e, f,* the short vowels may be either short *u* or *o,* § 128. *b.* (5) Polysyllabic nouns regulate their ultimate and penult syllables in conformity with the laws of other declensions ; as in the cases *g, h,* the former with a *pure* penult vowel, the latter with an *impure* one. (6) Nouns of the forms in *i,* make the const. in ‍ִי, except in the phrase חַי יְהוָֹה. Nouns in ‍ִי double the Yodh; as לֵוִי, לְוִיִּים.

Note 1. When the final letter is a Resh or a Guttural and cannot be doubled, the compensation for Daghesh excluded is as usual ; see § 112. This brings the words in question within other declensions; e. g. שֹׁר, const. שֹׁר, with light suff. שֹׁרִי (for שַׁהְרִי § 112), plur. שְׁוָרִים, const. שָׂרֵי etc. with Qamets immutable, i. e. the sing. belongs to Dec. II. *c, d,* and the plur. to Dec. I. So לַח, const. לַח, with suff. לַחִי, plur. לַחִים (for לַחִים § 112), belongs to Dec. I., the vowel throughout being immutable.

Note. 2. A few nouns belong to this declension in some of their forms, and to other declensions in others; e. g. מַעֲדַנִּים, אֵת, etc.; for which, see the lexicons.]

General Remark. Nouns of *various* declensions as to their *vowels,* belong to this declension. It is only the doubling of the *final consonant,* which makes the peculiarity of it. The vowel-changes are all governed by laws, belonging to the general principles adopted respectively in other declensions.

Ninth declension.

§ 377. This comprises *all those words ending in* הָ‑, *which are derived from verbs* לָ"ה.

§ 378. *Changes.* (*a*) In the const. singular, final Seghol is changed to Tseri. (*b*) With suffixes, etc., the ending הָ‑ is dropped. (*c*) Penultimate vowels, if mutable, conform to the usual rules respecting the vowel-changes.

[§ 379. *Notes on the paradigm.* (1) It is only the final ending הָ‑ which characterises this declension. The penult vowel may be *immutable*, as in *a;* or *mutable*, as in *b.* It is treated according to the general laws of the vowel changes. (2) With suffixes, these nouns imitate the verbs from which they are derived, and throw away their final consonant and vowel, as in *a, b.* (3) The const. vowel Tseri, (*longer* than the Seghol of the ground-form), is altogether a peculiarity in the phenomena of declension.

NOUNS FEMININE.

Tenth declension.

§ 380. This includes *all nouns with the feminine ending* הָ‑ *and the preceding vowels immutable.*

§ 381. *Changes.* In the const. state הָ‑ becomes תַ‑; before suffixes it becomes תְ‑ or תָ‑. The plural is usually וֹת.

[§ 382. *Notes on the paradigm.* (1) In regard to the fem. ending הָ‑ in the abs. state; although its vowel coalesces with a Quiescent, and on general grounds would be immutable, yet in this case the law of the vowels yields to the demands of case or relation, i. e. a change of the vowel is effected by a more imperious law, which requires a change in order to designate the relation in which the noun in question may stand to other parts of the sentence connected with it. (2) The reader will see that Qamets is retained under the penult letter, whenever it stands in a simple syllable ; according to § 130.

Eleventh declension.

§ 383. This comprehends *all nouns with the fem. ending* הָ‑ *and a mutable Qamets or Tseri in the penult syllable.*

§ 384. *Changes.* These are the same as in Dec. X; except that here, the vowel of the penult being mutable, it falls away in the const. state and before suffixes.

[§ 385. *Notes on the paradigm.* (1) The cases *a, b,* simply follow the analogy of Dec. X., with the exception, that the penult vowel undergoes the mutations which the general laws of declension demand. (2) In *c, d, e,* after the penult vowel falls away, there would remain two Shevas at the beginning of a syllable; which being impossible, a new vowel arises, agreeably to §§ 137, 138. (3) Many nouns of Dec. XI. as to the *absolute* state, conform out of this altogether to Dec. XIII; so that only the abs. state belongs to Dec. XI., and all the rest to Dec. XIII. Such are *f, g;* and such are many which are noted in the lexicons.]

[§ 386. *Remarks.* (1) Many fem. nouns apparently belong here, but in reality to Dec. I., because the *penult* vowel is immutable; e. g. אָלָה, תְּלָאָה, גְּזֵלָה, בְּרָכָה, etc.; all such a good lexicon notes.

(2) A few nouns (by usage) are employed as belonging both to Dec. X. and XI.; e. g. יָפָה, const. יְפַת, with suff. יָפָתִי, Dec. X.; so נְבֵלָה, with suff. נְבֵלָתִי, Dec. X., but commonly the const. is as נִבְלַת, with suff. נִבְלָתוֹ, etc. The lexicon should designate such.]

Twelfth declension.

§ 387. This includes *all those fem. nouns in* הָ which *are derived from Segholates of Dec. VI.*

The feminine ending is attached to the original masc. form of the Segholate, as מֶלֶךְ, original form מַלְךְ, fem. מַלְכָּה; so that these nouns have the appearance of belonging to Dec. X.

§ 388. *Changes.* Nouns belonging here are declined exactly like those of Dec. X. in the *singular;* but the *plural* conforms to the model of the plurals in Dec. VI.

[389. *Notes on the paradigm.* (1) The example *a* is a derivate of the *A* class of Segholates; *b, c,* of the *E* class; *d,* of the *O* class. (2) The form in *e* exhibits the effects of Ayin Guttural upon the vowel-points of a word.

Remark. There is a number of nouns which in appearance belong to this declension, e. g. מַרְאָה, מִצְוָה, etc., but which in reality belong to Dec. X. The plural at once distinguishes them; e. g. plur. מִצְוֹת, not מְצָווֹת, etc. as it would be in Dec. XII.]

Thirteenth declension.

§ 390. This includes all fem. Segholates in תֶ֫ and תָ֫;
i. e. *all those which have the tone on the penult and a furtive vowel in the final syllable.*

The furtive vowel here is Seghol or Pattahh; and as it is *factitious*, it appears only in the abs. and const. state. The *original* vowel reappears, as in Dec. VI., whenever the word receives any accession. All fem. Infinitives and participles in הֶ֫ or הַ֫, fall under this declension.

§ 391. *Changes.* The sing. number is declined as in Dec. VI. The plur. absolute is quite anomalous, sometimes dropping the original final vowel of the groundform, and sometimes retaining it.

[§ 392. *Notes on the paradigm.* (1) The example *a* exhibits the manner of Segholates belonging to the *A* class; *b, c,* those of the *E* class; *d, e,* those of the *O* class, whose short vowel may be short *o* or *u*. (2) The fem. Inf. const. forms are declined as in *f, g, h.*

Remark. Some nouns of the *E* class take Pattahh in the syllable which precedes a suffix; e. g. יוֹנַקְתִּי, יוֹנַקְתְּ ; Inf. form, שָׁבְתִּי, שִׁבְתָּם, Ps. 23: 6.]

NOUNS OF THE DUAL NUMBER.

[§ 393. These are exhibited in Par. XXVII. (*a*) From the paradigm it appears, that the *construct* state of the dual is the same as that of the plur. masc. in יִם֫ . To this form the grave suffixes are attached, as in the plural; see § 344. (*b*) The dual in general causes the same contraction of the vowels of the sing. ground-form, as the plural; but in Dec. VI., the contraction is still greater; e. g. בֶּ֫רֶךְ, dual בִּרְכַּ֫יִם; the plur. would be בְּרָכִים.

Note. There are but a few nouns of the *dual* form. Dec. IX. exhibits none. Of those that actually occur, some have no *singular;* others have no *construct* form. The nouns שָׁמַ֫יִם and מַ֫יִם are of the dual form, but are used as *plurals.*]

ANOMALOUS NOUNS.

[§ 394. Such are בַּ֫יִת, אִשָּׁה, אָמָה, אִישׁ, אָחוֹת, אֶחָד, אָח, אָב, רֹאשׁ, פֶּה, עִיר, מַ֫יִם, כְּלִי, יוֹם, חָם, בַּת, בֵּן; the peculiar derivative forms of which the lexicon exhibits.]

NUMBERS.

[§ 395. *Cardinal numbers.* (*a*) From 1 to 10 the forms of cardinal numbers have the distinction of gender, and generally also that of the abs. and const. states. From 3 to 10 however, the primitive forms are of the *fem.* gender; while the derivative forms (in הָ‎ and תָ‎) are of the *masc.* gender.

(*b*) From 11 to 19, the cardinal numbers are of a *compound* form, i. e. they are made up by joining the word עָשָׂר‎ in the masc., and עֶשְׂרֵה‎ in the fem., to the units. These numerals thus formed have no const. state, but are put in apposition with other nouns, or are used adverbially.

Note. The words עָשָׂר‎ and עֶשְׂרֵה‎ are found only in the above connections, and are evidently derived from עֶשֶׂר‎ *ten;* somewhat like the termination *-teen* for *ten*, in the English *thirteen, fourteen,* etc.

(*c*) From 20 to 90, the cardinal numbers are the *plural* forms of the corresponding *units;* except that the form for 20, is the plural of the form for 10. All these are of common gender, and have no const. state.

Note. When intermediate units are to be expressed, they may either precede or follow the tens; as שִׁבְעִים וְשֶׁבַע‎=שֶׁבַע וְשִׁבְעִים‎ =77.

(*d*) *Hundreds* are expressed by the plural of the word מֵאָה‎ preceded by the nine units; *thousands*, by the plural of אֶלֶף‎ with the same units; *ten thousands* in a similar manner by the forms of רִבּוֹ‎, רְבָבָה‎ or רִבּוֹא‎; see in the Par. under D. E.

Note. In expressing a sum of *hundreds*, with intervening *tens* and *units*, the smaller numbers may either precede or follow the hundreds; as שְׁנָה וּמֵאָה שָׁנָה וְשִׁשִּׁים שְׁתַּיִם‎=162 *years*, Gen. 5: 18; or שְׁלֹשׁ מֵאוֹת שִׁבְעִים וּשְׁנַיִם‎=372, Ezra 2: 4. The latter mode prevails in the later Hebrew.

In expressing *thousands* with intervening smaller numbers, the former are placed first; as שְׁמֹנַת אֲלָפִים חֲמֵשׁ מֵאוֹת וּשְׁמֹנִים‎=8580. Num. 4: 48.]

[§ 396. *Ordinal numbers.* The ordinal numbers extend only from *two* to *ten.* Beyond this last number, and sometimes also below it, the *cardinal* numbers are used as ordinals.

The ordinals are derived from the cardinals by annexing to them the termination יִ‎. Most of them likewise insert יִ‎ before the final letter of the ground-form.

Note. The ordinals sometimes have a fem. form in ית‎, and sometimes in יָה‎. In this shape, they are commonly employed to denote *part;* as עֲשִׂירִית‎, *the tenth part.*]

[§ 397. *Notes on the paradigm.* (1) The class *A* exhibits the usual forms of the cardinals from *one* to *ten*. The fem. אַחַת is for אֶחְדֶת. The form שְׁנַיִם is dual, as if from שֵׁן; the fem. שְׁתַּיִם (for שִׁנְתַיִם) is also dual, as from an obsolete root שָׁנָה. The Daghesh in שְׁתַּיִם is regarded as Daghesh lene, or rather as a Daghesh compensative for the נ which is dropped. (2) There is a dual form of masc. cardinals, which is used adverbially; as שִׁבְעָתַיִם *sevenfold*, Gen. 4: 15, 24, etc. אַרְבַּעְתַּיִם *fourfold*, 2 Sam. 12: 6. (3) The plurals of some of these forms likewise appear; as אֲחָדִים, Gen. 27: 44; עֶשְׂרוֹת *tens*, Ex. 18: 21, 25, etc. (4) A few of these cardinals are also found with suffixes; as שְׁנֵינוּ, *both of us*; שְׁלָשְׁתְּכֶם, *ye three*, quasi *trias vestrûm*.

(5) The class *B* presents the forms of cardinals from *eleven* to *nineteen*. Those for *eleven* and *twelve* have *two* forms; and שְׁנֵים and שְׁתֵּים coincide with the Aramaean dual. The form שְׁמֹנַת עָשָׂר, *eighteen*, occurs once, Judg. 20: 25.]

[§ 398. *Method of notation.* The Hebrews made use of the letters of the alphabet, in order to denote numbers. Like the Greeks, they divided the letters (including the final ones) into three classes; of which the first denoted *units*, the second *tens*, the third *hundreds*. After 400 the *final* letters were sometimes employed, as in the paradigm. To express thousands and higher numbers, they began the alphabet anew, placing two dots over each letter. When more than one letter was employed, the accent called *Garshayim* or *double Geresh* was sometimes used to mark them as numerals. In designating *composite* numbers, the letters which represent the larger numbers are placed *first*; as חכט = 429; דתצח = 4898; אתלא = 1831.

Note. *Fifteen* is denoted by טו = 9+6 = 15; never by יה, because this last is the contraction for the word יְהֹוָה.]

ADJECTIVES.

§ 399. Hebrew adjectives have no peculiar and appropriate forms, but *only* such as are common to nouns. The fem. form of the adjective is derived from the masculine in the same manner as the fem. nouns, § 323. The dual number does not occur here.

<small>Whatever has been said of the forms of *nouns*, in the preceding sections, applies also to *adjectives*; so that the latter do not need to be treated of separately.</small>

Note. Comparison in adjectives is formed by *periphrasis*, for which see § 454 seq. The const. state of adjectives appears most frequently when they are used as nouns, or with a noun understood; as יִשְׁרֵי־לֵב *the upright of heart*, Ps. 6: 11.

PARTICLES.

§ 400. Under the general appellation of *particles*, are comprehended *adverbs, prepositions, conjunctions,* and *interjections*.

§ 401. Like nouns, some of these are *primitive*, but most of them *derivative*. Of the derivates some have an ending appropriated solely to the form of particles, as אָמְנָם, *truly* from אֹמֶן *truth;* while most retain the form of verbs, nouns, or pronouns.

Note 1. *Compound* words are more frequent among particles, than among the leading parts of speech. *Apocope* is also more common; all the prepositions, etc. which consist of only one letter, being doubtless apocopated words; as לְ for אֶל, מְ for מִן, etc.

Note 2. The older grammarians have, for the most part, considered all the particles as *derivative* nouns; but this is hardly probable, as primitives are found in all other parts of speech. It is, however, very difficult to draw the exact line between the primitive and derivative forms, as the etymology is often much obscured by the changes which the particles have undergone.

ADVERBS.

[§ 402. Some *derivative* adverbs have appropriate endings; e. g. (*a*) In ־ָם; as אָמְנָם *truly*, from אֹמֶן *truth*. (*b*) In ־ֹם; as פִּתְאֹם *suddenly*, from פֶּתַע *the wink of an eye*. (*c*) In ־ִית; as שֵׁנִית, *a second time*. (*d*) In ־ַי; אֲזַי, from אָז *then*.]

[§ 403. Many derivative adverbs have the forms of other parts of speech; e. g. (*a*) Of nouns with a preposition; as לְפָנִים *before*, מַעְלָה *upwards*, etc. (*b*) Of nouns in the Accusative, either sing. or plural; as sing. בֶּטַח *securely*, plur. מֵישָׁרִים *uprightly*. Some of these forms are no longer used as nouns; as אַיִן *not*. (*c*) Of adjectives; as masc. טוֹב *well*, fem. מְהֵרָה *quickly*, plur. נוֹרָאוֹת *fearfully*, in the const. state רַבַּת *much*. These are used in a neuter sense, like *multum, πόλλα,* etc. (*d*) Of the Inf. absolute, especially in Hiphil; as עוֹד *again* literally *redeundo,* הַרְבֵּה *much* lit. *multiplicando,* הַשְׁכֵּם *early*. Sometimes with a preposition; as לָרוֹב *abundantly*. (*e*) Of pronouns; as זֶה *here*, מָה *how*, etc.]

[§ 404. Some adverbs are compounded of other words. (*a*) Of prepositions and adverbs; as עַל־כֵּן *wherefore*, עַד־אָנָה *how long?* (*b*) Of two adverbs; as אֵיפֹה *where*, from אֵי and פֹּה, etc.]

[§ 405. Several adverbs receive after them *verbal* suffixes; in which connection the suffixes are generally in the Nom. case; e. g. עוֹדֶנִּי *I* [am] *yet*, עוֹדֶנּוּ *he* [is] *yet;* אֵינֶנּוּ *he* [is] *not;* אַיּוֹ *where* [is] *he?* Gen. 3: 9, אַיֶּכָּה (for אַיֶּךָ) *where* [art] *thou?* The suffixes are usually those with an epenthetic Nun, which belong to the Fut. tense.]

PREPOSITIONS.

[§ 406. Four prepositions, בְּ, כְּ, לְ, מִ, (·מִ), consisting of only one letter, are united with the words which they govern. Probably they are all derivates of roots which were of a more complete form. This is certain as to מִ (which comes from מִן), and probable as to the others; see the articles in the lexicon. For the various vowel pointing of these prepositions, see § 152. *b*.

[§ 407. Derivative prepositions making words by themselves, (and most of them are of this kind), have the forms of other parts of speech; viz. (*a*) Of nouns sing. in the Acc. case, or const. state; as יַעַן *causâ, on account of,* נֶגֶד, *before,* תַּחַת, *under,* etc. (*b*) Of nouns plural in the const. or suff. state; as אֶל, *to, for,* אֱלֵי poetic; מִן, מִנֵּי, etc. Several prepositions take suffixes of such a form as are usually attached to the plural, as well as such as are attached to the singular; as תַּחַת, תַּחְתַּי, תַּחְתָּיו, but also with sing. suff. תַּחְתָּם; so אֵלָיו, *to him*, etc. In like manner עַל *upon*, plur. const. עֲלֵי poetic, with suff. עָלַי, עָלֶיךָ, עֲלֵיכֶם. (*c*) Of nouns in the const. state with prefix-prepositions; as בְּיַד *by*, לִפְנֵי *before*, etc. (*d*) Of adverbs with prefix-prepositions; as לְבִלְתִּי, בְּאֵין *without*, מֵאָז *since*, etc. (*e*) Of adverbs followed by a preposition, so as to denote but one idea; as סָבִיב לְ *around*, מֵעַל לְ *above*, חוּץ מִן *without*, etc. (*f*) Of a double preposition; as מֵעִם *from with*, מִבֵּין *between*, אֶל תַּחַת *under;* like the French *d'aupres, de chez*. (*g*) Of a paragogic letter or suffix, viz. ה ָ *towards, to;* as סְדֹמָה *towards Sodom*, אַרְצָה *to the ground*, etc. So also ה ֵ and ה ִ, in a few cases; as סְוֵנֵה *to Syene,* Ezek. 29: 10; נֹבֶה *to Nob,* 1 Sam. 21: 2.

Note. Prepositions take *noun-suffixes*, in the manner of both sing. and plur. nouns; very seldom are *verbal-suffixes* appended to them, like בַּעֲדֵנִי, תַּחְתֶּנָּה, תַּחְתֵּנִי, etc.]

[§ 408. Several prepositions and particles are united with the pronouns in a peculiar way. The following table exhibits a view of these peculiarities.

§§ 408. 409. PREPOSITIONS—CONJUNCTIONS.

מִן	כְּ (כְּמוֹ)	לְ	בְּ
מִמֶּנִּי } מִמֶּנִּי	כָּמוֹנִי	לִי	בִּי
מִמְּךָ (מִמֶּךָ) מִמֵּךְ	כָּמוֹךָ	לְךָ (לָךְ) לָךְ	בְּךָ (בָּךְ) בָּךְ
מִמֶּנְהוּ } מִמֶּנּוּ	כָּמוֹהוּ	לוֹ	בּוֹ
מִמֶּנָּה	כָּמוֹהָ	לָהּ	בָּהּ
מִמֶּנּוּ	כָּמוֹנוּ	לָנוּ	בָּנוּ
מִכֶּם	כָּכֶם (כְּמוֹכֶם)	לָכֶם	בָּכֶם
מִכֶּן	....	לָכֶן	בָּכֶן
מֵהֶם (מִמֶּהֶם)	כְּמוֹדָם כָּהֶם	לָהֶם, לָמוֹ	בָּם
מֵהֶן	....	לָהֶן	בָּהֶן (בָּהֵן)

אֵת of the Acc.		אֵת with.	
אֹתִי, אוֹתִי	אֹתָנוּ	אִתִּי	אִתָּנוּ
אֹתְךָ (אֹתָךְ) אֹתָךְ	אֶתְכֶם, אֶתְכֶן	אִתְּךָ (אִתָּךְ) אִתָּךְ	אִתְּכֶם ....
אֹתוֹ	אֶתְהֶם, אֹתָם	אִתּוֹ	אִתָּם
אֹתָהּ	אֶתְהֶן, אֹתָן	אִתָּהּ	....

Notes on the paradigm. (1) The suff. ךָ sometimes takes the parag. ה_ָ; e. g. בְּךָ = בְּכָה, לָךְ = לָכָה, etc. (2) Before suffixes, כְּ requires the parag. מוֹ as a union-syllable; as in the table. (3) מִן becomes מִמֶּן (= מִנְמֶן i. e. מִן doubled) before most of the pronouns; not before all, e. g. מִכֶּם = מִנְכֶם, etc. (4) אֵת the sign of the Accus., (also standing sometimes before other cases, § 427. Note 2), in union with pronouns, always assumes the form אֹת, or (as it is often written *plenè*) אוֹת. (5) אֵת *with* appears to be derived from a root עלל, or to stand (as Gesenius supposes) for אֱיָת. It is imitated throughout, in its Daghesh and its mode of taking suffixes, by עִם *with*; as עִמִּי, עִמְּךָ, etc.

Note. The parag. forms, הֵמָּה, הֵנָּה, take prepositions without change; as מֵהֵמָּה, בָּהֵנָּה, בָּהֵמָּה, etc.]

CONJUNCTIONS.

[§ 409. Of *primitive* conjunctions there are only a few; and most of these are monosyllabic. *Derived* conjunctions have the forms, (a) Of pronouns; as אֲשֶׁר (שֶׁ) *because*, *that*, like ὅτι, *quod*, etc. (b) Of pronouns preceded by prepositions; as יַעַן־אֲשֶׁר *because*, עַד־אֲשֶׁר

until, etc. (c) Of a double conjunction; as גַּם כִּי *although;* כִּי אִם *but, unless.*]

INTERJECTIONS.

[§ 410. Interjections being exclamations expressive of joy or sorrow, are for the most part *primitive*.

Derived interjections have the forms, (a) Of verbs in the Imperative, both of the sing. and plur. forms; as הָבָה *age!* plur. הָבוּ, from יָהַב; הַס *hush, be still!* plur. הַסּוּ in Piel, from הָסָה; רְאֵה *ἰδού, ecce!*
(b) Of nouns; as אַשְׁרֵי *O the blessedness of!* חָלִילָה *far be it from, God forbid!* בִּי *O hear;* רַב *enough, hold!*

Note. The interjection הִנֵּה takes after it *verbal* suffixes in the Nom. case; as הִנְנִי, הִנֶּנִּי *ecce ego!* הִנְּךָ *ecce tu!* etc.]

PART IV.

SYNTAX.

In the syntax *etymological* arrangement is not followed, but that which is most convenient and simple in the natural order of sentences.

ARTICLE.

The article in Hebrew, like that in Greek, seems originally to have been a *demonstrative* pronoun, *this, that;* and sometimes to have been used also as a *relative* pronoun; in both which senses it is occasionally employed in our present Heb. Scriptures; see § 412. Note 1.

Insertion of the Article.

§ 411. In general the Hebrew article (§ 162), like *the* in English, is used in speaking of a definite, before-mentioned, well known, or monadic object.

E. g. הַמֶּלֶךְ *the king;* Gen. 2: 7, הָאָדָם *the man* before mentioned; הַשֶּׁמֶשׁ *the sun;* הָאָרֶץ, etc. But in *poetry*, definite objects are often designated without the article; as Ps. 48: 3, 'the city מֶלֶךְ רָב *of the great king;*' Ps. 72: 1. In a similar manner the earlier Greek poets omit the article where the Attic prose writers insert it.

§ 412. The article is commonly (but not always) used in cases such as the following, viz.

(*a*) Before a noun in the Genitive, when the first noun requires the article.

E. g. מַלְכֵי הָאָרֶץ *the kings of the land;* אַנְשֵׁי הַמִּלְחָמָה *the men of war,* i. e. the warriors.

(*b*) Before a noun of multitude in the singular.

E. g. הָרָשָׁע *the wicked,* הַצַּדִּיק *the righteous,* הַכְּנַעֲנִי *the Canaanite.*

(*c*) Before generic nouns, when used with a particular, individual signification.

§§ 412. 413. SYNTAX; ARTICLE. 153

E. g. הַנָּהָר *the river*, i. e. the Euphrates; הַמִּדְבָּר *the desert*, i. e. the Arabian desert; הַשָּׂטָן *the adversary*, i. e. Satan, ὁ διάβολος.

(*d*) Often before the Vocative.

E. g. הַשָּׁמַיִם *O heavens!* הַיָּם *O sea!* Frequently omitted in poetry.

Note 1. The article is sometimes used as a pronoun, either demonstrative or relative; e. g. הַיּוֹם *this day*, הַלַּיְלָה *this night*, הַפַּעַם *this time*. So also Jos. 10: 24, 'the warriors הֶהָלְכוּא אִתּוֹ *who accompanied him*;' Judg. 13: 8, 'the child הַיּוּלָּד *which is born*;' etc.

Note 2. The Hebrews sometimes joined the article with a noun which we should use in an *indefinite* signification (prefixing the article *a* or *an*); e. g. 1 Sam. 17: 34, הָאֲרִי *a lion;* Num. 11: 27, הַנַּעַר *a youth;* Ex. 2: 15, הַבְּאֵר *a well*, etc. So in Is. 7: 14, הָעַלְמָה may, in conformity with such usage, be rendered *a virgin* and not *the maiden*, as Gesenius and others have translated it. It should be remarked, however, that we can hardly believe the Hebrew article to have been employed, in cases where to the mind of the writer the object was wholly *indefinite*. E. g. Gen. 19: 11, 'he smote them בַּסַּנְוֵרִים (for בְּהַסַּנְוֵרִים) *with blindness;* not *a blindness* (as we might say), but *the blindness*, i. e. the disease of blindness; just as we say, *the pestilence, the plague*, etc. So in cases of this nature, where we may employ the indefinite article *a* in translating Hebrew words with the article הַ, it seems quite probable that circumstances rendered the object definite in the mind of the writer. Such may have been the case in regard to the prophet's mind, in Is. 7: 14.

Where a properly *indefinite* sense is designed to be expressed, the article is omitted; as Job. 1: 1, 'there was אִישׁ *a man*.'

Note 3. The indefinite article *a* or *an*, is sometimes expressed by אֶחָד *one;* as 1 Sam. 1: 1, 'there was אִישׁ אֶחָד *a man*,' etc. 1 Sam. 16: 18. 25: 14. Job 2: 10. Ex. 29: 3. 1 K. 19: 4. This construction is usual in Chaldee and Syriac. So in Greek, Matt. 21: 19, συκῆ μία, *a fig-tree;* Mark 14: 51, εἷς τις νεανίσκος, *a certain young man*, etc.

Omission of the article.

§ 413. (1) Proper names, especially those of persons, countries, rivers, mountains, and places, frequently omit it, although they might have it.

There are so many exceptions to the omission, that it can by no means be regarded as a general principle of the language. Thus פְּרָת *the Euphrates* always omits the article, but הַיַּרְדֵּן *the Jordan* almost always has it. So סִינַי *Sinai*, צִיּוֹן *Sion*, etc. are always without it; but הַלְּבָנוֹן *Lebanon*, הַכַּרְמֶל *Carmel*, etc. usually with it.

20

(2) It is omitted before a noun in the const. state followed by a Genitive.

E. g. דְּבַר יְהוָה *the word of Jehovah,* instead of הַדְּבַר יְהוָה. But there are some exceptions here, which shew that the usage is variable. Thus (*a*) When the *following* Gen. is a proper name which excludes the article, the *first* noun may take it; as Gen. 31: 13, הָאֵל בֵּית־אֵל, *the God of Bethel;* Gen. 24: 67, הָאֹהֱלָה שָׂרָה, *to the tent of Sarah.* (*b*) So where two Genitives come together; as Ezek. 45: 16, כֹּל הָעָם הָאָרֶץ, *all the people of the land.* (*c*) In some other cases also, it is used without any such reasons; e. g. הַכְּתֹנֶת שֵׁשׁ, *the coat of fine linen,* Ex. 28: 39; הַמִּזְבֵּחַ הַנְּחֹשֶׁת, *the altar of brass,* 2 K. 16: 14. Jer. 32: 12 (comp. v. 11). Ps. 123: 4. In most cases of such a nature, the Genitive relation that follows, is made by לְ, § 421. *d.*

(3) Before a noun which has a suffix pronoun.

But here also the article is sometimes used, especially before a word in the Genitive, or for the sake of emphasis, etc.; as Josh. 7: 21, בְּתוֹךְ הָאֹהֳלִי, *in the midst of my tent,* Mic. 2: 12. Lev. 27: 23. Before participles with a suff. pronoun, the article is very common; Deut. 13: 6, 11. 8: 14—16. 20: 1. etc.

Note. Before the predicate of a sentence, it is more usually omitted; but still, it is often inserted when *definiteness* is required.

General Remark. In all the cases where the article is omitted, and in which the object still is *definite,* either the nature of the thing itself, or of its adjuncts, marks that definiteness. E. g. in No. 1. above, a *proper* name makes the noun *definite;* in No. 2, the following Gen. makes it definite; in No. 3, the pronoun does this; and so in other cases of omission which from their nature are *definite.* The reader will see, moreover, that there are scarcely any cases in which the omission of the article is uniformly a matter of necessity.

Article before adjectives.

§ 414. (1) In general where a noun has the article, the adjective or pronoun-adjective agreeing with it, must also have the article.

E. g. Gen. 10: 12, הָעִיר הַגְּדֹלָה *the great city;* Num. 11: 34, הַמָּקוֹם הַהוּא, *this place.* But this principle is not uniform; for sometimes the noun has an article, and the adjective omits it; as Gen. 29: 2, הָאֶבֶן גְּדֹלָה, *the great stone;* 2 Sam. 6: 3, הָעֲגָלָה חֲדָשָׁה, *the new wagon.*

(2) The article is usually *omitted* before adjectives, (*a*) When the noun to which the adjective belongs, omits the article; i. e. כֶּבֶשׂ אַלּוּף, *a lame lamb,* etc.

Note. But when the noun omits an article required by the sense, merely through the influence of a suffix pronoun, or of a Gen. which follows it, the adjective which belongs to it may still take the article; as 2 Chr. 6: 32, שִׁמְךָ הַגָּדוֹל, *thy great name;* Deut. 11: 7, מַעֲשֵׂה יְהוָֹה הַגָּדוֹל, *the great work of Jehovah.*

(*b*) When the adjective is the predicate of a sentence. E. g. טוֹב הָאֱלֹהִים, *God is good;* בָּרוּךְ שֵׁם יְהוָֹה, *the name of Jehovah be blessed.* Compare § 413. 3. Note.

N. B. Practice is *not* uniform in regard to the article, in any of the cases under § 414. Instances are not rare, where the noun omits the article (without any of the reasons for it assigned in § 413 above), and the adjective still has it; e. g. 1 Sam. 19: 22, בּוֹר הַגָּדוֹל, *the great cistern;* Jer. 38: 14. 46: 16. 50: 16, etc. In some cases apparently of this nature, the article is to be rendered as a pronoun; e. g. גָּדֵר הַדְּחוּיָה [like] '*a wall which is tottering.*'

NOUNS.

Case absolute.

§ 415. By this is meant, the case of a noun or pronoun which stands in the beginning of a sentence, without any verb or predicate directly belonging to it. The case absolute is more commonly, but not always, of the form of the Nominative.

§ 416. *Modes of construction.* (*a*) When the noun in the case absolute is the real subject of the sentence which follows, a Vav copulative succeeds it; as Job 36: 26, מִסְפַּר שָׁנָיו וְלֹא חֵקֶר, '*as to the number of his years,* surely there is no computation,' i. e. his years cannot be computed. (*b*) The case absolute is sometimes used where the sense requires an *oblique* case, and then the oblique case is most commonly made by a pronoun; e. g. Ps. 18: 31, הָאֵל תָּמִים דַּרְכּוֹ, '*as to God,* perfect is the way *of him,*' i. e. the way of God is perfect, where as to the sense the Gen. of הָאֵל is required; for the Accusative, Ps. 74: 17, קַיִץ וָחֹרֶף אַתָּה יְצַרְתָּם, '*as to summer and winter,* thou hast made *them.*' So Jer. 6: 19, תּוֹרָתִי וַיִּמְאֲסוּ בָהּ, '*as to my law,* they have abhorred *it.*' (*c*) Sometimes a participle is joined with the Nom., like the English case absolute; as 1 Sam. 2: 13, כָּל־אִישׁ זֹבֵחַ זֶבַח, '*any man offering a sacrifice,* the servant of the priest came, etc.' 1 Sam. 9: 11. Gen. 4: 15.

Note. *Pronouns* are often found in the case absolute, as well as nouns.

§ 417. The case absolute is sometimes made, (*a*) By the Acc.; as

Gen. 47: 21, אֶת־הָעָם, 'as to the people, he led them from one town to another.' (b) By the Dat.; as Ps. 16: 3, לִקְדוֹשִׁים, 'as to the saints who are in the land, all my delight is in them.' (c) By the Abl.; as Gen. 2: 17, מֵעֵץ הַדַּעַת טוֹב וָרָע, 'in respect to the tree of knowledge of good and evil, thou shalt not eat of it,' etc.

Cases relative.

§ 418. Declension in the Latin or Greek sense of the word, the Hebrew has not. The *case* of a noun is marked therefore, as in English, either by the relation which it sustains to the sentence, as *subject, object,* etc.; or by its relation to some specific part of it, as *regimen* or *const.* state; or by prepositions connected with it, either expressed or understood.

Nominative case.

§ 419. This is known by its being the *subject* of a sentence.

This may be either one noun or several, either sing. or plural; and the nouns may be of the ground-form, or in the state of regimen which belongs also to all *cases*, § 434. See also § 426. Note. § 427. Note 2.

Genitive case.

§ 420. This is most commonly made by a noun or adjective preceding it in the const. state, § 332 seq. The noun itself which is in the Genitive, undergoes no change of form.

The Gen. is nearly always placed *immediately after* its antecedent, i. e. the noun, etc., which causes it to be put in the Genitive; but in a few cases, some word closely connected with the clause is inserted between the Gen. and its antecedent. Thus Gen. 7: 6, מַבּוּל הָיָה מַיִם, *a flood of waters was,* [Heb. a flood was of waters]; Hos. 14: 3, כָּל־תִּשָּׂא עָוֹן, *thou wilt forgive all transgression,* [Heb. all thou-wilt-forgive transgression]; Is. 40: 12. Job 15: 10. Is. 19: 8. One can scarcely refrain from believing that such cases, so contrary to the common usage of the Hebrews, must have originated from error in transcribing.

§ 421. Besides the usual method of expressing the Genitive, as designated in § 420, it is often marked by the particle לְ, *to, belonging to, of.*

In many cases the expression of a Gen. is needed, where no noun

§ 421. SYNTAX OF NOUNS ; GENITIVE CASE. 157

preceding it in regimen is employed, or where the usual form of regimen would mark a closer connection than the writer designed, or where the preceding noun is so conditioned as to render the usual form of regimen undesirable or inexpediént. In all such cases, the Hebrews usually expressed the Genitive by the use of לְ. E. g.

(a) Where the preceding noun is omitted; as לְדָוִד, [a psalm] of David, (this is called לְ auctoris); so where בֶּן (son) is omitted, as יִתְרְעָם לְעֶגְלָה, Ithream [the son] of Eglah.

(b) Where the first noun is an indefinite one, the second a definite one; as בֶּן לְיִשַׁי a son of Jesse, (בֶּן־יִשַׁי would be, the son of Jesse). 2 Sam. 9: 3. 1 K. 2: 39. 2 Sam. 2: 8 לְשָׁאוּל. . . . שַׂר, a leader of Saul's. Is. 37: 13. Num. 1: 4.

(c) When several nouns follow each other in succession, where the sense of the Gen. is required, it is usual to put לְ before the second Gen. case; e. g. חֶלְקַת הַשָּׂדֶה לְבֹעַז, a field-portion of Boaz, (in the const. state it would mean, a portion of the field of Boaz), Ruth 2: 3.

Note. In such cases, however, אֲשֶׁר is very often inserted before the לְ, e. g. Ruth 4: 3. Gen. 41: 43. Cant. 1: 1. Ezra 1: 5. Judg. 3: 28. 12: 5. 1 K. 15: 20. 22: 31, et saepe. See General Remark below.

(d) As the article is usually omitted before the first of two nouns in regimen (§ 413. 2), so where it is inserted because the sense imperiously demands it, the following Genitive is usually made by לְ, in order that the form of regimen may be dispensed with in respect to the first noun. E. g. 1 K. 4: 2, אֵלֶּה הַשָּׂרִים אֲשֶׁר לוֹ, these are the princes which were his (Solomon's); 1 Chron. 11: 10, הַגִּבּוֹרִים אֲשֶׁר לְדָוִיד, the heroes who were David's. 1 Chron. 11: 11. 27: 31. Ruth. 2: 21. 2 Sam. 14: 31. Gen. 29: 9. 47: 4, et alibi saepe.

Note. In nearly all cases of this nature, the article is expressed before the preceding noun. In poetry there are a few exceptions, by virtue of poetic license.

(e) When a Genitive by anticipation precedes its natural place, it is made by לְ; e. g. Jer. 22: 4, לְדָוִיד עַל כִּסְאוֹ, lit. of David on his throne, i. e. on the throne of David.

(f) When an adjective intervenes between the first and second noun; e. g. בֶּן אֶחָד לַאֲחִימֶלֶךְ, a son of Ahimelek; especially after a numeral, as Hag. 1: 1, בִּשְׁנַת שְׁתַּיִם לְדָרְיָוֶשׁ, in the second year of Darius. Gen. 7: 11. 1 K. 3: 18.

(g) In designating time, after a numeral when יוֹם etc. is omitted; Deut. 1: 3, בְּאֶחָד לַחֹדֶשׁ, on the first [day] of the month. Ezek 1: 2.

(h) In describing the materials of which a thing consists; e. g. Ez. 1: 11, כֵּלִים לַזָּהָב, vessels of gold. Lev. 13: 48.

GENERAL REMARK. It will be seen by a careful inspection of the above examples, that the Hebrew very often admits a Gen. relation to be expressed, without the form of regimen. Strictly speaking, however, there is no case of this sort which does not admit of another solution, viz. one which resembles the Greek, Latin, and French methods of expressing *possession* or *property* ; e. g. ἐστί μοι, *est mihi, c'est à moi.* The later Hebrew, which frequently employs אֲשֶׁר לְ to express a Gen. relation, proffers the solution in question. Thus לְדָוִיד is an elliptical expression for מִזְמוֹר אֲשֶׁר לְדָוִיד ; בֶּן לְיִשַׁי is used instead of בֶּן אֲשֶׁר לְיִשַׁי ; הַצּוֹפִים לְשָׁאוּל *the watchers which belonged to Saul,* is used for הַצּוֹפִים אֲשֶׁר הָיוּ לְשָׁאוּל, etc. The very frequent cases where אֲשֶׁר is actually employed in this way, point us of course to such an obvious solution.

As to the לְ *auctoris* (*a* above), however, Gesenius solves it by rendering לְ *by, through,* thus designating the efficient cause ; which seems to be well supported by analogies. See his Lex. art. לְ.

§ 422. In Hebrew the Gen. frequently stands where we might naturally expect *apposition*.

E. g. נְהַר פְּרָת, *the river of Euphrates,* i. e. the river Euphrates ; 1 K. 10: 15, אַנְשֵׁי הַתָּרִים, *the men of the merchants,* i. e. the merchant-men.

§ 423. The Gen. frequently follows such adjectives or participles, as express qualities belonging to the subject designated by such Genitive.

E. g. 2 Sam. 4: 4, נְכֵה רַגְלַיִם, *lame of feet,* i. e. in his feet ; Ps. 24: 4, נְקִי כַפַּיִם, *pure of hands,* i. e. of pure hands ; Prov. 6: 32, חֲסַר־לֵב *deficient of* [in] *understanding.* So in Latin, *integer vitae scelerisque purus,* etc.

§ 424. *Significations of the Genitive.* This case marks a great variety of relations and dependencies in Hebrew ; which are generally comprehended in the expressions, *Gen. of the subject,* and *Gen. of the object.*

Note. These two designations, viz. *the Gen. of the subject and object,* do not by any means convey an adequate idea of all the various relations which the Gen. sustains or expresses. These may be better distributed thus : viz. (1) *Genitive of the subject;* e. g. חֲמַת יְהוָה, the *anger of Jehovah,* i. e. the anger which he feels, or of which he is the subject. This is frequent. (2) *Genitive of the object;* e. g. Prov. 1: 7, יִרְאַת יְהוָה, *the fear of Jehovah,* i. e. the fear of which Jehovah is the object ; Prov. 20: 2, אֵימַת מֶלֶךְ, *the terror of the king,* i. e. the terror of which the king is the object, (this may be ranked under No. 5) ; זִכְרְךָ, *the memory of thee,* i. e. of which thou art the object. This class of meanings is of wide extent. (3) *The Genitive of possession*, not merely as property, but as quality, attribute, etc. etc.; e. g. יַד יְהֹוָה, *the hand of Jehovah*, i. e. which belongs to him; נֶפֶשׁ דָּוִד, *the soul of David*. (4) *The Genitive of material;* e. g. כְּלִי כֶסֶף, *vessels of silver*, i. e. made of silver, Ex. 11: 2. (5) *The Genitive of cause (Genitivus auctoris);* 1 Sam. 14: 15, חֶרְדַּת אֱלֹהִים, *the terror of God*, i. e. what God inspires, or of which he is the author; Ezek. 12: 19, חֲמַס הַיֹּשְׁבִים, *the injury of the inhabitants*, i. e. the injury of which the inhabitants were the cause or authors. There is a great variety of shades under this head of meaning. (6) *The Genitive of consequence*; e. g. Ezek. 35: 5, עֲוֹן קֵץ, *the sin of the end*, i. e. the sin which is followed by consummation or destruction. (7) *The Gen. of relation;*[*] e. g. Is. 54: 9, מֵי נֹחַ, *the waters of Noah*, i. e. to which Noah stood related, viz. as described in the history of the flood, or waters in the time of Noah; 1 Sam. 16: 20, חֲמוֹר לֶחֶם, *the ass of bread*, i. e. the ass which carries bread. There is a great variety here. (8) *The Genitive of quality;* i. e. אִמְרֵי אֱמֶת *words of truth*, i. e. true words. This is a widely extended usage; see § 440. Other divisions of meaning conveyed by the Gen., might be added; but these are the leading ones. The attentive reader of the Scriptures will soon find, that the *Genitivus subjecti et objecti* is very far from expressing all relations designated by this case; and indeed, that no formal divisions can reach all the niceties of the examples which now and then occur. In fact, almost every and any kind of relation of one thing to another, is expressed by the Genitive case.

§ 425. Sometimes the Genitive following an adjective, is used as a noun of multitude, and the adjective then denotes a part of this multitude.

E. g. Prov. 15: 20. 21: 20, כְּסִיל אָדָם, *the foolish of men*, i. e. foolish men; 1 Sam. 17: 40, 'five חַלֻּקֵי אֲבָנִים, *smooth of stones*,' i. e. smooth stones; Job 41: 7, אֲפִיקֵי מָגִנִּים, *the strong of shields*, i. e. strong shields.

Dative case.

§ 426. This case is marked by לְ signifying *to* or *for*.

Note 1. In a few cases לְ stands before the Nom.; as 1 Chron. 3: 2, 'the third was לְאַבְשָׁלוֹם, *Absalom*.' Sometimes before the Acc.; as Ezra 8: 16, 'I sent לֶאֱלִיעֶזֶר, *Eliezer*.' Lam. 4: 5. 2 Sam. 3: 30. Job 5: 2. The latter usage is common in Syriac.

---

[*] All Genitives express *relation*, and this name might therefore be given to all. But as more *specific* names are here assigned to other Genitives, I have used *relation* to designate a *sui generis* connection which I can find no other word satisfactorily to express.

Note 2. The Dative case is very common after the verb הָיָה, either implied or expressed, when it signifies *possession, belonging to;* like *sum* put for *habeo,* in Latin.

Accusative case.

§ 427. This is sometimes designated by אֵת, אֶת־; otherwise it is without any distinctive sign.

Note 1. The use of אֵת with the Acc. is limited, (*a*) To nouns with the article. (*b*) To nouns having a Gen. or suffix after them. (*c*) To proper names. Consequently it is used only in cases where a *definite* idea is conveyed by the noun. But in poetry, this usage is not observed with any strictness.

Note 2. Sometimes אֵת is used before the Nom.; as 2 K. 6: 5, וְאֶת־הַבַּרְזֶל, '*and the iron* fell into the water.' Especially before the Nom. of *passive* verbs; as Gen. 17: 5, אֶת־שִׁמְךָ, '*thy name* shall no more be called Abram.' Sometimes before the Nom. of neuter verbs; as 2 Sam. 11: 25, אֶת־הַדָּבָר הַזֶּה, '*this matter,* may it not displease thee;' Ezek. 35: 10, אֶת־שְׁנֵי הַגּוֹיִם, '*the two nations* are mine.' See אֵת in the Lex.

§ 428. *Use of the Accusative case.* This commonly, as in other languages, denotes, (1) The *object* of a transitive verb. (2) In a great number of cases, it forms *adverbial* designations of time, place, measure, etc. (3) It is also used in all those cases where the Greeks understand κατά, and the Latins, *secundum, quoad,* etc. E. g.

(*a*) Place whither; as 2 Chr. 20: 36, לָלֶכֶת תַּרְשִׁישׁ, *to go to Tarshish.* (*b*) Place where; as Gen. 18: 1, פֶּתַח־הָאֹהֶל, *at the door of the tent.* (*c*) Time when and how long; as עֶרֶב, *in the evening;* בֹּקֶר, *in the morning.* So Gen. 27: 44, יָמִים אֲחָדִים, *during certain days.* (*d*) Measure; as Gen. 7: 20, 'the waters rose fifteen אַמָּה cubits.' (*e*) The material from which any thing is made; as Gen. 2: 7, 'God formed man עָפָר, *of dust* from the earth;' § 511. Note. (*f*) Cases where κατά would be implied in Greek; as 1 K. 16: 23, 'lame אֶת־רַגְלָיו *as to his feet;*' Ps. 3: 8, 'thou hast smitten all thine enemies לֶחִי, *as to* [on] *the cheek bone.*' (*g*) Cases where a noun is taken in an adverbial signification; as Deut. 23: 24, נְדָבָה, *voluntarily;* Ezek. 11: 19, לֵב אֶחָד, *unanimously;* Ex. 24: 3, קוֹל אֶחָד, *unanimously,* etc.

N. B. It will be very convenient to name these various cases, the *Acc. of place; of time; of quantity; of material; of manner.* The student has only to recollect that all these are designated by the Acc., and this without its bearing a special relation to any active verb.

(4) The Accusative is sometimes put after participles, or verbals with an active signification, and is governed by them.

E. g. 2 K. 4: 1, יָרֵא אֶת־יְהוָֹה, *fearing Jehovah;* Is. 11: 9, דֵּעָה אֶת־יְהוָֹה, *the knowledge of Jehovah,* lit. *tò cognoscere Jehovam.*

Vocative and Ablative.

§ 429. The Vocative sometimes has the article to designate it; but not always. It can be distinguished only by the sense of the passage.

§ 430. The Ablative case takes מִן *from, out of;* בְּ *in, by;* עִם *with,* etc. In many cases, the preposition is merely implied.

Construct State.

§ 431. A noun is said to be in this state, when it precedes another noun in the Genitive. This rarely admits any intervening word, § 420. Note.

As to the changes in the form of the noun in the const. state; see § 333.

§ 432. The *form* of the const. state, however, is not limited to nouns before a Gen. case; it often appears. (*a*) Before nouns in other cases governed by prepositions. (*b*) Before verbs and parts of sentences which express the same sense as nouns might express. (*c*) Before adjectives. (*d*) Before אֲשֶׁר. (*e*) Before וְ copulative.

(*a*) Before nouns governed by prepositions; e. g. (1) Nouns with בְּ; as Is. 9: 2, שִׂמְחַת בַּקָּצִיר, *the joy in* [of] *harvest;* Is. 5: 11, מַשְׁכִּימֵי בַבֹּקֶר, *who rise early in the morning.* (2) With לְ; as Is. 56: 10, אֹהֲבֵי לָנוּם, *lovers of slumber.* (3) With אֶל; as Is. 14: 20, יוֹרְדֵי אֶל־אַבְנֵי־בוֹר, *going down to the stones of the pit.* (4) With אֵת; as Jer. 33: 22, *the Levites* מְשָׁרְתֵי אֹתִי, *who served me.* (5) With מִן; as Jer. 23: 23, אֱלֹהֵי מִקָּרוֹב, *a God near at hand.* (6) With עַל; as Judg. 5: 10, הֹלְכֵי עַל־דֶּרֶךְ, *who go on the way.*

(*b*) Before verbs and parts of sentences expressing ideas that might be designated by nouns; as 1 Sam. 25: 15, כָּל־יְמֵי הִתְהַלַּכְנוּ אִתָּם, *all the days of our walking with them,* where יְמֵי is in the const. state before the verb that follows. Job 18: 21, מְקוֹם לֹא יָדַע אֵל, *the place of him who knows not God.* Is. 29: 1, קִרְיַת חָנָה דָוִד, *the city of David's dwelling.* The like in Lev. 14: 46. Is. 30: 29. Hos. 1: 2; also in Ex. 6: 28. Lev. 7: 35. Num. 3: 1. Zech. 8: 9. Jer. 36: 2. 48: 36. Lam. 1: 14. Ps. 81: 6.

(c) Before adjectives; as 2 K. 12: 10, אֲרוֹן אֶחָד, *one coffer* (§ 440. a); Is. 17: 10, נִטְעֵי נַעֲמָנִים, *pleasant plants*; see § 445. § 440.

(d) Before אֲשֶׁר; as Lev. 4: 24, מְקוֹם אֲשֶׁר, *the place which.* Gen. 40: 3. See also 1 Sam. 3: 13.

(e) Before וְ copulative; as Is. 33: 6, חָכְמַת וָדַעַת, *wisdom and knowledge.* So also, Is. 35: 2. Is. 51: 21.

§ 433. In a few cases, the const. form seems to be employed where we might naturally expect the absolute.

But most of these are cases of such a nature, as to shew that some noun in the Gen. after such const. form is *implied*, although not expressed. E. g. 2 K. 9: 17, 'I see שִׁפְעַת, *a multitude*,' i. e. the multitude of Jehu, as the preceding part of the verse shews. Ps. 74: 19, 'give not לְחַיַּת, *to the beasts*,' i. e. to the beasts of the forest (הַיַּעַר), or to the wild beast. Both of these cases, however, may be mere examples of the unusual fem. in ־ָה, see § 319. Note 3. So in Ps. 16: 3, אַדִּירֵי is probably for אַדִּירֵי הָאָרֶץ, as supplied from the preceding part of the verse.

For the supposed use of the *abs.* instead of the *const.*, see § 435.

§ 434. *Const. state* or *regimen* has reference solely to the relation of the two nouns, etc., connected together in this state; but not to the relation these may sustain in regard to the rest of the sentence.

Hence the const. state is found in all the cases of nouns; e. g. (a) In the Nom.; as 1 K. 12: 22, דְּבַר הָאֱלֹהִים, 'the word of God came to Shemaiah.' (b) In the Gen.; as Job 12: 24, לֵב רָאשֵׁי עַם־הָאָרֶץ, *the heart of the princes of the people of the land;* where רָאשֵׁי is in the Gen. in regard to לֵב, and in the const. as it respects עַם; while עַם is in the Gen. with regard to רָאשֵׁי, and in the const. as it respects הָאָרֶץ. (c) In the Dat.; as Job 3: 20, לְמָרֵי נָפֶשׁ, *to those who are grieved in spirit,* where the former word is in the const. state and Dative. (d) In the Acc.; as 1 Sam. 9: 27, 'that I may show thee אֶת־דְּבַר אֱלֹהִים, *the word of God,*' where דְּבַר is in the const. state Accusative. (e) In the Voc.; as 2 K. 1: 13, אִישׁ הָאֱלֹהִים, *O man of God.* (f) In the Abl.; as Ps. 17: 4, בִּדְבַר שְׂפָתֶיךָ, *by the word of thy lips,* where the first noun is in the const. state Ablative.

Apposition.

§ 435. In Hebrew, two nouns designating the same thing, are not only placed in apposition (as is usual in other languages), but apposition is frequently employed where the Gen. might be used and would naturally be expected. E. g. Prov. 22: 21, אֲמָרִים אֱמֶת, *words* [which are] *truth*, i. e. *words of truth*; Zech. 1: 13, דְּבָרִים נִחֻמִים, *words* [which are] *consolations*, i. e. *words of consolation*; Ex. 24: 5, זְבָחִים שְׁלָמִים, *offerings* [which are] *peace offerings*.

Note. Of two nouns thus placed, one is frequently used as an adjective; as in the examples above, we may render *true words, consolatory words*, etc. See § 440 seq.

§ 435 a. Nouns are apparently, but not really in apposition, which designate *weight, measures, time*, etc.

E. g. 2 K. 7: 1, סְאָה סֹלֶת, *a seah* [of] *fine meal;* 2 K. 5: 23, כִּכְּרַיִם כֶּסֶף, *two talents* [of] *silver;* Gen. 41: 1, שְׁנָתַיִם יָמִים, *two years* [of] *time;* 1 K. 7: 42, שְׁנֵי טוּרִים רִמֹּנִים, *two rows* [of] *pomegranates;* Ezek. 22: 18, סִגִּים כֶּסֶף, *dross* [of] *silver*. Comp. § 463.

N. B. In these instances the second nouns are all the Acc. of measure, material, time, manner, etc.; comp. § 428. N. B.

Note 1. Sometimes nouns are put in apposition, where the latter noun designates a *whole* or *genus*, of which the former designates only a *part* or *species*; e. g. Judg. 5: 13, אַדִּירִים עָם, *the nobles* [of, among] *the people*.

Note 2. Some examples occur of apparent apposition, in which the latter noun is probably in the Gen., by reason of a word *implied;* e. g. יְהוָֹה [אֱלֹהֵי] צְבָאוֹת, *Jehovah* [God of] *hosts*. So probably, Is. 30: 20, מַיִם [מֵי] לַחַץ, *water* [water of] *trouble;* אַפּוֹ [חֲמַת] חֵמָה, *the glow* [the glow of] *his anger*.

Gender of Nouns and Adjectives.

§ 436. The Hebrew having no neuter gender, it commonly employs the fem. to express it; but sometimes the masculine, § 321. Note 1.

E. g. Ps. 27: 4, 'I have asked אַחַת, *one thing;*' Ps. 12: 4, גְּדֹלוֹת, *great things;* Gen. 42: 30, קָשׁוֹת, *hard things*, etc. Less often is the masculine employed; as Prov. 8: 6, נְגִידִים, *noble things*.

Note. The fem. is sometimes used also in a *collective* sense, for objects which are properly masculine; as Mic. 1: 11, 12, יוֹשֶׁבֶת, *inhabitress*, i. e. inhabitants; Mic. 7: 8, 10, אֹיֶבֶת, *enemies*. So עֵץ *a tree*, עֵצָה *a grove of trees*, etc. So in Arabic, the *pluralis fractus*, which is used as a collective, very often has a fem. form.

Number of Nouns.

§ 437. (1) The Hebrews often employed nouns sing. in a *collective* sense, especially national denominations.

E. g. צֹאן *small cattle*, זָהָב *gold*, הַכְּנַעֲנִי *the Canaanite*, i. e. the inhabitants of Canaan, etc.

(2) For the sake of emphasis, the Hebrews commonly employed most of the words which signify *Lord, God*, etc. in the plur. form, but with the sense of the singular. This is called *pluralis excellentiae*.

Examples. (*a*) אָדוֹן *lord*, is so used in all the forms of the plural, except אֲדֹנָי *my masters.* The form אֲדֹנָי is always used in the sense of the singular for *God.* (*b*) אֱלוֹהַ *God*, in all the forms of the plural. (*c*) בַּעַל *lord*, in all its forms. (*d*) קְדֹשִׁים, *the most Holy One*, Hos. 12: 1. Prov. 9: 10. 30: 3. Jos. 24: 19. (*e*) שַׁדַּי *the Almighty*, is probably of the plural form, § 325. *b*. (*f*) תְּרָפִים *household god*, as sing. 1 Sam. 19: 13, 16. (*g*) Occasionally a few other words are used in the like way; as Job 35: 10, ' God עֹשָׂי, *my Maker ;*' Ecc. 12: 1, בֹּרְאֶיךָ, *thy Creator.* See also Is. 22: 11. 42: 5. Ps. 149: 2. Comp. § 484.

(3) The plural, especially in poetry, is not unfrequently used where we might expect the singular.

E. g. Job 6: 3, ' the sand יַמִּים, *of the seas*,' i. e. of the sea. Even where only *one* can possibly be meant, is this the case; as Judg. 12: 7, ' he was buried בְּעָרֵי, *in the towns* of Gilead,' i. e. in a town; Gen. 8: 4, ' the ark rested הָרֵי, *on the mountains* of Ararat,' i. e. on the mountain; Job 21: 32, צְבָרוֹת, *the graves*, i. e. the grave. Ps. 46: 5.

Peculiar significancy attached to nouns in certain cases.

Repetition of nouns.

§ 438. The Hebrews frequently repeated nouns *without* the copula וְ between them, for various purposes; viz.

(*a*) To denote multitude; e. g. Gen. 14: 10, בֶּאֱרֹת בֶּאֱרֹת חֵמָר, *pits pits of bitumen*, i. e. many pits, etc.; see *d* below. (*b*) To denote distribution; e. g. Gen. 32: 17, עֵדֶר עֵדֶר לְבַדּוֹ *flock flock by itself*, i. e. each flock by itself. (*c*) To denote *all, every ;* e. g. Deut. 14: 22, שָׁנָה שָׁנָה, *year year*, i. e. every year. Sometimes also *with* a copula; as Deut. 32: 7, דּוֹר וָדוֹר, *generation and generation*, i. e. all generations. (*d*) To denote intensity; e. g. Ecc. 7: 24, עָמֹק עָמֹק, *deep deep*, i. e. very deep; comp. *a* above. So earnestness in warning or threatening, in grief, joy, etc., is usually expressed by *repetition*.

§§ 439—441. SYNTAX OF NOUNS; PECULIAR SIGNIF. 165

Note. In order to denote *intensity*, it is not always necessary that the *same* word should be repeated; but a *synonymous* word, or a word of *similar sound* and *signification*, is often substituted with the same effect; as Ps. 40: 3, טִיט הַיָּוֵן, *clay of mire*, i. e. the miry clay; Job 30: 3, שׁוֹאָה וּמְשֹׁאָה, *wasting and destruction*, i. e. great wasting, etc.

§ 439. Repetition *with* the copula וְ, usually denotes *diversity*.

E. g. Deut. 25: 13, אֶבֶן וָאָבֶן, *stone and stone*, i. e. different stones or weights; Ps. 12: 3, בְּלֵב וָלֵב, *with a heart and a heart*, i. e. with different hearts, with deceit.

Nouns employed as Adjectives.

§ 440. Of two nouns in regimen, one is frequently employed as an adjective, in order to qualify the other.

The principle is regulated thus: (*a*) The second or Gen. noun *commonly* qualifies the first; e. g. כְּלִי כֶסֶף, *vessels of silver*, i. e. silver vessels; אֲחֻזַּת עוֹלָם, *possession of eternity*, i. e. everlasting possession; Is. 24: 10, קִרְיַת־תֹּהוּ, *city of desolation*, i. e. desolate city; Gen. 34: 30, מְתֵי מִסְפָּר, *men of number*, i. e. which can be numbered, few men.

(*b*) Sometimes the first noun qualifies the second; e. g. קוֹמַת אֲרָזָיו, *the tallness of his cedars*, i. e. his tall cedars; מִשְׁמַן בְּשָׂרוֹ, *the fatness of his flesh*, i. e. his fat flesh; כָּל־הָאָדָם, *the whole of men*, i. e. all men. Ex. 13: 3. But this construction is less frequent than the other.

Note. This principle is more or less common to all languages, specially the one designated under *a*; but the Hebrew having only a few adjectives, resorts to it more frequently than almost any other language. In particular, the Hebrew is almost entirely wanting in adjectives designating the *material* of which any thing is made. Hence כְּלִי כֶסֶף, *vessels of silver*, and other expressions of the like nature, are a matter of necessity. But this form of expression is sometimes used where there is no necessity, i. e. where adjectives might be employed; e. g. בִּגְדֵי הַקֹּדֶשׁ, *garments of holiness;* כֹּהֵן הָרֹאשׁ, *priest of the head*, i. e. high priest, instead of הַכֹּהֵן הַגָּדוֹל.

§ 441. When two or more nouns are connected by the verb of existence (הָיָה) expressed or understood, such nouns as designate *quality* are usually employed as *adjectives*.

E. g. Gen. 1: 2, 'the earth הָיְתָה תֹהוּ וָבֹהוּ, *was desolation and emptiness*,' i. e. desolate and empty; Ps. 10: 5, מָרוֹם מִשְׁפָּטֶיךָ, *highness* [are] *thy statutes*, i. e. they are high, out of sight; Job 8: 9, תְּמוֹל אֲנַחְנוּ, *yesterday* [are] *we*, i. e. of yesterday, *hesterni sumus*. Lev. 21: 6.

§ 442. Nouns with prepositions prefixed, are sometimes used as adjectives.

E. g. Ps. 77: 14, בְּקֹדֶשׁ דַּרְכֶּךָ, *in holiness* [is] *thy way,* i. e. thy way is holy; 1 Chr. 26: 14, יוֹעֵץ בְּשֵׂכֶל, *a counsellor with wisdom,* i. e. a wise counsellor; Ps. 17: 9, אֹיְבַי בְּנֶפֶשׁ, *my enemies in respect to life,* i. e. my deadly enemies.

§ 443. When two nouns are connected by a conjunction, one of them is occasionally employed as an adjective.

E. g. Gen. 4: 4, מִבְּכֹרוֹת צֹאנוֹ וּמֵחֶלְבֵהֶן, *of the firstlings of his flock and of the fat of them,* i. e. of the fat firstlings, etc.; Gen. 3: 16, עִצְּבוֹנֵךְ וְהֵרֹנֵךְ, *thy pain and thy conception,* i. e. thy painful conception. Perhaps Ps. 119: 168. The construction may be called *Hendiadys,* ἓν διὰ δυοῖν.

§ 444. To express qualities which in other languages are usually designated by adjectives, the Hebrews employed the words אִישׁ, בַּעַל, בֶּן, בַּת, followed by a noun expressive of *quality.*

Examples. (*a*) אִישׁ *man;* as אִישׁ דְּבָרִים *a man of words,* i. e. an eloquent man; אִישׁ חֶסֶד, *a man of piety,* i. e. a pious man. (*b*) מְתִים *men;* as מְתֵי רָעָב, *men of hunger,* i. e. hungry men. (*c*) בַּעַל *lord, possessor;* as בַּעַל שֵׂעָר, *possessor of hair,* i. e. hairy; בַּעֲלֵי בְרִית, *possessors of a covenant,* i. e. bound together by a covenant. (*d*) בֶּן *son,* and בַּת *daughter;* as בֶּן־חַיִל, *son of strength,* i. e. a hero; בֶּן־מָוֶת *son of death,* i. e. condemned, worthy of death; בֶּן שָׁנָה, *son of a year,* i. e. a yearling. So בְּנוֹת הַשִּׁיר, *the daughters of song.* i. e. singing women, Ecc. 12: 4; see Lex. The student will see that these cases are only a peculiar modification of the principle in § 440. *a*.

Note. The first noun in constructions of this kind is sometimes omitted, and can be supplied only from the sense of the passage; as Job 31: 32, אֹרַח *way,* for בֶּן אֹרַח, *son of the way,* i. e. a traveller; Prov. 17: 4, שֶׁקֶר *falsehood,* for *a man of falsehood,* i. e. a liar. So Gen. 15: 2, דַּמֶּשֶׂק, for *son of Damascus,* i. e. a native of Damascus. Job 34: 18.

ADJECTIVES.

§ 445. The Hebrew, like other languages, often supplies the place of nouns by adjectives taken in an abstract or neuter sense.

E. g. Jos. 24: 14, תָּמִים, *integrity,* lit. upright, innocent; Job 20: 22, עָמָל, *trouble,* lit. troublesome, etc. Ps. 10: 10. So אֵשֶׁת רָע, *a woman*

§§ 445—447. SYNTAX; ADJECTIVES. 167

of evil, i. e. an evil woman, where רַע is constructed as a noun in the Gen.; מֵי מָלֵא, *waters of fulness*, i. e. full streams, instead of מַיִם מְלֵאִים Comp. in Greek, τὸ καλόν, τὸ σοφόν, etc.

Note. In this way some adjectives are constantly used as epithets of persons or things; as אָבִיר *strong*, for 'God;' אַבִּיר *strong*, for 'bull, horse, hero;' חַמָּה *hot*, for 'the sun;' לְבָנָה *white*, for 'the moon' etc. So for *God*, we say in English, *the Almighty, the Omnipotent*, etc.; in French, *l'Eternel*, etc. This is called the *epitheton ornans*.

Adjectives as predicates of a sentence.

§ 446. (*a*) When an adjective is the predicate of a sentence, and the verb of existence (הָיָה) is omitted, the adjective stands regularly *before* the noun, and is usually without the article.

E. g. Gen. 4: 13, גָּדוֹל עֲוֹנִי, *great* [is] *my iniquity*. In a very few cases the adjective seems to stand *after* the noun; as in Gen. 19: 20. 1 Sam. 12: 17. But in the first case, the expression seems to be elliptical, viz. קְרוּבָה [הִיא]; in the second, רַבָּה is probably a *verb*. Hab. 1: 16.

(*b*) Such adjective generally agrees in number and gender with the noun to which it relates; but there are many apparent exceptions.

Note. These exceptions may be explained on the principle, that when adjectives are used as predicates, they are often to be taken in an *abstract* sense as *nouns* of the *neuter* gender; § 445. Thus Ps. 73: 28, קִרְבַת אֱלֹהִים לִי טוֹב, *approach to God* [is] *to me delightful*, lit. a pleasant or delightful thing, the noun being in the fem., and the adj. in the masc. and used as a *neuter* noun, § 436. So Gen. 27: 29, אֹרְרֶיךָ אָרוּר, *the cursers of thee* [are] *cursed*, lit. an accursed thing; Ps. 119: 137, מִשְׁפָּטֶיךָ יָשָׁר, *upright* [quoddam rectum] *are thy statutes*. Ps. 66: 3. So Virgil, Aen. IV. 569, *varium et mutabile semper femina;* Statius, Theb. II. 399, *blandum potestas;* Achill. Tat., πονηρὸν μὲν γυνή. So τὸ πᾶν, τὰ πάντα, *the universe*, rational or material.

§ 447. *Article before an adjective used as a predicate.* When this occurs, the verb of existence הָיָה, or its equivalent the pronoun הוּא, is usually inserted.

E. g. 1 Sam. 17: 14, דָּוִד הוּא הַקָּטָן *David was the smallest*, i. e. the youngest. In cases of this kind, the adjective is placed *after* the noun to which it relates.

Note. In like manner, participles used for the Pres. tense of verbs sometimes stand as predicates *after* the noun, and take the article; e. g. Deut. 3: 21, עֵינֶיךָ הָרֹאֹת, *thine eyes see.*

Adjectives qualifying nouns.

§ 448. Adjectives used as epithets, i. e. simply qualifying nouns, (so also participial and pronominal adjectives), generally agree with the noun in gender and number.

§ 449. EXCEPTIONS. (*a*) The *pluralis excellentiae*, commonly but not always, takes an adjective singular, § 437. 2; e. g. Is. 19: 4. אֲדֹנִים קָשֶׁה *a hard master*. On the contrary, Jos. 24: 19, אֱלֹהִים קְדֹשִׁים, *a holy God*, falling in with the general analogy. (*b*) Nouns of multitude in the singular, commonly but not always, require a plural adjective;* e. g. Jer. 50: 6, צֹאן אֹבְדוֹת, *a wandering flock.*

§ 450. Dual nouns take plural adjectives; e. g. יָדַיִם רָפוֹת, *weak hands.*

§ 451. Nouns of *common* gender, having more than one adjective, admit both the masc. and fem. forms in the adjectives.

E. g. 1 K. 19: 11, רוּחַ גְּדוֹלָה וְחָזָק, *a great and strong wind.*

Position of Adjectives.

§ 452. When they qualify nouns, they are usually put *after* them.

The number of apparent exceptions to this rule is so very small, and some of them so equivocal, that it appears dubious whether *real* exceptions are to be admitted. See however, Ps. 89: 51, כָּל־רַבִּים עַמִּים, *all the numerous people;* also Is. 53: 11. Jer. 3: 7, 10. 16: 16.

Note. The pronominal adjective זֶה *this*, not unfrequently precedes the noun with which it agrees.

§ 453. When an adjective serves to qualify two or more nouns, it is usually put *after* them; and the gender of it may be either masc. as the more worthy, or the same as the gender of the last noun.

E. g. Neh. 9: 13, חֻקִּים וּמִצְוֹת טוֹבִים, *good laws and statutes;* Ezek. 1: 11, פְּנֵיהֶם וְכַנְפֵיהֶם פְּרֻדוֹת, *their faces and wings were separated.* Here פְּרֻדוֹת, a part. adjective, is fem.; as is the noun also which next precedes it.

---

* Note. When the concord is directed by the sense, as in *a, b*, rather than by the grammatical form of the noun, we may call it *constructio ad sensum*.

Construct state of adjectives.

§ 453 a. They are often put in this state, even when they qualify the noun with which they stand in regimen.

E. g. נְקִי כַפַּיִם, *clean of hands* ; בַּר לֵבָב, *pure of heart* ; יְפֵה תֹאַר *beautiful of form*, etc. This construction is of wide extent in Hebrew, and is often used in respect to participles partaking of the nature of adjectives. Ps. 19: 3, 9. Jer. 1: 8.

Comparison of adjectives.
Comparative degree.

§ 454. (a) The comparative degree in adjectives, is made by using מִן (*prae, in comparison of*) after the adjective, and before the noun with which the comparison is made.

E. g. Judg. 14: 18, מָתוֹק מִדְּבַשׁ, *sweeter than honey* ; Ps. 19: 11.

Note. In the same manner also מִן is used, to make a comparison after nouns or verbs signifying condition or quality. E. g. Is. 52: 14, 'his visage מִשְׁחַת מֵאִישׁ, *was marred more than any man's* ; Gen. 41: 40, אֶגְדַּל מִמֶּךָ, *I will be greater than thou.*

(b) But מִן before the Inf. mood, implies a *negative*.

In this case it may be translated *so that not*, or *than that*, according as the sentence is constructed ; e. g. Gen. 4: 13, גָּדוֹל עֲוֹנִי מִנְּשׂוֹא, *my iniquity is great so that it cannot be pardoned*, or *greater than that it can be pardoned.*

(c) Sometimes the adjective necessary to make out fully the comparison, is omitted ; as Is. 10: 10, ' their gods מִירוּשָׁלַםִ, [were more powerful] *than those of Jerusalem.*'

Note. In the Rabbinic, comparison is made by יוֹתֵר, *more*. In the N. Test., the *positive* degree of adjectives is not unfrequently used for both the other degrees; an imitation of the Hebrew, which does not vary the form of adjectives for the sake of comparison.

Superlative degree.

§ 455. The Hebrew has no appropriate form to mark this, but expresses it by various circumlocutions.

E. g. (a) By the article prefixed to an adjective of the positive degree ; as 1 Sam. 16: 11, ' David was הַקָּטָן, *the smallest.*' The Arabian makes his superlative, by prefixing the article to the comparative form. (b) By a Gen. or suffix following the adjective ; as 2 Chr. 21: 17, קְטֹן בָּנָיו, *the smallest of his sons*; Mic. 7: 4, טוֹבָם, *the best of them.* (*c*) A superlative of intensity is formed, when a word is repeated and put in the Gen. plural; as קֹדֶשׁ הַקֳּדָשִׁים, *holy of holies,* i. e. the the most holy place; Ecc. 1: 1, הֲבֵל הֲבָלִים, *vanity of vanities,* i. e. exceedingly vain. So 1 K. 8: 27, *heaven of heavens,* i. e. the highest heaven; Gen. 9: 25, *servant of servants,* i. e. a most abject servant; Deut. 10: 17, *God of gods,* i. e. the supreme God, etc. (*d*) The comparative degree sometimes necessarily expresses the sense of the superlative; as Gen. 3: 1, 'now the serpent was עָרוּם מִכֹּל חַיַּת הַשָּׂדֶה, *cunning above all the beasts of the field,*' i. e. the most cunning of all. (*e*) Some *nouns* necessarily imply a superlative in themselves; viz. (1) רֹאשׁ *head,* as Ps. 137: 6, רֹאשׁ שִׂמְחָתִי, *the head of my joy,* i. e. my highest joy. (2) בְּכוֹר, *first born,* as Is. 14: 30, בְּכוֹרֵי דַלִּים, *first born of the wretched,* i. e. most wretched; Job 18: 13, בְּכוֹר מָוֶת, *the first born of death,* i. e. the most terrible death.

§ 456. Besides the above modes of expressing a *superlative,* the Hebrew exhibits a variety of methods by which *intensity* of meaning is denoted.

E. g. (*a*) מְאֹד *very,* or מְאֹד מְאֹד *very very;* as Gen. 7: 19, 'the waters increased מְאֹד מְאֹד, *very exceedingly,*' etc. (*b*) By repeating the same word; see § 438. (*c*) By two synonymous words, see § 438. *d.* and Note. (*d*) By repeating the same word and putting it in the Gen. when repeated; as Hos. 10: 15, רָעַת רָעַתְכֶם, *the evil of your evil,* i. e. your base wickedness. Sometimes a synonyme is used in the Gen., instead of the same word being repeated, § 438. *d,* Note. (*e*) The name of God placed after a noun sometimes makes it specially intensive; as Jonah 3: 3, a great city לֵאלֹהִים *before God,*' i. e. really or truly very great; Gen. 10: 9, 'Nimrod was a mighty hunter לִפְנֵי יְהוָֹה, *before Jehovah,*' i. e. exceedingly expert in hunting. So Acts 7: 20, 'Moses was ἀστεῖος τῷ Θεῷ, *fair to God,*' i. e. very fair; Luke 1: 6, 'righteous ἐνώπιον τοῦ Θεοῦ, *before God,*' i. e. really or eminently pious.

NUMERALS.

§ 457. The cardinal numbers 2—10, are commonly joined with *plural* nouns, and follow the same gender. They may be put (*a*) In the const. state with nouns to which they relate; e. g. שְׁלֹשֶׁת יָמִים, *three days,* lit. a threeness of days. (*b*) In apposition, or perhaps *adverbially,* with the nouns to which they relate, and either before or after them; e. g. שְׁלֹשָׁה בָנִים *three sons,* בָּנוֹת שָׁלוֹשׁ *three daughters.* The position of the cardinal number *after* the noun, is less common, and belongs rather to the later Hebrew.

§§ 458—465. SYNTAX; NUMERALS.   171

§ 458. The cardinal numbers 11—19, are put in apposition, or rather *adverbially*, with nouns plural or singular, and commonly stand before the noun, but sometimes after it. The gender is usually the same as that of the noun. E. g. Num. 1: 44, שְׁנֵים עָשָׂר אִישׁ, *twelve men;* 2 Sam. 9: 10, חֲמִשָּׁה עָשָׂר בָּנִים, *fifteen sons,* etc.

§ 459. The tens (20—90) are of common gender; are put in apposition with nouns either sing. or plural; and may stand either before or after the noun. E. g. Judg. 11: 33, עֶשְׂרִים עִיר *twenty cities;* Gen. 32: 15, אֵילִים עֶשְׂרִים, *twenty rams.*

§ 460. Numbers composed of tens and units (e. g. 26, 34, 48, etc.), when standing before a noun, require it to be in the *singular;* but when the noun precedes, it is in the *plural.* In both cases the gender of the smaller numeral is the same as that of the noun. E. g. Deut. 2: 14, שְׁלֹשִׁים וּשְׁמוֹנֶה שָׁנָה, *thirty and eight years;* Jos. 19: 30, עָרִים עֶשְׂרִים וּשְׁתַּיִם, *cities twenty and two,* etc.

§ 461. The numerals מֵאָה *a hundred* and אֶלֶף *a thousand,* may be put in either the abs. or const. state with nouns either sing. or plural, and may stand either before or after the noun. E. g. Gen. 17: 17, מֵאָה־שָׁנָה, *a hundred years;* 25: 7, 17, מְאַת שָׁנָה, *a hundred of years;* 2 Chr. 3: 16, רִמּוֹנִים מֵאָה, 100 *pomegranates;* Is. 7: 23, אֶלֶף גֶּפֶן, *a thousand of vines;* Ezra 8: 27, אֲדַרְכֹּנִים אֶלֶף, 1000 *Darics.*

§ 462. Numbers composed of thousands and smaller numbers, follow the same rule as composite numerals in § 460.

§ 463. In many cases the numerals are used alone to designate weights, measures in common use, and time, the noun being omitted. E. g. Gen. 20: 16, אֶלֶף כֶּסֶף, *a thousand* [shekels] *of silver;* Ruth 3: 15, שֵׁשׁ שְׂעֹרִים, *six* [measures] *of barley;* 1 Sam. 10: 4, שְׁתֵּי־לֶחֶם, *two* [loaves] *of bread.* The word אַמָּה *cubit,* commonly takes the preposition בְּ after the numeral; as Ex. 27: 18, מֵאָה בָּאַמָּה, *one hundred in cubits,* i. e. 100 cubits. Gen. 8: 5, בְּאֶחָד לַחֹדֶשׁ, *on the first* [day] *of the month.* Comp. § 551.

§ 464. The cardinal numbers beyond ten are also used as *ordinals;* and they are either put *before* the noun and in apposition with it, or are put in the Gen. *after* the noun.

E. g. Gen. 7: 11, בְּשִׁבְעָה עָשָׂר יוֹם, *on the seventeenth day;* 1 K. 16: 10, בִּשְׁנַת עֶשְׂרִים וָשֶׁבַע, *in the year of* 27, i. e. the 27th year.

For the *ordinal* numbers below 10, see § 396.

§ 465. The cardinal numbers below ten are also used as *ordinals,* in designating years, and days of the month.

E. g. 2 K. 18: 10, שְׁנַת שֵׁשׁ, *the sixth year*, lit. the year of six; Gen. 8: 5, בְּאֶחָד לַחֹדֶשׁ [day] *of the month;* Lev: 23: 32, בְּתִשְׁעָה לַחֹדֶשׁ, *on the ninth of the month*, etc. as in English.

§ 466. The cardinal numbers are used *distributively*, when repeated without a copula.

E. g. Gen. 7: 8, שְׁנַיִם שְׁנַיִם, *two and two*, or *two by two;* Gen. 7: 3, שִׁבְעָה שִׁבְעָה, *seven and seven*, or *by sevens*.

PRONOUNS.

Primitive pronouns.

§ 467. These are more usually omitted before verbs; but when employed, they seem intended to give more energy to the expression.

Such pronouns are commonly found only in the Nominative; but occasionally they occupy the oblique cases as the following section shews.

§ 468. When a pronoun of any form is to be repeated for the sake of emphasis, it is done by using the *primitive* form; and this form thus repeated, is in any case required by the nature of the sentence. E. g.

(*a*) In the Nom.; as Ps. 9: 7, אָבַד זִכְרָם הֵמָּה, *the memory of them of them has perished*, i. e. the very memory of them, etc. (*b*) In the Gen.; as 1 K. 21: 19, 'the dogs shall lick אֶת־דָּמְךָ גַּם אָתָּה, *the blood of thee even of thee.*' (*c*) In the Dat.; as Hag. 1: 4, הָעֵת לָכֶם אַתֶּם, *is it a time for you yourselves?* (*d*) In the Acc.; as Gen. 27: 34, בָּרֲכֵנִי גַם־אָנִי, *bless me even me.* (*e*) In the Abl.; as 1 Sam. 25: 24, בִּי אֲנִי הֶעָוֹן, *with me even me* [be] *this evil.*

Note 1. The primitive pronoun is sometimes placed first; as Gen. 49: 8, 'Judah אַתָּה יוֹדוּךָ אַחֶיךָ, *thee thee shall thy brethren praise.*'

Note 2. The primitive pronoun appears sometimes to be used by way of emphasis, instead of repeating a noun; e. g. Gen. 4: 27, וּלְשֵׁת גַּם־הוּא יֻלָּד, *and to Seth even to him was born a son.*

§ 469. *Primitive pronouns used for the verb of existence.* (*a*) When a personal pronoun is the *subject* of a sentence, it implies the verb of existence (הָיָה) after it; the verb itself being usually omitted.

E. g. Gen. 42: 11, כֵּנִים אֲנַחְנוּ, *we* [are] *righteous;* Gen. 29: 4, מֵאַיִן אַתֶּם, *whence* [are] *ye?* Gen. 3: 10, עֵירֹם אָנֹכִי, *I* [am] *naked.*

Note. *Personal pronouns of the* THIRD *person, sometimes stand simply in the place of the verb of existence;* e. g. Gen. 9: 3, 'every thing which moves אֲשֶׁר הוּא חַי, *which is alive;*' Ps. 16: 3, 'the saints אֲשֶׁר בָּאָרֶץ הֵמָּה, *who are in the land;*' Zech. 1: 9, מָה הֵמָּה אֵלֶּה, *what are these?* Plainer still is this principle in such cases as follow; viz. Zeph. 2, 12, 'ye Cushites, victims of my sword אַתֶּם הֵמָּה, *are ye;*' 2 Sam. 7: 28, אַתָּה־הוּא הָאֱלֹהִים, *thou art God,*' Ezra 5: 11, "the servants of God אֲנַחְנָא הִמּוֹ (Chaldaic), *are we,*' answering to the Heb. אֲנַחְנוּ הֵמָּה. In Syriac and Arabic, this use of the personal pronoun is very common.

§ 469. *a.* Primitive pronouns of the third person, viz. הֵן, הֵם, הִיא, הוּא, are very frequently employed as demonstrative pronouns.

E. g. בַּיּוֹם הַהוּא, *in that day;* הַגּוֹיִם הָהֵם *those nations.* Comp. § 167. Note.

Suffix Pronouns.

§ 470. In general the pronouns suffixed to verbs are in the Acc. case; those suffixed to nouns are in the Gen. case.

§ 471. *Exceptions as to verbal suffixes.* (*a*) These sometimes express the sense of the Dative; as Jos. 15: 19, נְתַתָּנִי, *thou hast given* TO *me;* Zech. 7: 5, הֲצֹמְתֻּנִי אָנִי, *have ye fasted* FOR *me* FOR *me,* i. e. on my account; Job 10: 14, 'if I sin וּשְׁמַרְתָּנִי, *then thou watchest it* FOR *me,* i. e. on my account; Prov. 13: 20, שֹׁחֵרוֹ מוּסָר, *he seeks* FOR *him correction;* Ps. 94: 20, יָחָבְרְךָ, *is it bound* TO *thee?* (*b*) They sometimes denote relations which are usually expressed by particles; as Is. 65: 5, קְדַשְׁתִּיךָ, *I am more holy* THAN *thou;* 1 K. 21: 10, וִיעִדֻהוּ, *aud caused them to testify* AGAINST *him;* Ps. 42: 5, אֶדַּדֵּם, *I moved along* WITH *them,* etc. This usage is more frequent in Arabic.

§ 472. *Exceptions as to the suffixes of nouns.* (*a*) These sometimes express the sense of the Dative; as Ps. 115: 7, יְדֵיהֶם—רַגְלֵיהֶם, *they have hands—they have feet,* for יָדַיִם לָהֶם, *hands are to them,* etc. (*b*) They express the sense of the preposition עַל; as Ex. 15: 7, קָמֶיךָ, *those who rise up* AGAINST *thee,* instead of קָמִים עָלֶיךָ. So Ps. 53: 6, חֹנָךְ, *him who encampeth* AGAINST *thee.*

Note. The suffixes of nouns may have either an active or a passive sense: e. g. (*a*) Active; as חֲמָסִי, *my violence,* i. e. that which I do; סִפְרִי, *my book,* i. e. that which I possess. This sense of the suffixes is the common one. (*b*) Passive; as Jer. 51: 35, חֲמָסִי, *my violence,* i. e. that which is done upon me; Ex. 20: 20, יִרְאָתוֹ, *his fear,* i. e. which he inspires; Is. 56: 7, תְּפִלָּתִי, *my prayer,* i. e. the prayer offered to me; Ps. 56: 13, נְדָרֶיךָ, *thy vows*, i. e. vows made to thee; Is. 21: 2, אַנְחָתָהּ, *her sighing*, i. e. the sighing over her, or on her account. Comp. § 424.

N. B. For the *pleonasm* and *ellipsis* of personal pronouns, see § 543 seq. § 552 seq.

Position of pronouns.

§ 473. (*a*) When a noun in the Gen. is used merely to qualify a preceding noun, the suffix pronoun (which as to sense belongs to the *first* noun) is usually placed after the *second.*

E. g. Dan. 9: 24, עִיר קָדְשֶׁךָ, *thy holy city*, lit. the city of thy holiness; Is. 2: 20, אֱלִילֵי כַסְפּוֹ, *his silver idols*, lit. the idols of his silver; Zeph. 3: 11, עַלִּיזֵי גַאֲוָתֵךְ, *thy proud exulters*, lit. the exulters of thy pride, etc.

(*b*) In a very few cases, the suffix is attached to the *first* noun.

E. g. Ps. 71: 7, מַחֲסִי־עֹז, *my strong refuge*, lit. my refuge of strength. Ezek. 16: 27. Lev. 6: 3. But this construction is not altogether certain, as it admits of another solution, viz. by the ellipsis of the first noun before the second.

§ 474. Pronouns usually stand *after* the noun to which they relate.

But sometimes this noun is not mentioned until after the pronoun, either immediately, or perhaps at the distance of several sentences; and sometimes it is to be supplied only from the general sense of the passage, e. g. Ps. 87: 1. יְסוּדָתוֹ בְּהַרְרֵי־קֹדֶשׁ, *its foundation* [is] *in the holy mountain*, i. e. Zion's, as appears from v. 2; Is. 8: 21, עָבַר בָּהּ, *he passes through it*, i. e. the land, see v. 22; Ps. 9: 13, 'when he taketh vengeance for blood אוֹתָם זָכָר, *he remembereth them*,' i. e. the afflicted, as in the second part of the parallelism; Ps. 65: 10. 68: 15. 18: 15, comp. v. 18. Job 37: 4.

Note. Sometimes, although the pronoun is immediately preceded by a noun, it does not refer to that noun, but to one which must be supplied from the sense; as Ps. 44: 3, 'by thy hand thou didst drive out the nations, וַתִּטָּעֵם *and didst plant* THEM,' i. e. the Israelites, as appears from v. 2. So Ps 81: 16, comp. v. 14. Ps. 105: 37. Gen. 10: 12, where הוּא probably refers to *Nineveh* in v. 11.

Nouns used for pronouns.

§ 475. (1) In addressing a superior, the Hebrews commonly employed words descriptive of the relation which the speaker, or the person

§§ 475. 476. SYNTAX; ANOMALIES OF PRONOUNS.

addressed, sustained, instead of using pronouns; e. g. Gen. 44: 16, 'what shall we say *to my lord?*' i. e. to thee; 'lo, we are servants *to my lord*,' i. e. to thee. Verse 19, '*my lord* asked *his servants*,' etc. i. e. *thou* didst inquire of *us*.

(2) The place of the personal pronouns, especially in a *reflexive* sense, is often supplied by the most distinguished and essential parts of either the *external* or *internal* man.

E. g. (*a*) By נֶפֶשׁ *soul*, most frequently; as Job 9: 21, לֹא אֵדַע נַפְשִׁי, *I know not myself;* Ps. 7: 3, 'lest like a lion יִטְרֹף נַפְשִׁי, *he rend me;*' Ps. 3: 3, לְנַפְשִׁי, *to me;* Ps. 11: 1. 16: 10. 35: 3. Amos 1: 8, 'Jehovah hath sworn בְּנַפְשׁוֹ, *by himself.*' (*b*) By פָּנִים *person;* as Prov. 7: 15, לְשַׁחֵר פָּנֶיךָ, *to seek thee;* Ezek. 6: 9, נָקֹטּוּ בִּפְנֵיהֶם, *they abhor themselves*, etc. (*c*) By לֵב *heart;* as Ex. 9: 14, לִבְּךָ, *thyself;* Ps. 16: 9, לִבִּי, *I myself*, etc. (*d*) Occasionally by several other words; as Ps. 7: 6. 16: 9, חַיִּים *life*, and כָּבוֹד *heart* or *soul;* Is. 26: 9, רוּחַ *spirit;* Ps. 6: 8, עַיִן *eye;* Ps. 16: 9, בָּשָׂר *flesh;* Ps. 17: 14, בֶּטֶן *belly;* Ps. 6: 3, עֶצֶם *bone;* 1 Sam. 20: 17, יָד *hand*, etc. The same usage prevails very extensively in Aramaean and Arabic.

Anomalies of pronouns.

§ 476. Departures from concord in respect to gender, number, etc., are called anomalies here. These are somewhat frequent, and may be ranked under several heads; comp. §§ 484—496.

E. g. (*a*) *In regard to number;* for a pronoun sing. not unfrequently relates to a noun plural, i. e. it is used in a collective sense, like a noun of multitude; as Deut. 21: 10, 'when thou goest against אֹיְבֶיךָ, *thine enemies*, and God נְתָנוֹ *gives* HIM (sing.) into thine hand,' etc. Josh. 2: 4, ' and the women took the two spies, וַתִּצְפְּנוֹ *and hid him.*' So Deut. 28: 48. Ps. 5: 10. Mal. 2: 2. Jer. 31: 15. Ecc. 10: 15. Is. 5: 23, et saepe passim.

Note. Pronouns singular being often employed in a *generic* or *collective* sense, in the same way as nouns of multitude, they exhibit the like appearances in regard to concord with verbs, adjectives, etc.

(*b*) *In regard to gender.* (1) The masc. is used for the feminine; as אַתֶּם for אַתֵּן, Ezek. 13: 20. הֵמָּה for הֵנָּה, Ruth 1: 22. Cant. 6: 8. Zach. 5: 10. So the suff. כֶם for כֶן, Ruth 1: 8, 11, 13. הֶם for הֶן, Ruth 1: 19. Ex. 1: 21. Is. 3: 16. Dan. 8: 9, 2. Ezek. 1: 6, 7, 8 saepe. ם ֵ for ן ֵ, Judg. 19: 24. ם ָ for ן ָ, 2 K. 18: 16. 2 Chron. 29: 3. (2) The fem. for the masculine; as הֵנָּה instead of הֵמָּה, 2 Sam. 4: 6. Jer. 50: 5. אַתְּ for אַתָּה, Deut. 5: 24. Ezek. 28: 14. In Arabic and Rabbinic such anomalies are very frequent.

(c) *In respect both to number and gender;* e. g. Job 14: 19, סְפִיחֶיהָ, where the antecedent of הָ is מַיִם plur. masc. Is. 35: 7, רִבְצָה [in] *the laier of her,* i. e. of the תַּנִּים plur. masc.

Relative pronouns.

§ 477. The relative אֲשֶׁר (also זֶה and זוּ when used as relatives, § 169) is used in respect to antecedents of all persons, numbers, and genders, § 168.

§ 478. The relative אֲשֶׁר is often joined in sense with other words, merely to give them a *relative* meaning; e. g.
(a) With nouns and pronouns; as Gen. 13: 16, אֲשֶׁר אֶת־עָפָר, *which dust;* אֲשֶׁר לוֹ, *to whom;* אֲשֶׁר אֹתוֹ, *whom;* Deut. 28: 49, אֲשֶׁר לְשֹׁנוֹ, *whose language;* Ps. 1: 4, אֲשֶׁר תִּדְּפֶנּוּ רוּחַ, *which the wind scatters,* etc. (b) With adverbs; as אֲשֶׁר שָׁם, *where;* אֲשֶׁר מִשָּׁם, *whence,* etc.

Note. The word אֲשֶׁר is commonly, but not always, separated from the word which it qualifies, by another intervening word. The word qualified, moreover, is often omitted; as Ezek. 21: 35, 'in the place [בּוֹ] אֲשֶׁר נִבְרֵאת, *where thou wast created;* Ex. 32: 34, אֶל־ [מָקוֹם] אֲשֶׁר, *to what* [place]; Is. 43: 4, מֵאֲשֶׁר [עֵת], *from what* [time], etc. For the *ellipsis* of this pronoun, see § 553.

Note 2. אֲשֶׁר not only designates a relative sense, but often includes with it the sense of *these* or *those;* e. g. אֲשֶׁר תָּאֹר, THOSE WHOM *thou shalt curse,* Num. 22: 6; לַאֲשֶׁר, *to those which,* etc.

VERBS.

Usual principles of concord.

§ 479. In general a verb agrees with its Nom. case in number, gender, and person.

§ 480. Nouns of multitude in the singular often take a verb in the plural.

E. g. Gen. 33: 13, וָמֵתוּ כָּל־הַצֹּאן, *then all the flock will die;* comp. § 449. *b.* Sometimes verbs in the singular only are employed after nouns of multitude; in other cases, a sentence begins with a verb sing., and proceeds with plur. verbs; e. g. Ex. 1: 20. 33: 4. Is. 2: 20. Ps. 14: 1, etc. See further on nouns of multitude, § 500.

§ 481. Several connected Nominatives, either all masc., or of different genders, usually take a verb in the plur. masculine.

E. g. Ex. 17: 10, 'and Moses and Aaron and Hur עָלוּ *ascended;'* Ps. 85: 11, חֶסֶד־וֶאֱמֶת נִפְגָּשׁוּ, *mercy and truth are met together;* Gen. 8: 22, etc.

Note. *Exceptions.* Cases occur rarely, where a verb sing. is used after several Nominatives; e. g. Ex. 21: 4, הָאִשָּׁה וִילָדֶיהָ תִּהְיֶה, *the woman and her children shall be*, (verb sing.)

§ 482. When the subject and predicate of a sentence are connected by the verb of existence (הָיָה), this verb often agrees with the latter.

E. g. Gen. 27: 39, מִשְׁמַנֵּי הָאָרֶץ יִהְיֶה מוֹשָׁבֶךָ, *rich countries shall be thine abode;* Gen. 31: 8. Lev. 25: 33. Ezek. 35: 15, etc.

§ 483. Dual nouns take verbs like nouns plural.

Anomalies in the concord of verbs.

I. As to number.

§ 484. The *pluralis excellentiae* commonly, but not always, takes a verb in the singular, § 437. 2.

E. g. Gen. 1: 1, בָּרָא אֱלֹהִים, *God created;* Ex. 21: 29, בְּעָלָיו יוּמָת, *his owner shall be put to death.* But in a few cases the *pluralis excellentiae* takes a verb in the *plural;* e. g. Gen. 20: 13. 31: 53. 35: 7. Ex. 32: 4, 8. 2 Sam. 7: 23.

§ 485. Plural Nominatives of the fem. gender, which relate to *beasts* or *things* and not to persons, frequently take a verb singular whether it precede or follow them.*

E. g. Ezek. 26: 2, נִשְׁבְּרָה דַלְתוֹת, *broken is* [are] *the gates;* Joel 1: 20, בַּהֲמוֹת שָׂדֶה *the beasts cry* [cries]; Gen. 49: 22. Jer. 4: 14. 48: 41. 51: 29, 56. Ps. 119: 98. 87: 3. Job 27: 20, etc.

§ 486. *Vice versâ*, the plur. fem. of verbs is sometimes used, where the usual concord would demand the singular.

E. g. Ex. 1: 10, כִּי־תִקְרֶאנָה מִלְחָמָה, *when there shall happen war;* Judg. 5: 26. Job 17: 16. Is. 28: 3. Obad. 13.

§ 487. When a Nom. plural is used in a *distributive* sense, viz. to denote *each* or *every one* of the subjects in question, it often takes a verb in the singular.

E. g. Ex. 31: 14, מְחַלְלֶיהָ יוּמָת, *they who profane it,* i. e. every one who profanes it [the Sabbath], *shall be put to death;* Prov. 27: 16. 3: 18. 28: 1. Gen. 47: 3. Ex. 31: 14.

§ 489. When the verb *precedes* a plural Nominative, it

---

* Note. This construction of the feminine plural with a verb singular, is technically called the *pluralis inhumanus.* Compare the Greek neuter plurals, as joined with verbs singular.

is not unfrequently put in the singular; and sometimes when it follows one.

E. g. 1 Sam. 1: 2, וַיְהִי לִפְנִנָּה יְלָדִים, *and there was to Peninnah children*, i. e. Peninnah had children; Is. 13: 22, עָנָה אִיִּים, *the jackals shall howl;* Deut. 5: 7. Judg. 13: 12. 2 Sam. 21: 6. Ps. 124: 5. In all such cases, the verb is used in a kind of impersonal way, like the French *il vient des hommes, there comes some men.* So occasionally, even when the verb *follows* a plur. Nom.; as Ecc. 2: 7, בְּנֵי בַיִת הָיָה לִי, *there were slaves to me,* i. e. I had slaves; Gen. 46: 22, 'these were the sons of Rachel אֲשֶׁר יֻלַּד *which were* [lit. was] *born to Jacob;*' Gen. 35: 26. Dan. 9: 24. Is. 64: 10.

Note. Sentences not unfrequently begin with a verb singular, and then proceed with a verb plural; as Gen. 1: 14, מְאֹרוֹת, יְהִי, *let there be lights,* ... וְהָיוּ *and let them be* for signs, etc.' Num. 9: 6. Ezek. 14: 1. Esth. 9: 23.

II. As to gender.

§ 490. Feminine Nominatives, either sing. or plural, sometimes take a verb masc. whether it precedes or follows them.

E. g. 1 Sam. 25: 27, הֵבִיא שִׁפְחָתְךָ, *thine handmaid brought;* 1 Chr. 2: 48, פִּילֶגֶשׁ יָלַד, *the concubine bore;* Judg. 21: 21, אִם יֵצְאוּ בְנוֹת, *if the daughters go out;* Ruth 1: 8, 'even as *ye* [Ruth and Orpah] עֲשִׂיתֶם *have done* to the dead;' Is. 57: 8, וַתִּכְרָת־לָךְ *and thou hast made a covenant for thyself,* where the subject of the verb is fem. So Lev. 2: 8. 11: 32. 1 K. 22: 36. Ecc. 7: 7. 12: 5. Jer. 3: 5. Cant. 3: 5. 5: 8. 8: 4. 2 K. 3: 26. Gen. 15: 17.

Note. In a *very few* cases, a masc. Nominative singular is followed by a verb fem.; e. g. Ecc. 7: 27, אָמְרָה קֹהֶלֶת *saith the Preacher*, where the verb follows the grammatical *form* of the Nom. rather than the *sense* of it; Judg. 11: 39, וַתְּהִי־חֹק, *and it became a custom,* where the verb is employed in an impersonal manner.

§ 491. Nouns of common gender take either a masc. or fem. verb; and sometimes both, in the same construction.

E. g. Is. 33: 9, אָבַל אֻמְלְלָה אֶרֶץ, *the land mourns and is withered;* 14: 9. Job 20: 26. Lev. 3: 1. 5: 1. etc.

Note. There are more nouns of the common gender in Hebrew, than has been generally supposed, (Ges. Lehrgeb. p. 472); which accounts for many supposed anomalies of gender.

§ 492. Nouns of multitude, (among which the names of nations may be ranked), frequently take a verb feminine; and in some cases they admit no other; comp. § 480.

§§ 493—495. SYNTAX OF VERBS; ANOMALIES. 179

E. g. Ex: 5: 16, חָטָאת עַמֶּךָ, *thy people have sinned.* So the name of a nation, as Ps. 114: 2. This construction resembles that of the *pluralis fractus* in Arabic, which often takes a verb feminine, whatever the sense of the noun may be.

Note. The names of *nations, countries*, and *towns* are of the masc. gender, when they are used to denote the *inhabitants*; but they are fem., when they only designate *place*; comp. § 320.

§ 493. When several Nominatives of different genders are connected, the verb sometimes agrees with a masc. noun as the most worthy; and sometimes it conforms to the noun which stands nearest; e. g.

(*a*) With a masc. noun; as Prov. 27: 9, שֶׁמֶן וּקְטֹרֶת יְשַׂמַּח לֵב, *ointment and perfume make* [makes] *glad the heart;* Hos. 9: 2, etc.

(*b*) With the nearest noun; as Num. 12: 1, וַתְּדַבֵּר מִרְיָם וְאַהֲרֹן, *then spake Miriam and Aaron;* Num. 20: 11, וַתֵּשְׁתְּ הָעֵדָה וּבְעִירָם, *and the multitude and their cattle drank;* Gen. 7: 7. 1 K. 17: 15. Esth. 9: 29. 2 Sam. 3: 22. Comp. § 481.

For the *general* rule respecting the composite Nominatives, see § 481.

Note. Where there are several Nominatives connected, and the sentence begins with a verb singular, it *commonly* proceeds with a verb plural; as Gen. 21: 32. 24: 61. 31: 14. 33: 7. Comp. § 489. Note. § 480.

III. Number and gender.

§ 494. Feminine nouns of multitude in the singular, often take a verb in the plur. masculine.

E. g. 1 Sam. 2: 33, 'all מַרְבִּית *the increase* of thy house יָמוּתוּ, *shall die;*' Jer. 44: 12, שְׁאֵרִית '*the remainder* of Judah who שָׂמוּ *set their faces;*' Zeph. 2: 9. Gen. 48: 6. This is *constructio ad sensum*, § 449. *b.* Note.*

§ 495. (*a*) Plural Nominatives of the fem. gender sometimes take a verb in the sing. masc., whether they precede or follow the verb. (*b*) *Vice versâ,* nouns plur. masculine (specially a *pluralis inhumanus*), sometimes take a verb sing. feminine.

E. g. (*a*) Job 42: 15, לֹא נִמְצָא נָשִׁים יָפוֹת, *there were* [was] *not found women so beautiful;* Jer. 48: 15, עָרֶיהָ עָלָה *her towns ascended in the flames;* Ex. 13: 7. 1 K. 11: 3. Is. 17: 6. Mic. 2: 6. Hab. 3: 17. Ps. 57: 2. 87: 3. Job 22: 9. Comp. § 489. § 490. (*b*) לֹא חָמְעַד אֲשֻׁרָיו, *his steps totter* [totters] *not;* Job 14: 19, תִּשְׁטֹף סְפִיחֶיהָ, *its floods overflow* [overflows]; also when the verb *follows,* as Jer. 49: 24, חֲבָלִים אֲחָזַתָּה *distresses take* [takes] *hold on her.*

§ 496. *Peculiar Anomaly.* When the subject of a verb is a noun in the const. state followed by a Genitive, the verb sometimes agrees in number, or in number and gender, with the noun in the Genitive.

E. g. 2 Sam. 10: 9, 'and Joab saw that הָיְתָה פְנֵי מִלְחָמָה, *the front of the battle was* against him;' where the verb agrees with מִלְחָמָה. Is. 22: 7, מִבְחַר עֲמָקַיִךְ מָלְאוּ, *the choice part of thy vallies,* i. e. thy choice vallies, *shall be filled;* where the verb agrees with עֲמָקַיִךְ. So Job 29: 10. 38: 21. Is. 2: 11. Jer. 10: 21, etc.

Note. The solution of this seems to be the intimate connection or oneness of two nouns in regimen; § 332.

§ 497. *Anomalies as to the Dual.* We have seen that the dual takes a verb in the same manner as the plural, there being no dual number of verbs, § 483. Like the plural too (§ 489), it can take a verb in the singular, whether it follows or precedes the verb; e. g. Ex. 17: 12, וַיְהִי יָדָיו, *his hands* [was] *were,* Josh. 8: 20. Mic. 4: 11. So 1 Sam. 4: 15, וְעֵינָיו קָמָה, *and his eyes* [was] *were dim;* Deut. 27: 7, *Kethibh.*

Note. For anomalies of the like character with these in §§ 481—496, in regard to pronouns, see § 476.

Impersonal verbs.

§ 498. These are made in Hebrew by the 3d pers. masc. or fem. sing. of either the Praet. or Fut. tense; and sometimes by the Inf. mood.

E. g. וַיְהִי, *and it happened;* מַר לִי, *it is bitter to me;* יָנוּחַ לִי, *I am quiet,* lit. it is quiet to me; צַר לוֹ, or וַיֵּצֶר לוֹ, *it was grievous to him;* 1 Sam. 30: 6, וַתֵּצֶר לְדָוִד, *and it was grievous to David;* Job 4: 5, 'but now תָּבוֹא אֵלֶיךָ, *it comes upon thee;*' Ps. 18: 7, Inf. בַּצַּר לִי, *when it was ill with me.* In Gen. 4: 26, הוּחַל (pass.) *it was begun.*

§ 499. Impersonal verbs commonly take after them a Dative case with the preposition לְ.

E. g. צַר לִי *it is grievous to me,* i. e. I am grieved; בַּצַּר לִי, *when it was ill to me.*

§ 500. *Verbs with indefinite Nominatives.* These are frequent, e. g.

(a) The third pers. sing. or plur. of the verb is used in this way; as Gen. 11: 9, קָרָא [one] *called;* Gen. 48: 1, וַיֹּאמֶר [and one] *told;* 1 Sam. 26: 20, יִרְדֹּף [one] *pursues;* 16: 23. Is. 9: 5. 64: 3, 'from everlasting לֹא שָׁמְעוּ [they] *have not heard;*' 47: 1, לֹא יִקְרָאוּ־לָךְ [they]

§§ 500—503. VERBS; PRAETER TENSE. 181

shall not call thee, etc. Dan. 1: 12. Hosea 2: 9. This construction answers to the use of *on, tout le monde,* etc. in French, or to the Greek λέγουσι, etc. and is quite common in Hebrew.

Note 1. Sometimes the Nom. is expressed by אִישׁ, אָדָם, etc.; and sometimes the act. Part. of the verb is employed as the Nom., as Is. 16: 10, יִדְרֹךְ הַדֹּרֵךְ, *the treader shall tread,* i. e. one shall tread; Is. 28: 4, יִרְאֶה הָרֹאֶה, *the seer sees,* i. e. one sees; 2 Sam. 17: 9. Deut. 22: 8. So plur., Jer. 31: 5, נָטְעוּ הַנֹּטְעִים, *the planters shall plant,* i. e. one shall plant; Nah. 2: 3.

Note 2. The 3 pers. plural, or a Part. plural used as a verb, is often to be rendered *passively* in such cases; as Job 34: 20, יָסִירוּ אַבִּיר, *the mighty one is removed,* lit. they remove the mighty one; Prov. 9: 11, 'for by me יִרְבּוּ *are increased* [lit. they increase] thy days, and years יוֹסִיפוּ *are added* [lit. they add] to thee;' Gen 39: 22, 'all which עָשִׂים שָׁם *was done there,*' lit. they did or were doing there. Job 4: 19. 7: 3. 17: 12. 19: 26. 32: 15. Comp. Luke 12: 20, τὴν ψυχήν σου ἀπαιτοῦσι, *thy soul shall they require,* i. e. thy soul shall be required; 16: 9, *that when ye die* δέξωνται, *ye may be received,* lit. they may receive you, etc.

(*b*) Occasionally the *second* person of the verb is employed in a similar way; e. g. Is. 7: 25, לֹא תָבוֹא שָׁמָּה, *one shall not come there,* lit. thou shalt not come; Job 18: 4. Lev. 2: 4. Also in the common phrase with the Inf., עַד בֹּאֲךָ *until thou comest,* i. e. till one comes.

TENSES.

§ 501. As the Hebrew has but two distinct *forms* of tense, it is obvious that these must have had a diverse, various, and extended use.

§ 502. The Praeter and Future forms can be used indifferently, in a great many cases, to express the same idea. Both of them may be made *Aorists* by prefixing Vav, § 208, § 209, and by some other particles placed before them; but the *predominant* use of the Praeter is to express *past* time of some shade or other; and the *predominant* use of the Future is to designate some shade of *future* time.

§ 503. *The Praeter tense* of verbs is used to designate the meaning of various tenses.

(*a*) For the Perfect tense, which is its appropriate use; e. g. Gen. 3: 13, 'what is this which עָשִׂית, *thou hast done?* 3: 11, 'who הִגִּיד *has told* thee?' 3: 14, 17, 22.

(*b*) For the Pluperfect tense; e. g. Gen. 2: 2, 'God finished the work עָשָׂה, *he had made;* 2: 5, 'Jehovah לֹא הִמְטִיר, *had not caused it to rain.*'

(c) For the past tense of narration or historic tense; e. g. Gen. 1: 1, 'God בָּרָא *created*;' 1: 2, 'the earth הָיְתָה *was*;' 29: 17, 'Rachel הָיְתָה יְפַת־תֹּאַר, *was beautiful in appearance.*'

The Fut. with Vav conversive commonly follows the Praeter, in the same sentence or in a succeeding one, in order to avoid repeating the Praeter. This form of tense is common, where a subsequent narration is connected with a preceding one. Comp. Gen. 4: 2—5. 1 Sam. 7: 15, 16.

(d) For the present tense; (1) In verbs signifying quality or condition; as גָּדַל *he is great,* חָכַם *he is wise,* etc. (2) When the object of the verb is to express *a state of acting*; as Ps. 119: 28, 'my soul דָּלְפָה *weeps* for trouble;' 119: 30, 'the way of truth בָּחָרְתִּי *I choose*;' Is. 1: 15, 'your hands מָלֵאוּ *are full* of blood.' (3) In general propositions designating action at *any* time; as Ps. 1: 1, 'blessed is the man who לֹא הָלַךְ *walketh not*—לֹא דָרָךְ *treadeth not*—לֹא יָשָׁב *sitteth not;* and so often. The Fut. is employed in the same way.

(e) For the Fut. tense; (1) In prophecies, protestations, and assurances; as Is. 9: 1, 'the people who have walked in darkness רָאוּ (see) *shall see* a great light;' Is. 2: 2, וְהָיָה *and it shall come to pass*; 2: 3, 4, 11, 17, 19, et saepe. (2) When a Fut. form (with a future meaning) precedes the Praeter in the same construction; as Is. 1: 30, 31, תִּהְיוּ *ye shall be* as an oak—וְהָיָה הֶחָסֹן *and the mighty man shall be,* etc.; 3: 25, 28, 'thy men יִפֹּלוּ *shall fall* by the sword—and her gates וְאָנוּ וְאָבְלוּ *shall mourn and lament;*' and so often.

Note 1. The conjunction Vav in such cases may precede the verb itself, as in *e.* 2.; or precede the Nom. when this stands before the verb; e. g. Job 19: 27, 'I shall see רָאוּ וְעֵינַי *and my eyes shall behold,*' where רָאוּ is made Fut. by the Vav before its Nominative. In some cases Vav is omitted, particularly by poetic license, and the Praeter still designates the sense of a Future.

Note 2. *Any* word expressive of Future time and standing in connection with any construction, requires the Praet. that follows (with a Vav prefixed) to be rendered as a Future; e. g. 1 Sam. 2: 31, 'behold the days בָּאִים *are coming,* וְגָדַעְתִּי *when I will cut off,* etc. So with an Inf.; as Deut. 4: 30, בַּצַּר לְךָ *when thou shalt be troubled,* וּמְצָאוּךָ *and these things shall overtake thee*; Gen. 2: 5. So also, Ex. 17: 4, עוֹד מְעַט *yet a little time,* וּסְקָלֻנִי *and they will stone me;* Ex. 16: 1, 'at evening וִידַעְתֶּם *ye shall know.*'

(f) For the Imp. mood; (1) When an Imp. precedes, and the Praet. is connected with it by Vav; as Gen. 6: 21, קַח לְךָ *take for thyself,* וְאָסַפְתָּ *and collect;* comp. above in *e.* 2. (2) Sometimes when

§ 504. SYNTAX OF VERBS; FUTURE TENSE. 183

Vav is prefixed without a preceding Imp.; as Gen. 33: 10, 'if I have found favor in thine eyes, וְלָקַחְתָּ then take, etc. Ruth 3: 9. Gen. 47: 23. Deut. 29: 7, 8.

(g) For the Subj. mood in all its tenses, especially when a Fut. with a Subj. meaning precedes in the same construction, § 504. h; e. g. (1) For the Present; as Gen. 3: 22, פֶּן־יִשְׁלַח lest he put forth his hand, וְלָקַח and [lest he] take, וְאָכַל and [lest he] eat, etc. (2) For the Imperf.; as Is. 1: 9, הָיִינוּ 'we should be as Sodom, דָּמִינוּ we should be like Gomorrha;' Gen. 13: 13, דְפָקוּם—וָמֵתוּ, should one hurry them— then they would die; Ruth 1: 12. Judg. 8: 19. (3) For the Pluperf.; as Is. 1: 9, 'unless Jehovah הוֹתִיר had left us a remnant, etc.' 2 K. 13: 19, ' then הִכִּיתָ thou wouldest have smitten the Syrians.' Job 10: 19. Num. 22: 33. (4) For the *Futurum exactum* or Fut. perfect, as it is named; as Ruth 2: 21, עַד אִם־כִּלּוּ, until they shall have finished; 3: 18. Is. 4: 4. Gen. 24: 19.

§ 504. The *Future tense* of verbs is used with a variety of meaning; viz.

(a) To indicate future time; which is its *appropriate* use.

(b) For the present tense; e. g. לֹא אֵדַע, *I know not*; אֹל אוּכַל, *I cannot*; מֵאַיִן תָּבוֹא, whence comest thou? מַה־תְּבַקֵּשׁ, what seekest thou? Also in general propositions; as ' a wise son יְשַׂמַּח makes glad his father.' Such a use of the Fut. is very common, and agrees with the common use of it in Arabic.

(c) To designate *past* time; e. g. (1) Often when preceded by particles that indicate *past* time. (a) By אָז *then*; as Jos. 10: 12, אָז יְדַבֵּר, *then spake he*. (b) By טֶרֶם, *not yet*; as Gen. 2: 5, טֶרֶם יִהְיֶה *was not yet*, or *before it was*. But sometimes the sense is *future* after these particles; as Ex. 12: 48. Job 10: 21. (2) Sometimes (not very frequently) it indicates the *past* time of narration, i. e. it is employed as the *historic* tense; e. g. Gen. 2: 6, ' and a mist יַעֲלֶה *went up*, etc.' 2: 10, ' and thence יִפָּרֵד *it was divided*, etc.' 2: 25, וְלֹא יִתְבּוֹשָׁשׁוּ *and they were not ashamed*. Is not this occasioned by the Vav which precedes? Comp. § 503. e. 2. Note 1.

(d) With Vav conversive the Fut. forms a common historic tense.

Note. Vav does not always stand before the verb itself in such cases, but may stand before some word intimately connected with it; e. g. Gen. 2: 10, וּמִשָּׁם יִפָּרֵד, *and thence it was divided*.

⁎ (e) Without such Vav it is sometimes employed to denote *habitual* or *continued* action; as 1 K. 5: 25, ' thus much Solomon יִתֵּן *gave* to Hiram yearly;' Job 1: 5, ' thus יַעֲשֶׂה *did* Job continually; 2 Sam. 12: 31. 2 Chr. 25: 14.

§§ 504. 505. SYNTAX OF VERBS; IMPER. MOOD.

(*f*) For the Imp.; viz. (1) Always where the *first* or *third* person of the Imp. is needed; as Gen. 1: 26, נַעֲשֶׂה אָדָם *let us make man;* 1: 3, יְהִי־אוֹר *let there be light,* etc. Where excitement, urging, entreaty, etc., is to be expressed, the parag. Fut. is usually employed; as אָגִילָה, *let me rejoice now;* אָקוּמָה, *let me arise now.* (2) In prohibitions; because the Hebrew Imp. is not used with negatives; e. g. Ex. 20: 15, לֹא תִגְנֹב, *steal not,* lit. thou shalt not steal.

(*g*) For the Optative; especially when the particle נָא is subjoined; e. g. Ps. 7: 10, יִגְמָר־נָא *O that it might come to an end!* Cant. 7: 9, יִהְיוּ־נָא *O may they be!* 1 K. 17: 21. Is. 19: 12. 47: 13. For the Optative use of the parag. and apoc. Fut., see § 203. seq.

(*h*) For the Subjunctive; especially after particles signifying *that, so that, in order that,* etc. E. g. after אֲשֶׁר *that,* בַּעֲבוּר *that,* וְ *that,* כִּי *that,* לְ *that,* לְמַעַן אֲשֶׁר *in order that,* אַל *that not,* בַּל *that not,* פֶּן *that not.* But the Fut. often follows particles such as the above, when a Subj. sense is not required but a Fut. one.

(*i*) The Fut. designates all those shades of meaning, which we express in English by the auxiliaries, *may, can, must, might, could, should, would,* etc. E. g. Gen. 3: 2, נֹאכֵל, *we may eat;* 30: 31, מָה־אֶתֶּן־לָךְ, *what must* [shall] *I give thee?* Judg. 14: 16, וְלָךְ אַגִּיד, *and should I tell thee?* Prov. 20: 9, מִי־יֹאמַר, *who can* [will] *say?* So Job 10: 18, אֶגְוַע, *I should have died;* Gen. 31: 37, וַאֲשַׁפְּטֶךָ, *that I might take my leave of thee;* 28: 8, 'until that all יֵאָסְפוּ *shall have been gathered;* comp. § 503. *g.* 4.

(*j*) The Fut. with Vav conversive (which commonly indicates *past* time), is sometimes used as a proper Future, the Vav being rendered merely as a *conjunction;* e. g. Is. 9: 5, 'to us a son shall be given, and the government וַתְּהִי *shall be* upon his shoulder, etc.' Is. 9: 10, 13, 15, 17. 51: 12, 13.

(*k*) The Fut. with Vav is sometimes also used, (1) For the Present Indic.; as 2 Sam. 19: 2, 'behold the king weeps וַיִּתְאַבֵּל *and mourns;* Ps. 102: 5, וַיִּבַשׁ, *and is dried up.* (2) For the present Subj.; as Jos. 9: 21, 'let them live, וַיִּהְיוּ *and let them be,* or *may they be,* etc.' Job 14: 10. But such uses of the Fut. with Vav *conversive,* are not frequent.

Note. In respect to the *forms,* etc., of the Fut., comp. § 203. seq.

Imperative mood.

§ 505. The Imp. mood and the Fut. tense are nearly related to each other, and often they are used almost in-

§ 505. 507. SYNTAX OF VERBS; COMPOSITE VERBS.   185

discriminately; comp. § 504. *f.* § 201. The Imp., besides its *proper* sense, is employed for the Future; viz.

(*a*) When two Imperatives immediately succeed each other; in which case the latter often has a Fut. sense, and the former a conditional one; e. g. Gen. 42: 18, עֲשׂוּ וָחְיוּ, *do this and live,* i. e. do this and ye shall live; Prov. 3: 3, 4, 7. 4: 4. 7: 2. 9: 6. Is. 8: 9. 36: 16. 45: 22. 55: 2.

(*b*) When an Imp. is connected with a Fut. in the same construction, it often has a Fut. meaning; e. g. (1) Sometimes when it stands *before* the Fut.; as Is. 45: 11, שְׁאָלוּנִי WILL *ye inquire of me*—and תְּצַוֻּנִי *will ye prescribe to me?* 6: 9. (2) When it stands *after* the Fut.; as Gen. 45: 18, וְאֶתְּנָה *and I will give you*.... וַאֲכָלוּ *and ye shall eat,* lit. eat ye. Gen. 20: 7. Is. 54: 14. Ruth 1: 9.

Use of composite Verbs.

§ 506. The Hebrew does not form composite verbs, like the Greek and Latin, by *prefixing* prepositions to them; but it inserts a preposition *between* them and the noun or pronoun which follows them.

<small>Different prepositions are used in order to vary the shades of meaning; and in this way a great variety of forms of verbs are made in Hebrew, Aramaean, and Arabic, which may be called *composite;* like our English, *put, put by, put up, put in, put down, put aside, put away,* etc.</small>

E. g. נָפַל *to fall;* נָפַל עַל *to fall over to, to fall away;* נָפַל מִן *to leave, to depart from;* נָפַל לִפְנֵי *to fall down before* any one. קָרָא *to call;* קָרָא בְּ *to call to, to invoke;* קָרָא לְ *to name.* שָׁאַל *to ask* with an Acc. of the *person;* שָׁאַל *to demand,* with an Acc. of the *thing* demanded; שָׁאַל בְּ *to consult* any one.

§ 507. No definite rules can be made out, for the very various usage of prepositions in these cases. The lexicons and practice only can give the requisite information. The following distinctions may aid the learner, in a few cases; viz.

(*a*) The preposition בְּ is often put after verbs signifying *to be angry, to trust, to hold, to sin against, to reprove,* etc.; also *to pray to, to invoke, to worship, to testify against, to look upon, to hear* or *listen to, to smell, to touch,* etc.

(*b*) The preposition לְ is often put after verbs signifying, *to make, to attain to, to become* any thing: as 2 Sam. 7: 14, 'I will be to him לְאָב, *for a father* [a father], and he shall be to me לְבֵן, *for a son* [a son];' 1 Sam. 4: 9, הֱיוּ לַאֲנָשִׁים, *be ye for men,* i. e. be men, act courageously; Gen. 2: 22, 'and Jehovah made the rib לְאִשָּׁה, *for a woman;*'

i. e. a woman. The later Hebrew makes more frequent use of לְ in this way, than the early; e. g. Jon. 4: 6, comp. Ex. 12: 27.

Note. This is the habitual construction after the verb הָיָה signifying *to become;* e. g. Gen. 2: 7, הָיָה לְנֶפֶשׁ חַיָּה, *became an animated being.*

(c) The particles לְפָנֵי, אַחֲרֵי, בְּעַד, בֵּין, עַל, מִן, כְּ, etc. are often put after verbs; and they modify, in various ways, the simple meaning of them.

Cases governed by Verbs.

§ 508. Active transitive verbs govern the Accusative case.

Note. Many verbs have both a trans. and intrans. sense; consequently they are sometimes *with*, and sometimes *without* an Acc. after them; e. g. בָּכָה *to weep*, and *to bemoan;* הָלַךְ *to go*, and *to pass through*, Gen. 2: 14; יָשַׁב *to dwell*, and *to inhabit;* Ps. 22: 4, זָמַר *to sing*, and *to celebrate with praise;* so שִׁיר, רִנֵּן, etc.

§ 509. Many verbs in Hebrew govern an Acc. directly, without any intervening preposition, which we can translate only by inserting a preposition before the noun.

E. g. בִּשֵּׂר *to bring good tidings* TO *any one*, מָרָה *to be refractory* AGAINST *any one*, עָרַב *to give a pledge* FOR *any one*, etc. Among these are, verbs of *putting off* and *on*, of *ornamenting;* of *plenty* and *want;* of *dwelling in* or *among;* of *going out, coming in, coming upon, happening to*, etc. Verbs of *overflowing, overspreading*, etc. take the Acc. of the thing with which they overflow, etc.; as Ex. 3: 8, 'a land which זָבַת חָלָב וּדְבָשׁ *overflows* with *milk and honey;* Joel 4: 18. Jer. 9: 17. Lam. 3: 48.

§ 510. Neuter verbs sometimes take an Acc. case.

E. g. חָגַג חָג, *to celebrate a feast;* חוּד חִידָה, *to propose an enigma*, etc. Comp. the English, *to run a race, to fight a fight*, etc. Gen. 27: 34. Neh. 2: 10. Ps. 25: 19, etc.

§ 511. *Verbs governing two Accusatives.* All verbs which have a *causative* meaning, (of course the conj. Piel and Hiphil generally), may govern two Accusatives; the one usually of a *person*, and the other of a *thing*.

E. g. Ezek. 8: 17, מָלְאוּ אֶת־הָאָרֶץ חָמָס, *they filled* [caused to be full] *the earth* with *violence;* Gen. 41: 42, וַיַּלְבֵּשׁ אֹתוֹ בִּגְדֵי־שֵׁשׁ, *and he clothed him* with [caused him to put on] *garments of fine linen*, etc.

Note. Many verbs in Kal have a kind of *causative* meaning, or one kindred to it, and may therefore govern two Accusatives; e. g. such as signify, *to anoint, to sow, to plant, to stone,* i. e. cover with stones, *to nourish, to furnish, to rob, to do good* or *evil to* any one, *to call* or *name, to command, to convert one thing into another,* as Job 28: 2, אֶבֶן יָצוּק נְחוּשָׁה, *stone he fuses* into *brass*; Gen. 2: 7, 'God made man עָפָר מִן הָאֲדָמָה with *dust* [out of dust] *from the earth,* where עָפָר is the Acc. of *the material,* as grammarians speak.

§ 512. But the insertion of appropriate prepositions, such as בְּ, לְ, מִן, עַל, etc. before the latter noun in cases like the above, is not unfrequent; so that the Hebrews practised both methods of constructing a sentence.

Many of the cases above may be regarded as having a preposition *implied* before the second noun in the Accusative.

Passive Verbs.

§ 513. The passive forms of verbs which govern two Accusatives, retain but one of them; the other being usually made a Nominative.

E. g. Ps. 80: 11, כָּסּוּ הָרִים צִלָּהּ, *the mountains were covered with the shadow of it.* Ex. 25: 40. 28: 11.

Note. Sometimes verbs of a passive *form* have an active *sense;* and in this case they may govern an Acc., like active verbs; e. g. Job 7: 3, הָנְחַלְתִּי יַרְחֵי שָׁוְא, *I have inherited months of vanity,* where the verb is in Hophal; Ex. 20: 5. Deut. 13: 3.

Infinitive absolute.

§ 514. (1) This is usually put *before* a finite tense of the same verb, and in this position serves to qualify its meaning in various ways; viz.

(*a*) It marks intensity of various degrees; as 1 Sam. 23: 22, עָרֹם יַעְרִם הוּא, *very subtilely will he deal;* 20: 6, נִשְׁאֹל נִשְׁאַל, *he has urgently requested;* Amos 9: 8, לֹא הַשְׁמֵיד אַשְׁמִיד, *I will not utterly destroy.* Gen. 31: 30. 43: 3, 7, הֲיָדֹעַ נֵדַע, *could we indeed know?* 37: 8, הֲמָלֹךְ תִּמְלֹךְ, *shalt thou indeed reign?*

(*b*) It denotes assurance, certainty; as Gen. 2: 17. מוֹת תָּמוּת, *thou shalt surely die;* 3: 4. 37: 33, טָרֹף טֹרַף, *he is surely torn in pieces;* Judg. 15: 2, אָמֹר אָמַרְתִּי, *surely I thought,* or *said.*

(*c*) In general, it gives intensity, energy, animation, vivacity, or some coloring of this nature, to the expression; although it is difficult always to express it in an English version.

So the *intensive* particles of the Greek, German, etc., cannot be well expressed in a translation

(2) Put *after* a finite tense, it marks *continued* action.

E. g. 2 Sam. 15: 30, עָלוּ עָלֹה וּבָכֹה *they went up continually weeping*; Gen. 8: 7, וַיֵּצֵא יָצוֹא וָשׁוֹב, *and it continued going and returning*; Gen. 19: 9, ' he is continually acting the part of a judge.' Is. 6: 9. Jer. 23: 17. 1 Sam. 6: 12. 1 K. 20: 37. 2 Sam. 3: 24. 26: 5. In such cases a participle is sometimes used as a second Inf., 2 Sam. 16: 5; or a noun, Is. 29: 14.

N. B. Although *continued* action, etc., is usually designated by the Inf. abs. placed *after* the finite verb, yet there are examples of this position which do not appear to differ from the cases under No. 1; e. g. Is. 22: 17. Jer. 22: 10. Gen. 31: 15. Dan. 11: 10, 13.

Note 1. The Inf. abs. is *commonly* of the same conjugation as the finite verb with which it is joined, but sometimes of a different one; as Job 6: 1, שָׁקוֹל יִשָּׁקֵל, with Inf. abs. in Kal and finite verb in Niphal; Ezek. 16: 4, הָחְתֵּל לֹא חֻתָּלְתְּ, Inf. in Hophal and finite verb in Pual.

Note 2. The Inf. abs. is sometimes taken from a kindred synonymous verb; as Is. 28: 28, אָדוֹשׁ יְדוּשֶׁנּוּ, *he will thoroughly thresh him*, roots אָדַשׁ and דּוּשׁ, both signifying *to thresh*.

§ 515. The Inf. abs. is sometimes used adverbially.

E. g. הֵיטֵיב *bene faciendo*, for *bene*; 1 Sam. 3: 12, הָחֵל וְכַלֵּה, *incipiendo et finiendo*, i. e. utterly.

§ 516. In a few cases, the Inf. const. is used as the Inf. absolute.

(*a*) Adverbially; as Is. 60: 14, שְׁחוֹחַ *incurvando*, for שָׁחוֹחַ; Hab. 2: 10, קְצוֹת for קָצֹה. (*b*) With a finite verb; as Num. 23: 25, קֹב לֹא תִקֳּבֶנּוּ, *thou shalt not curse at all*, for קָבוֹב: Ruth 2: 16, שֹׁל־תָּשֹׁלּוּ, for שָׁלֹל; Ps. 50: 21, הֱיוֹת־אֶהְיֶה for הָיֹה, etc. Instances of this nature are so rare, that one hardly knows whether to rank them under the head of established usage.

§ 517. The Inf. abs. is sometimes used instead of a finite verb; and this for any mood, tense, or person.

E. g. Deut. 5: 12, שָׁמוֹר simply, instead of שָׁמוֹר תִּשְׁמְרוּן, as it is in Deut. 6: 17; Ex. 20: 8, זָכוֹר for זָכֹר תִּזְכֹּר, as in Deut. 7: 18; Job 40: 2, הֲרֹב *an contendendo?* for הָרֹב רָב, as in Judg. 11: 25. So Dan. 9: 5, מָרַדְנוּ וְסוֹר, *we have rebelled and apostatized*; Est. 9: 6. Jer. 14: 5. Gen. 41: 43. Judg. 7: 19. Ecc. 8: 9. 9: 11. Ezek. 1: 14, ' the living creatures רָצוֹא וָשׁוֹב *ran and returned;* Ecc. 4: 2. Jer. 32: 44, ' fields shall they buy, וְכָתוֹב *and they shall write* bills of sale, וְחָתוֹם—וְהָעֵד *and they shall seal them—and take witnesses*,' etc. Num. 15: 35. Deut.

14: 21. Is. 5: 5. Ezek. 11: 7, you הוֹצֵיא *will I bring out,*' etc. 1 K. 22: 30. 2 Chr. 18: 29.

For the Imper.; Deut. 5: 12, שָׁמוֹר *keep*; 1: 16. Jer. 2: 2, הָלוֹךְ *go*; 13: 1, etc. Num. 25: 17. See the first examples above.

Note. The Inf. abs. is in some cases to be translated in a *passive* sense; as Prov. 12: 7, 'the wicked הָפוֹךְ, *are to be destroyed.*' This is elliptical; the full phrase would be הָפוֹךְ יֵהָפְכוּ. So הָפֵר, Prov. 15: 22.

§ 518. The Inf. abs. is also employed in an *energic* sense, as a kind of *nomen actionis,* or to denote the *practice* of doing any thing.

E. g. אָלֹה וְכַחֵשׁ וְרָצֹחַ וְגָנֹב פָּרָצוּ, *cursing, and dissembling, and murdering, and stealing, break out,* Hos. 4: 2. Is. 21: 5. 59: 4. Jer. 7: 9. 23: 14. 8: 15. 2 K. 4: 43. Prov. 12: 7. Ps. 22: 9.

Note. As the Inf. abs. has generally an *intensive* sense, whether employed with a finite verb or standing alone, it may be called the *energic* form of verbs. The usage adverted to in § 517, § 518, shews that the Heb. language possesses a most striking power of brevity and energy.

§ 518 *a.* The Inf. abs. is sometimes employed simply as a verbal noun in the Acc. after an active verb.

E. g. Is. 42: 24, לֹא אָבוּ הָלוֹךְ, *they would not go.* Is. 7: 15, לְדַעְתּוֹ מָאוֹס, *until he know how to refuse.* Jer. 9: 4.

Infinitive construct.

§ 519. The Inf. const. being a sort of verbal noun, it is used like one in respect to construction, position, government, and even form; the plural forms excepted, which it has not.

§ 520. Like nouns, the Inf. const. is used in the various cases; viz.

(*a*) In the Nom. case; e. g. Gen. 2: 18, הֱיוֹת הָאָדָם, '*the being of the man* alone is not good;' 29: 19, תִּתִּי (Inf. of נָתַן) '*my giving* is good;' 11: 6. 30: 15. (*b*) In the Gen.; e. g. Gen. 29: 7, עֵת הֵאָסֵף, *the time of collecting;* 2: 4, בְּיוֹם עֲשׂוֹת, *in the day of making,* Num. 9: 15. Ps. 128: 2, et passim. (*c*) In the Dat.; e. g. Num. 7: 5, וְהָיוּ, לַעֲבֹד *and let them be for serving,* i. e. let them serve. 8: 11; Ezek. 30: 16, תִהְיֶה לְהִבָּקֵעַ, *it shall be for being pierced through,* i. e. it shall be pierced through; comp. § 523. *d.* (*d*) In the Acc.; e. g. 1 K. 3: 7, '*I knew* not צֵאת וָבוֹא, *the going out or coming in;*' Jer. 5: 3. Gen· 21: 6. The Acc. here commonly has לְ before it; as Gen. 11: 8. Ex. 2: 15. Comp. § 522. § 523. (*c*) In the Abl.; e. g. Ps. 39: 2, 'I will guard my way מֵחֲטוֹא *from sinning.*'

§ 521. Like nouns, it takes prepositions before it, and suffixes after it.

In translating such Infinitives we must generally give them a *finite sense;* e. g. (a) With בְּ; as Gen. 2: 4, בְּהִבָּרְאָם, *when they were created,* lit. in the being created of them; Ex. 16: 7, בְּשָׁמְעוֹ *because he heard;* Is. 1: 15. (b) With כְּ; as Gen. 44: 30, כְּבֹאִי, *when I come;* 39: 18, כַּהֲרִימִי, *when I lifted up.* (c) With לְ; Gen. 2: 3, לַעֲשׂוֹת, *when he made* it; Is. 7: 15, לְדַעְתּוֹ, *until he know;* 1 K. 16: 7, 'to provoke him by his doings, לִהְיוֹת *in that he was,* or *in respect to his being.* In like manner, with אַחַר, תַּחַת, לְמַעַן, עַל, עַד, מִן, etc.

Note. The preposition מִן has often a *negative* sense in such cases; e. g. Gen. 27: 1, 'his eyes were dim מֵרְאֹת, *so that he could not see,* lit. from seeing; 16: 2. Ex. 14: 5. For מִן before the Inf. in comparisons, see § 454. b.

N. B. For the use of the Inf. const. instead of the Inf. abs., see § 516.

§ 522. The Inf. const. with לְ, in many cases, answers to the English Inf. preceded by the particle *to.*

E. g. Gen. 2: 5, 'and there was no man לַעֲבֹד, *to till* the ground;' v. 10, 'and a river went out from Eden לְהַשְׁקוֹת, *to water* the ground;' 11: 6, 'all which they may purpose לַעֲשׂוֹת *to do,'* etc. When בִּלְתִּי (*not*) comes before an Inf., the לְ is put before it; as Gen. 3: 11, 'which I commanded thee לְבִלְתִּי אֲכָל־ *not to eat ;'* i. e. the Inf. is used as a noun in regimen with בִּלְתִּי.

§ 523. The Inf. const. with לְ, and with the verb of existence (הָיָה) expressed or implied, constitutes a periphrasis expressing the meaning of several forms of the finite verb, viz.

(a) Of the Praeter; as 2 Chr. 26: 5, וַיְהִי לִדְרֹשׁ אֱלֹהִים, *and he sought God,* lit. and he was for seeking God; Gen. 15: 12, 'the sun וַיְהִי לָבוֹא *was about to go down,'* lit. was for going down; 2 Chr. 11: 22. Ezra 3: 12.

(b) Of the Present; as Is. 44: 14, [הָיָה] לִכְרָת־לוֹ, *he hews down for himself,* lit. [he is] for hewing down. Prov. 19: 8, 'he that is wise, [הָיָה] לִמְצֹא טוֹב, *findeth prosperity,'* lit. is for finding; Is. 21: 1.

(c) Of the Future; as Is. 38: 20, יְהוָֹה [וְיִהְיֶה] לְהוֹשִׁיעֵנִי, *Jehovah will deliver me,* lit. will be for the delivering of me; Ps. 25: 14, 'Jehovah [וְיִהְיֶה] לְהוֹדִיעָם] *will teach them,'* lit. will be for the teaching of them; 49: 15. 62: 10. Ecc. 3: 14. So Ps. 101: 8, ' soon אַצְמִית *will I destroy* the wicked of the land, לְהַכְרִית *I will cut off,'* etc.

(d) Of the Passive ; as Jos. 2: 5, ' and it came to pass הַשַּׁעַר לִסְגּוֹר when the gate was to be shut,' lit. at the shutting of the gate ; Deut. 31: 17, וְהָיָה לֶאֱכֹל, and they shall be devoured, lit. and it shall be for devouring them ; Is. 6: 13.

(e) Of the Latin participle in -dus, or the English auxiliaries shall, can, must, etc. ; as 2 K. 4: 13, מֶה [הָיָה] לַעֲשׂוֹת, what [is] to be done for thee ? 2 Chr. 19: 2, הֲלָרָשָׁע [הָיָה] לַעְזֹר, should one help the wicked ? Judg. 1: 19, לֹא [הָיָה] לְהוֹרִישׁ, he could not dispossess them : Hos. 9: 13. Amos 6: 10. 2 Chr. 20: 6.

§ 524. The Inf. const. (sometimes also the Inf. abs.) governs nouns in the oblique cases, like finite verbs.

The Inf. const. sometimes takes *verbal* suffixes, i. e. it governs pronouns in the Acc. The Inf. abs. also, in a very few cases, takes an Acc. after it ; as. Is. 22: 13, הָרֹג בָּקָר וְשָׁחֹט צֹאן וְאָכֹל בָּשָׂר, *caedendo boves, et jugulando oves, et edendo carnem*, etc.

§ 525. The *subject* of the Inf. const. (corresponding to the Nom. of finite verbs), is usually put in the Gen. after the verb.

E. g. Judg. 13: 20, בַּעֲלוֹת הַלַּהַב, *in the mounting up of the flame*, i. e. when the flame mounted up ; 1 Sam. 23: 6, בִּבְרֹחַ אֶבְיָתָר, *in the flying of Abiathar*, i. e. when Abiathar fled ; Ps. 66: 10. Here, also, belong those cases in which the Inf. const. takes *noun-suffixes*, i. e. suffixes in the Genitive.

§ 526. Besides the *subject* in the Gen. after the Inf. construct, it also takes the *object*, i. e. an Acc. case, and even two Accusatives.

E. g. Gen. 2: 4, בְּיוֹם עֲשׂוֹת יְהוָה אֶרֶץ וְשָׁמַיִם, *in the day of Jehovah's making the earth and heavens*, i. e. in the day when Jehovah made, etc. 1 K. 13: 4, כִּשְׁמֹעַ הַמֶּלֶךְ אֶת־דְּבַר אִישׁ, *when the king heard the word of the man*, etc. Is. 58: 5, ' a day עַנּוֹת אָדָם נַפְשׁוֹ, *when a man will afflict his soul*,' etc. So with the subject and two Accusatives ; as Gen. 41: 39, אַחֲרֵי הוֹדִיעַ אֱלֹהִים אוֹתְךָ אֶת־כָּל־זֹאת, *since God's showing you all this*, i. e. since God hath shewn etc.

Note. The Gen. or *subject* usually stands next to the verb ; but in a very few cases the Acc. is put first ; as Is. 5: 24, כֶּאֱכֹל קַשׁ לְשׁוֹן אֵשׁ, *as the flame of fire devours the stubble*; 20: 1. Gen. 4: 15.

PARTICIPLES.

§ 527. Active Participles are often used in the place of finite verbs; viz.

(a) For the present tense; e. g. Ecc. 1: 4, 'one generation הֹלֵךְ *passeth away,* and another generation בָּא *cometh;'* 1: 7, 8. Ps. 1: 6. 3: 2. 4: 7. Is. 1: 7. In this manner participles are used with pronouns of any person instead of verbs, in order to express the present tense; as יָרֵא אָנֹכִי, *I fear;* יָרֵא אַתָּה, *thou fearest;* יְרֵאִים אֲנַחְנוּ, *we fear;* etc. In intrans. verbs this use is very common.

(b) For the past tense in all its gradations; e. g. Gen. 2: 10, 'and a river יֹצֵא *issued* from Eden;' Deut. 4: 3, 'your eyes הָרֹאוֹת *have seen;'* Gen. 31: 17, 18, 19.

(c) For the Fut. in all its varieties; e. g. Gen. 17: 19, 'Sarah יֹלֶדֶת *shall bear* a son,' etc. 19: 13, מַשְׁחִיתִים 'we are about to destroy the city;' 6: 17, 'behold I מֵבִיא *will cause to come* a flood;' 48: 4. Ex. 9: 18. 1 K. 11: 31. 14: 10.

§ 528. Participles, when used as verbs, are subject to all the *anomalies* of concord which are found in verbs.

E. g. Gen. 4: 10, קוֹל דְּמֵי אָחִיךָ צֹעֲקִים, *the voice of thy brother's blood cries* [cry].

§ 529. The two Hebrew participles, active and passive, often have the sense of the Latin participles in *-rus* and *-dus.*

E. g. Gen. 19: 14, מַשְׁחִית יְהוָה הָעִיר, *Jehovah is about to destroy the city;* Ps. 76: 8, נוֹרָא, *metuendus;* Ps. 18: 4, מְהֻלָּל, *laudandus,* etc.

§ 530. The verb of existence (הָיָה) added to the participle, makes an Imperf. tense descriptive of continued action or condition.

E. g. Job 1: 14, 'the cattle הָיוּ חֹרְשׁוֹת, *were ploughing;'* Neh. 1: 4, וָאֱהִי צָם וּמִתְפַּלֵּל, *I was fasting and praying;* 2: 13, 15. 2 Chr. 24: 14. 36: 16. Gen. 4: 17. Deut. 9: 22, 24.

Note. In like manner יֵשׁ *there is,* and אֵין *there is not,* either with or without suffixes, are often connected with participles, and form a periphrasis for the Pres. tense of the finite verb; e. g. Judg. 6: 36, 'if יֶשְׁךָ מוֹשִׁיעַ *thou savest;'* Gen. 24: 49. 43: 5, 'if אֵינְךָ מְשַׁלֵּחַ, *thou dost not send away;'* Ex. 5: 16, 'straw אֵין נִתָּן *is not given;'* Lev. 26: 6.

§ 531. *Active participles* may govern the same cases as their verbs; but it is a more common construction to put them *in regimen* with the noun that follows.

E. g. Ps. 84: 5, יוֹשְׁבֵי בֵיתֶךָ, *inhabiters of thy house;* Ps. 28: 1, יוֹרְדֵי בוֹר, *the descenders of* [i. e. those who go down into] *the pit;* 5: 12, אֹהֲבֵי שְׁמֶךָ, *the lovers of thy name;* 19: 8. Prov. 2: 19. Such a Gen. is capable of all the varieties of rendering which belong to the Gen. after nouns, § 424. It also admits intervening prepositions, like nouns, § 432.

§ 532. Passive participles are constructed with cases in various ways; viz.

(*a*) With an Acc.; as Ezek. 9: 2, לָבוּשׁ בַּדִּים, *clothed* [with] *linen garments;* 1 Sam. 2: 18, חָגוּר אֵפוֹד, *girded* [with] *an ephod.* So in Greek ἀναιδείην ἐπιειμένος, Il. α. 149. (*b*) With the Gen.; as Ezek. 9: 11, לְבֻשׁ הַבַּדִּים, *clothed* [of] *linen garments;* Joel 1: 8, חֲגֻרַת־שַׂק *girded* [of] *sackcloth;* Ps. 32: 1, נְשׂוּי־פֶּשַׁע, *pardoned* [of] *sin,* etc.

Note. When there is but one form of the participle, as מֵת (from מוּת *to die*), this is capable of all the meanings and constructions of both the act. and pass. participles.

§ 532 *a.* Active participles are very often employed as mere *nomina agentis* vel *patientis*, i. e. are mere nouns in the sense of agents actively or passively considered.

Verbs used as adverbs.

§ 533. When two verbs *immediately* follow each other, either with or without the copula between them, the first of them may serve merely to qualify the second, and must then be rendered adverbially.

E. g. 1 Sam. 2: 3, אַל תַּרְבּוּ תְדַבְּרוּ, *do not make much* [and] *speak* i. e. do not say much; Job 19: 3, לֹא תֵבֹשׁוּ תַּהְכְּרוּ־לִי, *ye are not ashamed ye stun me,* i. e. in a shameless manner ye stun me; Gen. 26: 18, וַיָּשָׁב וַיַּחְפֹּר, *and he returned and dug,* i. e. he again dug; 19: 22. 27: 20. 30: 31. 31: 28. Hos. 1: 6. Ps. 51: 4. 71: 20. So הֵיטִיב is used for *well, skilfully,* Ps. 33: 3, הוֹסִיף for *again, once more,* Gen. 4: 2. 8: 12. כִּלָּה for *ad finem, entirely,* Gen. 24: 15. מִהַר for *hastily, quickly,* Gen. 27: 20. Ex. 2: 18. הִרְבָּה for *much, often,* 2 K. 21: 6. Ps. 51: 4. שׁוּב for *again,* 1 K. 19: 6. Job 7: 7. The same is true of some other verbs. In some cases the *second* verb is the Inf., as Gen. 27: 20. Ex. 2: 18, etc.

ADVERBS.

§ 534. Adverbs in Hebrew are often used in the place of nouns.

(a) In apposition with the nouns which they qualify: as Gen. 18: 4, מְעַט־מַיִם, *a little water*; Neh. 2: 12, אֲנָשִׁים מְעַט, *few persons*; Is. 30: 33, עֵצִים הַרְבֵּה, *much wood*, etc. (b) In the Gen. after nouns; as 1 K. 2: 31, דְּמֵי חִנָּם, *innocent blood*; Ezek. 30: 16, צָרֵי יוֹמָם, *daily persecutors*; Deut. 26: 5, מְתֵי מְעָט, *few men*, etc.

§ 535. Adverbs standing in the place of nouns, sometimes take prepositions before them in the manner of nouns.

E. g. Ezek. 6: 10, אֶל חִנָּם, *gratis*; 2 Chr. 19: 36, בְּפִתְאֹם, *suddenly*; 1 K. 22: 20, בְּכֹה, *so*, [lit. in the so]; Esth. 4: 16, בְּכֵן, *so*; Neh. 9: 19, בְּיוֹמָם, *daily*.

§ 536. The repetition of adverbs marks intensity.

E. g. Gen. 7: 19, מְאֹד מְאֹד, *very much*; Deut. 28: 43, מַעְלָה מַּעְלָה, *higher and higher*; מַטָּה מַטָּה, *deeper and deeper*; 1 K. 20: 40, הֵנָּה וָהֵנָּה, *hither and hither*, i. e. here and there, all around.

§ 537. Two negatives in Hebrew strengthen the negation.

E. g. 1 K. 10: 21, אֵין כֶּסֶף לֹא נֶחְשָׁב, *silver was not at all regarded*. In the parallel verse, 2 Chr. 9: 20, לֹא is omitted. Ex. 14: 11, הֲמִבְּלִי אֵין קְבָרִים, *because there were no graves at all*. Zeph. 2: 2. etc.

§ 538. A negative particle is often joined with nouns and adjectives, to qualify the sense of them.

E. g. Deut. 32: 6, לֹא חָכָם, *not wise*, i. e. foolish; Ps. 43: 1, לֹא חָסִיד, *unmerciful*; Job 30: 8, בְּלִי שֵׁם, *disgraced*; Deut. 32: 21, לֹא־אֵל, *no God*; לֹא־עָם, *not a nation*, i. e. not worthy of this appellation; Is. 31: 8, לֹא־אִישׁ, *not a mortal*; 10: 15, לֹא־עֵץ, *no wood at all*, etc. This mode of expression is called λιτότης.

Note. A negative is frequently *implied* in an interrogative sentence; e. g. 2 Sam. 7: 5, הַאַתָּה, *wilt thou build me an house?* i. e. thou shalt not; as in the parallel verse, 1 Chr. 17: 4. So Is. 27: 7. Prov. 24: 28. Ezek. 18: 23, comp. v. 32. 1 K. 8: 27. Gen. 30: 20. Job 16: 6, 'if I keep silence מַה־מִּמֶּנִּי יַהֲלֹךְ, *what departs from me?* i. e. I am not relieved; Cant. 8: 4. Prov. 20: 24. Dan. 1: 10.

PREPOSITIONS.

§ 539. Prepositions both simple and composite govern the oblique cases of nouns, pronouns, etc.

For the pleonasm and ellipsis of them, see § 547. § 559.

Note. The Hebrew language sometimes compounds two or more prepositions together, and employs them at one time in the sense of one part of this composite word, and at another in the sense that each of the prepositions separately used would convey; e. g. אַחֲרֵי = מֵאַחֲרֵי, מִן = לְמִן, עַל = מֵעַל, etc. Yet in most of such cases, the first preposition seems to indicate some relation which could not be expressed without it; e. g. לְמִן means *from* [something] *to* [something], an idea different from that conveyed by מִן simply.

CONJUNCTIONS.

§ 540. As the Hebrew language possesses but very few conjunctions, some of them are necessarily employed in a great variety of significations. This is particularly the case with the copulative וְ. But the various uses of this and others, are best learned from the lexicons and from practice.

For some peculiar uses of Vav, see § 558. Note. For the *ellipsis* of conjunctions, see § 561.

INTERJECTIONS.

§ 541. Interjections simply expressive of *calamity* or *imprecation*, often take a Dative after them.

E. g. 1 Sam. 4: 8, אוֹי לָנוּ, *wo to us!* Ezek. 30: 2, הָהּ לַיּוֹם, *wo for the day!*

§ 542. Interjections which have the forms of other parts of speech, take after them the cases required by those forms.

E. g. Ps. 1: 1, אַשְׁרֵי with a Gen. after it; 29: 1, 2, הָבוּ, with an Acc., etc.

PLEONASM.

§ 543. PERSONAL PRONOUNS. *Verbal suffixes* are not unfrequently pleonastic, being immediately followed by the noun to which they have relation.

E. g. Ex. 2: 6, וַתִּרְאֵהוּ אֶת־הַיֶּלֶד, *she saw him the child;* 1 Sam. 21: 14, וַיְשַׁנּוֹ אֶת־טַעְמוֹ *he changed it his understanding;* Job 33: 20, זִהֲמַתּוּ חַיָּתוֹ לָחֶם, *his soul abhors it bread;* Ps. 83: 12. Such is the predominant construction in the Chaldee and Syriac.

§ 544. *The suffixes of nouns* are sometimes pleonastic.

E. g. Is. 17: 6, בִּסְעִפֶיהָ פֹּרִיָּה, *in the twigs of it the fruit tree;* Prov. 14: 13, אַחֲרִיתָהּ שִׂמְחָה, *the end of it joy;* Cant. 1: 6, כַּרְמִי שֶׁלִּי, *my vineyard which* [is] *to me.* Such also is the general usage of the Chaldee and Syriac.

§ 545. The Dative case of pronouns after verbs, and especially verbs of motion, is often pleonastic.

E. g. Gen. 12: 1, לֶךְ־לְךָ, *go for thyself*, i. e. go; Cant. 2: 11, הָלַךְ לוֹ, *it has gone for itself*, i. e. has gone; Gen. 27: 43, בְּרַח־לְךָ, *flee for thyself*, i. e. flee; Is. 31: 8, נָס לוֹ, *he has fled for himself*, i. e. he has fled; Job 39: 4, לֹא־שָׁבוּ לָמוֹ, *they turned not back for themselves*, i. e. turned not back; Cant. 2: 17, דְּמֵה לְךָ, *compare for thyself*, i. e. compare; Job 12: 11, 'the palate וְטַעַם־לוֹ, *relishes for itself*,' i. e. relishes; 15: 28, 'houses which לֹא־יֵשְׁבוּ לָמוֹ, *they do not inhabit for themselves*,' i. e. which no one inhabits; Prov. 13: 13, יֵחָבֶל לוֹ, *he shall perish for himself*, i. e. shall perish; Job 19: 29, גּוּרוּ לָכֶם, *fear for yourselves*, i. e. fear ye. The Arabic has the same idiom; and it is also very common in Syriac.

§ 546. The Dative pleonastic also occurs after participles and adjectives; but more seldom than after verbs.

E. g. Hos. 8: 9, 'a wild ass בֹּדֵד לוֹ, *lonely for itself*,' i. e. alone, or lonely; Amos 2: 13, מְלֵאָה לָהּ, *full for itself*, i. e. full; Ps. 144: 2, מְפַלְּטִי־לִי, *my deliverer for me*, i. e. my deliverer.

547. Of Prepositions. The prepositions בְּ and מִן are sometimes pleonastic.

(*a*) בְּ; as Ex. 32: 22, 'thou knowest this people that בְּרָע הוּא, *they are evil*,' lit. that they are in evil; Hos. 13: 9, כִּי־בִי בְעֶזְרֶךָ, *for my help is in thee*, lit. in respect to me [I am] in thy help; Ps. 29: 4. Prov. 3: 26. Is. 26: 4. 45: 14, אַךְ בָּךְ אֵל, *only thou* [art] *God*, or *only in thee* [is] *God*; Job 18: 8. Ezra 3: 3. In the three last examples, it stands even before the subject of a sentence. This is technically called *Beth essentiae.*

Note. The name of *Beth essentiae* is also extended to בְּ used in cases like the following; as Ps. 118: 7, יְהוָה בְּעֹזְרָי, *Jehovah is among my helpers*, i. e. Jehovah is my helper. Ps. 54: 6. 99: 6. Job 24: 13. Judg. 13: 35.

(*b*) מִן; as Deut. 15: 7, 'a poor man מֵאַחַד אַחֶיךָ, *one of thy brethren*,' lit. from one of thy brethren; Lev. 4: 2. 5: 13. Ezek. 18: 10. This idiom is common in Arabic.

ELLIPSIS.

§ 548. Of Nouns. The Nom. case is sometimes omitted before verbs.

(a) Before verbs used in an intrans. way, in order to denote condition or state of feeling; e. g. Gen. 31: 36, וַיִּחַר לֹו *it was hot to him*, viz. אַף *anger*, i. e. his anger burned; Gen. 34: 7. comp. Gen. 30: 2. Ex. 4: 14, etc., where אַף is expressed. So 1 Sam. 24: 11, וַתָּחָס עָלֶיךָ, *and it pitied thee*, i. e. mine eye (עֵינִי) pitied; comp. Gen. 45: 20. Deut. 7: 16, etc. where עַיִן is expressed. (b) Words such as the mind of the reader will spontaneously supply, are sometimes omitted, viz. such as אֱלֹהִים, יְהוָֹה, etc.; e. g. Prov. 10: 24, *the desire of the righteous* יִתֵּן *he will grant*, i. e. Jehovah will grant; 12: 12. 13: 21. 21: 13. Job 3: 20. Ecc. 9: 9. Ps. 10: 4, comp. v. 13, and see below in § 555.

§ 549. The Acc. case after several verbs which are in frequent use, is often omitted as being unnecessary to render the language intelligible.

E. g. יָלְדָה *she bore*, i. e. children; כָּרַת *he concluded*, viz. בְּרִית *an agreement;* נָטָה *he inclined or spread*, i. e. אֹזֶן *the ear*, or אֹהֶל *the tent;* נָשָׂא *he lifted up*, i. e. קוֹל *the voice;* עָרַךְ *he arranged*, i. e. מִלִּים *words* in prayer, etc. These omissions are sometimes supplied; but more generally the noun is omitted.

§ 550. When the subject of a proposition is required by the sense to be repeated in the predicate with some addition, the actual repetition of it rarely takes place.

E. g. Cant. 1: 15, עֵינַיִךְ יוֹנִים *thine eyes* [are the eyes] *of doves;* Ps. 18: 34. 43: 7. 55: 7. Is. 52: 14.

§ 551. In the designation of weights and measures, the ordinary words which express the standard of them, are commonly omitted; days and months, also, are in like manner occasionally omitted.

E. g. אֶלֶף כֶּסֶף, *a thousand* [shekels] *of silver;* עֲשָׂרָה זָהָב, *ten* [shekels] *of gold;* שֵׁשׁ שְׂעֹרִים *six* [ephahs] *of barley;* שְׁתֵּי לֶחֶם *two* [loaves] *of bread;* comp. § 463. So in respect to time; as בְּאֶחָד לַחֹדֶשׁ *on the first* [day] *of the month.* Gen. 8: 15. Ex. 12: 18. Comp. § 465.

§ 552. OF PRONOUNS. The *personal* pronouns are often omitted; e. g.

(a) In the Nom. most commonly, as in Greek and Latin. (b) In the Gen. after the Inf. *nominascens*, or after a noun; e. g. Gen. 6: 19, לְהַחֲיוֹת, *to preserve* [them] *alive*, etc., instead of לְהַחֲיוֹתָם; Ex. 15: 2, ' Jehovah is my strength, וְזִמְרָת *and* [my] *song,*' for וְזִמְרָתִי; Ps. 40:

10, 11. 66: 6, etc. (e) In the Acc. after verbs; as Ex. 2: 25, 'and God וַיֵּדַע *observed* them,' for וַיֵּדָעֵם; so perhaps Ps. 137: 5, 'let my right hand תִּשְׁכַּח *forget* [me];' 139: 1. 17: 11. Gen. 9: 22, etc.

§ 553. The relative pronoun אֲשֶׁר is often omitted in various constructions; viz.

(a) In the Nom.; as Gen. 15: 13, 'in a land לֹא לָהֶם, [which] *is not theirs;'* Is. 40: 20. 51: 2. 54: 1. 55: 5. 61: 10, etc. (b) In the Gen. after a noun in the const. state; as Ex. 4: 13, 'send [אֲשֶׁר] תִּשְׁלַח *by the hand* [of him whom] *thou wilt send.'* See § 433. (c) In the Acc.; Prov. 9: 5, 'as wine [which] מָסָכְתִּי *I have mingled;'* Gen. 3: 13, מַה־זֹּאת עָשִׂית, *what is this* [which] *thou hast done?*

(d) When used to qualify pronouns, adverbs, etc. (§ 478); as Ex. 18: 20, 'the way יֵלְכוּ בָהּ [in which] *they go;'* Job 3: 3, 'perish the day [אֲשֶׁר] אִוָּלֶד בּוֹ, [in which] *I was born;'* Ps. 32: 2. Is. 1: 30. 23: 7, etc. Ecc. 1: 5, [אֲשֶׁר] זוֹרֵחַ הוּא שָׁם, [where] *he arose.* (e) Sometimes even the pronoun which אֲשֶׁר would qualify, is also omitted; as Ps. 4: 8, 'more than in the time [אֲשֶׁר] דְּגָנָם וְתִירוֹשָׁם רָבּוּ [בוֹ], [in which] *their corn and new wine increase,* etc. Comp. § 478. Note.

(f) אֲשֶׁר in the sense of *that which, he who, those who,* etc., is often omitted; e. g. Job 24: 19, 'Sheōl takes away חָטָאוּ [those who] *have sinned;'* Ps. 12: 6, 'I will place in safety יָפִיחַ לוֹ [him whom] *one puffs at,'* i. e. who is contemned. (g) In an *adverbial* sense; as 1 Chr. 15: 12, אֶל הֲכִינוֹתִי לוֹ *to* [the place which] *I have prepared for it;* comp. § 478. Note.

Note. The omission of אֲשֶׁר is much more common in poetry than in prose. In prose, it is generally inserted after a *definite* noun, and omitted after an indefinite one, as in Arabic. (De Sacy, Gramm. Arabe II. § 363.)

§ 554. Of Verbs. The verb of existence (הָיָה) is commonly omitted between a subject and its predicate, especially when the predicate stands first; see § 446.

E. g. Gen. 3: 11, כִּי־עֵירוֹם אָנֹכִי, *for naked* [am] *I;* 4. 13, גָּדוֹל עֲוֹנִי, *great* [is] *my iniquity,* etc.

555. When the words of any one are repeated, the verb אָמַר (which marks quotation) is very often omitted, and must be supplied from the sense of the passage.

E. g. Ps. 8: 4, when I behold the heavens, [אֹמַר אֲנִי *I exclaim*], Lord, what is man!' 10: 4, 'the wicked in his pride [אָמַר *has said*], בַּל־יִדְרֹשׁ [Jehovah] *will not punish;'* comp. v. 13, where the ellipsis is supplied; Ps. 52: 8, 9. 59: 8. Job 8: 18. Ecc. 8: 2, אֲנִי, i. e. [אוֹמֵר] אֲנִי.

§§ 556—559. ELLIPSIS OF ADVERBS—PREPOSITIONS. 199

§ 556. When a finite verb would be preceded by an Inf. abs. of the same verb, the former is sometimes omitted; comp. § 517.

Note. Besides the above common cases of ellipsis in respect to the the verb, there are many others, especially in poetry, which cannot be made the subject of rules, but must be supplied in conformity with the context; e. g. in Job 39: 24. Is. 66: 6. Ps. 3: 9. 4: 3. 6: 4. 7: 9. Jer. 11: 15. 2 Sam. 23: 17, comp. 1 Chr. 11: 19. 1 K. 11: 25. 2 K. 6: 33. Hos. 8: 1. Prov. 6: 26.

§ 577. Of Adverbs. The interrogative הֲ is often omitted.

E. g. Gen. 27: 24, אַתָּה זֶה בְּנִי, *art thou my very son*, for הַאַתָּה; 3: 1, אַף כִּי, *is it so then that*, for הַאַף כִּי; 1 Sam. 16: 4. 30: 8. 2 Sam. 9: 6. 18: 29. Job 40: 25. Such ellipsis often takes place in a *negative* interrogation before לֹא; as Jon. 4: 11, וַאֲנִי לֹא אָחוּס, *and should not I spare* Nineveh? instead of הֲלֹא; Lam. 1: 12. 3: 36. Ex. 8: 22. 2 K. 5: 26. Job 14: 16, וְלֹא תִשְׁמֹר, *and wilt thou not keep watch* over my sins? So also before אַל, 1 Sam. 27: 10.

§ 558. When two negative propositions follow each other in the same construction, especially in poetic parallelism, the *negative* adverb is sometimes omitted in the second proposition, and must be supplied.

E. g. 1 Sam. 2: 3, 'speak not proudly, יֵצֵא עָתָק, *let* [not] *any rash thing proceed* from your mouth;' Ps. 9: 19, 'for he will not always forget the poor, the expectation of the afflicted תֹּאבַד, *shall* [not] *always perish;* Ps. 75: 6. Job 28: 17. 30: 20. Is. 23: 4. 38: 18.

Note. When a negative is expressed in the first member of a parallelism, and the second has a Vav prefixed to it, that Vav should be rendered disjunctively, viz. *nor, but,* etc.; e. g. Ps. 44: 19, 'our heart has not turned back from thee, וַתֵּט אֲשֻׁרֵינוּ, NOR *our steps declined;* Is. 41: 28, וְיָשִׁיבוּ NOR *did any answer,* or BUT *none gave answer;* Job 3: 10. Is. 28: 27. Deut. 33: 6.

§ 559. Of Prepositions. The prepositions בְּ, לְ, etc., are not unfrequently omitted where the sense requires them.

(*a*) The prefix בְּ; as Ps. 66: 17, אֵלָיו פִּי־קָרָאתִי, *I cried to him* [with] *my mouth,* for בְּפִי; 12: 3. 17: 10, 13, 14. 60: 7, 'help me יְמִינְךָ [with] *thy right hand;* 108: 7. 109: 2, etc. Note also that the prefix כְּ, when used as a conjunction, usually excludes בְּ; as Am. 9: 11,

200 §§ 560—562. SYNTAX; ELLIPSIS OF CONJUNCTIONS, ETC.

כִּימֵי עוֹלָם, as [in] the days of old, for כְּבִימֵי. (b) The prefix לְ; as Prov. 27: 7, נֶפֶשׁ רְעֵבָה, [to] the hungry soul, for לְנֶפֶשׁ; 13: 18. 14: 22. Jer. 9: 2. (c) The preposition מִן; Ecc. 2: 24, 'nothing is better for a man שֶׁיֹּאכַל [than] that he should eat,' for מִשֶּׁיֹּאכַל.

§ 560. OF CONJUNCTIONS. Conjunctions which would express some particular relation of the latter part of a *sentence* to the former, are sometimes omitted, and their place is supplied by the copulative Vav.*

§ 561. Conjunctions which serve to connect words and phrases are often omitted.†

(a) The copulative Vav; as Gen. 31: 2, תְּמוֹל שִׁלְשׁוֹם *yesterday* [and] *the day before;* Judg 19: 2, יָמִים אַרְבָּעָה חֳדָשִׁים, *a year* [and] *four months;* Hab. 3: 11, שֶׁמֶשׁ יָרֵחַ, *sun* [and] *moon;* Nah. 3: 1. Is. 63: 11. Ex. 15: 9. Judg. 5: 27. Ps. 10: 3. The asyndetic construction occurs principally in poetry, or in the phraseology of common life. (b) The disjunctives וְ, אוֹ, *or;* as 2 K. 9: 32, שְׁנַיִם שְׁלֹשָׁה *two* [or] *three eunuchs;* 1 Sam. 20: 12. Is. 17: 6. (c) The sign of comparison כְּ, כַּאֲשֶׁר, *as;* Is. 21: 8, יִקְרָא אַרְיֵה *he will roar* [as] *a lion;* Ps. 11: 1, נוּדוּ הַרְכֶם צִפּוֹר, *fly to your mountain* [as] *a bird;* Is. 51: 12, 'who shall be made חָצִיר [as] *grass;* Job 24: 5. Ps. 40: 8. Nah. 3: 12, 13. Especially when the second member of a sentence has כֵּן *so,* the first member often omits כְּ; as Is. 55: 9, 'for [as] the heavens are higher than the earth, כֵּן *so* are his ways,' etc. Ps. 48: 6. Job 7: 9. Judg. 5: 15 (d) The particles כִּי, אֲשֶׁר, *that;* as Ps. 9: 21, 'the nations shall know אֱנוֹשׁ הֵמָּה, [that] *they are mere men;'* 50: 21. 71: 8. Job 19: 25. Lam. 1: 21.

Ellipsis in poetic parallelism.

§ 562. In poetry, a noun, pronoun, verb, adverb, or preposition, expressed in the first member of a parallelism, is frequently omitted in the second member; and *vice versâ*.

In the second member. (a) A noun; as Ps. 24: 1, לַיהוָה '*Jehovah's is* the earth and all that is in it, [*Jehovah's is*] the world and they who dwell therein.' (b) A pronoun; Ps. 22: 6, אָנֹכִי 'I am a worm and no man, [*I am*] the scorn of men;' so אַתָּה, in v. 10. (c) A verb; as Ps. 23: 3, 'O my God, אֶקְרָא *I call* all the day, ... and all the night

---

* In technical language, that part of the sentence which in cases like the above precedes Vav is called *protasis;* that which follows, *apodosis.*

† This is called the *constructio asyndetica* or *asyndetic construction;* i.e. without the σύνδεσμος or conjunction.

§§ 562—565. SYNTAX; CHANGE OF CONSTRUCTION. 201

[*do I call*];' 13: 3, עַד אָנָה אָשִׁית, '*how long shall I have* anxiety in my soul, [*how long shall I have*] sorrow in my heart?' Is. 49: 7, 'kings יִרְאוּ *shall behold* and rise, princes [*shall behold*] and do reverence, etc. (*d*) An adverb; as Ps. 10: 5, לָמָה, '*why*, Jehovah, standest thou afar off, [*why*] hidest thou thyself;' 13: 3. 22: 2, etc. For the omission of לֹא, see § 558. (*e*) A preposition; as Job 12: 12, בִּישִׁישִׁים, *with the aged* is wisdom, וְאֹרֶךְ and [*with*] *length* of days is understanding;' 15: 3. Is. 28: 7. 44: 28, 'saying to Jerusalem—וְהֵיכָל and [to] the temple, 'for וְלַהֵיכָל; 28: 6. Job 34: 10. Gen. 49: 25, מֵאֵל '*from the God* of thy father—וְאֵת שַׁדַּי and [*from*] the Almighty,' for מֵאֵת; Ps. 22: 2, ' why art thou distant דִּבְרֵי [*from*] the words of my cry,' for מִדִּבְרֵי; Job 30: 5. Is. 48: 9. 49: 7. 61: 7.

In the first member; e. g. Is. 48: 11, 'for how how shall [*my glory*] be profaned, for I will not give כְּבֹדִי, *my glory* to another?' And so often.

Remark. These principles of ellipsis are by no means limited to *poetry*; oftentimes they for substance occur in prosaic parts of the Hebrew Scriptures; e. g. Ex. 6: 3, 4. A multitude of obscurities in the English translation of the Old Testament might be removed by the aid of these principles, and much light diffused over the sacred writings.

CHANGE OF CONSTRUCTION.

563. When a sentence begins with a verb in the Inf., preceded by a preposition and used in a finite sense, it often proceeds with a *finite* verb.

E. g. Ps. 60: 2, בְּהַצּוֹתוֹ—וַיָּשָׁב, *when he strove—and returned*; Gen. 39: 18, כַּהֲרִימִי קוֹלִי וָאֶקְרָא, *when I raised my voice and cried*; Is. 18: 5. 30: 12. 49: 5 Qeri. Amos. 1: 11. 2: 4. Gen. 27: 45. Job 28: 25. 29: 6. 38: 7.

§ 564. Sentences often begin with a participle, and proceed with a *finite* verb.

E. g. Prov. 19: 28, מְשַׁדֶּד־אָב יַבְרִיחַ אֵם, *he who abuses his father,* [*and*] *chases away his mother*; 2: 14. Is. 5: 11. 48: 1. 57: 3. Gen. 27: 33. Ps. 15: 2, 3, etc.

§ 565. Sentences often exhibit a change of *person*, especially in poetry; viz.

(*a*) A transition from the *third* person to the *second*; and *vice versâ*. E. g. Is. 1: 29, ' for THEY shall be ashamed of the groves, which YE have loved;' Gen. 49. 4, 'THOU wentest up to thy father's bed—HE went up to my couch;' Mic. 7: 18. Mal. 2: 15.

(b) A transition from the *first* person to the *third*. E. g. Is. 42: 24. 44: 24, 25, '*I* am Jehovah who made the universe,—HE frustrates the signs, etc. This transition, however, is not very frequent, and for the most part it is altered in the Qeri.

Note. The same changes of person occur also in the use of suffix-pronouns, a transition being often made from the *first* or *second* person to the *third*, and *vice versâ;* as Prov. 8: 17 (Kethib), 'I love אֹהֲבֶיהָ, *his* lovers, i. e. those who love me; Mic. 1: 2, 'hear ye people, כֻּלָּם *all of them*, i. e. all of you; Job 18: 4. Is. 22: 16, etc.

CONSTRUCTIO PRAEGNANS.

§ 566. The name of *constructio praegnans* is applied to phrases, which imply more than the words literally express, although there is no direct ellipsis.

E. g. Ps. 22: 22, מִקַּרְנֵי רֵמִים עֲנִיתָנִי, *answer* [and deliver] *me from the horns of the wild bulls,* comp. v. 13 ; Ps. 74: 7, לָאָרֶץ חִלְּלוּ מִשְׁכַּן שְׁמֶךָ *to the earth have they* [cast down and] *defiled thy dwelling ;* 1 Sam. 10: 9, וַיַּהֲפָךְ־לוֹ אֱלֹהִים לֵב אַחֵר, *and God changed* [his heart and gave] *to him another heart;* 1 Chr. 12: 17, לְרַמּוֹתַנִי לְצָרַי, *but if to deceive* [and betray] *me to my enemies;* Ps. 118: 5. Is. 38: 17. Jos. 4: 18. 2 Sam. 18: 19. Hos. 1: 2, etc.

ZEUGMA.

§ 567. The name of *Zeugma* is applied to a construction, where two subjects have a verb in common, but this verb expresses action, etc., which can with propriety be predicated of only *one* of the subjects; e. g. Job 4: 10, 'the voice of the lion, and the teeth of the young lions, *are broken out*,' i. e. the roaring of the lion [is made to cease], and the teeth, etc. Gen. 47: 19, 'wherefore should we die, *we and our land*,' i. e. we die, and our land [become desolate] ; Is. 55: 3. Hos. 1: 2. Jer. 15: 8. Est. 4: 1.

§ 568. The figure *Zeugma* also includes those cases where nouns are grammatically connected with preceding nouns, when in respect to *sense* strictly considered such connection cannot be admitted; e. g. Ps. 65: 9, ' thou makest מוֹצָאֵי , *the outgoings* of the morning and the evening to rejoice, ' where *outgoings* cannot be predicated of evening ; Gen. 2: 1, ' the heavens, and the earth, and all צְבָאָם *the host of them,* i. e. the host of the heavens, viz. the stars. Compare Neh. 9: 6.

HENDIADYS.

§ 569. The name *Hendiadys* is applied to a construction, in which two nouns are put in the same case, and connected by a copula, while in respect to *sense* one of them must be taken as a Gen. following the other, or as an *adjective* qualifying the other, § 443.

E. g. Gen. 1: 14, 'and they shall be for signs, וּלְמוֹעֲדִים *and for seasons*,' i. e. they shall be for signs of seasons, etc. 3: 16, *I will multiply thy sorrows and thy conception*, i. e. I will multiply the pains of thy conception; Job 10: 17, *misfortunes and a host*, i. e. a host of misfortunes; 4: 16, *stillness and a voice*, i. e. a low voice; comp. 1 K. 19: 12. 2 Chr. 16: 14. Jer. 29: 11. The origin of the word is, ἓν διὰ δυοῖν, *one thing by two*.

PARONOMASIA.

§ 570. The name *paronomasia* is given to an expression, which contains two or more words selected in such a manner that they may resemble each other in *sound*, while in *sense* they may differ.

Paronomasia is a very favorite figure of rhetoric among the Hebrews, and is common in all the oriental languages. It differs from our rhyme, inasmuch as the words which constitute it do not necessarily stand at the end of parallelisms or strophes, but may be placed together in any part of a sentence, and are found in prose as well as poetry.*

§ 571. There are various modes of constructing paronomasia, of which the following are the principal.

(*a*) By placing together like sounding words; as Gen. 1: 2, תֹּהוּ וָבֹהוּ, *desolate and empty*; 4: 12, נָע וָנָד, *a fugitive and a vagabond*; 18: 27, עָפָר וָאֵפֶר, *dust and ashes*; Job 30: 19. Is. 28: 10, צַו לָצַו צַו לָצָו קַו לָקָו קַו לָקָו, *law here and law there, precept here and precept there*; 24: 17, פַּחַד וָפַחַת וָפָח, *terror and a snare and a sling*; Ps. 18: 8. Lam. 3: 47. Jer. 48: 43. Is. 24: 3, 4.

(*b*) By using like sounding words in different parts of a sentence; as Hos. 8: 2, צָמָח *the stalk* yields no קֶמַח *meal*; Is. 5: 7, 'and he looked לְמִשְׁפָּט *for equity*, and lo מִשְׂפָּח *shedding of blood*, for לִצְדָקָה *righteousness*, and lo צְעָקָה *the cry* of the oppressed;' 7: 9, 'if לֹא תַאֲמִינוּ *ye will not believe*, then לֹא תֵאָמֵנוּ *ye shall not be established*;' 61: 3, 'he shall appoint פְּאֵר תַּחַת אֵפֶר, *beauty instead of ashes*;' Ps. 40: 4. 52: 8. 68: 3. Zech. 9: 5. Gen. 42: 35. Amos 5: 26.

---

* Besides the name παρονομασία, the Greek rhetoricians also called this figure παρήχησις and παρωνυμία; the Latins, *agnominatio*.

§ 571. SYNTAX; PARONOMASIA.

(c) By changing sometimes the ordinary forms of words, in order to produce similarity of sound; as Ezek. 43: 11, מוֹצָאָיו וּמוֹבָאָיו, where מוֹבָא stands for מָבוֹא; Ps. 32: 1, נְשׂוּי־פֶּשַׁע כְּסוּי־חֲטָאָה, where נְשׂוּי stands for נָשׂוּא. See Mic. 1: 8. Ezek. 4: 11. Amos 5: 26.

(d) By employing, in some cases, a word sounding *in some degree* like another; as Joel 1: 15, 'it shall come כְּשֹׁד מִשַּׁדַּי, *as destruction from the Almighty;*' Jer. 51: 2, 'I will send against Babylon זָרִים *barbarians*, וְזֵרוּהָ *and they shall scatter her;*' Is. 32: 7, כֵּלָיו כֵּלָיו, '*the armour of the crafty* is evil;' Ezek. 7: 6, קֵץ בָּא בָּא הַקֵּץ הֵקִיץ אֵלָיִךְ, *the end is come, come is the end, it is waked up against thee;* Is. 1: 23, שָׂרַיִךְ סוֹרְרִים *thy princes are revolters,* comp. Hos. 9: 15. Is. 57: 6. Amos 8: 2.

(e) By repeating the *same* word in a different signification; as Ecc. 7: 6, 'like the noise [crackling] הַסִּירִים *of thorns* under הַסִּיר *a pot;*' Judg. 10: 4, 'Jair had thirty sons, and they rode upon thirty עֲיָרִים, *asses' colts*, and had thirty עֲיָרִים, *cities;*' 15: 16, 'with the jaw bone הַחֲמוֹר *of an ass,* have I slain חֲמוֹר חֲמֹרָתָיִם *one heap two heaps;*' 1 Sam. 1: 24, 'and הַנַּעַר נָעַר *the lad was yet a lad;*' Jer. 1: 11, 12, 'what seest thou, Jeremiah? Ans. A rod שָׁקֵד *of the almond tree.* Then God said, Well, for שֹׁקֵד *I watch* over, etc.

(f) Proper names are frequently made the occasion of paronomasia; as Mic. 1: 10, בְּבָכוֹ אַל תִּבְכּוּ, *in Acco weep not,* בְּבֵית לְעַפְרָה *in Beth Leaphra* roll thyself עָפָר *in the dust;* 1: 14, 'the houses אַכְזִיב *of Achzib* לְאַכְזָב *are liars;*' Zeph. 2: 4, עַזָּה עֲזוּבָה, *Gaza is forsaken;* Gen. 9: 27, 'God יַפְתְּ לְיֶפֶת *will enlarge Japhet;*' 49: 8, 'יְהוּדָה *O Judah,* thy brethren יוֹדוּךָ *shall praise thee;*' 49: 16, דָּן יָדִין, *Dan shall judge;* 49: 19, גָּד גְּדוּד יְגוּדֶנּוּ, *Gad, a host shall press upon him;* Ruth 1: 20. Neh. 9: 24. Num. 18: 2. Is. 21: 2. Jer. 6: 1. 48: 2. Ezek. 25: 16. Hos. 2: 25. Amos 5: 5, 6.

Note. Paronomasia is very common in the New Testament; as Matt. 8: 22, ἄφες τοὺς νεκροὺς θάψαι τοὺς ἑαυτῶν νεκρούς *let the dead bury their own dead;* see above in c. In Latin are found *capiatur Capua, cremetur Cremona;* and Cicero exclaims (*in Verrem* IV. 24), *quod nunquam hujusmodi* EVERRICULUM *in provinciâ ullâ fuit.* In the writings of the monks of the middle ages, and of the older English divines, paronomasia abounds to excess.

PARADIGMS

OF

VERBS AND NOUNS.

Par. I. Regular Verb transitive. §§ 212—219.

		Kal.	Kal.	Niphal.	Piel.
Praet.	3 m. (sing.)	קָטַל	רָכַב	נִקְטַל	קִטֵּל (קִטַּל)
	3 f.	קָטְלָה	רָכְבָה	נִקְטְלָה	קִטְּלָה (etc).
	2 m.	קָטַלְתָּ	רָכַבְתָּ	נִקְטַלְתָּ	קִטַּלְתָּ
	2 f.	קָטַלְתְּ	רָכַבְתְּ	נִקְטַלְתְּ	קִטַּלְתְּ
	1	קָטַלְתִּי	רָכַבְתִּי	נִקְטַלְתִּי	קִטַּלְתִּי
	3 (plur.)	קָטְלוּ	רָכְבוּ	נִקְטְלוּ	קִטְּלוּ
	2 m.	קְטַלְתֶּם	רְכַבְתֶּם	נִקְטַלְתֶּם	קִטַּלְתֶּם
	2 f.	קְטַלְתֶּן	רְכַבְתֶּן	נִקְטַלְתֶּן	קִטַּלְתֶּן
	1	קָטַלְנוּ	רָכַבְנוּ	נִקְטַלְנוּ	קִטַּלְנוּ
Inf.	abs.	קָטוֹל	רָכוֹב	הִקָּטֵל (נִקְטֹל)	קַטֵּל (קַטֹּל)
	const.	קְטֹל	רְכֹב	הִקָּטֵל	קַטֵּל
Fut.	3 m. (sing.)	יִקְטֹל	יִרְכַּב	יִקָּטֵל	יְקַטֵּל
	3 f.	תִּקְטֹל	תִּרְכַּב	תִּקָּטֵל	תְּקַטֵּל
	2 m.	תִּקְטֹל	תִּרְכַּב	תִּקָּטֵל	תְּקַטֵּל
	2 f.	תִּקְטְלִי	תִּרְכְּבִי	תִּקָּטְלִי	תְּקַטְּלִי
	1	אֶקְטֹל	אֶרְכַּב	אֶקָּטֵל	אֲקַטֵּל
	3 m. (plur.)	יִקְטְלוּ	יִרְכְּבוּ	יִקָּטְלוּ	יְקַטְּלוּ
	3 f.	תִּקְטֹלְנָה	תִּרְכַּבְנָה	תִּקָּטַלְנָה	תְּקַטֵּלְנָה
	2 m.	תִּקְטְלוּ	תִּרְכְּבוּ	תִּקָּטְלוּ	תְּקַטְּלוּ
	2 f.	תִּקְטֹלְנָה	תִּרְכַּבְנָה	תִּקָּטַלְנָה	תְּקַטֵּלְנָה
	1	נִקְטֹל	נִרְכַּב	נִקָּטֵל	נְקַטֵּל
Fut. apoc.					
Imp.	2 m. (sing.)	קְטֹל	רְכַב	הִקָּטֵל	קַטֵּל
	2 f.	קִטְלִי	רִכְבִי	הִקָּטְלִי	קַטְּלִי
	2 m. (plur.)	קִטְלוּ	רִכְבוּ	הִקָּטְלוּ	קַטְּלוּ
	2 f.	קְטֹלְנָה	רְכַבְנָה	הִקָּטַלְנָה	קַטֵּלְנָה
Part.	act.	קוֹטֵל	רוֹכֵב		מְקַטֵּל
	pass.	קָטוּל	רָכוּב	נִקְטָל	

Par. I. Regular Verb transitive. §§ 212—219.

Pual.	Hiphil.	Hophal.	Hithpael.
קֻטַּל (קֻטֹּל)	הִקְטִיל	הָקְטַל (הֻקְטַל)	הִתְקַטֵּל (הִתְקַטֹּל)
קֻטְּלָה (etc.)	הִקְטִילָה	הָקְטְלָה (etc.)	הִתְקַטְּלָה (etc.)
קֻטַּלְתָּ	הִקְטַ֫לְתָּ	הָקְטַ֫לְתָּ	הִתְקַטַּ֫לְתָּ
קֻטַּלְתְּ	הִקְטַלְתְּ	הָקְטַלְתְּ	הִתְקַטַּלְתְּ
קֻטַּ֫לְתִּי	הִקְטַ֫לְתִּי	הָקְטַ֫לְתִּי	הִתְקַטַּ֫לְתִּי
קֻטְּלוּ	הִקְטִ֫ילוּ	הָקְטְלוּ	הִתְקַטְּלוּ
קֻטַּלְתֶּם	הִקְטַלְתֶּם	הָקְטַלְתֶּם	הִתְקַטַּלְתֶּם
קֻטַּלְתֶּן	הִקְטַלְתֶּן	הָקְטַלְתֶּן	הִתְקַטַּלְתֶּן
קֻטַּ֫לְנוּ	הִקְטַ֫לְנוּ	הָקְטַ֫לְנוּ	הִתְקַטַּ֫לְנוּ
קֻטֹּל (הֻקְטֹל) הַקְטִיל		הֻקְטַל	
קֻטַּל	הַקְטֵיל	הָקְטַל	הִתְקַטֵּל
יְקֻטַּל (יְקֻטֹּל)	יַקְטִיל	יָקְטַל (יֻקְטַל)	יִתְקַטֵּל (יִתְקַטֹּל)
תְּקֻטַּל (etc.)	תַּקְטִיל	תָּקְטַל (etc.)	תִּתְקַטֵּל (etc.)
תְּקֻטַּל	תַּקְטִיל	תָּקְטַל	תִּתְקַטֵּל
תְּקֻטְּלִי	תַּקְטִ֫ילִי	תָּקְטְלִי	תִּתְקַטְּלִי
אֲקֻטַּל	אַקְטִיל	אָקְטַל	אֶתְקַטֵּל
יְקֻטְּלוּ	יַקְטִ֫ילוּ	יָקְטְלוּ	יִתְקַטְּלוּ
תְּקֻטַּ֫לְנָה	תַּקְטֵ֫לְנָה	תָּקְטַ֫לְנָה	תִּתְקַטֵּ֫לְנָה
תְּקֻטְּלוּ	תַּקְטִ֫ילוּ	תָּקְטְלוּ	תִּתְקַטְּלוּ
תְּקֻטַּ֫לְנָה	תַּקְטֵ֫לְנָה	תָּקְטַ֫לְנָה	תִּתְקַטֵּ֫לְנָה
נְקֻטַּל	נַקְטִיל	נָקְטַל	נִתְקַטֵּל
	יַקְטֵל		
(wanting)	הַקְטֵל	(wanting)	הִתְקַטֵּל (הִתְקַטֹּל)
	הַקְטִ֫ילִי		הִתְקַטְּלִי (etc.)
	הַקְטִ֫ילוּ		הִתְקַטְּלוּ
	הַקְטֵ֫לְנָה		הִתְקַטֵּ֫לְנָה
	מַקְטִיל		מִתְקַטֵּל
מְקֻטָּל (מְקֻטָּל)		מָקְטָל (מֻקְטָל)	

Par. II. Reg. Verbs intransitive. §§ 220—222.

		Kal.	Kal.	Kal.	Kal.
Praet.	3 m. (sing.)	שָׁפֵל	שָׁאֵל	יָלַד	יָגֹר
	3 f.	שָׁפְלָה	שָׁאֲלָה	יָלְדָה	יָגְרָה
	2 m.	שָׁפַלְתָּ	שָׁאַלְתָּ (יָלַדְתָּ) יָלַדְתָּ	יָגֹרְתָּ
	2 f.	שָׁפַלְתְּ	שָׁאַלְתְּ (יָלַדְתְּ) יָלַדְתְּ	יָגֹרְתְּ
	1	שָׁפַלְתִּי	שָׁאַלְתִּי (יָלַדְתִּי) יָלַדְתִּי	יָגֹרְתִּי
	3 (plur.)	שָׁפְלוּ	שָׁאֲלוּ	יָלְדוּ	יָגְרוּ
	2 m.	שְׁפַלְתֶּם	שְׁאֶלְתֶּם	יְלַדְתֶּם	יְגָרְתֶּם
	2 f.	שְׁפַלְתֶּן	שְׁאֶלְתֶּן	יְלַדְתֶּן	יְגָרְתֶּן
	1	שָׁפַלְנוּ	שָׁאַלְנוּ	יָלַדְנוּ	יָגֹרְנוּ
Inf.	abs.	שָׁפוֹל	שָׁאוֹל	(The other forms in these two words belong to the irregular verbs.)	
	const.	שְׁפַל	שְׁאַל		
Fut.	3 m. (sing.)	יִשְׁפַּל	יִשְׁאַל	יִשְׁכֹּן	
	3 f.	תִּשְׁפַּל	תִּשְׁאַל	תִּשְׁכֹּן	
	2 m.	תִּשְׁפַּל	תִּשְׁאַל	etc.	
	2 f.	תִּשְׁפְּלִי	תִּשְׁאֲלִי	(derived from שָׁכֵן, שְׁכֹן)	
	1	אֶשְׁפַּל	אֶשְׁאַל		
	3 m. (plur.)	יִשְׁפְּלוּ	יִשְׁאֲלוּ		
	3 f.	תִּשְׁפַּלְנָה	תִּשְׁאַלְנָה		
	2 m.	תִּשְׁפְּלוּ	תִּשְׁאֲלוּ		
	2 f.	תִּשְׁפַּלְנָה	תִּשְׁאַלְנָה		
	1	נִשְׁפַּל	נִשְׁאַל		
Imp.	2 m. (sing.)	שְׁפַל	שְׁאַל		
	2 f.	שִׁפְלִי	שַׁאֲלִי		
	2 m. (plur.)	שִׁפְלוּ	שַׁאֲלוּ		
	2 f.	שְׁפַלְנָה	שְׁאַלְנָה		
Part.	act.	שָׁפֵל	שׁוֹאֵל		
	pass.		שָׁאוּל		

Par. III. Verbs פּ Gutt., smooth enunciation. § 224.

	Kal.	Niphal.	Hiphil.	Hophal.
Praet.	עָמַד	נֶעֱמַד	הֶעֱמִיד	הָעֳמַד
	עָמְדָה	נֶעֶמְדָה	הֶעֱמִידָה	הָעָמְדָה
	עָמַדְתָּ	נֶעֱמַדְתָּ	הֶעֱמַדְתָּ	הָעֳמַדְתָּ
	עָמַדְתְּ	נֶעֱמַדְתְּ	הֶעֱמַדְתְּ	הָעֳמַדְתְּ
	עָמַדְתִּי	נֶעֱמַדְתִּי	הֶעֱמַדְתִּי	הָעֳמַדְתִּי
Plur.	עָמְדוּ	נֶעֶמְדוּ	הֶעֱמִידוּ	הָעָמְדוּ
	עֲמַדְתֶּם	נֶעֱמַדְתֶּם	הֶעֱמַדְתֶּם	הָעֳמַדְתֶּם
	עֲמַדְתֶּן	נֶעֱמַדְתֶּן	הֶעֱמַדְתֶּן	הָעֳמַדְתֶּן
	עָמַדְנוּ	נֶעֱמַדְנוּ	הֶעֱמַדְנוּ	הָעֳמַדְנוּ
Inf. abs.	עָמוֹד	נַעֲמוֹד	הַעֲמֵיד	
const.	עֲמֹד	הֵעָמֵד	הַעֲמִיד	הָעֳמַד
Fut.	יַעֲמֹד יֶחֱזַק	יֵעָמֵד	יַעֲמִיד	יָעֳמַד
	תַּעֲמֹד תֶּחֱזַק	תֵּעָמֵד	תַּעֲמִיד	תָּעֳמַד
	תַּעֲמֹד תֶּחֱזַק	תֵּעָמֵד	תַּעֲמִיד	תָּעֳמַד
	תַּעַמְדִי תֶּחֶזְקִי	תֵּעָמְדִי	תַּעֲמִידִי	תָּעָמְדִי
	אֶעֱמֹד אֶחֱזַק	אֵעָמֵד	אַעֲמִיד	אָעֳמַד
Plur.	יַעַמְדוּ יֶחֶזְקוּ	יֵעָמְדוּ	יַעֲמִידוּ	יָעָמְדוּ
	תַּעֲמֹדְנָה תֶּחֱזַקְנָה	תֵּעָמַדְנָה	תַּעֲמֵדְנָה	תָּעֳמַדְנָה
	תַּעַמְדוּ תֶּחֶזְקוּ	תֵּעָמְדוּ	תַּעֲמִידוּ	תָּעָמְדוּ
	תַּעֲמֹדְנָה תֶּחֱזַקְנָה	תֵּעָמַדְנָה	תַּעֲמֵדְנָה	תָּעֳמַדְנָה
	נַעֲמֹד נֶחֱזַק	נֵעָמֵד	נַעֲמִיד	נָעֳמַד
Fut. apoc.			יַעֲמֵד	
Imp.	עֲמֹד חֲזַק	הֵעָמֵד	הַעֲמֵד	
	עִמְדִי חִזְקִי	הֵעָמְדִי	הַעֲמִידִי	
Plur.	עִמְדוּ חִזְקוּ	הֵעָמְדוּ	הַעֲמִידוּ	
	עֲמֹדְנָה חֲזַקְנָה	הֵעָמַדְנָה	הַעֲמֵדְנָה	
Part. act.	עֹמֵד		מַעֲמִיד	
pass.	עָמוּד	נֶעֱמָד		מָעֳמָד

Par. IV. Verbs פ Gutt., rough enunc. § 225.

	Kal.	Kal.	Niphal.	Hiphil.	Hophal.
Praet.	חָדַל (חָדֵל)	חָגַר	נֶהְפַּךְ	הֶחְסִיר	הָהְפַּךְ
3 f.	חָדְלָה	חָגְרָה	נֶהְפְּכָה	הֶחְסִירָה	הָהְפְּכָה
2 m.	חָדַלְתָּ	etc.	etc.	etc.	etc.
2 f.	חָדַלְתְּ				
1.	חָדַלְתִּי				
3 (plur.)	חָדְלוּ		נֶהְפְּכוּ	הֶחְסִירוּ	הָהְפְּכוּ
2 m.	חֲדַלְתֶּם		etc.		
2 f.	חֲדַלְתֶּן				
1.	חָדַלְנוּ				
Inf. abs.	חָדוֹל	חָגוֹר		הַחְסִיר	
const.	חֲדֹל	חֲגֹר	הֵהָפֵךְ	הַחְסִיר	הָהְפַּךְ
Fut.	יֶחְדַּל	יַחְגֹּר	יֵהָפֵךְ	יַחְסִיר	יָהְפַּךְ
3 f.	תֶּחְדַּל	תַּחְגֹּר	תֵּהָפֵךְ	תַּחְסִיר	תָּהְפַּךְ
2 m.	תֶּחְדַּל	תַּחְגֹּר	etc.	etc.	etc.
2 f.	תֶּחְדְּלִי	תַּחְגְּרִי			
1	אֶחְדַּל	אַחְגֹּר			
3 m. (pl.)	יֶחְדְּלוּ	יַחְגְּרוּ			
2 f.	תֶּחְדַּלְנָה	תַּחְגֹּרְנָה			
2 m.	תֶּחְדְּלוּ	תַּחְגְּרוּ			
2 f.	תֶּחְדַּלְנָה	תַּחְגֹּרְנָה			
1	נֶחְדַּל	נַחְגֹּר			
Imper. 2 m.	חֲדַל	חֲגֹר	הֵהָפֵךְ	הַחְסֵר	
2 f.	חִדְלִי	חִגְרִי	הֵהָפְכִי		etc.
2 m. (pl.)	חִדְלוּ	חִגְרוּ	הֵהָפְכוּ		
2 f.	חֲדֶלְנָה	חֲגֹרְנָה	הֵהָפַכְנָה		
Part. act.	חָדֵל	חוֹגֵר		מַחְסִיר	
pass.		חָגוּר	נֶהְפָּךְ		מָהְפָּךְ

Par. V. Verb ע״ Guttural. §§ 229—232.

Kal.	Niphal.	Piel.	Pual.	Hithpael.
זָעַק	נִזְעַק	בֵּרַךְ (רִחַץ) (נִהַג)	בֹּרַךְ	הִתְבָּרֵךְ
זָעֲקָה	נִזְעֲקָה	בֵּרְכָה (etc.)	בֹּרְכָה (etc.)	הִתְבָּרְכָה
זָעַקְתָּ	נִזְעַקְתָּ	בֵּרַכְתָּ	בֹּרַכְתָּ	הִתְבָּרַכְתָּ
זָעַקְתְּ	נִזְעַקְתְּ	בֵּרַכְתְּ	בֹּרַכְתְּ	הִתְבָּרַכְתְּ
זָעַקְתִּי	נִזְעַקְתִּי	בֵּרַכְתִּי	בֹּרַכְתִּי	הִתְבָּרַכְתִּי
זָעֲקוּ	נִזְעֲקוּ	בֵּרְכוּ	בֹּרְכוּ	הִתְבָּרְכוּ
זְעַקְתֶּם	נִזְעַקְתֶּם	בֵּרַכְתֶּם	בֹּרַכְתֶּם	הִתְבָּרַכְתֶּם
זְעַקְתֶּן	נִזְעַקְתֶּן	בֵּרַכְתֶּן	בֹּרַכְתֶּן	הִתְבָּרַכְתֶּן
זָעַקְנוּ	נִזְעַקְנוּ	בֵּרַכְנוּ	בֹּרַכְנוּ	הִתְבָּרַכְנוּ
זָעוֹק				
זְעֹק	הִזָּעֵק	בָּרֵךְ	בֹּרַךְ	הִתְבָּרֵךְ
יִנְהַם יִזְעַק	יִזָּעֵק	יְבָרֵךְ (יְנַהֵג) יְבָרֶךְ־(יְרַחֵץ)	יְבֹרַךְ	יִתְבָּרֵךְ
תִּנְהַם תִּזְעַק	תִּזָּעֵק	תְּבָרֵךְ (etc.)	תְּבֹרַךְ (etc.)	תִּתְבָּרֵךְ
תִּנְהַם תִּזְעַק	תִּזָּעֵק	תְּבָרֵךְ	תְּבֹרַךְ	תִּתְבָּרֵךְ
תִּנְהֲמִי תִּזְעֲקִי	תִּזָּעֲקִי	תְּבָרְכִי	תְּבֹרְכִי	תִּתְבָּרְכִי
אֶנְהַם אֶזְעַק	אֶזָּעֵק	אֲבָרֵךְ	אֲבֹרַךְ	אֶתְבָּרֵךְ
יִנְהֲמוּ יִזְעֲקוּ	יִזָּעֲקוּ	יְבָרְכוּ	יְבֹרְכוּ	יִתְבָּרְכוּ
תִּנְהֶמְנָה תִּזְעַקְנָה	תִּזָּעַקְנָה	תְּבָרֵכְנָה	תְּבֹרַכְנָה	תִּתְבָּרֵכְנָה
תִּנְהֲמוּ תִּזְעֲקוּ	תִּזָּעֲקוּ	תְּבָרְכוּ	תְּבֹרְכוּ	תִּתְבָּרְכוּ
תִּנְהֶמְנָה תִּזְעַקְנָה	תִּזָּעַקְנָה	תְּבָרֵכְנָה	תְּבֹרַכְנָה	תִּתְבָּרֵכְנָה
נִנְהַם נִזְעַק	נִזָּעֵק	נְבָרֵךְ	נְבֹרַךְ	נִתְבָּרֵךְ
זְעַק	הִזָּעֵק	בָּרֵךְ (נַהֵג)		הִתְבָּרֵךְ
זַעֲקִי	הִזָּעֲקִי	בָּרְכִי (etc.)		הִתְבָּרְכִי
זַעֲקוּ	הִזָּעֲקוּ	בָּרְכוּ		הִתְבָּרְכוּ
זְעַקְנָה	הִזָּעַקְנָה	בָּרֵכְנָה		הִתְבָּרֵכְנָה
זוֹעֵק		מְבָרֵךְ (מְנַהֵג)		מִתְבָּרֵךְ
זָעוּק	נִזְעָק		מְבֹרָךְ	

Par. VI. Verb ל" Guttural. §§ 233—236.

		Kal.	Niphal.		Piel.
Praet.	3 m. (sing.)	שָׁמַע	נִשְׁמַע	(שִׁמַּע)	שִׁמַּע
	3 f.	שָׁמְעָה	נִשְׁמְעָה	etc.	שִׁמְּעָה
	2 m.	שָׁמַעְתָּ	נִשְׁמַעְתָּ		שִׁמַּעְתָּ
	2 f.	שָׁמַעַתְּ	נִשְׁמַעַתְּ		שִׁמַּעַתְּ
	1	שָׁמַעְתִּי	נִשְׁמַעְתִּי		שִׁמַּעְתִּי
	3 (plur.)	שָׁמְעוּ	נִשְׁמְעוּ		שִׁמְּעוּ
	2 m.	שְׁמַעְתֶּם	נִשְׁמַעְתֶּם		שִׁמַּעְתֶּם
	2 f.	שְׁמַעְתֶּן	נִשְׁמַעְתֶּן		שִׁמַּעְתֶּן
	1	שָׁמַעְנוּ	נִשְׁמַעְנוּ		שִׁמַּעְנוּ
Inf.	abs.	שָׁמוֹעַ	נִשְׁמֹעַ		שַׁמֵּעַ
	const.	שְׁמֹעַ	הִשָּׁמֵעַ		שַׁמֵּעַ
Fut.	3 m. (sing.)	יִשְׁמַע	יִשָּׁמַע	(יְשַׁמַּע)	יְשַׁמַּע
	3 f.	תִּשְׁמַע	תִּשָּׁמַע	etc.	תְּשַׁמַּע
	2 m.	תִּשְׁמַע	תִּשָּׁמַע		תְּשַׁמַּע
	2 f.	תִּשְׁמְעִי	תִּשָּׁמְעִי		תְּשַׁמְּעִי
	1	אֶשְׁמַע	אֶשָּׁמַע		אֲשַׁמַּע
	3 m. (plur.)	יִשְׁמְעוּ	יִשָּׁמְעוּ		יְשַׁמְּעוּ
	3 f.	תִּשְׁמַעְנָה	תִּשָּׁמַעְנָה		תְּשַׁמַּעְנָה
	2 m.	תִּשְׁמְעוּ	תִּשָּׁמְעוּ		תְּשַׁמְּעוּ
	2 f.	תִּשְׁמַעְנָה	תִּשָּׁמַעְנָה		תְּשַׁמַּעְנָה
	1	נִשְׁמַע	נִשָּׁמַע		נְשַׁמַּע
Fut. apoc.					
Imp.	2 m. (sing.)	שְׁמַע	הִשָּׁמַע	(שַׁמַּע)	שַׁמַּע
	2 f.	שִׁמְעִי	הִשָּׁמְעִי	etc.	שַׁמְּעִי
	2 m. (plur.)	שִׁמְעוּ	הִשָּׁמְעוּ		שַׁמְּעוּ
	2 f.	שְׁמַעְנָה	הִשָּׁמַעְנָה		שַׁמַּעְנָה
Part.	act.	(שֹׁמֵעַ) שֹׁמֵעַ		(מְשַׁמֵּעַ)	מְשַׁמֵּעַ
	pass.	שָׁמוּעַ (נִשְׁמָע) נִשְׁמָע			

Par. VI. Verb לֹ״ Guttural. §§ 233—236.

Pual.	Hiphil.	Hophal.	Hithpael.
שֻׁמַּע	הִשְׁמִיעַ	הָשְׁמַע	הִשְׁתַּמֵּעַ (הִשְׁתַּמַּע)
שֻׁמְּעָה	הִשְׁמִיעָה	הָשְׁמְעָה	הִשְׁתַּמְּעָה (etc.)
שֻׁמַּעַתָּ	הִשְׁמַעְתָּ	הָשְׁמַעְתָּ	הִשְׁתַּמַּעְתָּ
שֻׁמַּעַתְּ	הִשְׁמַעַתְּ	הָשְׁמַעַתְּ	הִשְׁתַּמַּעַתְּ
שֻׁמַּעְתִּי	הִשְׁמַעְתִּי	הָשְׁמַעְתִּי	הִשְׁתַּמַּעְתִּי
שֻׁמְּעוּ	הִשְׁמִיעוּ	הָשְׁמְעוּ	הִשְׁתַּמְּעוּ
שֻׁמַּעְתֶּם	הִשְׁמַעְתֶּם	הָשְׁמַעְתֶּם	הִשְׁתַּמַּעְתֶּם
שֻׁמַּעְתֶּן	הִשְׁמַעְתֶּן	הָשְׁמַעְתֶּן	הִשְׁתַּמַּעְתֶּן
שֻׁמַּעְנוּ	הִשְׁמַעְנוּ	הָשְׁמַעְנוּ	הִשְׁתַּמַּעְנוּ
	הַשְׁמֵעַ		
שֻׁמַּע	הַשְׁמִיעַ	הָשְׁמַע	הִשְׁתַּמֵּעַ
יְשֻׁמַּע	יַשְׁמִיעַ	יָשְׁמַע	יִשְׁתַּמַּע (יִשְׁתַּמֵּעַ)
תְּשֻׁמַּע	תַּשְׁמִיעַ	תָּשְׁמַע	תִּשְׁתַּמַּע (etc.)
תְּשֻׁמַּע	תַּשְׁמִיעַ	תָּשְׁמַע	תִּשְׁתַּמַּע
תְּשֻׁמְּעִי	תַּשְׁמִיעִי	תָּשְׁמְעִי	תִּשְׁתַּמְּעִי
אֲשֻׁמַּע	אַשְׁמִיעַ	אָשְׁמַע	אֶשְׁתַּמַּע
יְשֻׁמְּעוּ	יַשְׁמִיעוּ	יָשְׁמְעוּ	יִשְׁתַּמְּעוּ
תְּשֻׁמַּעְנָה	תַּשְׁמַעְנָה	תָּשְׁמַעְנָה	תִּשְׁתַּמַּעְנָה
תְּשֻׁמְּעוּ	תַּשְׁמִיעוּ	תָּשְׁמְעוּ	תִּשְׁתַּמְּעוּ
תְּשֻׁמַּעְנָה	תַּשְׁמַעְנָה	תָּשְׁמַעְנָה	תִּשְׁתַּמַּעְנָה
נְשֻׁמַּע	נַשְׁמִיעַ	נָשְׁמַע	נִשְׁתַּמַּע
	יַשְׁמֵעַ		
	הַשְׁמַע		הִשְׁתַּמַּע (הִשְׁתַּמֵּעַ)
	הַשְׁמִיעִי		הִשְׁתַּמְּעִי (etc.)
	הַשְׁמִיעוּ		הִשְׁתַּמְּעוּ
	הַשְׁמַעְנָה		הִשְׁתַּמַּעְנָה
	מַשְׁמִיעַ		מִשְׁתַּמֵּעַ (מִשְׁתַּמַּע)
מְשֻׁמָּע		מָשְׁמָע	

Par. VII. Verbs פ"א §§ 240. 241.

		Kal.	Kal.	Niphal.	Hiphil.	Hophal.
Praet.	3 m.	אָכַל	אָמַר	נֶאֱכַל	הֶאֱכִיל	הָאֳכַל
	3 f.	(regular)	(regular)	(as פּ Gutt.)	(as פּ Gutt.)	(as פּ Gutt.)
Inf.	abs.	אָכוֹל	אָמוֹר			
	const.	אֱכֹל	אֱמֹר	הֵאָכֵל	הַאֲכִיל	הָאֳכַל
Fut.	3 m.	יֹאכַל	יֹאמַר	יֵאָכֵל	יַאֲכִיל	יָאֳכַל
	3 f.	תֹּאכַל	תֹּאמַר	תֵּאָכֵל	(etc.)	(etc.)
	2 m.	תֹּאכַל	תֹּאמַר	תֵּאָכֵל		
	2 f.	תֹּאכְלִי	תֹּאמְרִי	תֵּאָכְלִי		
	1	אֹכַל	אֹמַר	אֵאָכֵל		
Plur.	3 m.	יֹאכְלוּ	יֹאמְרוּ	יֵאָכְלוּ		
	3 f.	תֹּאכַלְנָה	תֹּאמַרְנָה	תֵּאָכַלְנָה		
	2 m.	תֹּאכְלוּ	תֹּאמְרוּ	תֵּאָכְלוּ		
	2 f.	תֹּאכַלְנָה	תֹּאמַרְנָה	תֵּאָכַלְנָה		
	1	נֹאכַל	נֹאמַר	נֵאָכֵל		

Fut. apoc.   וַיֹּאכַל

Imp.	2 m. (sing.)	אֱכֹל	אֱמֹר	הֵאָכֵל	הַאֲכֵל	
	2 f.	אִכְלִי	אִמְרִי		(etc.)	
	2 m. (plur.)	אִכְלוּ	אִמְרוּ			
	2 f.	אֲכֹלְנָה	אֱמֹרְנָה			
Part.	act.	אֹכֵל (אֹמֵר) אֹרֵב			מַאֲכִיל	
	Pass.	אָכוּל		נֶאֱכָל		מָאֳכָל

The *derivative* conjugations of verbs פ"א are declined in the same manner as those of פּ *Guttural;* א being treated (out of Kal) as a *Guttural,* and not as a *Quiescent;* see Niphal, etc., in the paradigm. In like manner, Piel אִכֵּל, Pual אֻכַּל, Hithp. הִתְאַכֵּל; compare verbs פּ Guttural, עָמַד and חָזַק, for the mode of inflection.

Par. VIII. Verbs orig. פ״וֹ; I. Class פ״יֹ. §§ 243—247.

	Kal.	Kal.	Niphal.	Hiphil.	Hophal.
Praet.	יָשַׁב	יָרַשׁ	נוֹשַׁב	הוֹשִׁיב	הוּשַׁב
3 f.	(regular)	(regular)	נוֹשְׁבָה	הוֹשִׁיבָה	הוּשְׁבָה
2 m.			נוֹשַׁבְתָּ	הוֹשַׁבְתָּ	הוּשַׁבְתָּ
2 f.			נוֹשַׁבְתְּ	הוֹשַׁבְתְּ	הוּשַׁבְתְּ
1.			נוֹשַׁבְתִּי	הוֹשַׁבְתִּי	הוּשַׁבְתִּי
Plur. 3.			נוֹשְׁבוּ	הוֹשִׁיבוּ	הוּשְׁבוּ
2 m.			נוֹשַׁבְתֶּם	הוֹשַׁבְתֶּם	הוּשַׁבְתֶּם
2 f.			נוֹשַׁבְתֶּן	הוֹשַׁבְתֶּן	הוּשַׁבְתֶּן
1.			נוֹשַׁבְנוּ	הוֹשַׁבְנוּ	הוּשַׁבְנוּ
Inf. abs.	יָשׁוֹב	יָרוֹשׁ		הוֹרֵשׁ	
const.	(יבוֹ) שֶׁבֶת	רֶשֶׁת (יְבֹשׁ)	הִוָּשֵׁב	הוֹשִׁיב	הוּשַׁב
Fut.	יֵשֵׁב	יִירַשׁ (יְרַשׁ)	יִוָּשֵׁב	יוֹשִׁיב	יוּשַׁב
3 f.	תֵּשֵׁב	תִּירַשׁ (etc.)	תִּוָּשֵׁב	תּוֹשִׁיב	תּוּשַׁב
2 m.	תֵּשֵׁב	תִּירַשׁ	תִּוָּשֵׁב	תּוֹשִׁיב	תּוּשַׁב
2 f.	תֵּשְׁבִי	תִּירְשִׁי	תִּוָּשְׁבִי	תּוֹשִׁיבִי	תּוּשְׁבִי
1	אֵשֵׁב	אִירַשׁ	אִוָּשֵׁב	אוֹשִׁיב	אוּשַׁב
3 m. (plur.)	יֵשְׁבוּ	יִירְשׁוּ	יִוָּשְׁבוּ	יוֹשִׁיבוּ	יוּשְׁבוּ
3 f.	תֵּשַׁבְנָה	תִּירַשְׁנָה	תִּוָּשַׁבְנָה	תּוֹשִׁיבְנָה	תּוּשַׁבְנָה
2 m.	תֵּשְׁבוּ	תִּירְשׁוּ	תִּוָּשְׁבוּ	תּוֹשִׁיבוּ	תּוּשְׁבוּ
2 f.	תֵּשַׁבְנָה	תִּירַשְׁנָה	תִּוָּשַׁבְנָה	תּוֹשִׁיבְנָה	תּוּשַׁבְנָה
1	נֵשֵׁב	נִירַשׁ	נִוָּשֵׁב	נוֹשִׁיב	נוּשַׁב
Fut. apoc.				יוֹשֵׁב	
Imp. m. (sing.)	שֵׁב	יְרַשׁ (רֵשׁ)	הִוָּשֵׁב	הוֹשֵׁב	
f.	שְׁבִי	יִרְשִׁי	הִוָּשְׁבִי	הוֹשִׁיבִי	
m. (pl.)	שְׁבוּ	יִרְשׁוּ	הִוָּשְׁבוּ	הוֹשִׁיבוּ	
f.	שֵׁבְנָה	יְרַשְׁנָה	הִוָּשַׁבְנָה	הוֹשֵׁבְנָה	
Part. act.	יוֹשֵׁב	יוֹרֵשׁ		מוֹשִׁיב	
pass.	יָשׁוּב	יָרוּשׁ	נוֹשָׁב		מוּשָׁב

Par. IX. Verbs פִי. II. Class. | Par. X. פִי. III. Class.

	Kal.	Hiphil.	Kal.	Kal.
Praet. 3 m. (sing.)	יָטַב (הֵיטִיב)	הֵיטִיב	יָצַת	יָצַק
3 f.	regular	הֵיטִיבָה	regular.	etc.
3 (plur.)		הֵיטִיבוּ		
Inf. abs.	יָטוֹב		יָצוֹת	יָצוֹק
const.	יְטֹב	הֵיטִיב		יְצֹק
Fut. 3 m. {יִיטַב / הִוָּצֵר}	יִיטַב (יֵטִיב)	יֵיטִיב	יִיצַת	יִיצֹק
3 f.	תִּיטַב	תֵּיטִיב	תִּיצַת	תִּיצֹק
2 m.	תִּיטַב	תֵּיטִיב	תִּיצַת	תִּיצֹק
2 f.	תִּיטְבִי	תֵּיטִיבִי	תִּיצְתִי	תִּיצְקִי
1	אִיטַב	אֵיטִיב	אִיצַת	אִיצֹק
3 m. (pl.)	יִיטְבוּ	יֵיטִיבוּ	יִיצְתוּ	יִיצְקוּ
3 f.	תִּיטַבְנָה	תֵּיטֵבְנָה	תִּצַּתְנָה	תִּצַּקְנָה
2 m.	טִיטְבוּ	תֵּיטִיבוּ	תִּצַּתוּ	תִּצַּקוּ
2 f.	תִּיטַבְנָה	תֵּיטֵבְנָה	תִּצַּתְנָה	תִּצַּקְנָה
1	נִיטַב	נֵיטִיב	נִצַּת	נִצֹּק
Fut. apoc.	וַיִּיצֶר	יֵיטֵב		
Imp. m. (sing.)	יְטַב	הֵיטֵב		
f.	יִטְבִי	הֵיטִיבִי		
m. (plur.)	יִטְבוּ	הֵיטִיבוּ		
f.	יְטֹבְנָה	הֵיטֵבְנָה		
Part. act.	יוֹטֵב	מֵיטִיב	יוֹצֵת	יוֹצֵק
pass.	יָטוּב		יָצוּת	יָצוּק

Remarks. Niphal, in verbs of this species, does not occur. The daghesh'd conjugations are regular throughout; e. g. Piel יִטֵּב, Pual יֻטַּב, Hithpael הִתְיַטֵּב. Hophal conforms to the model in Par. VIII; e. g. יוּטַב, etc. Only Hiphil, therefore, distinguishes the II. class of verbs פִי from those of the I. class.

Remarks. The conj. Niphal, Hiphil, and Hophal, are declined in the same manner as these conjugations are in verbs Pe Nun, Par. XI. E. g. Niph. נִצָּה, Hiph. הִצִּית, Hoph. הֻצַּת, etc.

Par. XI. Verbs פ״ן. §252.

		Kal.	Kal.	Niphal.	Hiphil.	Hophal.
Praet.	3 m.	נָפַל	נָגַשׁ	נִגַּשׁ	הִגִּישׁ	הֻגַּשׁ
	3 f.	[regular]	[regular]	נִגְּשָׁה	הִגִּישָׁה	הֻגְּשָׁה
	2 m.			נִגַּשְׁתָּ	הִגַּשְׁתָּ	הֻגַּשְׁתָּ
	2 f.			נִגַּשְׁתְּ	הִגַּשְׁתְּ	הֻגַּשְׁתְּ
	1			נִגַּשְׁתִּי	הִגַּשְׁתִּי	הֻגַּשְׁתִּי
	3 m. (plur.)			נִגְּשׁוּ	הִגִּישׁוּ	הֻגְּשׁוּ
	2 m.			נִגַּשְׁתֶּם	הִגַּשְׁתֶּם	הֻגַּשְׁתֶּם
	2 f.			נִגַּשְׁתֶּן	הִגַּשְׁתֶּן	הֻגַּשְׁתֶּן
	1			נִגַּשְׁנוּ	הִגַּשְׁנוּ	הֻגַּשְׁנוּ
Inf.	abs.	נָפוֹל	נָגוֹשׁ	הִנָּגֹשׁ	הַגֵּישׁ	
	const.	נְפֹל	גֶּשֶׁת		הַגִּישׁ	הֻגַּשׁ
Fut.		יִפֹּל	יִגַּשׁ	יִנָּגֵשׁ	יַגִּישׁ	יֻגַּשׁ
	3 f.	תִּפֹּל	תִּגַּשׁ	תִּנָּגֵשׁ	תַּגִּישׁ	תֻּגַּשׁ
	2 m.	תִּפֹּל	תִּגַּשׁ	תִּנָּגֵשׁ	תַּגִּישׁ	תֻּגַּשׁ
	2 f.	תִּפְּלִי	תִּגְּשִׁי	תִּנָּגְשִׁי	תַּגִּישִׁי	תֻּגְּשִׁי
	1	אֶפֹּל	אֶגַּשׁ	אֶנָּגֵשׁ	אַגִּישׁ	אֻגַּשׁ
	3 m. (plur.)	יִפְּלוּ	יִגְּשׁוּ	יִנָּגְשׁוּ	יַגִּישׁוּ	יֻגְּשׁוּ
	3 f.	תִּפֹּלְנָה	תִּגַּשְׁנָה	תִּנָּגַשְׁנָה	תַּגֵּשְׁנָה	תֻּגַּשְׁנָה
	2 m.	תִּפְּלוּ	תִּגְּשׁוּ	תִּנָּגְשׁוּ	תַּגִּישׁוּ	תֻּגְּשׁוּ
	2 f.	תִּפֹּלְנָה	תִּגַּשְׁנָה	תִּנָּגַשְׁנָה	תַּגֵּשְׁנָה	תֻּגַּשְׁנָה
	1	נִפֹּל	נִגַּשׁ	נִנָּגֵשׁ	נַגִּישׁ	נֻגַּשׁ
Fut. apoc.					יַגֵּשׁ	
Imp.	m.	נְפֹל	גַּשׁ	הִנָּגֵשׁ	הַגֵּשׁ	
	f.	[regular]	גְּשִׁי	הִנָּגְשִׁי	הַגִּישִׁי	
	m. (plur.)		גְּשׁוּ	הִנָּגְשׁוּ	הַגִּישׁוּ	
	f.		גַּשְׁנָה	הִנָּגַשְׁנָה	הַגֵּשְׁנָה	
Part.	act.	נֹפֵל	נֹגֵשׁ		מַגִּישׁ	
	pass.		נָגוּשׁ	נִגָּשׁ		מֻגָּשׁ

Par. XII. Verbs עע. §§ 256—266.

	Kal.	Kal.	Niphal.	Hiphil.
Praet. 3 m.	סַב	סָבַב	נָסַב (הֵסַב)	הֵסֵב (הֲסִבּוֹ)
3 f.	סַבָּה	סָבְבָה	נָסַבָּה	הֵסֵבָּה
2 m.	סַבּוֹתָ	סָבַבְתָּ	נְסַבּוֹתָ	הֲסִבּוֹתָ
2 f.	סַבּוֹת	סָבַבְתְּ	נְסַבּוֹת	הֲסִבּוֹת
1	סַבּוֹתִי	סָבַבְתִּי	נְסַבּוֹתִי	הֲסִבּוֹתִי
3 (plur.)	סַבּוּ	סָבְבוּ	נָסַבּוּ	הֵסֵבּוּ
2 m.	סַבּוֹתֶם	סְבַבְתֶּם	נְסַבּוֹתֶם	הֲסִבּוֹתֶם
2 f.	סַבּוֹתֶן	סְבַבְתֶּן	נְסַבּוֹתֶן	הֲסִבּוֹתֶן
1	סַבּוֹנוּ	סָבַבְנוּ	נְסַבּוֹנוּ	הֲסִבּוֹנוּ
Inf. abs.	סָבוֹב		הִסּוֹב	הָסֵב
const.	סֹב (גַּל)		הִסֵּב (הֵחֵל)	הָסֵב
Fut.	יָסֹב יִסֹּב	יִסֹּב	יִקַּל	יָסֵב (יָדַע) יָסֵב (יַתֵּם)
3 f.	תָּסֹב	תָּסֹב	תִּקַּל	תָּסֵב	תָּסֵב
2 m.	תָּסֹב	תָּסֹב	תִּקַּל	תָּסֵב	תָּסֵב
2 f.	תָּסֹבִּי	תִּסְבִּי	תִּקַּלִּי	תָּסֵבִּי	תָּסֵבִּי
1	אָסֹב	אֶסֹּב	אֶקַּל	אֶסַּב	אָסֵב
3 m. (plur.)	יָסֹבּוּ	יִסְבּוּ	יִקַּלּוּ	יָסַבּוּ	יָסֵבּוּ (יַתֵּמוּ)
3 f.	תְּסֻבֶּינָה	תִּסֹּבְנָה	תִּקַּלְנָה	תְּסֻבֶּינָה	תְּסִבֶּינָה
2 m.	תָּסֹבּוּ	תִּסְבּוּ	תִּקַּלּוּ	תָּסַבּוּ	תָּסֵבּוּ
2 f.	תְּסֻבֶּינָה	תִּסֹּבְנָה	תִּקַּלְנָה	תְּסֻבֶּינָה	תְּסִבֶּינָה
1.	נָסֹב	נִסֹּב	נִקַּל	נָסַב	נָסֵב
Fut. conv.	וַיָּסָב				וַיָּסֵב
Imp. m.	סֹב			הִסַּב	הָסֵב
f.	סֹבִּי			הִסַּבִּי	הָסֵבִּי
m.	סֹבּוּ			הִסַּבּוּ (הֵרָפוּ)	הָסֵבּוּ
f.	סֻבֶּינָה			הִסַּבֶּינָה	הֲסִבֶּינָה
Part. act.	סוֹבֵב				מֵסֵב
pass.	סָבוּב			נָסָב	

Par. XII. Verbs עע. §§ 256—266.

Hophal.	Poel.	Poal.	Pilpel.	Pulpal.
הוּסַב (הֻשַׁם)	סוֹבֵב	סוֹבַב	סִבְסֵב	סֻבְסַב
הוּסַבָּה	סוֹבְבָה	סוֹבְבָה	סִבְסְבָה	סֻבְסְבָה
הוּסַבֹּתָ	סוֹבַ֫בְתָּ	סוֹבַ֫בְתָּ	סִבְסַ֫בְתָּ	סֻבְסַ֫בְתָּ
הוּסַבּוֹת	סוֹבַ֫בְתְּ	סוֹבַ֫בְתְּ	סִבְסַ֫בְתְּ	סֻבְסַ֫בְתְּ
הוּסַבֹּ֫תִי	סוֹבַ֫בְתִּי	סוֹבַ֫בְתִּי	סִבְסַ֫בְתִּי	סֻבְסַ֫בְתִּי
הוּסַ֫בּוּ	סוֹבְבוּ	סוֹבְבוּ	סִבְסְבוּ	סֻבְסְבוּ
הוּסַבּוֹתֶם	סוֹבַבְתֶּם	סוֹבַבְתֶּם	סִבְסַבְתֶּם	סֻבְסַבְתֶּם
הוּסַבּוֹתֶן	סוֹבַבְתֶּן	סוֹבַבְתֶּן	סִבְסַבְתֶּן	סֻבְסַבְתֶּן
הוּסַבּ֫וֹנוּ	סוֹבַ֫בְנוּ	סוֹבַ֫בְנוּ	סִבְסַ֫בְנוּ	סֻבְסַ֫בְנוּ

| הוּסַב | סוֹבֵב | סוֹבַב | סַבְסֵב | סֻבְסַב |

יוּסַב (יֻכַּת)	יְסוֹבֵב	יְסוֹבַב	יְסַבְסֵב	יְסֻבְסַב
תּוּסַב	תְּסוֹבֵב	תְּסוֹבַב	תְּסַבְסֵב	תְּסֻבְסַב
תּוּסַב	תְּסוֹבֵב	תְּסוֹבַב	תְּסַבְסֵב	תְּסֻבְסַב
תּוּסַ֫בִּי	תְּסוֹבְבִי	תְּסוֹבְבִי	תְּסַבְסְבִי	תְּסֻבְסְבִי
אוּסַב	אֲסוֹבֵב	אֲסוֹבַב	אֲסַבְסֵב	אֲסֻבְסַב
יוּסַ֫בּוּ	יְסוֹבְבוּ	יְסוֹבְבוּ	יְסַבְסְבוּ	יְסֻבְסְבוּ
תּוּסַבֶּ֫ינָה	תְּסוֹבַ֫בְנָה	תְּסוֹבַ֫בְנָה	תְּסַבְסֵ֫בְנָה	תְּסֻבְסַ֫בְנָה
תּוּסַ֫בּוּ	תְּסוֹבְבוּ	תְּסוֹבְבוּ	תְּסַבְסְבוּ	תְּסֻבְסְבוּ
תּוּסַבֶּ֫ינָה	תְּסוֹבַ֫בְנָה	תְּסוֹבַ֫בְנָה	תְּסַבְסֵ֫בְנָה	תְּסֻבְסַ֫בְנָה
נוּסַב	נְסוֹבֵב	נְסוֹבַב	נְסַבְסֵב	נְסֻבְסַב

	סוֹבֵב		סַבְסֵב	
	סוֹבְבִי		סַבְסְבִי	
	סוֹבְבוּ		סַבְסְבוּ	
	סוֹבֵ֫בְנָה		סַבְסֵ֫בְנָה	

| | מְסוֹבֵב | | מְסַבְסֵב | |
| מוּסָב | | מְסוֹבָב | | מְסֻבְסָב |

Par. XIII. Verbs ע"וֹ. §§ 267--271.

		Kal.	Kal.	Niphal.	Hiphil.
Praet.	3 m. (sing.)	קָם	מֵת	נָקוֹם	הֵקִים
	3 f.	קָ֫מָה	מֵ֫תָה	נָק֫וֹמָה	הֵקִ֫ימָה
	2 m.	קַ֫מְתָּ	מַ֫תָּה	נְקוּמ֫וֹתָ	הֲקִימ֫וֹתָ
	2 f.	קַמְתְּ	מַתְּ	נְקוּמוֹת	הֲקִימוֹת
	1	קַ֫מְתִּי	מַ֫תִּי	נְקוּמ֫וֹתִי	הֲקִימ֫וֹתִי
	3 (plur.)	קָ֫מוּ	מֵ֫תוּ	נָק֫וֹמוּ	הֵקִ֫ימוּ
	2 m.	קַמְתֶּם	מַתֶּם	נְקוּמוֹתֶם	הֲקִימוֹתֶם
	2 f.	קַמְתֶּן	מַתֶּן	נְקוּמוֹתֶן	הֲקִימוֹתֶן
	1	קַ֫מְנוּ	מַ֫תְנוּ	נְקוּמ֫וֹנוּ	הֲקִימ֫וֹנוּ
Inf.	abs.	קוֹם	מוֹת		הָקֵם
	const.	קוּם	מוּת	הִקּוֹם	הָקִים
Fut.	3 m. (sing.)	יָקוּם	יָמוּת	יִקּוֹם	יָקִים
	3 f.	תָּקוּם	(etc.)	תִּקּוֹם	תָּקִים
	2 m.	תָּקוּם		תִּקּוֹם	תָּקִים
	2 f.	תָּק֫וּמִי		תִּק֫וֹמִי	תָּקִ֫ימִי
	1	אָקוּם		אֶקּוֹם	אָקִים
	3 m. (plur.)	יָק֫וּמוּ		יִקּ֫וֹמוּ	יָקִ֫ימוּ
	3 f.	תְּקוּמֶ֫ינָה		תִּקּ֫וֹמְנָה	תָּקֵ֫מְנָה
	2 m.	תָּק֫וּמוּ		תִּקּ֫וֹמוּ	תָּקִ֫ימוּ
	2 f.	תְּקוּמֶ֫ינָה		תִּקּ֫וֹמְנָה	תָּקֵ֫מְנָה
	1	נָקוּם		נִקּוֹם	נָקִים
Fut. apoc.		יָקֹם	יָמֹת		יָקֵם
Imp.	2 m. (sing.)	קוּם	מוּת (מֵת)	הִקּוֹם	הָקֵם
	2 f.	ק֫וּמִי	(etc.)	הִק֫וֹמִי	הָקִ֫ימִי
	2 m. (plur.)	ק֫וּמוּ		הִק֫וֹמוּ	הָקִ֫ימוּ
	2 f.	קֹ֫מְנָה		הִקֹּ֫מְנָה	הָקֵ֫מְנָה
Part. act.		קָם	מֵת		מֵקִים
	pass.	קוּם		נָקוֹם	

Par. XIII. Verbs ע״ו. §§ 267—271.			P. XIV. ע״י. 221
Hophal.	Polel.	Polal.	Kal.
הוּקַם	קוֹמֵם	קוֹמַם	בָּן
הוּקְמָה	קוֹמְמָה	קוֹמֲמָה	בָּנָה
הוּקַמְתָּ	קוֹמַ֫מְתָּ	קוֹמַ֫מְתָּ	בַּ֫נְתָּ
הוּקַמְתְּ	קוֹמַמְתְּ	קוֹמַמְתְּ	בַּנְתְּ
הוּקַ֫מְתִּי	קוֹמַ֫מְתִּי	קוֹמַ֫מְתִּי	בָּ֫נְתִּי
הוּקְמוּ	קוֹמְמוּ	קוֹמֲמוּ	בָּ֫נוּ
הוּקַמְתֶּם	קוֹמַמְתֶּם	קוֹמַמְתֶּם	בְּנְתֶּם
הוּקַמְתֶּן	קוֹמַמְתֶּן	קוֹמַמְתֶּן	בְּנְתֶּן
הוּקַ֫מְנוּ	קוֹמַ֫מְנוּ	קוֹמַ֫מְנוּ	בַּ֫נּוּ
			בּוֹן
הוּקַם	קוֹמֵם	קוֹמַם	בִּין
יוּקַם	יְקוֹמֵם	יְקוֹמַם	יָבִין
תּוּקַם	תְּקוֹמֵם	תְּקוֹמַם	תָּבִין
תּוּקַם	תְּקוֹמֵם	תְּקוֹמַם	תָּבִין
תּוּקְמִי	תְּקוֹמְמִי	תְּקוֹמֲמִי	תָּבִ֫ינִי
אוּקַם	אֲקוֹמֵם	אֲקוֹמַם	אָבִין
יוּקְמוּ	יְקוֹמְמוּ	יְקוֹמֲמוּ	יָבִ֫ינוּ
תּוּקַ֫מְנָה	תְּקוֹמַ֫מְנָה	תְּקוֹמַ֫מְנָה	תְּבִינֶ֫ינָה
תּוּקְמוּ	תְּקוֹמְמוּ	תְּקוֹמֲמוּ	תָּבִ֫ינוּ
תּוּקַ֫מְנָה	תְּקוֹמַ֫מְנָה	תְּקוֹמַ֫מְנָה	תְּבִינֶ֫ינָה
נוּקַם	נְקוֹמֵם	נְקוֹמַם	נָבִין
			יָבֵן
	קוֹמֵם		בִּין
	קוֹמְמִי		בִּ֫ינִי
	קוֹמְמוּ		בִּ֫ינוּ
	קוֹמַ֫מְנָה		
	מְקוֹמֵם		בָּן
מוּקָם		מְקוֹמָם	

Par. XV. Verbs לא׳‎. §§ 276—279.

		Kal.	Niphal.	Piel.
Praet.	3 m. (sing.)	מָצָא	נִמְצָא	מִצָּא
	3 f.	מָצְאָה	נִמְצְאָה	מִצְּאָה
	2 m.	מָצָאתָ	נִמְצֵאתָ	מִצֵּאתָ
	2 f.	מָצָאת	נִמְצֵאת	מִצֵּאת
	1	מָצָאתִי	נִמְצֵאתִי	מִצֵּאתִי
	3 (plur.)	מָצְאוּ	נִמְצְאוּ	מִצְּאוּ
	2 m.	מְצָאתֶם	נִמְצֵאתֶם	מִצֵּאתֶם
	2 f.	מְצָאתֶן	נִמְצֵאתֶן	מִצֵּאתֶן
	1	מָצָאנוּ	נִמְצֵאנוּ	מִצֵּאנוּ
Inf.	abs.	מָצוֹא		מַצֹּא
	const.	מְצֹא	הִמָּצֵא	מַצֵּא
Fut.	3 m. (sing.)	יִמְצָא	יִמָּצֵא	יְמַצֵּא
	3 f.	תִּמְצָא	תִּמָּצֵא	תְּמַצֵּא
	2 m.	תִּמְצָא	תִּמָּצֵא	תְּמַצֵּא
	2 f.	תִּמְצְאִי	תִּמָּצְאִי	תְּמַצְּאִי
	1	אֶמְצָא	אֶמָּצֵא	אֲמַצֵּא
	3 m. (plur.)	יִמְצְאוּ	יִמָּצְאוּ	יְמַצְּאוּ
	3 f.	תִּמְצֶאנָה	תִּמָּצֶאנָה	תְּמַצֶּאנָה
	2 m.	תִּמְצְאוּ	תִּמָּצְאוּ	תְּמַצְּאוּ
	2 f.	תִּמְצֶאנָה	תִּמָּצֶאנָה	תְּמַצֶּאנָה
	1	נִמְצָא	נִמָּצֵא	נְמַצֵּא
Fut. apoc.				
Imp.	2 m. (sing.)	מְצָא	הִמָּצֵא	מַצֵּא
	2 f.	מִצְאִי	הִמָּצְאִי	מַצְּאִי
	2 m. (plur.)	מִצְאוּ	הִמָּצְאוּ	מַצְּאוּ
	2 f.	מְצֶאנָה	הִמָּצֶאנָה	מַצֶּאנָה
Part.	act.	מוֹצֵא		מְמַצֵּא
	pass.	מָצוּא	נִמְצָא	

Par. XV. Verbs ל"א. §§ 276—279.

Pual.	Hiphil.	Hophal.	Hithpael.
מֻצָּא (מֻצָּא)	הִמְצִיא	הֻמְצָא (הָמְצָא)	הִתְמַצָּא
מֻצְּאָה etc.	הִמְצִיאָה	הֻמְצְאָה etc.	הִתְמַצְּאָה
מֻצֵּאת	הִמְצֵאת	הֻמְצֵאת	הִתְמַצֵּאת
מֻצֵּאתָ	הִמְצֵאתָ	הֻמְצֵאתָ	הִתְמַצֵּאתָ
מֻצֵּאתִי	הִמְצֵאתִי	הֻמְצֵאתִי	הִתְמַצֵּאתִי
מֻצְּאוּ	הִמְצִיאוּ	הֻמְצְאוּ	הִתְמַצְּאוּ
מֻצֵּאתֶם	הִמְצֵאתֶם	הֻמְצֵאתֶם	הִתְמַצֵּאתֶם
מֻצֵּאתֶן	הִמְצֵאתֶן	הֻמְצֵאתֶן	הִתְמַצֵּאתֶן
מֻצֵּאנוּ	הִמְצֵאנוּ	הֻמְצֵאנוּ	הִתְמַצֵּאנוּ
	הַמְצֵא		
מֻצָּא	הַמְצִיא	הֻמְצָא	הִתְמַצֵּא
יְמֻצָּא (יְמֻצָּא)	יַמְצִיא	יֻמְצָא (יָמְצָא)	יִתְמַצֵּא
תְּמֻצָּא etc.	תַּמְצִיא	תֻּמְצָא etc.	תִּתְמַצֵּא
תְּמֻצָּא	תַּמְצִיא	תֻּמְצָא	תִּתְמַצֵּא
תְּמֻצְּאִי	תַּמְצִיאִי	תֻּמְצְאִי	תִּתְמַצְּאִי
אֲמֻצָּא	אַמְצִיא	אֻמְצָא	אֶתְמַצֵּא
יְמֻצְּאוּ	יַמְצִיאוּ	יֻמְצְאוּ	יִתְמַצְּאוּ
תְּמֻצֶּאנָה	תַּמְצֶאנָה	תֻּמְצֶאנָה	תִּתְמַצֶּאנָה
תְּמֻצְּאוּ	תַּמְצִיאוּ	תֻּמְצְאוּ	תִּתְמַצְּאוּ
תְּמֻצֶּאנָה	תַּמְצֶאנָה	תֻּמְצֶאנָה	תִּתְמַצֶּאנָה
נְמֻצָּא	נַמְצִיא	נֻמְצָא	נִתְמַצֵּא
	יַמְצֵא		
	הַמְצֵא		הִתְמַצֵּא
	הַמְצִיאִי		הִתְמַצְּאִי
	הַמְצִיאוּ		הִתְמַצְּאוּ
	הַמְצֶאנָה		הִתְמַצֶּאנָה
	מַמְצִיא		מִתְמַצֵּא
מְמֻצָּא (מְמֻצָּא)		מֻמְצָא (מָמְצָא)	

Par. XVI. Verbs לָ"ה. §§ 280—292.

		Kal.	Niphal.	Piel.	Pual.
Praet.	3. m.	גָּלָה	נִגְלָה	גִּלָּה	גֻּלָּה
	3 f. (גָּלַת)	גָּלְתָה	נִגְלְתָה	גִּלְּתָה	גֻּלְּתָה
	2 m.	גָּלִיתָ (גָּלֵיתָ)	נִגְלֵיתָ (נִגְלִיתָ)	גִּלִּיתָ	גֻּלֵּיתָ
	2 f.	גָּלִית	נִגְלֵית etc.	גִּלִּית	גֻּלֵּית
	1	גָּלִיתִי	נִגְלֵיתִי	גִּלִּיתִי	גֻּלֵּיתִי
	3 (pl.) (גָּלָיוּ)	גָּלוּ	נִגְלוּ	גִּלּוּ	גֻּלּוּ
	2 m.	גְּלִיתֶם	נִגְלֵיתֶם	גִּלִּיתֶם	גֻּלֵּיתֶם
	2 f.	גְּלִיתֶן	נִגְלֵיתֶן	גִּלִּיתֶן	גֻּלֵּיתֶן
	1	גָּלִינוּ	נִגְלֵינוּ	גִּלִּינוּ	גֻּלֵּינוּ
Inf.	abs.	גָּלֹה	נִגְלֹה	גַּלֵּה (גַּלֹּה)	גֻּלֹּה
	const.	גְּלוֹת	הִגָּלֹת	גַּלּוֹת	גֻּלֹּת
Fut.	3 m.	יִגְלֶה	יִגָּלֶה	יְגַלֶּה	יְגֻלֶּה
	3 f.	תִּגְלֶה	תִּגָּלֶה	תְּגַלֶּה	תְּגֻלֶּה
	2 m.	תִּגְלֶה	תִּגָּלֶה	תְּגַלֶּה	תְּגֻלֶּה
	2 f.	תִּגְלִי	תִּגָּלִי	תְּגַלִּי	תְּגֻלִּי
	1	אֶגְלֶה	אֶגָּלֶה	אֲגַלֶּה	אֲגֻלֶּה
	3 m. (plur.)	יִגְלוּ	יִגָּלוּ	יְגַלּוּ	יְגֻלּוּ
	3 f.	תִּגְלֶינָה	תִּגָּלֶינָה	תְּגַלֶּינָה	תְּגֻלֶּינָה
	2 m.	תִּגְלוּ	תִּגָּלוּ	תְּגַלּוּ	תְּגֻלּוּ
	2 f.	תִּגְלֶינָה	תִּגָּלֶינָה	תְּגַלֶּינָה	תְּגֻלֶּינָה
	1	נִגְלֶה	נִגָּלֶה	נְגַלֶּה	נְגֻלֶּה
Fut. apoc.		יִגֶל	יִגָּל	יְגַל (יְגַל)	
Imp.	2 m. (sing.)	גְּלֵה	הִגָּלֵה	גַּלֵּה (גַּל)	
	2 f.	גְּלִי	הִגָּלִי	גַּלִּי	
	2 m. (plur.)	גְּלוּ	הִגָּלוּ	גַּלּוּ	
	2 f.	גְּלֶינָה	הִגָּלֶינָה	גַּלֶּינָה	
Part.	act.	גּוֹלֶה		מְגַלֶּה	
	pass.	גָּלוּי	נִגְלֶה		מְגֻלֶּה

Par. XVI. Verbs לה. 280—292.

Hiphil.	Hophal.	Hithpael.	Hithpalel.
הִגְלָה	הָגְלָה	הִתְגַּלָּה	הִשְׁתַּחֲוָה
הִגְלְתָה	הָגְלְתָה	הִתְגַּלְּתָה	
הִגְלִיתָ (הִגְלִיתָ)	הָגְלִיתָ	הִתְגַּלִּיתָ	הִשְׁתַּחֲוִיתָ
הִגְלִית etc.	הָגְלִית	הִתְגַּלִּית	
הִגְלִיתִי	הָגְלִיתִי	הִתְגַּלִּיתִי	הִשְׁתַּחֲוֵיתִי
הִגְלוּ	הָגְלוּ	הִתְגַּלּוּ	הִשְׁתַּחֲווּ
הִגְלִיתֶם	הָגְלִיתֶם	הִתְגַּלִּיתֶם	הִשְׁתַּחֲוִיתֶם
הִגְלִיתֶן	הָגְלִיתֶן	הִתְגַּלִּיתֶן	
הִגְלִינוּ	הָגְלִינוּ	הִתְגַּלִּינוּ	
הַגְלֵה	הָגְלֵה	הִתְגַּלֵּה	
הַגְלֹת	הָגְלֹת	הִתְגַּלֹּת	הִשְׁתַּחֲוֹת
יַגְלֶה	יָגְלֶה	יִתְגַּלֶּה	יִשְׁתַּחֲוֶה
תַּגְלֶה	תָּגְלֶה	תִּתְגַּלֶּה	תִּשְׁתַּחֲוֶה
תַּגְלֶה	תָּגְלֶה	תִּתְגַּלֶּה	תִּשְׁתַּחֲוֶה
תַּגְלִי	תָּגְלִי	תִּתְגַּלִּי	
אַגְלֶה	אָגְלֶה	אֶתְגַּלֶּה	אֶשְׁתַּחֲוֶה
יַגְלוּ	יָגְלוּ	יִתְגַּלּוּ	יִשְׁתַּחֲווּ
תַּגְלֶינָה	תָּגְלֶינָה	תִּתְגַּלֶּינָה	
תַּגְלוּ	תָּגְלוּ	תִּתְגַּלּוּ	תִּשְׁתַּחֲווּ
תַּגְלֶינָה	תָּגְלֶינָה	תִּתְגַּלֶּינָה	
נַגְלֶה	נָגְלֶה	נִתְגַּלֶּה	נִשְׁתַּחֲוֶה
יֶגֶל		יִתְגַּל	יִשְׁתַּחוּ
הַגְלֵה (הֶגֶל)		הִתְגַּלֵּה	
הַגְלִי		הִתְגַּלִּי	הִשְׁתַּחֲוִי
הַגְלוּ		הִתְגַּלּוּ	הִשְׁתַּחֲווּ
הַגְלֶינָה		הִתְגַּלֶּינָה	
מַגְלֶה		מִתְגַּלֶּה	מִשְׁתַּחֲוֶה
	מָגְלֶה		

29

226 Par. XVII. פ"י & ל"ה. | Par. XVIII. Verbs פ"ן & ל"א.

	Kal.	Hiphil.	Kal.	Niphal.	Hiphil.
Praet.	יָרָה	הוֹרָה	נָשָׂא	נִשָּׂא	הִשִּׂיא*
3 f.	יָרְתָה	הוֹרָתָה	נָשְׂאָה	נִשְּׂאָה	הִשִּׂיאָה
2 m.	יָרִיתָ	הוֹרִיתָ	(לֹא as) נָשֵׂאתָ	נִשֵּׂאתָ	הִשֵּׂאתָ
2 f.	יָרִית	הוֹרִית	נָשֵׂאת	נִשֵּׂאת	הִשֵּׂאת
1	יָרִיתִי	הוֹרֵיתִי	נָשֵׂאתִי	נִשֵּׂאתִי	הִשֵּׂאתִי
3 [plur.]	יָרוּ	הוֹרוּ	נָשְׂאוּ	נִשְּׂאוּ	הִשִּׂיאוּ
2 m.	יְרִיתֶם	הוֹרִיתֶם	נְשָׂאתֶם	נִשֵּׂאתֶם	הִשֵּׂאתֶם
2 f.	יְרִיתֶן	הוֹרִיתֶן	נְשָׂאתֶן	נִשֵּׂאתֶן	הִשֵּׂאתֶן
1	יָרִינוּ	הוֹרֵינוּ	נָשָׂאנוּ	נִשֵּׂאנוּ	הִשֵּׂאנוּ
Inf. abs.	יָרֹה		נָשׂוֹא	הִנָּשֵׂא	הַשֵּׂא
const.	יְרוֹת	הוֹרֹת	שְׂאֵת		הַשִּׂיא
Fut.	יִירֶה	יוֹרֶה	יִשָּׂא	יִנָּשֵׂא	יַשִּׂיא
3 f.	תִּירֶה	תּוֹרֶה	תִּשָּׂא	(לֹא as)	
2 m.	תִּירֶה	תּוֹרֶה	תִּשָּׂא		
2 f.	תִּירִי	תּוֹרִי	תִּשְׂאִי		
1	אִירֶה	אוֹרֶה	אֶשָּׂא		
3 [plur.]	יִירוּ	יוֹרוּ	יִשְׂאוּ	יִנָּשְׂאוּ	יַשִּׂיאוּ
3 f.	תִּירֶינָה	תּוֹרֶינָה	תִּשֶּׂאנָה		
2 m.	תִּירוּ	תּוֹרוּ	תִּשְׂאוּ		תַּשִּׂיאוּ
2 f.	תִּירֶינָה	תּוֹרֶינָה	תִּשֶּׂאנָה		
1	נִירֶה	נוֹרֶה	נִשָּׂא		
Fut. apoc.	וַיֹּר				
Imp.	יְרֵה	הוֹרֵה	שָׂא		
2 f.	יְרִי	הוֹרִי	שְׂאִי		
2 m. [plur.]	יְרוּ	הוֹרוּ	שְׂאוּ		
2 f.	יְרֶינָה	הוֹרֶינָה	שֶׂאנָה		
Part. act.	יוֹרֶה	מוֹרֶה	נֹשֵׂא	* (From נָשָׂא, not	
pass.	יָרוּי		נָשׂוּא	נָשָׂא.)	

	Par. XIX. פ״ן & ל״ה.		Par. XX. Verb בּוֹא. 227		
	Kal.	Hiphil.	Kal.	Hiphil.	Hophal.
Praet.	נָטָה	הִטָּה	בָּא	הֵבִיא	הוּבָא
3 f.	נָטְתָה	הִטְּתָה	בָּאָה	הֵבִיאָה	הוּבָאת
2 m.	(as ל״ה)	הִטִּיתָ	בָּאתָ	הֵבֵאתָ	הוּבֵאתָה
2 f.		הִטִּית	בָּאת		
1		הִטִּיתִי	בָּאתִי	הֵבֵאתִי	
3 (plur.)		הִטּוּ	בָּאוּ (בָּאוּ)	הֵבִיאוּ	הוּבָאוּ
2 m.		הִטִּיתֶם	בָּאתֶם	הֲבֵאתֶם	
2 f.		הִטִּיתֶן	. . .	. . . .	
1		הִטִּינוּ	בָּאנוּ	הֲבִיאֹנוּ	
Inf. abs.	נָטֹה		בּוֹא		
const.	נְטוֹת	הַטּוֹת	בּוֹא (בֹּא)	הָבִיא	
Fut.	יִטֶּה	יַטֶּה	יָבוֹא	יָבִיא	יוּבָא
3 f.	תִּטֶּה	תַּטֶּה	תָּבוֹא	תָּבִיא	
2 m.	תִּטֶּה	תַּטֶּה	תָּבוֹא	תָּבִיא	
2 f.	תִּטִּי	תַּטִּי	תָּבוֹאִי		
1	אֶטֶּה	אַטֶּה	אָבוֹא	אָבִיא	
3 (plur.)	יִטּוּ	יַטּוּ	יָבֹאוּ	יָבִיאוּ	יוּבָאוּ
3 f.	תִּטֶּינָה	תַּטֶּינָה	תְּבֹאנָה	תְּבִיאֶינָה	
2 m.	תִּטּוּ	תַּטּוּ	תָּבֹאוּ	תָּבִיאוּ	
2 f.	תִּטֶּינָה	תַּטֶּינָה	. . .	. . . .	
1	נִטֶּה	נַטֶּה	נָבוֹא	נָבִיא	
Fut. apoc.	יֵט	יַט		וַיָּבֹא	
Imp.	נְטֵה (הַט) הַטֵּה		בּוֹא	הָבִיא(הָבֵא)	
2 f.	(as ל״ה)	הַטִּי	בּוֹאִי	הָבִיאִי	
2 m. (plur.)		הַטּוּ	בּוֹאוּ	הָבִיאוּ	
2 f.		הַטֶּינָה	. . .	. . . .	
Part. act.	נוֹטֶה	מַטֶּה	בָּא	מֵבִיא	מוּבָא
pass.	נָטוּי				

Par. XXI. Participles. § 301.

		Kal.		
		Masc.	Fem.	Fem. Segh.
Verbs final Pattahh	act.	קוֹטֵל	קֹטְלָה (קֹטְלָֽה־)	קֹטֶ֫לֶת
——	pass.	קָטוּל	קְטוּלָה	
— Tseri	act.	יָשֵׁן	יְשֵׁנָה	יְשֵׁנֶת
— Hholem	act.	יָגֹר	יְגֹרָה	
ע״ gutt.	act.	זֹעֵק	זֹעֲקָה	זֹעֶ֫קֶת
ל״ gutt.	act.	שֹׁמֵעַ	שֹׁמְעָה	שֹׁמַ֫עַת
עו״	act.	קָם	קָמָה	
לה״	act.	גֹּלֶה	גֹּלָה (גֹּלִיָּה)	
	pass.	גָּלוּי	גְּלוּיָה	

	Niphal.		
regular	נִקְטָל	נִקְטָלָה	נִקְטֶ֫לֶת
פ״ gutt.	נֶעֱמָד	נֶעֱמָדָה	נֶעֱמֶ֫דֶת
עע״	נָסָב	נְסַבָּה	
עו״	נָקוֹם	נְקוֹמָה	

	Piel.		
regular	מְקַטֵּל	מְקַטְּלָה	מְקַטֶּ֫לֶת
ער״	מְבָרֵךְ	מְבָרְכָה	מְבָרֶ֫כֶת
לה״	מְגַלֶּה	מְגַלָּה	
Poel of ע״ע	מְסוֹבֵב	מְסוֹבְבָה	מְסוֹבֶ֫בֶת

	Pual.		
regular	מְקֻטָּל	מְקֻטָּלָה	מְקֻטֶּ֫לֶת

	Hiphil.		
regular	מַקְטִיל	מַקְטִילָה	מַקְטֶ֫לֶת
פ״ gutt.	מַעֲמִיד	מַעֲמִידָה	מַעֲמֶ֫דֶת
עע״	מֵסֵב	מְסִבָּה	
עו״	מֵקִים	מְקִימָה	

	Hophal.		
regular	מָקְטָל	מָקְטָלָה	מָקְטֶ֫לֶת

	Hithpael.		
regular	מִתְקַטֵּל	מִתְקַטְּלָה	מִתְקַטֶּ֫לֶת

Par. XXI. Participles. § 301.

Kal.

Plur. masc.	Plur. fem.	Masc.	Fem.
קֹטְלִים	קֹטְלוֹת	Dec. VII. b.	Dec. X. XIII.
קְטוּלִים	קְטוּלוֹת	III. c.	X.
יְשֵׁנִים	יְשֵׁנוֹת	V. e.	XI. XIII.
יְגֵרִים	יְגֵרוֹת	III. c.	X.
זְעֵקִים	זְעֵקוֹת	VII.	X. XIII.
שֹׁמְעִים	שֹׁמְעוֹת	VII.	X. XIII.
קָמִים	קָמוֹת	I.	X.
גָּלִים	גָּלוֹת	IX. a.	X.
גְּלוּיִים	גְּלוּיוֹת	III. c.	X.

Niphal.

נִקְטָלִים	נִקְטָלוֹת	II.	XI. XIII.
נֶעֱמָדִים	נֶעֱמָדוֹת	II.	XI. XIII.
נְסִבִּים	נְסִבּוֹת	VIII.	X.
נְקוֹמִים	נְקוֹמוֹת	III. c.	X.

Piel.

מְקַטְּלִים	מְקַטְּלוֹת	VII. c.	X. XIII.
מְבָרְכִים	מְבָרְכוֹת	VII.	X. XIII.
מְגַלִּים	מְגַלּוֹת	IX.	X.
מְסוֹבְבִים	מְסוֹבְבוֹת	VII. b.	X. XIII.

Pual.

מְקֻטָּלִים	מְקֻטָּלוֹת	II.	XI. XIII.

Hiphil.

מַקְטִילִים	מַקְטִילוֹת	I.	X. XIII.
מַעֲמִידִים	מַעֲמִידוֹת	I.	X. XIII.
מְסִבִּים	מְסִבּוֹת	VIII.	X.
מְקִימִים	מְקִימוֹת	III.	X.

Hophal.

מָקְטָלִים	מָקְטָלוֹת	II.	XI. XIII.

Hithpael.

מִתְקַטְּלִים	מִתְקַטְּלוֹת	VII. c.	X. XIII.

Par. XXII. Verbs with suffix-pronouns. §§ 303—312.

Suffixes.	Sing. 1.	2 masc.	2 fem.	3 masc.	3 fem.
Kal. Praet.	קְטָלַ֫נִי	קְטָלָ֑ךְ	קְטָלֵךְ	קְטָלוֹ / קְטָלָ֫הוּ	קְטָלָהּ
3 f.	קְטָלַ֫תְנִי	קְטָלַ֫תֶךְ	קְטָלַ֫תֶךְ	קְטָלַ֫תְהוּ / קְטָלַ֫תּוּ	קְטָלַ֫תָּה
2 m.	קְטַלְתַּ֫נִי / קְטַלְתָּ֫נִי	—	—	קְטַלְתָּ֫הוּ / קְטַלְתּוֹ	קְטַלְתָּהּ
2 f.	קְטַלְתִּ֫ינִי	—	—	קְטַלְתִּ֫יו / קְטַלְתִּ֫יהוּ	קְטַלְתִּ֫יהָ
1	—	קְטַלְתִּ֫יךָ	קְטַלְתִּיךְ	קְטַלְתִּ֫יו	קְטַלְתִּ֫יהָ
3 (plur.)	קְטָל֫וּנִי	קְטָל֫וּךָ	קְטָל֫וּךְ	קְטָל֫וּהוּ	קְטָל֫וּהָ
2 m.	קְטַלְתּ֫וּנִי	—	—	קְטַלְתּ֫וּהוּ	קְטַלְתּ֫וּהָ
1	—	קְטַלְנ֫וּךָ	קְטַלְנ֫וּךְ	קְטַלְנ֫וּהוּ	קְטַלְנ֫וּהָ
Inf.	קָטְלֵ֫נִי / קָטְלִי(בְּקָצְרִי)קָבְלִי (בְּחָרְיִ)	קָטְלְךָ / קָטְלָ֑ךְ	קָטְלֵךְ	קָטְלוֹ (פָּעֳמוֹ)	קָטְלָהּ (חֲנֹתָהּ)
Fut.	יִקְטְלֵ֫נִי	יִקְטָלְךָ	יִקְטְלֵךְ	יִקְטְלֵ֫הוּ	יִקְטְלֶ֫הָ / יִקְטְלָהּ
3 m. with epenth. נ	יִקְטְלֵ֫נִי	יִקְטָלֶ֑ךָּ	—	יִקְטְלֶ֫נּוּ	יִקְטְלֶ֫נָּה
3 (plur.)	יִקְטְל֫וּנִי (יִקְטְלֻ֫נְנִי)	יִקְטְל֫וּךָ	יִקְטְלוּךְ	יִקְטְל֫וּהוּ (יִקְטְלֻ֫נְהוּ)	יִקְטְל֫וּהָ
Imp.	קָטְלֵ֫נִי / שְׁמָעֵ֫נִי	—	—	קָטְלֵ֫הוּ	קָטְלֶ֫הָ / קָטְלָהּ
Piel	קַטְּלֵ֫נִי	קַטֶּלְךָ	קַטְּלֵךְ	קַטְּלוֹ	קַטְּלָהּ
Hiph. fut.	יַקְטִילֵ֫נִי	יַקְטִילְךָ	יַקְטִילֵךְ	יַקְטִילֵ֫הוּ	יַקְטִילָהּ

Par. XXII. Verbs with suffix-pronouns. §§ 303—312.

Plur. 1.	2 masc.	2 fem.	3 masc.	3 fem.
קְטָלָ֫נוּ	קְטָלְכֶם	קְטָלְכֶן	קְטָלָם	קְטָלָן
קְטָלַ֫תְנוּ	קְטָלַתְכֶם	קְטָלַתְכֶן	קְטָלַ֫תַם	קְטָלַ֫תַן
קְטַלְתָּ֫נוּ	—	—	קְטַלְתָּם	קְטַלְתָּן
קְטַלְתִּ֫ינוּ	—	—	קְטַלְתִּים	קְטַלְתִּין
—	קְטַלְתִּיכֶם	קְטַלְתִּיכֶן	קְטַלְתִּים	קְטַלְתִּין
קְטָלֹ֫נוּ	קְטָלוּכֶם	קְטָלוּכֶן	קְטָלוּם	קְטָלוּן
קְטַלְתֹּ֫נוּ	—	—	קְטַלְתּוּם	קְטַלְתּוּן
—	קְטַלְנוּכֶם	קְטַלְנוּכֶן	קְטַלְנוּם	קְטַלְנוּן
קְטָלֵ֫נוּ	⎰ קְטָלְכֶם ⎱ בְּקָעָם (אֲהָבָם)	⎰ קְטָלְכֶן ⎱ קְטָלְכֶן	⎰ קְטָלָם ⎱ קְטָלְכֶן (חֲנֻנֵּם)	קְטָלָן
יִקְטְלֵ֫נוּ	יִקְטָלְכֶם	יִקְטָלְכֶן	⎰ יִקְטְלֵם ⎱ יִלְבָּשָׁם (יִמְצָאֵם)	יִקְטְלֵן
יִקְטְלֻ֫נוּ יִקְטְלוּנוּ	יִקְטְלוּכֶם	יִקְטְלוּכֶן	יִקְטְלוּם	יִקְטְלוּן
קָטְלֵ֫נוּ שְׁמָע֫וּנוּ	—	—	קָטְלֵם	—
קָטְלֵ֫נוּ	קְטָלְכֶם	קְטָלְכֶן	קְטָלָם	קְטָלָן
יַקְטִילֵ֫נוּ	יַקְטִילְכֶם	יַקְטִילְכֶן	יַקְטִילֵם	יַקְטִילֵן

Par. XXIII. Verbs לה with suffixes. § 313.

Suffixes.	Sing. 1.	2 masc.	3 masc.	Plur. 3 masc.
Kal. Praet.	עָשַׂנִי	עָשְׂךָ	עָשָׂהוּ	עָשָׂם
3 f.	עָשַׂתְנִי	עָשַׂתְךָ	עָשַׂתּוּ	עָשָׂתַם
2 m.	עָשִׂיתָנִי / עָשִׂיתַנִי	—	עָשִׂיתוֹ / עָשִׂיתָהוּ	עֲשִׂיתָם
1	—	עֲשִׂיתִיךָ	עֲשִׂיתִיו / עֲשִׂיתִיהוּ	עֲשִׂיתִים
3 (plur.)	עָשׂוּנִי	עָשׂוּךָ	עָשׂוּהוּ	עָשׂוּם
Inf.	עֲשֹׂתִי	עֲשֹׂתְךָ	עֲשֹׂתוֹ / עֲשֹׂהוּ	עֲשֹׂתָם
Fut. 3 m.	יַעֲשֵׂנִי	יַעַשְׂךָ	יַעֲשׂוֹ / יַעֲשֵׂהוּ	יַעֲשֵׂם
3 m. with epenth. נ	יַעֲשֶׂנִּי	יַעַשְׂךָ	יַעֲשֶׂנּוּ	
1	—	אֶעֶשְׂךָ	אֶעֱשֵׂהוּ	אֶעֱשֵׂם
3 m. (plur.)	יַעֲשׂוּנִי	יַעֲשׂוּךָ	יַעֲשׂוּהוּ	יַעֲשׂוּם
Imp. m.	עֲנֵנִי	—	עֲנֵהוּ	עֲנֵם
Piel. Praet. 3 m.	צִוַּנִי	צִוְּךָ	צִוָּהוּ	צִוָּם
Fut. 3 m.	יְצַוֵּנִי	יְצַוְּךָ	יְצַוֵּהוּ	יְצַוֵּם
3 m. with epenth. נ	יְצַוֵּנִי	יְצַוְּךָ	יְצַוֶּנּוּ	—
Hiph. Praet.	הִכַּנִי	הִכְּךָ	הִכָּהוּ	הִכָּם
Fut. with epenth. נ	יַכֵּנִי	יַכְּךָ	יַכֵּנּוּ	—

Par. XXIV. Nouns with suffixes. § 334—340.

No. I. Noun masc. ending with a consonant.

Abs. (sing.)	סוּס	a horse.	(plur.)	סוּסִים	horses.
Suff. 1	סוּסִי	my horse,		סוּסַי	my horses.
2 m.	סוּסְךָ	thy —		סוּסֶיךָ	thy —
2 f.	סוּסֵךְ	thy —		סוּסַיִךְ	thy —
3 m.	סוּסוֹ	his —		סוּסָיו	his —
3 f.	סוּסָהּ	her —		סוּסֶיהָ	her —
1 (plur.)	סוּסֵנוּ	our —		סוּסֵינוּ	our —
2 m.	סוּסְכֶם	your —		סוּסֵיכֶם	your —
2 f.	סוּסְכֶן	your —		סוּסֵיכֶן	your —
3 m.	סוּסָם	their —		סוּסֵיהֶם	their —
3 f.	סוּסָן	their —		סוּסֵיהֶן	their —

No. II. Noun masc. ending with a Quiescent.

Abs. (sing.)	אָב	father.	Abs. (sing.)	אָב	father.
Suff. (sing.)	אָבִי	my father.	Suff. (pl.)	אָבִינוּ	our father.
2 m.	אָבִיךָ	thy —	2 m.	אֲבִיכֶם	your —
2 f.	אָבִיךְ	thy —	2 f.	אֲבִיכֶן	your —
3 m.	אָבִיו, אֲבִיהוּ	his —	3 m.	אֲבִיהֶם	their —
3 f.	אָבִיהָ	her —	3 f.	אֲבִיהֶן	their —

No. III. Noun feminine.

Abs. (sing.)	תּוֹרָה	a law.	(plur.)	תּוֹרוֹת	laws.
Suff. 1	תּוֹרָתִי	my law.		תּוֹרוֹתַי	my laws.
2 m.	תּוֹרָתְךָ	thy —		תּוֹרוֹתֶיךָ	thy —
2 f.	תּוֹרָתֵךְ	thy —		תּוֹרוֹתַיִךְ	thy —
3 m.	תּוֹרָתוֹ	his —		תּוֹרוֹתָיו	his —
3 f.	תּוֹרָתָהּ	her —		תּוֹרוֹתֶיהָ	her —
1 (plur.)	תּוֹרָתֵנוּ	our —		תּוֹרוֹתֵינוּ	our —
2 m.	תּוֹרַתְכֶם	your —		תּוֹרוֹתֵיכֶם	your —
2 f.	תּוֹרַתְכֶן	your —		תּוֹרוֹתֵיכֶן	your —
3 m.	תּוֹרָתָם	their —		תּוֹרוֹתֵיהֶם	their —
3 f.	תּוֹרָתָן	their —		תּוֹרוֹתֵיהֶן	their —

Par. XXV. Nouns Masculine. §§ 345 seq.

	Sing. abs.	Const.	Light suff.	Grave suff.
		Dec. I. Singular. § 345.		
(a)	סוּס	סוּס	סוּסִי	סוּסְכֶם
(b)	גִּבּוֹר	גִּבּוֹר	גִּבּוֹרִי	גִּבּוֹרְכֶם
(c)	שָׁפוֹט	שָׁפוֹט	שְׁפוֹטִי	שְׁפוֹטְכֶם
(d)	אֱלוֹהַּ	אֱלוֹהַּ	אֱלוֹהִי	אֱלוֹהֲכֶם
		Dec. II. Singular. § 347.		
(a)	דָּם	דַּם	דָּמִי	(once) דִּמְכֶם
(b)	כּוֹכָב	כּוֹכַב	כּוֹכָבִי	כּוֹכַבְכֶם
(c)	כּוֹבַע	כּוֹבַע	כּוֹבָעִי	כּוֹבַעֲכֶם
(d)	שַׂד	שַׂד	שָׂדִי	שַׂדְכֶם
		Dec. III. Singular. § 350.		
(a)	פָּקִיד	פָּקִיד	פְּקִידִי	פְּקִידְכֶם
(b)	מֵלִיץ	מֵלִיץ	מְלִיצִי	מְלִיצְכֶם
(c)	קָטוּל	קָטוּל	קְטוּלִי	קְטוּלְכֶם
(d)	זִכְרוֹן	זִכְרוֹן	זִכְרוֹנִי	זִכְרוֹנְכֶם
(e)	חִזָּיוֹן	חִזָּיוֹן (עִצָּבוֹן)	חִזְיוֹנִי	חִזְיוֹנְכֶם
(f)	מָנוֹס	מָנוֹס	מְנוּסִי	מְנוּסְכֶם
(g)	אֵבוּס	אֵבוּס	אֲבוּסִי	אֲבוּסְכֶם
(h)	גָּדוֹל	גְּדָל-		
		Dec. IV. Singular. § 353.		
(a)	דָּבָר	דְּבַר	דְּבָרִי	דְּבַרְכֶם
(b)	לֵבָב	לְבַב	לְבָבִי	לְבַבְכֶם
(c)	חָכָם	חֲכַם	חֲכָמִי	חֲכַמְכֶם
(d)	שַׁעַר	שַׁעַר	שַׁעֲרִי	שַׁעַרְכֶם
(e)	עָמֵק	עֲמֵק	עֲמֵקִי	עֲמֵקְכֶם
(f)	כָּנָף	כְּנַף	כְּנָפִי	כְּנַפְכֶם
(g)	צָבָא			

Par. XXV. Nouns Masculine. § 345 seq.

Plural abs.	Light suff.	Const.	Grave suff.
Dec. I. Plural.			
סוּסִים	סוּסַי	סוּסֵי	סוּסֵיכֶם
גְּבוֹרִים	גִּבּוֹרַי	גִּבּוֹרֵי	גִּבּוֹרֵיכֶם
שְׁפוּטִים	שְׁפוּטַי	שְׁפוּטֵי	שְׁפוּטֵיכֶם
אֱלֹהִים	אֱלֹהַי	אֱלֹהֵי	אֱלֹהֵיכֶם
Dec. II. Plural.			
דָּמִים	דָּמַי	דְּמֵי	דְּמֵיכֶם
כּוֹכָבִים	כּוֹכָבַי	כּוֹכְבֵי	כּוֹכְבֵיכֶם
כּוֹבְעִים	כּוֹבָעַי	כּוֹבְעֵי	כּוֹבְעֵיכֶם
שָׂדִים	שָׂדַי	שְׂדֵי	שְׂדֵיכֶם
Dec. III. Plural.			
פְּקִידִים	פְּקִידַי	פְּקִידֵי	פְּקִידֵיכֶם
מְלִיצִים	מְלִיצַי	מְלִיצֵי	מְלִיצֵיכֶם
קְטוּלִים	קְטוּלַי	קְטוּלֵי	קְטוּלֵיכֶם
זִכְרוֹנִים	זִכְרוֹנַי	זִכְרוֹנֵי	זִכְרוֹנֵיכֶם
חֶזְיוֹנוֹת (חֶשְׁבּוֹנוֹת)	(as Dec. X.)		
מְנוּסִים	מְנוּסַי	מְנוּסֵי	מְנוּסֵיכֶם
אֲבוּסִים	אֲבוּסַי	אֲבוּסֵי	אֲבוּסֵיכֶם
Dec. IV. Plural.			
דְּבָרִים	דְּבָרַי	דִּבְרֵי	דִּבְרֵיכֶם
לְבָבִים	לְבָבַי	לִבְבֵי	לִבְבֵיכֶם
חֲכָמִים	חֲכָמַי	חַכְמֵי	חַכְמֵיכֶם
שְׁעָרִים	שְׁעָרַי	שַׁעֲרֵי	שַׁעֲרֵיכֶם
עֲמֻקִּים	עֲמֻקַּי	עִמְקֵי	עִמְקֵיכֶם
כְּנָפִים	כְּנָפַי	כַּנְפֵי	כַּנְפֵיכֶם
צְבָאוֹת	צְבָאוֹת		(צִבְאוֹתָם)

Par. XXV. Nouns Masculine. §§ 356 seq.

	Sing. abs.	Const.	Light suff.	Grave suff.
(h)	עָשָׁן	עֲשַׁן (עֳשֶׁן)		
(i)	צֵלָע	צְלַע (צֶלַע)	צַלְעִי	

Dec. V. Singular. § 356.

	Sing. abs.	Const.	Light suff.	Grave suff.
(a)	זָקֵן	זְקַן	זְקֵנִי	זְקַנְכֶם
(b)	חָצֵר	חֲצַר	חֲצֵרִי	חַצְרְכֶם
(c)	כָּתֵף	כְּתֵף	כְּתֵפִי	כִּתְפְכֶם
(d)	כָּבֵד	כְּבַד (בְּבַד)	כְּבֵדִי	כְּבַדְכֶם

Dec. VI. Singular. A class. § 359.

	Sing. abs.	Const.	Light suff.	Grave suff.
(a)	מֶלֶךְ (מַלְךּ)	מֶלֶךְ	מַלְכִּי	מַלְכְּכֶם
(b)	נַעַר	נַעַר	נַעֲרִי	נַעַרְכֶם
(c)	זֶרַע (זַרְע)	זֶרַע	זַרְעִי	זַרְעֲכֶם

E class.

	Sing. abs.	Const.	Light suff.	Grave suff.
(d)	סֵפֶר	סֵפֶר	סִפְרִי	סִפְרְכֶם
(e)	קֶבֶר	קֶבֶר	קִבְרִי	קִבְרְכֶם
(f)	חֵלֶק	חֵלֶק	חֶלְקִי	חֶלְקְכֶם
(g)	חֵלֶד	חֵלֶד	חֶלְדִי	חֶלְדְּכֶם
(h)	נֵצַח	נֵצַח	נִצְחִי	נִצְחֲכֶם

O class.

	Sing. abs.	Const.	Light suff.	Grave suff.
(i)	בֹּקֶר	בֹּקֶר	בָּקְרִי	בָּקְרְכֶם
(j)	קֹמֶץ	קֹמֶץ	קָמְצִי	קָמְצְכֶם
(k)	פֹּעַל	פֹּעַל	פָּעֳלִי (פֹּעֲלִי)	פָּעָלְכֶם
(l)	קֹדֶשׁ	קֹדֶשׁ	קָדְשִׁי	קָדְשְׁכֶם

Par. XXV. Nouns Masculine. §§ 356 seq.

Plur. abs.	Light suff.	Const.	Grave suff.
עֲשָׁנִים	עֲשָׁנַי	עַשְׁנֵי	עַשְׁנֵיכֶם
צְלָעִים	צְלָעַי	צַלְעֵי	צַלְעֵיכֶם

Dec. V. Plural.

זְקֵנִים	זְקֵנַי	זִקְנֵי	זִקְנֵיכֶם
חֲצֵרִים	חֲצֵרַי	חַצְרֵי	חַצְרֵיכֶם
כְּתֵפוֹת	(as Dec. XI.)		
כְּבֵדִים	כְּבֵדַי	כִּבְדֵי	כִּבְדֵיכֶם

Dec. VI. Plural. *A* class.

מְלָכִים	מְלָכַי	מַלְכֵי	מַלְכֵיכֶם
נְעָרִים	נְעָרַי	נַעֲרֵי	נַעֲרֵיכֶם
זְרָעִים	זְרָעַי	זַרְעֵי	זַרְעֵיכֶם

E class.

סְפָרִים	סְפָרַי	סִפְרֵי	סִפְרֵיכֶם
קְבָרִים	קְבָרַי	קִבְרֵי	קִבְרֵיכֶם
חֲלָקִים	חֲלָקַי (חִקְרֵי)	חֶלְקֵי	חֶלְקֵיכֶם
חֲלָדִים	חֲלָדַי	חֶלְדֵי	חֶלְדֵיכֶם
נְצָחִים	נְצָחַי	נִצְחֵי	נִצְחֵיכֶם

O class.

בְּקָרִים	בְּקָרַי	בָּקְרֵי	בָּקְרֵיכֶם
קְמָצִים	קְמָצַי	קָמְצֵי	קָמְצֵיכֶם
פְּעָלִים	פְּעָלַי	פָּעֳלֵי	פָּעֳלֵיכֶם
קֳדָשִׁים	קֳדָשַׁי	קָדְשֵׁי	קָדְשֵׁיכֶם

Par. XXV. Nouns Masculine. §§ 371 seq.

Segholates of roots עוּ and עִי. (q) דּוּד, const. דּוּד, pl. דּוָדִים
(m) מָוֶת, const. מוּת   (r) שׁוֹר —— שׁוֹר - שְׁוָרִים
(n) תָּוֶךְ —— תּוֹךְ   Segholates of roots לה.
(o) חַיִל —— חַיִל   (s) פְּרִי(פֶּרִי)const.פְּרִי, suff. פֶּרְיוֹ, פֶּרְיְךָ
(p) עִיר —— עִיר, pl.עָרִים (t) —— חֲצִי (חֵצִי) חֲצִי—חֶצְיוֹ, חֶצְיְךָ

Dec. VII. Singular. § 371.

	Sing. abs.	Const.	Light suff.	Grave suff.
(a)	שֵׁם	שֵׁם (שֶׁם־)	שְׁמִי	שִׁמְכֶם
(b)	אוֹיֵב	אוֹיֵב	אוֹיְבִי	אוֹיִבְכֶם
(c)	מִקְטָל	מִקְטָל	מִקְטָלִי	מִקְטָלְכֶם
(d)	מִזְבֵּחַ	מִזְבַּח	מִזְבְּחִי	מִזְבַּחֲכֶם
(e)	מַקֵּל	מַקֵּל	מַקְלִי	מַקֶּלְכֶם
(f)	מַפְתֵּחַ	מַפְתֵּחַ	—	—
(g)	עֵץ	עֵץ	עֵצִי	עֶצְכֶם
(h)	אֶשְׁכֹּל	—		

Dec. VIII. Singular. § 374.

(a)	יָם	יַם (יָם־)	יַמִּי	יַמְּכֶם
(b)	אַף	אַף	אַפִּי	אַפְּכֶם
(c)	מַד	מַד	מַדִּי	מִדְּכֶם
(d)	לֵב	לֵב (לֶב־)	לִבִּי	לִבְּכֶם
(e)	חֹק	חֹק (חָק־)	חֻקִּי	חָקְּכֶם
(f)	עֹז	עֹז (עָז־)	עֻזִּי (עָזִּי)	עֻזְּכֶם
(g)	גָּמָל			
(h)	מָגֵן	מָגֵן	מָגִנִּי	מָגִנְּכֶם
(i)	חַי	חֵי		

Dec. IX. Singular. § 377.

(a)	חֹזֶה	חֹזֵה	חֹזִי	חֹזְכֶם
(b)	שָׂדֶה	שָׂדֵה	שָׂדִי	שָׂדְכֶם

Par. XXV. Nouns Masculine. §§ 371 seq.

Segholates of לה continued.				Inf. Segholates.	
(u) חֲלִי (חֳלִי), const. חֳלִי, suff. חָלְיוֹ	(x) דְּבַשׁ, const. דְּבַשׁ, suff. דִּבְשׁוֹ
(v) גְּדִי, plur. גְּדָיִים [pl. חֲלָיִים] (y) שֶׁכֶם — שְׁכֶם — שִׁכְמוֹ
(w) צְבִי, — צְבָיִים	(z) בְּאֵר — בְּאֵר, pl. בְּאֵרוֹת
	(yy) קְטֹל, קָטְלוֹ. (zz) פַּעַם, פַּעֲמוֹ

Dec. VII. Plural.

Plural abs.	Light suff.	Const.	Gravo suff.
שֵׁמוֹת	שְׁמוֹתַי	שְׁמוֹת	שְׁמוֹתֵיכֶם
אוֹיְבִים	אוֹיְבַי	אוֹיְבֵי	אוֹיְבֵיכֶם
מְקַטְּלִים	מְקַטְּלַי	מְקַטְּלֵי	מְקַטְּלֵיכֶם
מִזְבְּחוֹת	מִזְבְּחוֹתַי	מִזְבְּחוֹת	מִזְבְּחוֹתֵיכֶם
מַקְלוֹת	(as Dec. XIII.)		
מַפְתְּחִים			
עֵצִים	עֵצַי	עֲצֵי	עֲצֵיכֶם
אֶשְׁכֹּלוֹת			אֶשְׁכֹּלֹתֵיהֶם

Dec. VIII. Plural.

יָמִים	יָמַי	יְמֵי	יְמֵיכֶם
אַפִּים	אַפַּי	אַפֵּי	אַפֵּיכֶם
מָדִים	מַדַּי	מַדֵּי	מַדֵּיכֶם
לְבֻאוֹת	לְבֻאוֹתַי	לְבֻאוֹת	לְבֻאוֹתֵיכֶם
חֻקִּים	חֻקַּי	חֻקֵּי	חֻקֵּיכֶם
גְּמַלִּים	גְּמַלַּי	גְּמַלֵּי	גְּמַלֵּיכֶם
מָגִנִּים	מָגִנַּי	מָגִנֵּי	מָגִנֵּיכֶם
חַיִּים	חַיַּי	חַיֵּי	חַיֵּיכֶם

Dec. IX. Plural.

חֹזִים	חֹזַי	חֹזֵי	חֹזֵיכֶם
שָׂדִים	שָׂדַי	שְׂדֵי	שְׂדֵיכֶם

Par. XXVI. Nouns Feminine. §§ 380—392.

	Sing. abs.	Const.	Light suff.	Grave suff.
		Dec. X. Singular. § 380.		
(a)	תּוֹרָה	תּוֹרַת	תּוֹרָתִי	תּוֹרַתְכֶם
(b)	בְּתוּלָה	בְּתוּלַת	בְּתוּלָתִי	בְּתוּלַתְכֶם
		Dec. XI. Singular. § 383.		
(a)	שָׁנָה	שְׁנַת	שְׁנָתִי	שְׁנַתְכֶם
(b)	שֵׁנָה	שְׁנַת	שְׁנָתִי	שְׁנַתְכֶם
(c)	צְדָקָה	צִדְקַת	צִדְקָתִי	צִדְקַתְכֶם
(d)	חָכְמָה	חָכְמַת	חָכְמָתִי	חָכְמַתְכֶם
(e)	עֶגְלָה	עֶגְלַת	עֶגְלָתִי	עֶגְלַתְכֶם
(f)	מַמְלָכָה	מַמְלֶכֶת	מַמְלַכְתִּי (etc.)	as Dec. XIII.
(g)	מִשְׁפָּחָה	מִשְׁפַּחַת	מִשְׁפַּחְתִּי (etc.)	as Dec. XIII.
		Dec. XII. Singular. § 387.		
(a)	מַלְכָּה	מַלְכַּת	מַלְכָּתִי	מַלְכַּתְכֶם
(b)	שִׂמְלָה	שִׂמְלַת	שִׂמְלָתִי	שִׂמְלַתְכֶם
(c)	חֶרְפָּה	חֶרְפַּת	חֶרְפָּתִי	חֶרְפַּתְכֶם
(d)	חָרְבָּה	חָרְבַּת	חָרְבָּתִי	חָרְבַּתְכֶם
(e)	נַעֲרָה	נַעֲרַת	נַעֲרָתִי	נַעֲרַתְכֶם
		Dec. XIII. Singular. § 390.		
(a)	מִסְגֶּרֶת	מִסְגֶּרֶת	מִסְגַּרְתִּי	מִסְגַּרְתְּכֶם
(b)	גְּבֶרֶת	גְּבֶרֶת	גְּבִרְתִּי	גְּבִרְתֵּךְ
(c)		אֵשֶׁת	אִשְׁתִּי (אִשְׁתְּךָ)	אִשְׁתֵּךְ
(d)	כֻּתֹּנֶת	כְּתֹנֶת	כֻּתָּנְתִּי	כֻּתָּנְתֵּךְ
(e)	נְחֹשֶׁת	נְחֹשֶׁת	נְחֻשְׁתִּי	נְחֻשְׁתֵּךְ
(f)		לֶכֶת	לֶכְתִּי	לֶכְתְּךָ
(g)		שֶׁבֶת	שִׁבְתִּי	שִׁבְתְּךָ
(h)		קַחַת	קַחְתִּי	קַחְתְּךָ

Par. XXVI. Nouns Feminine. §§ 380—392.

Plural abs.	Const.	Suffix sing.	Suff. plural.

Dec. X. Plural.

| תּוֹרוֹת | תּוֹרוֹת | תּוֹרוֹתַי | תּוֹרוֹתֵיכֶם |
| בְּתוּלוֹת | בְּתוּלוֹת | בְּתוּלוֹתַי | בְּתוּלוֹתֵיכֶם |

Dec. XI. Plural.

שָׁנוֹת	שְׁנוֹת	שְׁנוֹתַי	שְׁנוֹתֵיכֶם
שְׁנוֹת	שְׁנוֹת	שְׁנוֹתַי	שְׁנוֹתֵיכֶם
צְדָקוֹת	צִדְקוֹת	צִדְקוֹתַי	צִדְקוֹתֵיכֶם
חֲכָמוֹת	חַכְמוֹת	חַכְמוֹתַי	חַכְמוֹתֵיכֶם
עֲגָלוֹת	עֶגְלוֹת	עֶגְלוֹתַי	עֶגְלוֹתֵיכֶם

Dec. XII. Plural.

מְלָכוֹת	מַלְכוֹת	מַלְכוֹתַי	מַלְכוֹתֵיכֶם
שְׂמָלוֹת	שִׂמְלוֹת	שִׂמְלוֹתַי	שִׂמְלוֹתֵיכֶם
חֲרָפוֹת	חֶרְפּוֹת	חֶרְפּוֹתַי	חֶרְפּוֹתֵיכֶם
חֲרָבוֹת	חַרְבוֹת	חַרְבוֹתַי	חָרְבוֹתֵיכֶם
נְעָרוֹת	נַעֲרוֹת	נַעֲרוֹתַי	נַעֲרוֹתֵיכֶם

Dec. XIII. Plural.

| מִסְגְּרוֹת | מִסְגְּרוֹת | מִסְגְּרוֹתַי | מִסְגְּרוֹתֵיכֶם |
| כֻּתֳּנוֹת | כָּתְנוֹת | כָּתְנוֹתַי | כָּתְנוֹתֵיכֶם |

Par. XXVII. Nouns Dual. § 393.

Sing. abs.	Dual abs.	Const.	Sing. abs.	Dual abs.	Const.
I.			צֹהַר	צָהֳרַיִם	
יוֹם	יוֹמַיִם		עַיִן	עֵינַיִם	עֵינֵי
רִבּוֹת	רִבּוֹתַיִם		לְחִי	לְחָיַיִם	
II.			**VII.**		
יָד	יָדַיִם	יְדֵי	מֹאזְנַיִם		מֹאזְנֵי
	מֶלְקָחַיִם		**VIII.**		
III.			כַּף	כַּפַּיִם	כַּפֵּי
שָׁבוּעַ	שְׁבֻעַיִם		שֵׁן	שִׁנַּיִם	שִׁנֵּי
IV.			**X.**		
כָּנָף	כְּנָפַיִם	כַּנְפֵי	אַמָּה	אַמָּתַיִם	
	חֲלָצַיִם		**XI.**		
V.			שָׂפָה	שְׂפָתַיִם	שִׂפְתֵי
עָקֵב	עֲקֵבַיִם	עִקְּבֵי	פֵּאָה	פֵּאָתַיִם	פֵּאֲתֵי
VI.			**XII.**		
רֶגֶל	רַגְלַיִם	רַגְלֵי	יַרְכָה	יַרְכָתַיִם	יַרְכְתֵי
בֶּרֶךְ	בִּרְכַּיִם	בִּרְכֵּי	רִקְמָה	רִקְמָתַיִם	
	מָתְנַיִם	מָתְנֵי	**XIII.**		
נַעַל	נַעֲלַיִם	נַעֲלֵי	נְחֹשֶׁת	נְחֻשְׁתַּיִם	

Par. XXVIII. Numerals, etc. §§ 395—398.

(A) Cardinals etc. from 1 to 10.

No.	Signs.	Masc. abs.	Const.	Fem. abs.	Const.	Ordinals.
1	א	אֶחָד (חַד)	אַחַד	אַחַת	אַחַת	שֵׁנִי
2	ב	שְׁנַיִם	שְׁנֵי	שְׁתַּיִם	שְׁתֵּי	שֵׁנִי
3	ג	שְׁלֹשָׁה	שְׁלֹשֶׁת	שָׁלֹשׁ	שְׁלֹשׁ	שְׁלִישִׁי
4	ד	אַרְבָּעָה	אַרְבַּעַת	אַרְבַּע	אַרְבַּע	רְבִיעִי
5	ה	חֲמִשָּׁה	חֲמֵשֶׁת	חָמֵשׁ	חֲמֵשׁ	חֲמִשִּׁי (חֲמִישִׁי)
6	ו	שִׁשָּׁה	שֵׁשֶׁת	שֵׁשׁ	שֵׁשׁ	שִׁשִּׁי
7	ז	שִׁבְעָה	שִׁבְעַת	שֶׁבַע	שְׁבַע	שְׁבִיעִי
8	ח	שְׁמֹנָה	שְׁמֹנַת	שְׁמֹנֶה		שְׁמִינִי
9	ט	תִּשְׁעָה	תִּשְׁעַת	תֵּשַׁע	תְּשַׁע	תְּשִׁיעִי
10	י	עֲשָׂרָה	עֲשֶׂרֶת	עֶשֶׂר	עֶשֶׂר	עֲשִׂירִי

(B) Cardinals from 11 to 19.

		Masculine.	Feminine.
11	יא״	אַחַד עָשָׂר	אַחַת עֶשְׂרֵה
		עַשְׁתֵּי עָשָׂר	עַשְׁתֵּי עֶשְׂרֵה
12	יב״	שְׁנֵים עָשָׂר	שְׁתֵּים עֶשְׂרֵה
		שְׁנֵי עָשָׂר	שְׁתֵּי עֶשְׂרֵה
13	יג״	שְׁלֹשָׁה עָשָׂר	שְׁלֹשׁ עֶשְׂרֵה
14	יד״	אַרְבָּעָה עָשָׂר	אַרְבַּע עֶשְׂרֵה
15	טו״	חֲמִשָּׁה עָשָׂר	חֲמֵשׁ עֶשְׂרֵה
16	יו״	שִׁשָּׁה עָשָׂר	שֵׁשׁ עֶשְׂרֵה
17	יז״	שִׁבְעָה עָשָׂר	שְׁבַע עֶשְׂרֵה
18	יח״	שְׁמֹנָה עָשָׂר	שְׁמֹנֶה עֶשְׂרֵה
19	יט״	תִּשְׁעָה עָשָׂר	תְּשַׁע עֶשְׂרֵה

Par. XXVIII. Numerals, etc. §§ 395—398.

(C) *Cardinals from 20 to 90.*

20	כ	עֶשְׂרִים	60	ס	שִׁשִּׁים
30	ל	שְׁלֹשִׁים	70	ע	שִׁבְעִים
40	מ	אַרְבָּעִים	80	פ	שְׁמֹנִים
50	נ	חֲמִשִּׁים	90	צ	תִּשְׁעִים

(D) *Hundreds.*

100	ק	מֵאָה	600	תר״(ס)	שֵׁשׁ מֵאוֹת
200	ר	מָאתַיִם	700	תש״(ן)	שְׁבַע מֵאוֹת
300	ש	שְׁלֹשׁ מֵאוֹת	800	תת״(ף)	שְׁמֹנֶה מֵאוֹת
400	ת	אַרְבַּע מֵאוֹת	900	תת״ק(ץ)	תְּשַׁע מֵאוֹת
500	תק״(ד)	חֲמֵשׁ מֵאוֹת			

(E) *Thousands.*

1,000	א	אֶלֶף	10,000	רְבָבָה, רִבּוֹ, רִבּוֹא
2,000	ב	אַלְפַּיִם	20,000	שְׁתֵּי רִבּוֹת
3,000	ג	שְׁלֹשֶׁת אֲלָפִים	30,000	שְׁלֹשׁ רִבּוֹת
4,000	ד	אַרְבַּעַת אֲלָפִים	40,000	אַרְבַּע רִבּוֹא
5,000	ה	חֲמֵשֶׁת אֲלָפִים	120,000	שְׁתֵּים עֶשְׂרֵה רִבּוֹ
6,000	ו	שֵׁשֶׁת אֲלָפִים		or 12 times 10,000
7,000	ז	שִׁבְעַת אֲלָפִים	600,000	שֵׁשׁ מֵאוֹת אֶלֶף

INDEX.

PART I.

ORTHOGRAPHY AND ORTHOEPY.

	Page.
ALPHABETS	9
Ancient number of letters	12
Arrangement of letters	12
Age of their names	12
Significance of the same	12
Pronunciation of the same	12
Later Hebrew alphabet	13
Final forms of letters	13
Sounds of letters	13
Dilated letters	14
Unusual letters	15
Similar letters	15
Classification of the letters	16
Aspirates, Quiescents, Gutturals, Liquids	16
VOWELS	17
Not original	17
Vowel-letters	17
Ground of classification	18
Quality and quantity of vowels	18
Pure and impure vowels	18
Long and short	19
Long by nature, and by position	19
Pure long vowels	19
Impure long vowels	19
Doubtful appearances of them	20
Daghesh'd long vowels	20
Vowels long by position	21
Short vowels	21
Kind of syllables in which the various vowels may stand	22
Qibbuts vicarious	22
SHEVA	23
Design of it	23
When employed	23
Sheva vocal	23
Sheva silent	24
Composite Shevas	24
When employed	24
Used out of the common course	24
General principle in regard to Shevas	25
Not employed under Quiescents	25
COALESCENCE OF VOWELS AND QUIESCENTS	25
Table exhibiting this	26
Sound of coalescing Quiescents not lost	26
The Ehevi when they retain a consonant power	26
Otium of the Ehevi	27

	Page.
COALESCENCE of vowels and Dagh. letters	27
Vowels affected by omitted Gutturals and Resh	27
Vowels affected by the omission of other Daghesh'd letters	28
ORTHOGRAPHY OF THE VOWELS	28
Proper place of the Vowels	28
Diacritical point over Shin and Sin	29
Vav with Hholem over it	29
Orthography of the vowels as connected with the Quiescents	29
Words written *plene* and *defective*	29
No certain rule for them	30
ORTHOGRAPHY of QAMETS HHATEPH	30
In a mixed syllable	30
In a simple syllable	31
PATTAHH FURTIVE	31
DAGHESH	32
Daghesh forte	32
Orthography of it	32
Omission of it	32
Division of Daghesh forte	33
Euphonic Daghesh and its kinds	33
DAGHESH LENE	34
General rule for the insertion of it	34
—— for the rejection of it	35
General exceptions to the rules	35
Particular exceptions to the same	36
RAPHE	36
MAPPIQ	37
METHEGH	37
Distinguished from Silluq	37
Cases in which it is either uniformly or usually employed	37
Cases in which usage is various	38
Methegh before Maqqeph	38
Use of several Metheghs on the same word	39
Use of Conjunctives instead of Methegh	39
MAQQEPH	39
Effects of it on the vowel and tone	39
End answered by it	39
RULES FOR READING HEBREW	40
Exemplification	41
ACCENTS, table of them	43
Various alleged uses of them	45
Proper place of writing them	46
TONE-SYLLABLE	47
General rule for it; and exceptions	47
Shifting of the tone-syllable	49
Critical marks, and Masoretic notes	51

246   INDEX.

PART II.

CHANGES AND PECULIARITIES OF CONSONANTS AND VOWELS.

Letters of the same organ easily commuted	52
Assimilation of Consonants	52
Consonants cast away or dropped	53
Consonants added	53
Transposition of Consonants	53
PECULIARITIES OF THE GUTTURALS AND RESH	54
Daghesh forte omitted in them, and compensation for it	54
Gutturals prone to the *A* sound	54
Commonly take a composite Sheva	55
PECULIARITIES OF QUIESCENTS	55
General principles regulating them	55
Other ways in which quiescence is effected, besides those involved in the general principle	55
Peculiar usage of Aleph, He, Vav, Yodh, when they would have a vowel, and be preceded by a Sheva	56
Peculiarites of Aleph	57
Peculiarities of Vav and Yodh	58
Peculiarities of He	58
Commutation of the Quiescents for each other	58
Quiescents used as PARAGOGIC letters	59
CHANGES OF THE VOWELS	59
Vowels mutable and immutable	59
Composite Shevas commuted	60
Proper mutable vowels	60
Changes of vowels limited to their respective classes	60
Corresponding long and short vowels	61
Rules of exchanging long vowels for short	61
When short vowels become long	61
Pause-accents lengthen short vowels	61
Falling away of Vowels	62
—— when the tone is moved forward one syllable	62
—— moved forward two syllables	63
Changes in vowels by reason of const. state	63
—— by reason of accession at the end	63
Rise of new vowels	64
What these usually are	64
What they are before composite Shevas	64
New vowels when two Shevas come together, of which the first is composite	64
Rise of furtive vowels	65
Euphonic changes of the vowels	65
Vowels changed by Accents	66
Accents sometimes lengthen short vowels	66
They shorten long ones	66
They restore vowels that had been dropped	67
They turn simple Sheva into Seghol	67
—— composite Sheva into the corresponding long vowel	67
Effect of pause accents not uniform	67
Vowels changed by accession and transposition	68
Vowels changed by the position of certain letters and words	68
Changes in the vowel-points of the article	68
—— of the particles	68
—— of the conjunct. Vav	69
—— of the interrog. ה	69

PART III.

GRAMMATICAL STRUCTURE OF WORDS.

Radical words	70
Conformity to their principles	70
Biliteral roots	70
Quadriliteral and Quinqueliteral roots	71
Parts of speech	71
Grammatical structure of words	71
Various ways of expressing case, number, gender, person, etc.	71
Composite words	71
Mode of writing particles and oblique pronouns	71
ARTICLE	72
Assimilation of it	72
PRONOUNS	72
Pronouns personal [Nom.]	72
Oblique cases of them	73
Pronouns demonstrative	73
—— relative	73
—— interrogative	74
VERBS	74
Classification	74
Inflection	74
Conjugation	74
Usual conjugations	75
Peculiar conjugations	75
Unusual conjugations	76
Conjugations of pluriliteral verbs	76
All conjugations do not belong to any one verb	76
Names of the conjugations	76
Root of verb	77
Forms of the root	77
Niphal and its significations	77
Piel	78
Pual, Hiphil, Hophal, Hithpael	78
Transposition of the letters prefixed to Hithpael	79
Significations of this conjugation	79
Unusual conjugations	80
Mood, tense, number, person and gender of verbs	80
Ground-forms of verbs	80
Formation of the Praeterite tense	81
Inf. const. and absolute	81
Formation of the Fut. tense	81
The praeformative letters of the Fut. tense expel the praeformatives of the derived conjugations	82
Final vowels of the Future	82
Imper. mood	82
Participles of transitive verbs	83
—— of intransitive verbs	83
Subj. and Opt. moods	83

INDEX. 247

Paragogic and apoc. Futures	84
Imper. parag. and apoc.	85
Future with Vav conversive	85
Praeter with Vav	85
General remarks on paradigms of verbs	86
Paragogic letters suffixed to verbs	86
Verbs with Quiescents defectively written	86
REGULAR TRANSITIVE VERBS; notes and explanations	87
REGULAR VERBS INTRANSITIVE; notes	90
VERBS WITH GUTTURALS	91
Verbs Pe Guttural; characteristics etc.	91
Notes on Paradigm	92
Verbs Ayin Guttural; characteristics etc.	93
Notes on the Paradigm	93
Verbs Lamedh Guttural; characteristics, etc.	94
IRREGULAR VERBS; definition	95
First Class ; PE ALEPH, characteristics	95
Notes on the Paradigm	95
PE YODH; characteristics	95
First Class of verbs Pe Yodh; characteristics	96
Notes on the Paradigm	97
Second Class of verbs Pe Yodh; characteristics	98
Notes on the Paradigm	98
Third Class of verbs Pe Yodh; characteristics	98
VERBS PE NUN; characteristics	99
Notes on the Paradigm	99
Second Class	100
VERBS AYIN DOUBLED; characteristics etc.	100
Notes on the Paradigm	102
Peculiar anomaly of these verbs	104
VERBS AYIN VAV; characteristics, etc.	105
Notes on the Paradigm	106
VERBS AYIN YODH	109
Third Class	109
VERBS LAMEDH ALEPH; characteristics, etc.	109
Notes on the Paradigm	110
Interchange of forms between these Verbs, and Verbs Lamedh He	110
VERBS LAMEDH HE; characteristics, etc.	111
Notes on the Paradigm	112
Apocopate Future of Kal	112
—— —— of Hiphil	114
Peculiar Anomalies	115
Imitations of Verbs Lamedh Aleph	115
General Remarks on these	115
VERBS LAMEDH TAV	115

VERBS DOUBLY ANOMALOUS	115
Relation of irreg. verbs to each other	117
Pluriliteral Verbs	117
PARTICIPLES	118
VERBS WITH SUFFIX-PRONOUNS	118
Table of the Forms of such suffixes	120
Notes on the Table of them	120
Notes on the Par. of them as attached to the verb	121
Verbs Lamedh He with suffixes	123
NOUNS; derivation and declension	123
Nouns primitive, derivative, and denominative	124
Composite and proper	124
Gender of Nouns	125
—— of the plural	126
Formation of Fem. nouns, with Table,	127
Formation of the plural, masc. and fem.	128
Heteroclites	128
Formation and use of the Dual	129
DECLENSION OF NOUNS; const. state	130
Suffix-State	130
Table of suffix pronouns	131
Rules for suffixes	132
Vowel-changes in nouns on account of declension	133
Laws of such Vowel-changes	133
Suffixes attached to the plural	134
NOUNS MASC. Dec. I. II.	135
Dec. III. IV.	136
Dec. V. VI.	137
—— Notes on the A. E. O class of Dec. VI.	139
—— Segholates of verbs Ayin Vav, etc.	139
—— Segholates of Verbs Lamedh He	140
—— Infinitive Segholates	140
—— Anomalous Plurals of Segholates	140
Dec. VII. VIII.	141
Dec. IX.	143
NOUNS FEM. Dec. X. XI.	143
Dec. XII.	144
Dec. XIII.	145
Dual Number of nouns	145
Heteroclites or anomalous nouns	145
NUMBERS; cardinal and ordinal	146
Notes on the Paradigm	147
Method of notation	147
ADJECTIVES	147
PARTICLES	148
Adverbs	148
Prepositions	149
Table of them with pronouns, etc.	150
Conjunctions	150
Interjections	151

PART IV.

SYNTAX.

ARTICLE	152
Insertion of it	152
Omission	153
Article before Adjectives	154
NOUNS; case absolute	155
Cases relative; Nom. Gen.	156

Gen. with Lamedh	156
General remark on it	157
—— sometimes follows adjectives	158
—— various meanings of it	158
Dat. case	159
Accusative	160
Accus. put after Participles and Verbals	161

INDEX.

Voc. and Abl. cases	161
CONSTRUCT STATE	161
Form of it not confined to position before a Genitive	161
Refers solely to the relation of two nouns to each other	162
Apposition	163
Gender of nouns and Adjectives	163
Number of nouns used collectively	164
Pluralis Excellentiae	164
Use of the plural in poetry	164
Repetition of nouns	164
——— with the copula	165
Nouns employed as adjectives	165
When employed as adjectives	165
Circumlocutory phrases used in the room of adjectives	166
ADJECTIVES; often used as nouns	166
——— used as predicates of a sentence	167
——— article before them in this case	167
Adjectives qualifying nouns	168
Plur. adjectives with Dual Nouns	168
Adj. with nouns of common gender	168
Position of adjectives	168
Construct state of them	169
Comparative degree of adjectives	169
Superlative	169
Various methods of making a superlative	170
NUMERALS	170
Cardinal numbers used for Ordinals	171
PRONOUNS; use of the primitive ones	172
——— used for the verb of existence	172
Case of suffix-pronouns	173
Exceptions	173
Position of noun-suffixes	174
Position of pronouns in a sentence	174
Place of reflexive pronouns supplied by various noun	175
Anomalies of pronouns	175
Relative pronouns	176
VERBS; general principle of concord	176
Concord with nouns of multitude	176
Verbs with several connected Nominatives	176
Concord of nouns with the verb of existence	177
Anomalies in concord of verbs; number	177
——— as to gender	178
——— as to both number and gender	179
Peculiar Anomaly	180
Impersonal Verbs	180
Verbs with indefinite Nominatives	180
TENSES; various meaning of the Praeter	181
——— of the Future	183
IMPERATIVE MOOD	184
Use of Composite Verbs	185
Cases governed by Verbs	186
Verbs governing two Accusatives	186
Passive Verbs	187
INF. ABSOLUTE, and its various uses	187
Inf. const. and its various uses	189
PARTICIPLES	192
Verbs used as adverbs	193
PARTICLES; adverbs	193
Prepositions	194
Conjunctions and Interjections	195
PLEONASM	195
ELLIPSIS	196
——— of nouns	196
——— of pronouns	197
——— of the verb of existence	198
——— of adverbs	199
——— of prepositions	199
——— of conjunctions	200
——— in poetic parallelism	200
Change of construction	201
Constructio praegnans	202
Zeugma	202
Hendiadys	203
Paronomasia	203
Paradigms of verbs, nouns, etc.	206 seq.

ERRATA.

[After the printing of the preceding work was finished, an unexpected opportunity occurred of submitting the whole to the keen and practised eye of Mr Joshua Seixas; who being a Hebrew by birth, and the son of a Rabbi, has such a knowledge of the Hebrew language as may be called vernacular. Mr S. is at present employed as a teacher of the Hebrew; and I have availed myself of the opportunity of his aid to correct the errors of the press, because I know by experience that to print a Hebrew Grammar without errors is impossible; and because that of all the books which a student is called to use, grammars and lexicons ought to be the most accurate. The smallest mistake may mislead the unwary beginner. All the pains possible have been bestowed on this edition. Every sheet has passed through at least *five* revisions; and it is doubtless, on the whole, the most accurate of any edition which I have hitherto published. Yet Mr Seixas in running it through has detected some errors. Most of them, indeed, are so slight that I might venture to let them pass without notice, as the reader would spontaneously correct them, when he had acquired but a little knowledge of the Hebrew. But as my book is designed for mere beginners as well as others, I have thought it advisable to correct even the slightest mistakes, although at the expense of making out a list of *errata*, which at first view appears formidable to the reader. Almost every error can be corrected by a very slight alteration, with the aid of a fine pen and a knife proper for delicate erasure. I must beg the reader to do this, as soon as he obtains a sufficient knowledge of Hebrew to be able to distinguish things that differ. In the mean time, I can assure him, that mortifying as a list of *errata* is to the author of a book, I prefer submitting to this, rather than to deprive him of the advantages to be derived from such a list. I can also assure him, that although in two or three instances, some singular errors have escaped, in this edition, yet the list of *errata* in any other that I have published, would be still greater, if made out with as close observation.]

Page 21. § 33. Note, פָּדָה, insert Daghesh lene in פּ.—p. 31. *c. e. g.*, הָאָדָם, put הָ for חָ.—§ 67. *b.* Note, הָאֲנִיָּה, put הָ for הָ.—p. 32. § 73. Note 1, יְשָׁדֻם, write יְשָׁדֻם.—p. 33. § 74. *b.* Note, אֵת, write אֵת; כָּרַת, write כָּרַת.—§ 75. e. g. לִ, supply Hhireq under the ל, it being broken off in the printing.—p. 36. Note 2, in הִשְׁפִּיל, הִשְׁפִּיל, עֻפַּל, write שׂ instead of שׁ.—p. 39. top line, יִרְאָה, put אָ for אָ.—Note 2, צַאֲצָאֶיהָם, put אַ for אָ.—§ 89. e. g. דָּיִד, put וְ for ־ְ.—p. 41. § 91. last line, שִׂית, put שׂ for שׁ.—p. 44. No. 23, מַאֲרִיךְ, put רְ for רְ— p. 49. *j*, דְּבָרֶיךְ, for דָּב put דְּב.—p. 50. line 3, וְבָאתָ, וְבָלִיתָ, for וְ in both cases put וּ.—p. 53. § 108. *a.* 3, מִלְקַח, לֶקַח, put קַ for קָ—*b*, for פְּוִי read כְּוִי.—§ 109. *a*, תְּמוּל, put וּ for יּ.—§ 110, in כֶּבֶשׂ, כֶּבֶשׂ, put שׂ for שׁ.—p. 57. § 119. *d*, אֲהָלֶיךָ, read הָ for הֳ.—p. 59, line 2, הֻזַּב, put הֻ for הָ.—p. 60, line 2, הִקְטִילוּ, הִקְטְלָנָה, put הַ for הָ—p. 61. § 129, for (*b*) *Forwards*, write (1) *Forwards*.—§ 129. *b*, דְּבַד read דְּבַר.—p. 64 line 6, דְּבָרוֹ, the final וֹ is broken in some copies, and needs restoring.—p.

65. § 141. e. g. בַּיִת, insert Daghesh in Beth.—Note 1. שָׁמַעַתְּ, for ּת write תְּ.—p. 66. d, דָּרָף, חֶרֶף, put ה for ח.—p. 67. § 149. b, הָסִיָּה, put הָ for הָּ.—p. 68, § 151, בְּהִשָּׁמָּה, erase Methegh; בְּהִשָּׁמָּה, put Dagh. in שׁ.—§ 152. a. 1, הַנֻּהְשׁ, put הַ for הָ.—5, in הַיְאֹר, erase Methegh.—Note, בִּדְהָב, put ְ for ָ.—p. 72. § 164, הֵמָה, for הֵ put הֶ—p. 73, line 3, אַתְּ, אַתִּי, for ת write תְּ.—line 7, for *always*, put *often*.—p. 76. § 176. 1, דָתְקְטַל, for הָ put הָ.—4, הַצּוֹצֵר, for הַ put הֶ—p. 77. § 182. Note, הִקְטֵל, הֻנְקְטַל, for הִ put הַ—p. 78. b. 4, חִשְׁרִישׁ; § 185. a, הִקְטִיל; b. 1, הִקְדִּישׁ; b. 2, הֻשְׁחִית, הֻשְׁקְט, חֻלְבַּן; Note, חָבִיר; put הַ for הָ; a mistake unaccountable.—p. 81. § 196. Note, הֻקְטַל, erase Daghesh in ט—p. 82. 3d line from bottom, וַיֵּשֶׁב, write יֵשֶׁב.—p. 84, § 206, line 3d of the table, הֵמַת, put תָּ for הָ.—p. 85, § 208, Note 4, וַיְהִי, erase Daghesh.—p 90. § 218. 2, וְהִתְקַדִּשְׁתִּי, put תְּ for ת.—§ 221, שָׁכַלְתִּי, put תְּ for תְ—p. 93. c. 2, הַעֲבִיר, put ה for ח.—(3) יַעֲסִיר, put ה for ע.—§ 230. e. g. נְחָג, put הַ for חַ.—§ 232. 2, הִצְדַּק, put יָ for יְ.—p. 94, c, for יִגְאַל write גָּאַל.—d. הִתְנֶחֲמָתִי, for ת put תְּ.—p. 95, 6th line from the bottom, אֹהַב, for הַ put הֶ—p. 98, line 3d from the top, הוֹשַׁר, put ה for ח—p. 99. § 254. a. 1, גְּשִׁיתוֹ, put ג for ג.—p. 103, top line, גּוּל, put וֹ for וּ.—p. 104, top line, הַפְתִיךָ, put הָ for הַ—p. 105, a. e. g. מֵת, מֵתָה, erase Daghesh in Mem.—p. 107, 3d line from the bottom, חֲקַמְלוּנוּ, put הַ for חַ—p. 108. 3, נָפַל, put ר for ב.—p. 110. § 278. 4, יוֹצֵאת, for the latter צ put א—p. 114. § 287. 1, הִגְלֵיתִי, erase Daghesh in ג—(3) for *Future*, write *Practer*; and in the next line, before *once* insert *Future*.—p. 116. c, אוֹרֶךָ, put ה for ךָ.—Ps. 45: 8, for 8 put 5.—(e) יִנָּטֶה, put ט for טָ.—p. 122. 2. Note, אֲדֹנָתָה, put ה for הָ.—p. 123. § 313. Note 2, הָיְיהוּ, put ה for הַ; יְמַצִּימוֹ, put ב for מ.—p. 124. 4th line from the bottom, צְלְמָלֶת should be written צְלְמָוֶת.—p. 125. § 319. Note 1, שֵׁנָא, שֵׁנָה, put שֵׁ for שָׁ.—§ 320. 2, פָּחָה, insert Daghesh in פּ.—p. 128, 3d line from the bottom, אָבוֹת, write וֹ for וּ.—p. 137. §358. 4, שָׁמְטָ, for שָׁ put שָׁ.—p. 138. in note near the top, מַלְכּוֹ, for ל put לָ.—p. 139. § 365. ANOMALIES, לָבָה, put ה for ח.—p. 140. § 369, for שְׁלַו write שְׁלֵו; for שְׁלָוִים write שְׁלֵוִים.—Note, עֲשָׁבוֹת, עֲשָׁבוֹת, put *Sin* instead of *Shin*.—§ 370, קַדְמָה, for ק put קֳ—p. 141. § 373. 6, זֵן, erase the Daghesh.—p. 146. d. Note, וּבָאָה, read וּמָצָאת.—p. 147. 3d line from the top, for שְׁנָתַיִם read שְׁנָתַיִם.—p. 157. d and e, דָּיָר, put רְ for ר—p. 158, in lines 6, 7, from the top, correct the same error.—§ 423. e. g., כַּפִּים, for י put יְ—160, line 7th from the bottom, לֶחִי, write לֶחִי.—p. 161. line 4th from the top, יְהֹנָה, put ה for ח.—p. 164. § 437. 2. b, אֱלוֹהַּ, put הַ for הָ.—3. e. g., צְבָרוֹת, put ק for צ.—p. 167. § 446. a. e. g., קְרוּבָה, put וֹ for

ו.—p. 171. § 464. e. g., עָשָׂר, erase the dot over עָ—p. 175. § 476.
e. g., אֹיְבֶיךָ, erase the dot in בֶּ.—2nd line from the bottom, for אֵת
write אֶת.—p. 176, 3d line from the top, for laier write lair.—p. 178.
Note near the middle, מְאֹרוֹת, יְהִי, erase the comma.—p. 179. § 493.
b, וְאַחֲרוֹן, put הָ for חֲ.—p. 180. § 496. e. g., עִמְּקָךָ, put עָ for עִ.—
§ 497, וַיְהִי, erase Daghesh in the Yodh.—p. 183. § 504. b, אַל, read
אַל.—p. 188. Note 1, הַתַּחַת, put חַ for הַ.—§ 516. a, תִּקְבְּנוּ, for קָ put
קְ—p. 190. § 523. b, for לְכָרוֹת write לִכְרָת.—p. 191. top line, לַסְגֹּר,
put ג for ג.—p. 192. § 530. c. g. וּמִתְפַּלֵּל, put פַּ for פַּ—p. 193. § 533.
e. g., וַיֵּשֶׁב, put שָׁ for שֶׁ.—p. 194. § 538. Note, הָאַתָּה, put הַ for הָ—
p. 195. § 543. e. g., אַחֲרִיתָהּ, put ה for הּ.—p. 198. d. for אֲשֶׁר write
אֲשֶׁר.—p. 199. § 577. e. g., הָאַתָּה, הָאַף, put הַ for הָ—§ 558. e. g.,
עָתָק, erase the dot over Ayin.—p. 201. line 4, Ps. 10: 5, put 1 for 5.—
p. 201. § 563. e. g., וְאֶקְרָא, put יָ for יִ.—p. 202. § 566. c. g., אֱלֹחִים,
put הָ for חַ; וַיַּהֲפֹךְ, put הֲ for ךָ—p. 203. § 571. a, לָצוּ, לָקוּ, erase
the dot in וּ.—p. 209. Fut. יַעֲמֹד, in some copies wants the Hholem
over ד—Imp. 2 fem. and 2 plur. masc. should read חִזְקִי, חִזְקוּ.—p.
210, Fut. plur. יֶחְדְּלוּ etc. usually reads יַחְדְּלוּ etc. in most of the persons.—p. 211. Piel, בְּרַכְתִּי, erase the dot over the ב.—p. 216. Fut. 2
m. טִיטְבוּ, write תֵּיטִבוּ.—p. 220. Niph. 3 plur. נָקוּמוּ should read
נָקוֹמוּ.—p. 221. Imp. 2 masc. plur. בִּינוּ should be printed בִּינוּ.—p.
224, Niph. 2 masc. sing., נִגְלֵיתָ should have the accent over לֵ.—2 plur.
fem. Fut. should have a Daghesh in גַּ—p. 225, in יְהִשְׁתַּחֲוָה, the Hhireq under ה is broken off in some copies.—In the Fut. apoc. the accent should be over חַ—p. 227. Hiph. וַיָּבֵא, should be וַיָּבֵא.—p. 230.
2 m. plur. קְטַלְתּוּנִי, put Sheva under לְ.—Inf. קְטָלֵנִי, put accent over
לֵ.—Fut. יִקְטְלֵנִי, put accent over לֵ.—Imp. שְׁמָעֵנִי, put accent over
עֵ—p. 238. Dec. VIII. (חק) read חָק.—p. 240. Dec. XI. d, חָכְמָה
is fem. of חָכָם, and only a fem. adjective.—Dec. XIII. Const. אֵשֶׁת
read אֵשֶׁת.

[After the above errata were in type, some additional ones, the fruit of a second revision of Mr
Seixas, were received. I add them to the list already printed, that nothing in my power may be
wanting to enable the student to detect every mistake, and to rectify it. Most of the cases in both
lists might have been omitted, so far as any danger of being misled arose from them. But my desire of correctness goes beyond this; and I may safely add, that the only reasons why Hebrew
grammars in general have not a large list of *errata*, is because they are not subjected to such a
sharp-sighted revision as this has been.]

P. 21. § 34. Note 1, for *mĕ-lĕk* read *mĕ-lĕkh*.—p. 31. § 67. b. c. g.,
פָּעֲלוּ, put וֹ for וּ.—p. 48, line 7th from the bottom, נְקוּמָה, for בְּ put
בָּ.—p. 54. § 112. e. g., for בֵּרֵךְ read בֵּרֵךְ.—p. 59. § 125. d. for מָקִים

read בְּקָרִים.—p. 60. § 128. Note, מְדִים, erase the dot from מ —p. 63. § 135, for כְּבֵד write כָּבֵד.—p. 81. § 196. Note, for Hoph. read Pual.—p. 82. § 199. table, for יָקֻם עֹן read יָקֻם עֹו.—p. 88. § 213. 2, אֶדְרֵשׁ, הִדְּרֵשׁ, erase the Tseri under ר in both words.—p. 90. § 219, יוֹדַעְתִּי, put Dagh. in ת.—§ 222, for יָלַד read יָלַד.—p. 99. § 254, שׂוֹא, נָשָׂא, put שׂ for שׁ.—p. 103. b. 1, נְחַנְתִּי, put תּ for ת—Ibid. 2, הֻמַּם read חֻמַּס —p. 104. 2nd line, פָּתָה write פָּתָה.—p. 127. 4th line from bottom, for עֹשֵׂת read עֹשֶׂת.—p. 142. § 376. 6, *Nouns in* ִ-, read ֵ-.

www.ingramcontent.com/pod-product-compliance
Lightning Source LLC
Chambersburg PA
CBHW070247230426
43664CB00014B/2426